DEMOCRA

DEMOCRATIC LEFT

The Life and Death of an Irish Political Party

KEVIN RAFTER

IRISH ACADEMIC PRESS
DUBLIN • PORTLAND, OR

First published in 2011 by Irish Academic Press

2 Brookside,	920 NE 58th Avenue, Suite 300
Dundrum Road,	Portland, Oregon,
Dublin 14,	97213-3786
Ireland	USA

www.iap.ie

British Library Cataloguing in Publication Data
Rafter, Kevin.
Democratic Left : the life and death of an Irish political
party.
1. Democratic Left (Political Party : Ireland) 2. Ireland—
Politics and government—1949- 3. Northern Ireland—
Politics and government—1969-1994. 4. Northern Ireland—
Politics and government—1994-
I. Title
324.2'41507-dc22

ISBN 978 0 7165 3111 1 (cloth)
ISBN 978 0 7165 3112 8 (paper)

Library of Congress Cataloging-in-Publication Data
An entry can be found on request

Printed by Good News Digital Books, Ongar, Essex

Contents

Acknowledgements

This study is the end result of several years of work with Ellen Hazelkorn and Henry Patterson. As supervisors of my doctorate both Ellen and Henry offered invaluable advice, insightful comment and plenty of distracting conversations. I am, in particular, deeply grateful to Ellen for her mentoring and friendship. A considerable debt of gratitude is owed to the many individuals who assisted with deepening my understanding of what was the political party, Democratic Left. I refer not just to those who gave their time to talk and discuss but also those who provided documentation, answered queries and checked facts. I would especially like to single out Tony Heffernan who with huge generosity answered my initial query about party records with several boxes of his private papers. I am grateful to numerous friends for their support, for conversations or just enquiring after the project. I would like to acknowledge support for this publication from the Institute of Art, Design and Technology, Dun Laoghaire where I was Head of the Department of Film and Media from 2008 to 2010. Finally, this study would not have been finished without my loving family Oorla, Ben, Brian and Adam. This work is dedicated to them and to my late friend Peter Fitzgerald, who encouraged me to embark upon a PhD but who sadly did not live to see its completion.

List of Tables

List of Plates

1. Proinsias De Rossa and Des Geraghty at the Workers' Party conference in February 1992 where they failed to get the required two-thirds majority to reconstitute the party.
   Source: Photocall Ireland
2. Following the Workers' Party split Eamon Gilmore and Des Geraghty – seen here at the February 1992 reconstitution conference – went on to become influential members of Democratic Left.
   Source: Photocall Ireland
3. Operating under the temporary name of 'New Agenda' the De Rossa group sought the help of members in selecting the permanent name for their new organisation.
4. One of Democratic Left's leading figures Pat Rabbitte at the party's founding conference in March 1992.
   Source: Photocall Ireland
5. Proinsias De Rossa voting at the Democratic Left founding conference in March 1992.
   Source: Photocall Ireland
6. Without an invite Proinsias De Rossa joins other party leaders in welcoming President Mary Robinson to Leinster House as reported by *The Sun* in July 1992.
7. Liz McManus with Proinsias De Rossa, Kathleen Lynch and Eamon Gilmore at a Democratic Left press conference during the November 1992 general election.
   Source: Photocall Ireland
8. Democratic Left championed the so-called 'liberal agenda' and as part of the Rainbow government in 1996 the party campaigned for a 'yes' vote in the referendum to remove the constitutional ban on divorce legislation.
9. Democratic Left advisor Tony Heffernan, who worked for the party in government during the life of the Rainbow coalition.
   Source: Photocall Ireland
10. Taoiseach John Bruton and Minister for Social Welfare Proinsias

De Rossa welcome US President Bill Clinton to Government Buildings during the life of the 1994-97 Rainbow coalition.
11. The Democratic Left-Labour Party merger discussions as captured by cartoonist Gerard Crowley in the *Sunday Business Post* in July 1998.
   Source: Courtesy of Gerard Crowley.
12. Celebrating the party's fifth year in existence in March 1997. (L to R) Eamon Gilmore, Proinsias De Rossa, Catherine Murphy, Helen Lahart, Anthony Creevy and Liz McManus.
13. Having secured the support of their respective parties, Ruairi Quinn and Proinsias De Rossa celebrate the merger. The deal when it became official in January 1999 marked the demise of Democratic Left.
   Source: Photocall Ireland

PART 1
Birth

Introduction

Democratic Left was a small Left-leaning political party which was organised primarily in the Irish Republic but also in Northern Ireland for just short of seven years in the 1990s. Formed out of a split in the Workers' Party in early 1992, Democratic Left was formally disbanded in January 1999 following a merger agreement with the Irish Labour Party. The party participated in a coalition government involving Fine Gael and Labour between late 1994 and the summer of 1997. This followed a tradition in Irish politics of small political parties participating in multi-party governmental arrangements including Clann na Poblachta (1948–51), Clann na Talmhain (1948–51) and the Progressive Democrats (1989–92).[1]

The party from which Democratic Left emerged – the Workers' Party – participated in the European Left's ideological re-evaluation throughout the 1970s and into the 1980s. The Workers' Party structured its organisation on a Marxist–Leninist model based upon democratic centralist principles. Its self-image was of a revolutionary workers' party, with the organisation being shaped by membership of the broad Left family in European politics and also an Irish republican political heritage. The long-time Workers' Party leader Tomás MacGiolla once described the party he led as 'the only serious socialist party in the state with the determination to take up the challenge of the new right'.[2] But MacGiolla's replacement by Proinsias De Rossa as party president in 1987 allowed space to open up for consideration of where the party stood politically. In this way, the transition in Left politics in Ireland – like elsewhere in Europe – predated the Berlin Wall's collapse.

The Left – broadly defined as either social democratic, socialist or communist – has long been engaged in ideological reinvention. But no previous period of transition was as dramatic as the transformation from the 1970s onwards brought about by the impact of globalisation and the collapse of the Soviet system. Economic globalisation had a profound impact on Left politics – as it has had more recently on Right politics – and for both ideological persuasions in ways that have yet to be fully appreciated. From the 1970s onwards the changed global economy, driven increasingly by international capital mobility, limited the tools of macroeconomic management available to individual governments. Private-sector involvement was given preference over state interventionism while the traditional Keynesian policy prescription was restricted in the new international economic order. This re-ordering of the rules of economic management was underway when the Soviet system collapsed, bringing further uncertainties for the direction of Left political action.

By the final decade of the twentieth century the Left was without a unique narrative. The goals of economic fairness and poverty reduction remained, but the traditional pillar of ideological interventionism had crumbled. Attempts at ideological reinterpretation in the guise of a 'third way' – or Donald Sassoon's 'new revisionism' – failed to offer either coherence or clarity.[3] The dominant political and economic story was now told by the neo-liberal Right, and even in the financial crisis from late 2008 onwards when governmental intervention increased dramatically in the banking sector there has been little consideration that an overarching and cohesive alternative exists to the guiding principles of free-market economics. Across the European continent parties from the Left and from the Right swap government for opposition but all the public sees are variations on a theme. This ideological convergence left the post-1989 Left agenda without a 'big idea' which, in very many respects in terms of economic management, is now indistinguishable from the neo-liberal tradition.

The task of reinvention – and reinventing those to the Left of the more moderate social democracy – continued into the 1990s for various new political entities including Democratic Left (DL) in Ireland. There was a desire among many associated with the party's leading figure Proinsias De Rossa to renew their image of socialism and construct a set of policies that communicated radical distinctiveness. This search for a new radical agenda, in effect a reformist socialist party, was a challenge which Democratic Left embarked upon at a time of enormous change in Irish society. Roy Foster has used the word 'anarchy' to describe the final three decades of the twentieth century in Ireland:

The destabilising pressures of Irish history since 1970, which included political subversion, financial corruption, the challenge of immigration and a sometimes spectacularly unequal prosperity, have presented the Irish state with a series of challenges, often impressively surmounted.[4]

While the debate about change raged over the thirty-year period – as Foster identified – much of the actual change, and resolution, was realised in the 1990s. Ireland was transformed in the 1990s. The decade opened with debates about economic decline in the Irish Republic and continued violence in Northern Ireland. Over the ten years that followed, unprecedented economic growth was recorded in the South while north of the border a peace process was developed. As Neil Collins observed, 'The Republic's impressive economic perform-ance and the dramatic breakthrough in the peace process in Northern Ireland were predicted by few. The consequences of these and other changes have transformed politics on the island.'[5] This era of prosperity and peace was without parallel in the history of modern Ireland – and the accommodation between unionism and republicanism in Northern Ireland was matched by a new acceptance of difference in the Irish Republic. And while the early years of the twenty-first century have been marked by profound economic upheaval – undermining some of this progress – there can be no regression on the transformative societal changes of the 1990s.

Those involved in the formation of Democratic Left were, therefore, not just reacting to – and being shaped by – the wider Left identity debates, they also had to respond to varying forces transforming every facet of life in Ireland. The new party was re-evaluating its inherited economic dogma in the 1990s when the Irish economy was undergoing dramatic changes so much so that previous debates about unemploy-ment, emigration and national debt gave way to a nascent boom best exemplified by a cover story in *The Economist* magazine under the headline, 'Ireland: Europe's Shining Light'.[6] Alongside economic progress, the 1990s was the decade in the history of twentieth-century Ireland when change was confronted in many contentious areas. This was particularly true in relation to the social and moral issues about which individuals associated with Democratic Left had long adopted progressive stances, and whereas previously bitter debates raged in the 1990s there was political and public resolution on subjects such as divorce, contraception and homosexuality. In truth, few areas of Irish life were untouched by the forces of change. Wrongdoing in the worlds of politics and business – hidden from public view for decades – was exposed along with revelation after revelation about abusive Roman Catholic clergy. Diarmaid Ferriter accurately referred to the 'many difficult, challenging and sometimes horrendous aspects of Irish life in previous decades that were unleashed and exposed in the 1990s'.[7]

The forces of change were also evident in the Irish political system, which had been marked by great instability in the 1980s – a decade which saw five general elections, the formation of a new Rightist political party, the Progressive Democrats (PDs), and the largest party, Fianna Fáil, enter its first ever coalition government. There was little sense that relative stability would be a feature of Irish politics in the 1990s. Commenting on the 1989 general election outcome, Peter Mair observed that the results were seen to confirm a new direction in the Irish party system with 'a drift towards a more European-style politics in particular'.[8] Scholars of political science have long seen the political system in Ireland as an oddity in Europe, with party difference rooted in the 1922–3 civil war. Basil Chubb noted that 'the triad of parties that emerged after independence continued as the major vehicles for partisan politics long after the issues that threw them up had either been resolved or had ceased to have great importance in the minds of the public.'[9] The impact of the developments in the 1980s, however – as they played out in the 1990s – meant, in the words of one writer, that 'Irish voters and the Irish party system are no longer anchored in the past.'[10] While the three main political parties – Fianna Fáil, Fine Gael and the Labour Party – maintained their traditional dominance, the decade was marked by electoral volatility, the formation of previously unimaginable coalition administrations of different hues and, for the first time, the creation of a government without recourse to a general election.

It is not an understatement to say that throughout Irish life in the 1990s the forces of modernity and change were rampant at a time when the backers of Democratic Left sought to build a new political party positioned on the Left of the political spectrum. This Irish context in the 1990s is important when considering the history of Democratic Left. The party's agenda dovetailed with many of the 'zeitgeist' issues of Ireland in the 1990s. And yet Democratic Left did not see out the decade as an independent political party. Why was this? The answer to the latter question comes in several guises – the international ideological uncertainty of the Left in the 1990s; the societal changes underway in Ireland in that same decade; and the internal workings of Democratic Left as a small political organisation.

The discussion and analysis in the chapters that follow reveals significant new information about the workings and organisation of small political movements in Ireland, including their financial arrangements, structures, identity, relations with similar-minded but larger parties as well as participation in coalition governments and their impact on those governments. In addition to interview material, the study presents important new evidence in the form of private papers belonging to senior figures in Democratic Left and the Labour Party. None of this documentation has previously been made public. It comes in several forms – minutes of private Democratic Left meetings; internal Democratic Left memos and reports; and correspondence between senior figures in Democratic Left and the Labour Party. The content is structured into three parts, individually titled – birth, life and death. While this structure allows the material to be presented in a near chronicle manner the study is not a chronicle narrative, so on occasion in earlier chapters it is necessary to refer to issues and events treated in greater depth in later chapters.

Democratic Left was shaped by the debate in European Left politics in the late 1980s which was injected with renewed urgency after the fall of the Berlin Wall and the challenge created in articulating an alternative ideological position that was both distinctive and coherent. Moreover, specific pressures within the Workers' Party created a climate in which the formation of Democratic Left was most likely an inevitable outcome. The Democratic Left experience provides lessons – in terms of identity, organisation, leadership and finances – for other small political parties which seek to create a sustainable place in the Irish political system, which has been dominated for almost ninety years by three larger parties.

NOTES

1. The Progressive Democrats were also involved in three different coalition governments with Fianna Fáil formed after the general elections in 1997, 2002 and 2007. The party officially disbanded in 2009. The Green Party also joined the coalition arrangement formed after the 2007 general election, which remained in office until early in 2011.

2. P. Mair, *The Changing Irish Party System: Organisation, Ideology and Electoral Competition* (London: Pinter, 1987), p.40.
3. See D. Sassoon, *One Hundred Years of Socialism: The West European Left in the Twentieth Century* (New York: New Press, 1996).
4. R. Foster, *Luck and the Irish: A Brief History of Change, 1970–2000* (London: Penguin, 2007), p.188.
5. N. Collins (ed.), *Political Issues in Ireland Today* (Manchester: Manchester University Press, 1999), p.xiii.
6. 'Europe's Shining Light', editorial, *The Economist*, 343, 8017 (May 1997), pp.21–4.
7. D. Ferriter, *The Transformation of Ireland, 1900–2000* (London: Profile, 2004), p.4.
8. P. Mair (ed.), *The West European Party System* (Oxford: Oxford University Press, 1990), p.208.
9. B. Chubb, *The Government and Politics of Ireland* (London: Longman, 1992), p.96.
10. P. Mair, 'Fianna Fáil, Labour and the Irish Party System', in M. Gallagher and M. Laver, *How Ireland Voted, 1992* (Dublin: Political Studies Association of Ireland (PSAI), 1993), p.172.

1

Positioning Democratic Left

INTRODUCTION

Parties of the Left across Europe have for over half a century been engaged in a re-evaluation of their core identities and values. This reassessment of core ideology and outlook emerged from the pressures, tensions and challenges in Left politics in the latter half of the twentieth century, most particularly the advance of economic globalisation and the collapse of the European communist regimes after 1989. The changed global economy in the 1980s and 1990s limited the tools of macroeconomic management. The preference of the Left for a Keynesian policy prescription became more problematic for individual governments. The role of state-sponsored interventionism – and its ability to have an impact on economic life – was thrown into question by the free movement of capital. This transformation in economic management was already underway when the Soviet system collapsed, bringing only more uncertainty for the direction of Left political action.

In terms of a post-1989 Left agenda, one writer observed, 'it has been said that, paradoxically, the effective rejection of the notion of a "big idea" – a theory of institutional design for an entire socio-economic system – is probably the biggest idea that democratic socialists have come up with for years.'[1] But the downside for the Left, as this chapter argues, is that without big ideas the Left became indistinguishable from the neo-liberal tradition. The very meaning of Left itself has been reinterpreted, and this naturally has had repercussions for the identity labelling of political parties like Democratic Left. The party from which Democratic Left emerged – the Workers' Party – was like other Left parties in western and eastern Europe in having engaged in pre-1989 revisionism. The Workers' Party participated in the European Left's ideological re-evaluation throughout the 1970s and into the 1980s.

The evolution of the term 'Left' over the last half century, the motivators for change and the emergence of the new revisionist doctrine are
discussed below. Three broad strands in Left politics in Europe are identified – social democratic, socialist/Eurocommunist and communist.
The evolution of these ideological perspectives ultimately shaped the
meaning of the 'New Left'. This background and context is important
as it establishes Democratic Left as one of the parties which grappled
in the 1990s with finding a new political space for Left politics in
Europe.

CHANGING DEFINITIONS

In 2007 the journalist Nick Cohen published *What's Left? How Liberals
Lost Their Way*, in which he examined the position of the British Left.
Cohen, a writer from the liberal-Left in British journalism, had railed
against Conservative Party politics from a young age. He later gained
a reputation for his uncompromising writing in the *Observer* newspaper among other outlets. By 2007 Cohen had, however, become
disenchanted with Left's political positioning on a range of issues from
economic management to globalisation to the so-called 'war on terror'.
But the decline in Left politics was not new, he asserted, and could be
traced back almost two decades:

> Socialism had vanished in the Eighties. Long before the Berlin
> Wall came down people had stopped thinking about it or seeing
> it as a plausible answer to the problems of organising societies. It
> wasn't just that communism was clearly finished. In the free
> world, trade union membership fell, and all Left-wing parties with
> a chance of winning an election stopped pretending that they could
> and should nationalise the commanding heights of the economy
> … The political chasm that separates the twenty-first century from
> the twentieth is that socialism is no longer credible. The loss of …
> Marxism is no loss at all, but the enfeeblement of the humane and
> generous forces of social democracy in Europe, India and North
> America has been a disaster. There were plenty of leftists at the
> millennium, but no radical Left with a practical plan to transform
> society.[2]

Cohen's thesis echoed many years of deliberations and writings by numerous political thinkers and practising politicians. For example, Anthony Crosland's revisionist work, *The Future of Socialism*, published in 1956, argued that post-war capitalism had fundamentally changed, so much so that equality could be achieved in a capitalist economy. Crosland's arguments generated considerable controversy, and even led one Left journal to publish a headline, 'How dare he call himself a socialist'.[3] In the initial decades of the twentieth century, socialist and communist political activism provided the oxygen for European Left causes. The Left was a broad church although three specific strands can be identified – social democratic and communist in western European and Soviet-controlled communism in eastern Europe. Communist regimes dominated in eastern Europe, while the post-Second World War era was defined by the strength of social democratic politics in western Europe. In broad terms the Left in all it various hues was committed to extensive state intervention and a Keynesian framework to achieve economic growth, high wages, price stability and full employment. The Left also favoured state-controlled policies to redistribute income through welfare programmes, social insurance and taxation laws. Moreover, the Left was also associated with the working class and a trade union movement. The acceptance of a mixed economy provided a significant difference between social democratic parties – described as those who were socialists and democrats – and those further to the Left including the countries ruled under the Soviet model as well as socialist and communist parties elsewhere in western Europe who were communist in outlook but avoided the anti-democratic tendencies originating from Moscow.[4]

In the post-Second World War era the western world was changing with the decline of traditional industries and the shattering of class structures. Economic life was transformed. Structural changes in the labour force with fewer industrial and agricultural workers was evident, with increasing numbers employed in white-collar jobs and in the services sector. 'The changes in class structure, the spread of prosperity, and the decline in class conflict led social democrats to further weaken the class nature of their approval and to play down the role of ideology,' Paterson and Thomas observed.[5] From the 1960s onwards there was a fundamental change in the international political and economic environment. Change was driven by events such as the suppression of reformers in Soviet-controlled Czechoslovakia to the oil shock and international recession post-1973. Reinvention and realignment was required by all strands of Left political activism in western European and also in the Soviet-controlled eastern Europe.

Parties on the Left undertook ideological reassessments. In his introductory essay in *The New European Left*, Donald Sassoon referred to 'the last great bout of revisionism in the late 1950s and early 1960s. At that time, in Germany, France and Italy, Britain and elsewhere, socialists (and in some cases communists) re-examined their doctrine and freed themselves of the ideological baggage they regarded as counter productive.'[6] One example of this revisionism was when in the post-1968 period reformed communists in western Europe adopted the label 'Eurocommunism', which offered a future separate from the Soviet Union in which national democratic values were respected while structural reforms of the capitalist system led ultimately to a socialist future.[7]

The reassessment and reinterpretation of Left ideology, however, failed to deal with the challenges of an increasingly globalised world. Economic integration and the free movement of labour and capital fundamentally altered the traditional terms of economic debate. The reduction in trade and financial investment barriers had a dramatic impact on the power of individual states. The Left policy agenda pivoting around state activism and a Keynesian interventionist prescription was fundamentally challenged by internationalising economic policies. The central policy tenets of the Left were rendered obsolete in a globalised economy, although it may be argued that the motivators of the Left – poverty elimination and economic fairness – remained very much in place.

The reach and impact of globalisation grew significantly in the 1980s, especially as liberalised financial markets rewrote the economic textbook. Suddenly money markets with ever-increasing investment and capital flows dwarfed national budgets. A shift in economic power took place, with the private sector and the dominance of the market system driving the global economic agenda. The Left no longer had a coherent model of economic organisation. Even in the post-2008 credit crunch crisis and international economic recession the Left struggled to offer an alternative policy amid unprecedented governmental intervention in banking and financial sectors.

The broad strands in Left politics – socialism, communism and

social democracy – had been under review prior to the collapse of the
Soviet model in 1989. Indeed, Sassoon – in his history of socialism,
published in 1996 – argued that the west European socialist model:

> ... was already in crisis before the collapse of communism. Social
> democrats, by and large, had lost faith in traditional social democ-
> racy. They were not optimistic about their own future. They had
> doubts about themselves. They mentioned socialism less and less.
> In 1973 the [British] Labour Party could still state in its pro-
> gramme that 'Only a socialist strategy now makes any sense at all.'
> Twenty years later, such a statement – if made – would astonish
> almost all observers.[8]

The end of the Cold War in the late 1980s certainly gave critics of the
Left plenty to celebrate. 'Socialist aims and programmes are factually
impossible to achieve or execute; and they also happen, into the bargain
as it were, to be logically impossible,' Hayek wrote.[9] The collapse of the
communist regimes in eastern Europe – coupled with an identity crisis
in Left politics generally – led Francis Fukayama to herald the triumph
of liberal democracy. The politics of the Left had faltered – as
Fukayama's (original but subsequently revised) thesis went – with liberal democracy allied to the market economy winning out as the most
durable ideology:

> What we may be witnessing is not just the end of the Cold War, or
> the passing of a particular period of post-war history, but the end of
> history as such ... That is, the end point of mankind's ideological
> evolution and the universalisation of Western liberal democracy as
> the final form of human government.[10]

The fall of the Berlin Wall in an era of advancing economic globalisation
led to a fundamental questioning of the Left's ideological prescription.
The Left failed to offer a coherent response to the new global economic
order. The result was a Left identity crisis and a convergence of
economic ideology. The strains in the Keynesian solution to economic
management were apparent in the 1970s as the recession which
followed the oil price increase hurt social democratic politics with its
association with state interventionism and the welfare state. 'The
Golden Age of social democracy had ended, symbolically at least, with
the collapse of the Bretton Woods system in 1973 and the oil crisis of

1973–74,' Callaghan noted.[11] In his history of the Left in Europe, Geoff Eley argued that 'a deep crisis in the established forms of the Left's politics was already becoming apparent' in the 1980s.[12] A changing composition of social classes and a weakening of class affiliation featured strongly as 'social democracy's pillars – full employment and Keynesian economics, welfare states and expanding public sectors, corporatism and strong unions – were crumbling and under attack'.[13] Martin Bull identified a number of common factors at work which spurred forward this crisis, including the long-term decline of the working class, the changed socio-economic agenda, the rise of the 'New Right' and an 'anti-state' consensus along with the total discrediting of the Soviet model. 'The crisis did not affect all of the parties to the same degree and their varying fortunes depended much on their abilities to adapt to the changes and to exploit their peculiarities of party political competition in their respective countries,' Bull wrote.[14]

The Right argued as part of its renewed message that the market had to take precedent and that social welfare systems blocked the route to economic recovery. The torch carriers for the New Right – Margaret Thatcher in the United Kingdom and Ronald Reagan in the United States – dominated the political and economic agenda. The role of the state was questioned, the private market was stressed as the principal mechanism for delivering goods and services, privatisation was advocated to reduce the 'inefficient' state role in the economy, while reductions in taxation were promoted. The Left had no distinct answer for this new economic agenda. By 1986, Paterson and Thomas were concluding that 'ideologically social democracy is in a period of disarray.'[15] This situation became even more pronounced as the 1980s progressed. The search for a new political and ideological identity intensified against the backdrop of what was described as 'a crisis of multi-dimensional proportions'.[16]

It became increasingly difficult to isolate the different strands on the Left. The socialist alternative to more moderate social democracy was in ideological trouble in western Europe while social democracy itself was under considerable pressure; and by the end of the 1980s in eastern Europe the Soviet communist model had collapsed. The crisis – and the challenge – for socialist parties in Europe was signalled by the increasingly obvious lack of economic policy difference from their social democratic counterparts. The fall of the Berlin Wall further energised the debate about core values and beliefs in the socialist Left, the social democratic Left and the communist Left. 'No democratic socialist alternative emerged from the rubble; instead collapse of command economies saw a rush to embrace "the market", dovetailing with the resurgence of neo-liberalism in the West,' Callaghan concluded.[17] It was a difficulty shared by many European Left political parties but most particularly those who had evolved from, and operated within, a communist tradition. Some time after the foundation of Democratic Left in Ireland in 1992, Richard Dunphy succinctly summarised the challenge in finding a 'post-communist European Left'.

> The communist tradition is clearly in profound ideological crisis. Such 'sacred truths' as the class analysis of modern society, the role of the [communist] party, the nature of state power, the content of 'internationalism', the direction of history, etc have been shaken to the core. As a result, the communist and ex-communist parties in Europe face a multi-faceted challenge: to their value-systems, their party culture, their strategic orientations, their conceptual frameworks. Unless they resolve this crisis and re-equip themselves with a credible analysis of modern society, they risk losing the ability to communicate with their potential (or existing) constituencies. Political collapse may follow intellectual atrophy, where it has not already done so.[18]

In a sense, those seeking Dunphy's 'credible analysis' were searching for a middle way between the failed attempt at creating a socialist state and the apparently triumphant capitalist prescription for running a modern economy. In truth, all strands on the Left were seeking an alternative way forward. The challenge for the Left was to find a new agenda, especially in the economic sphere, which was credible and coherent.

NEW REVISIONISM

In responding to the ideological challenges laid down by Mikhail Gorbachev in the Soviet Union which cascaded across eastern Europe, the overwhelming majority on the broad Left accepted a reality of living within the constraints imposed by capitalism. Reform rather than revolution became the accepted way forward. Various labels were applied to this new thinking, including the 'third way' and 'new revisionism'. Sassoon defined this middle way as 'neo-revisionism'. It was, he concluded, driven by 'the idea that capitalism would not be destroyed by a self-generated crisis, or by a revolution, or by the steady expansion of public property'.[19]

> Neo-revisionism is not a finite doctrinal corpus which can be easily analysed. It implies that markets should be regulated by legislation and not through state ownership. It means accepting that the object of socialism is not the abolition of capitalism, but its co-existence with social justice; that regulation of the market will increasingly be a goal achieved by supra-national means; that national – and hence parliamentary – sovereignty is a limited concept; that the concept of national roads to socialism should be abandoned. It means that the historic link with the working class, however defined, is no longer of primary importance, and that the trade unions are to be regarded as representing workers' interests with no a priori claim to have a greater priority than in the past to the concern of consumers. Neo-revisionism entails accepting important aspects of the conservative critique of socialism – including the association between collective provision and bureaucratic inertia.[20]

There has been much discussion about what constitutes 'third way' politics. One writer saw 'third way' politics offering scope for renewal, or indeed survival, of the Left in a rapidly changing political environment: 'In principle, a "third space" opened between old polarized alternatives of Stalinism and right-wing social democracy – a ready-made "third way" but as a new set of parameters where Left initiatives might form.'[21]

New Labour in the United Kingdom became most closely associated with 'third way' politics, although elements of the Left in France and Germany were also taken with similar ideas, including Lionel Jospin's French Socialists and Gerhard Schröder's German Social Democrats. Tony Blair offered the view that the third way constituted 'a modernised social democracy, passionate in its commitment to social justice and the goals of the Centre-Left, but flexible, innovative and forward-looking in the means to achieve them'.[22]

The real difficulty with new revisionism or third way politics has been that the concept means different things to different people.

Despite the attempt to construct a new ideological framework, no coherent conceptual understanding of third way politics has emerged nor has agreement been reached on the required policy instruments to implement its aspirations. For example, Anthony Giddens described the third way as 'social democracy, revived and modernised', but another academic, Stuart Hall, said it was little more than a variation of neo-liberalism evident in its support for 'the deregulation of markets, the continued privatisation of public assets, low taxation, breaking the inhibitions to market flexibility and institutionalising the culture of private provision and personal risk'.[23]

In assessing these differing viewpoints, Eric Shaw offered a midpoint interpretation in that 'the third way represents a synthesis, a fluid and eclectic mix that pulls in ingredients from both social democracy and neo-liberalism – spiced with some communitarian toppings.'[24] The central weakness for third way politics remains the lack of a coherent programme, especially in the economic arena. The traditional tenets of Left politics such as full employment, income redistribution and labour protection combined to form a cohesive policy and ideological programme. There were variations in the interpretation of this programme, with the different groups broadly being classified as socialist, communist and social democratic. The evolution of the Left in the 1970s and 1980s was transformed into a revolution by globalisation and the events of 1989. The Left needed renewal and particularly a new ideological narrative against the neo-liberal ascendancy. The third way was one attempt, but as Callaghan concluded, 'Talk of a "third way" is evidence of the perceived need for post-socialist vision and – in its nebulosity – evidence that one has not yet been found.'[25] The end result remains that great ambiguities continue to dog the Left in the early years of the twenty-first century.

CONVERGENCE

Parties from the social democratic tradition played a lead role in several governments in western Europe in the early 1970s. But their core beliefs were under scrutiny and the ideology of the Left, one argument has been made, had 'lost its intellectual coherence ...'[26] The traditional Marxist ideological outlook had in most cases been revised to account for contemporary political life, but the pressures on social democratic principles were also challenged by participation in the democratic process. 'Pragmatic political debate exposed the inadequacy of social democrats' traditional economic nostrums – state planning, corporatism and welfare policy – under changed conditions,' Butler argued.[27]

Across western Europe, political parties from the Left tradition in its various guises were confronted by organisational decline, a crisis of identity and the challenge of finding a new ideological programme to fit a contemporary globalised society. The evolution of the programmes of two parties on the European Left – in Germany and in Spain – provides evidence of the ongoing process of ideological revision. For example, the German Social Democrats embarked on a revisionist process when references to Marxism were dropped in 1959 for a strategy that involved the market, where possible, and the state, where necessary. Twenty years later, in 1979, the Spanish Socialist Workers' Party abandoned its Marxist ideology at an extraordinary congress.

In a similar attempt at evolution, the 'Eurocommunism' experiment was undertaken by the communist parties in Spain, Italy and France, among others. This was a serious attempt to 'rethink' the Left in a space removed from the Soviet model and to deal with the ramifications from the changing socio-economic structure of west European society. These parties were trying to find a political position that was more flexible, less exclusive, more democratic and less revolutionary.[28] The principal distinction between the two ideological positions centred around interpretations of class politics and the governing principle of Marxism-Leninism which was accepted by Eurocommunists but rejected by social democrats. Godson and Hasler offered a less benign assessment: 'On the face of it, "Eurocommunism" cannot be clearly distinguished from traditional West European Social Democracy.'[29] Writing in 1978, these two authors with some foresight speculated about a form of ideological convergence between social democratic parties and those from the communist tradition. They were, in truth, two related ideological outlooks, and both were in crisis as they struggled to find a new way forward. The social democratic Left was without answers while, as one writer noted, 'Despite Eurocommunism, the Soviet Union under Brezhnev all but destroyed the space where Communist parties in the West might flourish. The Soviet example was the greatest weapon the Right could ever have wanted against the Left in Western Europe.'[30] The suppression of communist reform movements and a lack of momentum in the Eurocommunist model were the twin factors – according to Eley – in the Left's identity crisis:

> Communist electoral performance began slipping in Italy, and in France and Spain it entirely collapsed. Determined Eurocommunists drew their conclusions and began shedding their Communist identities altogether. Concurrently, social democratic parties fell into disarray. The British Labour Party and the German Social Democratic Party (SDP) entered a parliamentary wilderness for 18 and 16 years of opposition, respectively, in 1979 and 1982; the initial euphoria of socialist election victories in France, Greece and Spain in 1981–82 rapidly palled in the face of austerity programs and rising unemployment; governing socialists in Austria and the Low Countries vacated any distinctive policies, and the long-dominant Scandinavian socialists lost both their confidence and their lock on office.[31]

The arrival of Mikhail Gorbachev as communist leader in the Soviet Union in early 1985 certainly added impetus to the unravelling political situation. His decision to militarily disengage from eastern Europe precipitated a fundamental political reconfiguration of the entire continent. Nothing short of a political and democratic revolution followed which 'displayed a common pattern – replacement of single-party Communist governments and command economies by multiparty democracies and market capitalisms based on private property and the rule of law'.[32] For almost two decades, from the economic recession in the early 1970s to the fall of the Berlin Wall in 1989 – there had been a gradual but ultimately dramatic convergence of policy orientation across the political spectrum in Europe. The scenario in the 1990s was the Left converging around a neo-liberal model and grappling with the meaning of globalisation which, one writer summarised, made 'the distributional goals of social democracy unachievable, at least by traditional social democratic means' and placed the 'European model' of welfare and social market 'in long-term retreat'.[33] This convergence thesis was evidenced in policies to reduce social welfare, declining trade union influence and a widespread acceptance of the role of the market. 'These new policy-making logics trumped political differences of socialists and conservatives in government. Sometimes, the Left rather than the Right set the pace,' Eley asserted.[34]

The project, as discussed previously, was about finding a 'third way' between 'classical social democracy and the traditions of the communist movement'.[35] The most dramatic changes in the composition of Left party politics came in the aftermath of the fall of the Berlin Wall. Some parties folded while others changed their names and ideological direction. Few remained unchanged. The Left, in its various guises identified earlier – socialist, communist and social democratic – underwent nothing less than a revolution in its thinking: 'Established parties were melting away, and even where socialist parties kept support they became a different kind of party ...'[36] The fallout was dramatic. For example, the Italian Communist Party, with which Proinsias De Rossa identified, dissolved itself in March 1990 and re-emerged as the Democratic Party of the Left – a new non-communist party on the Left. Critics of the move argued that the party would be transformed into a pro-capitalist social democratic party. Others articulated an alternative opinion that the distinctiveness of the Left was, in general, up for grabs. This was the dilemma facing most Left parties, whose ambition to smash the capitalism model was ended. 'Making the case for socialist policies, in the relentlessly triumphalist neo-liberal climate that became generalized during the 1980s, has become extraordinarily difficult.'[37] There was also little comfort in the new environment for any political party on the Left, as Sassoon observed:

> Not even social democracy rejoiced at the collapse of the centrally planned economy, because it did not usher in a social-democratic alternative. On the contrary the 'market' turned out to be more uncritically worshipped in what was once 'the Motherland of Socialism' than it had ever been in the West.[38]

As events unfolded in eastern Europe, parties of the Left across the continent rapidly abandoned their ideological heritage.

> The Western parties were thrown into turmoil as they confronted a common dilemma: should they abandon their principles, names and heritage wholesale or, if not, how could they dissociate themselves from the failure of their Eastern counterparts while maintaining those principles intact and a degree of political relevance in their respective countries?[39]

Many parties dumped traditional images and symbols as they sought to communicate new meanings. The Italian Communist Party discarded its name, the hammer and the sickle, and adopted an oak tree as its new symbol; the Italian socialists chose a carnation as their symbol, while the French socialists and, later, the Labour Parties in the United Kingdom and Ireland opted for the rose. Sassoon observed that 'symbols and images define and sustain all great social and political movements. They communicate a meaning. To modify or dispose of them is the most effective indication of change.'[40]

The choice of the name 'Democratic Left' – by the political leaders and activists who departed the Workers' Party in Ireland in 1992 – points to the new formation as being part of this wider European experience. Indeed, the selection of the party name by its members at the founding conference placed Democratic Left alongside other Left groups which, Martin Bull argues, had

> ... chosen to avoid any reference to 'democratic socialism' or 'social democracy' in deciding their names, opting instead for names such as 'New Left', 'Democratic Left', 'Democratic Party of the Left', and 'Green Left'. Besides reflecting compromise forged inside (and beyond) the parties between different factions, the names amount to an implicit recognition that if the political movement the parties have just left is in crisis the one they are entering is not in much better shape.[41]

There was a desire among many associated with Proinsias De Rossa to renew their image of socialism and construct a set of policies that communicated radical distinctiveness. This was not a unique decision. Across Europe those sponsoring a new party on the Left were recasting – as Sassoon identified the British Labour Party as doing – 'traditional principles in ... more fashionable language'.[42] While Sassoon was sympathetic to the emergence of this 'New Left', others, including Bull, offered a more dispiriting assessment: 'Many Western Marxists were slow to recognise that the 1989 revolutions involved not only the overthrow of Stalinism but of socialism *per se*.'[43] Finding remedies for the malaise in Left politics was a huge challenge which recast the very meaning of the Left as many parties, including Democratic Left in Ireland, engaged in a near-permanent struggle for a new political and ideological identity.

A NEW LEFT?

Over the last two decades the advance of economic globalisation has reduced the individual influence of national governments. In this environment – as discussed previously – the power of the Keynesian economic tools traditionally favoured by the Left significantly weakened. Moreover, the fiscal rules laid down in the European Union's Maastricht Treaty in 1992 are closer to the neo-liberal thinking of the New Right than the economic policy prescription associated with Left politics. This transformation had been underway at a time when the Left was being challenged to comprehend and deal with the consequences of the collapse of the Soviet model. In this new world many parties on the Left struggled to forge a new political identity and distinctive economic policy agenda. John Ishiyama has written about the convergence of political action, regardless of ideological persuasion, where 'the social, economic and political systems of all industrial societies will converge because of the dominant effects of technological development.'[44] For many, socialism's theory and past practice has been hard to discern in the policies of Left governments in countries like Britain, France and Spain in the 1990s and the early years of the twenty-first century. The neo-liberal economic dogma has since the 1980s been in the ascendancy regardless of the political orientation of most European governments in office. Reviewing the developments of the last two decades, Gottfried argued that

> ... policy differences between the Right and the Left have narrowed down to mere detail. The Right accepts and even expands the welfare state, while the Left has scuttled plans for government control of industries. Talk about a 'third way' between capitalism and socialism has replaced the radical Left's appeal to class conflict; meanwhile Left-of-center governments in Germany, France, and England trim public budgets as well as redistribute incomes.[45]

Ironically, the Left thrived in electoral terms in the 1990s with the British Labour Party ending an eighteen-year governmental exile in 1997 and the Social Democrats entering government in Germany in 1998. There were also successes in France and Italy, along with Left victories in eastern Europe and a return to office of several Left-led parties in Scandinavia, all of which led Eley to assert that 'European government had a socialist uniformity unparalleled since the antifascist coalitions of 1945. Yet this was a chastened and cautious socialism.'[46]

The lasting impact of these dramatic developments, according to Gottfried, meant 'the Left is no longer Marxist and only intermittently socialist.'[47] Kate Hudson offered a harsher assessment of what the developments of the last two decades have done for the wider European Left: 'Social democratic parties embraced central tenets of the economic and social philosophy of Ronald Reagan and Margaret Thatcher.'[48] The political meaning of Left at the start of the twenty-first century is very different from what it had been prior to 1989. Attitudes have been overhauled in relation to the market, government intervention and the welfare state. The great clashes and visible differences with political opponents have become harder to discern. The laissez-faire script reached a crisis with the post-2008 financial crisis and international recession but, as one commentator observed, there was little comfort for those on the centre-Left:

> The prevailing economic model of the last thirty years has run out of road, just as the post-war social democratic model ran out of road after three (far more successful) decades in the mid-1970s. But it is a non-sequitur to assume, as some on the Left do, that the world has changed forever. This is lazy thinking. Without an intellectual critique of what has gone wrong and what needs to be done to put things right, matters will revert more or less to where they were before the flood.[49]

The three strands in Left politics identified previously have all been transformed, with the difference between social democracy and socialist in western Europe narrowing, while the Soviet model has disappeared. The British Labour Party is a good example of what can be described as 'ideological convergence' but, as one study of the French Left noted, the Lionel Jospin government in the 1990s showed itself 'willing to confound textbook accounts of how Left politics should be conducted' [and] 'this political agenda shares much with the French right.'[50] Some parties have, however, rejected the New Left prescription as identified with the Blair-type third way. They sought an alternative definition of Sassoon's new revisionism. In Hudson's discussion of parties to the Left of social democratic parties there is reference to the electoral successes of the Left Party in Sweden, which contested on a platform of increased welfare spending, opposition to Swedish participation in the European Monetary Union and a thirty-five-hour working week. Its programme adopted in 1996 stated: 'The Left Party strives for the abolition of capitalism.' According to March and Muddle, the Left's response to the events that flowed from 1989 may be classified into four categories:

- parties which renounced the 'communist' label and completed their development towards the democratic Left;

- parties which transformed into fully-fledged social democratic parties;

- parties which ceased to exist independently and re-emerged as part of 'new politics' parties;

- parties which remained loyal to communism.[51]

The same authors defined the 'radical Left' in Europe post-1989 as those who rejected the underlying socio-economic structure, values and practices of contemporary capitalism while advocating an alternative economic and power structure involving a major redistribution of resources from existing political elites.[52] Most parties on the Left, however, reached an accommodation with the capitalist model and the main economic policy instruments available in a mixed system influenced by global financial interactions. Sassoon neatly summarised the revisionism of Left politics: 'there are times when it looks as if, for the socialist parties, the world started yesterday, and the past is scorched earth.'[53] The process has not yet reached an end point: 'the post-socialist's future has not yet been found,' Shaw and Bell concluded.[54] This is the political environment in the era in which Democratic Left was formed, and ultimately folded, as its leading members eventually, and many reluctantly, came to accept that their future lay in a merger with the more moderate Irish Labour Party.

NOTES

1. D. Arter, 'Scandinavia: What's Left is the Social Democratic Consensus', *Parliamentary Affairs*, 36, 1 (2003).
2. N. Cohen, *What's Left?: How the Left Lost its Way* (London: Harper Collins, 2007).
3. See A. Crosland, *The Future of Socialism* (London: Robinson Publishing, 2006).
4. W.E. Patterson and A.H. Thomas (eds), *The Future of Social Democracy: Problems and Prospects of Social Democratic Parties in Western Europe* (Alderley: Clarendon Press, 1986), p.6.

5. Ibid., pp.5–6.
6. D. Sassoon, 'Introduction: Convergence, Continuity and Change on the European Left', in G. Kelly (ed.), *The New European Left* (London: Fabian Society, 1999), p.14.
7. G. Eley, *Forging Democracy: The History of the Left in Europe, 1850–2000* (Oxford: Oxford University Press, 2002), p.414.
8. D. Sassoon, *One Hundred Years of Socialism: The West European Left in the Twentieth Century* (New York: New Press, 1996), p.733.
9. F.A. Hayek, *The Fatal Conceit: The Errors of Socialism – The Collected Works of F.A. Hayek*, edited by W.W. Bartley III (Chicago: University of Chicago Press, 1991), p.7.
10. F. Fukuyama, 'The End of History?', *National Interest*, vol. 16 (Summer 1989), p.4.
11. J. Callaghan, 'Social Democracy in Transition', *Parliamentary Affairs*, 56, 1 (2003), p.125.
12. Eley, *Forging Democracy*, p.6.
13. Ibid.
14. M.J. Bull, 'The West European Communist Movement in the Late Twentieth Century', *West European Politics*, 18, 1 (1995), p.80.
15. Patterson and Thomas, *The Future of Social Democracy*, p.6
16. Bull, 'The West European Communist Movement in the Late Twentieth Century', p.80.
17. Callaghan, 'Social Democracy in Transition', p.125.
18. See R. Dunphy, 'From Eurocommunism to Eurosocialism: The Search for a Post-Communist European Left', *University of Dundee Occasional Papers*, Series 1:7 (1993).
19. D. Sassoon, *One Hundred Years of Socialism: The West European Left in the Twentieth Century* (New York: New Press, 1996), p.733.
20. Ibid., pp.734–5.
21. Eley, *Forging Democracy*, p.484.
22. T. Blair, *The Third Way: New Politics for the New Century* (London: Fabian Society, 1998), p.3.
23. Quoted in E. Shaw, 'Britain: Left Abandoned? New Labour in Power', *Parliamentary Affairs*, 36, 1 (2003), p.6.
24. Ibid.
25. Callaghan, 'Social Democracy in Transition', p.139.
26. Patterson and Thomas, *The Future of Social Democracy*, p.7.
27. A. Butler, *Transformative Politics: The Future of Socialism in Western Europe* (London: St Martin's Press, 1997), p.2.
28. R. Kindersley, 'In Lieu of a Conclusion: Eurocommunism and "the Crisis of Capitalism"', in R. Kindersley (ed.), *In Search of Eurocommunism* (London: Macmillan, 1981), p.194.
29. R. Godson and S. Haseler, *Eurocommunism: Implications for East and West* (London: Macmillan, 1978), pp.87–8.
30. Eley, *Forging Democracy*, p.437.
31. Ibid., p.7.
32. Ibid., p.443.
33. Quoted in Callaghan, 'Social Democracy in Transition', p.138.
34. Eley, *Forging Democracy*, p.427.
35. Dunphy, 'From Eurocommunism to Eurosocialism', p.17.
36. Eley, *Forging Democracy*, p.460.
37. Ibid., p.503.
38. Sassoon, *One Hundred Years of Socialism*, pp.732–3.
39. Bull, 'The West European Communist Movement in the Late Twentieth Century', p.87.
40. Sassoon, *One Hundred Years of Socialism*, p.734.
41. Bull, 'The West European Communist Movement in the Late Twentieth Century', p.94.
42. Sassoon, *One Hundred Years of Socialism*, p.738.
43. Bull, 'The West European Communist Movement in the Late Twentieth Century', p.91.
44. J.T. Ishiyama, 'Communist Successor Parties', *Politics and Society*, 34, 1 (March 2006), p.120.
45. P. Gottfried, *The Strange Death of Marxism: The European Left in the New Millennium* (Columbia: University of Missouri, 2005), p.2.
46. Eley, *Forging Democracy*, p.482.

47. Gottfried, *The Strange Death of Marxism*, p.7.
48. K. Hudson, *European Communism Since 1989: Towards a New European Left?* (London: Palgrave, 2000), p.5.
49. Larry Elliott in *The Guardian*, 22 December 2008.
50. L. Bouvet and F. Michel, 'Pluralism and the Future of the French Left', in G. Kelly (ed.), *The New European Left* (London: Fabian Society, 1999), pp.35, 38.
51. L. Marsh and C. Muddle, 'What's Left of the Radical Left? The European Radical Left After 1989: Decline and Mutation', *Comparative European Politics*, vol. 3 (2005), p.27.
52. Ibid., p.25.
53. D. Sassoon, 'Introduction: Convergence, Continuity and Change on the European Left', in G. Kelly (ed.), *The New European Left* (London: Fabian Society, 1999), p.13.
54. D. Bell and E. Shaw (eds), 'Introduction', in special issue on 'What's Left? The Left in Europe Today', *Parliamentary Affairs*, 56, 1 (2003), p.2.

2

Small Parties and Third Ways

The party system in the Irish Republic has been dominated, almost exclusively, by three parties – Fianna Fáil, Fine Gael and the Labour Party – and has frequently been labelled the 'two and a half party system' given the ongoing presence of two larger parties – Fianna Fáil and Fine Gael – alongside the smaller Labour Party.[1] When Ireland won its independence from Britain such were the dramatic changes that arose out of the stances adopted on ending the union with Britain that, as Chubb observed, 'the party system that emerged in the 1920s bore little resemblance to the system before independence.'[2] The moderate nationalist Irish Parliamentary Party disappeared, the Labour Party – formed in 1912 – continued while Sinn Féin divided into what was the first in a series of splits that would become a recurring feature associated with the party. Sinn Féin, which was established in 1905, is the starting point, albeit a distant one, for tracing the origins of many of the political parties that emerged post-independence, including Fianna Fáil, Fine Gael and Democratic Left.

In his overview of Irish political parties, Manning observed that 'in the twenty-one year period between 1905 and 1926 there were at least four successive parties bearing the name Sinn Féin.'[3] The first Sinn Féin – monarchical – was the party associated with the writings of its founder Arthur Griffith, who attempted to shape a workable political programme and socio-economic policy that could peacefully deliver Irish independence from Britain. The second Sinn Féin – separatist – was the party that emerged after the Easter 1916 Rising and which was closely linked with militant republicanism and the decision to bypass British rule in Ireland. The third Sinn Féin – republican – was the group associated with Éamon de Valera, who rejected the 1921 Anglo-Irish Treaty and opposed the new Irish Free State, politically and, for a time, violently. The fourth Sinn

Féin – isolationist – went through various organisational and ideological
shifts but always maintained its distance from the institutions established
under the 1921 peace treaty. Two further parties trading under the Sinn
Féin banner may also be added to Manning's list following on from the
divisions within the republican movement in 1969–70. These divisions
produced two separate organisations to which the labels Provisionals and
Officials were applied to broadly distinguish their respective attitudes to
violence and political involvement. Democratic Left emerged from the
evolution in the 'Official' side of the republican movement, which
moved in the direction of politics while the Provisionals maintained an
adherence to the physical force tradition.

Despite the continuous movement in republican politics, the traditional description of the mainstream Irish party political system has
been one marked by relative stability. Mair has shown how, unlike the
experience elsewhere in western Europe – where parties mainly grew
out of social conflicts – the Irish experience was defined by political
and military conflict. 'The Irish parties in fact emerged from a unique
experience in the period 1916–23, during which an intra-nationalist
conflict and civil war centring on the country's constitutional status
followed an armed independence struggle.'[4]

Nevertheless, new entrants have continuously challenged the dominance of the three traditional parties – over the last ninety years new parties have been persistent in seeking to break into the national political
arena. Throughout this time Irish voters have had considerable choice
beyond the three main parties, although at each general election they
have neither fully embraced nor fully rejected new parties. The relationship between the electorate and these small parties like Democratic Left
has been akin to a love affair never consummated. The new entrants have
periodically challenged the established order in terms of shaping policy
agendas, winning seats and participating in multi-party governmental
arrangements. A limited number of small parties have achieved these
three outcomes – impact on policy, Dáil representation and governmental involvement – including Clann na Poblachta, Clann na Talmhain, the
Progressive Democrats, Democratic Left and the Green Party. But these
new entrants have had a poor record in sustaining their challenge to the
traditional dominance of the three traditional parties. With the exception
of the Green Party, which entered office for the first time in 2007, none
of these smaller parties survived sufficiently long to establish a lasting

presence on the political landscape and judgement of the Green Party's participation in a coalition with Fianna Fáil (2007–11) will only emerge over time. Despite this mixed record small parties 'add a richness and depth that has an impact on democracy and representation beyond the limited success they achieve at the ballot box – locally and nationally'.[5]

Mair has suggested that a large party is one that normally polls on average at least 15 per cent of the national vote while small parties are those that receive on average between 1.5 per cent and 15 per cent of the national vote, and have had a life beyond three electoral contests.[6] This means of categorisation is unsatisfactory in the case of Irish party politics as it sees the Labour Party – depending upon its electoral performance – on occasion classified as a small party and, at other times, as a large party.

Alternative classification methods in the political science literature have focused on the two largest parties in a country and described all others as small, although in the Irish case Coakley argues for labelling as small all except the three largest parties. This latter suggestion makes sense, as the Labour Party has features more in common with Fianna Fáil and Fine Gael than the multitude of small parties that have attempted to secure a foothold in Irish politics, including a wider national organisation, repeated governmental participation, greater levels of national electoral support and longevity.

The multi-member constituency electoral system in Ireland has helped small parties (and independents) to secure election, although they have been less successful than their counterparts elsewhere in Europe in establishing longevity. The electoral outcomes for small Irish parties have experienced peaks and troughs. Smaller parties enjoyed electoral successes in the 1920s, in the late 1940s and again in the period since the 1980s. But there have been disappointing times. At the 1969 general election only one of the 144 TDs returned to Dáil Éireann was an independent member.

These small parties can be placed into different classification frameworks, including Left, Right, agrarian, religious, nationalist and environmental. The party types led Coakley to observe that, 'at first sight, the range of minor parties that have existed in Ireland since independence is bewildering.'[7] Many have, however, been merely pressure groups seeking to raise attention on a small number of specific issues – indeed, even a single issue – and in most instances without electoral success. These included the Ratepayers' Association, which contested in

1922, 1923 and 1957 with a total of four candidates and a highest vote share of 0.4 per cent; the Blind Men's Party, which contested the June 1927 general election on behalf of the Irish Association of the Blind with two candidates; Cine Gael, which nominated a single candidate in the 1954 general election seeking to expropriate land in foreign ownership; the Army Wives' Group, which campaigned on soldiers' pay and conditions in the 1989 general election, nominating three candidates; and the Natural Law Party, which advocated transcendental meditation to solve global conflict, nominating ten candidates in 1997.

None of these 'parties' secured even modest electoral success although they may have succeeded in promoting their main cause. Nevertheless, what their existence does highlight is the need to categorise small parties carefully. In electoral, political and governmental terms some small parties are more serious, and more important, than others. Similarly, attempts to include independent candidates in an analysis of small parties fail to acknowledge that independent politicians do not exist within an organisational framework with a constitution, procedures and membership.

The majority (76 per cent) of the 262 candidates elected to Dáil Éireann as members of smaller parties represented in total only eight political parties. Indeed, of the thirty-four smaller parties that contested Dáil elections since 1945 only fourteen had candidates elected. According to Pedersen's 1982 study, to have an impact on political life small parties must signal their arrival (declaration), contest elections (authorisation), experience electoral success (representation) and make an impact, most likely, on the policy formation process (relevance).

Relevance can be defined in different ways. At first sight relevance may be associated with electoral success. But winning seats is just one way of measuring impact or success. There are different degrees of relevance. Smaller parties can have influence without achieving significant electoral success. The very act of contesting elections – even without winning seats – can assist in raising the profile of issues that are core to the interests of a small party. Such involvement may bring attention onto previously ignored issues or help to generate greater media interest in under-reported policy areas.

In this way some small parties operate almost as opinion formers. Their very existence – and potential to be electorally successful – also acts as an influence on the actions of the main parties. By way of responding to the potential threat to their own support base the larger party will adopt key elements of the platform of the smaller party. In the case of Ireland the three main parties have shown themselves to be excellent policy poachers.

Small parties have done well at 'second order' elections – local and European contests – but those successes have done little to assist in challenging the dominance of the three main parties in Dáil elections. Most small parties in Ireland have been marginal to national political life in terms of their electoral or system-influence impact. Only a limited number of small parties have made an electoral breakthrough into national politics – even fewer have had a governmental impact. Since 1945 only Clann na Talmhain, Clann na Poblachta, National Labour, the Progressive Democrats, Democratic Left and the Green Party have participated in coalition governments. This grouping of small parties, which adheres to all four criteria defined by Pedersen, deserves a separate classification from the myriad of other small parties – and independent candidates – registered to contest national elections. These groups have a national electoral relevance and fit the description of 'hinge parties' in that they operate at the centre of national politics and hold some coalition potential. If the parliamentary numbers fall correctly, such a small party can have 'blackmail potential' in that its involvement is needed by one, or more, of the larger parties to form a secure governmental arrangement.

While the small parties that have experienced government come from different ideological perspectives, they all have in common initial electoral success followed by steady decline. On first analysis it would seem that participation in government shortened their respective life-cycles. Involvement in a coalition government with one or more of the three big parties – Fianna Fáil, Fine Gael or the Labour Party – may possibly have blurred the lines of difference with their rivals. These small parties were ultimately, to use O'Malley's phrase, 'smothered' by their larger governmental partner.[8]

But the challenges and threats to small parties are more fundamental than the dangers of cosying-up with their larger rivals in government. When faced with a multitude of challenges such as membership, organisation, leadership and, more recently, money new parties in Ireland have struggled to sustain their political involvement. They have also failed to deal with the larger parties 'stealing their clothes' by adapting programmes and positions to preserve their predominance. The durability of the main parties has been impressive – even when faced with a decline in their first-preference vote, Fianna Fáil, Fine Gael and the Labour Party have adapted to changes and challenges so that they continue to win more or less the same percentage of Dáil seats.[9]

The emergence of new small parties is often a reflection of a failure by the established parties to respond to new political agendas – the new entrants are more in tune with voter concerns. They also act as a means of registering protest or discontent with the political system, and represent certain principles. In this way small parties tend to be agenda-setters. But their agendas may be limited and once the large parties adjust their stance voters tend to gravitate away from the small parties. In this way, the electorate's support for small parties may be highly promiscuous beyond a limited core vote.

Fianna Fáil and Fine Gael – and to a lesser degree the Labour Party – as catch-all parties with a flexibility to reach accommodation with societal changes rely upon broad coalitions of support. McGraw has argued that 'this catch-all character of the major parties has reinforced the pragmatic nature of Irish politics.'[10] In general, catch-all parties dilute their ideological individuality in order to maximise their appeal to centre-orientated middle-class voters. They compete for votes not on significant policy difference but rather on competency and personality, with competency equating with economic management and personality defined by the likeability of a party leader. As is discussed in subsequent chapters, a narrowing of party difference has been evident in the main areas of political debate in Irish society over the last two decades – Northern Ireland, the economy and the liberal/moral agenda. This uniquely Irish convergence was played out as the global political scene was transformed in a post-Berlin Wall environment with a merging of economic ideology and a blurring in the differences in political orientation between most mainstream parties which had their origins in twentieth-century Left and Right politics.

Those involved in founding Democratic Left in early 1992 were aware of the poor record new entrants had in challenging the traditional dominance of Fianna Fáil, Fine Gael and the Labour Party in Irish electoral and governmental history. 'It is extremely difficult to build a new party in Ireland from the ground up,' Pat Rabbitte, a senior Democratic Left figure, acknowledged.[11] The challenge for Rabbitte and his colleagues was made even harder still by the uncertainty over their political identity in the context of Left politics in the 1990s; the rate of change in Ireland in the same decade as many of their core issues were resolved; and the specific organisational and financial demands placed upon small political parties. Rabbitte, a senior founding member, had departed the Labour Party in the mid-1970s for what he perceived as the more radical alternative offered by Sinn Féin The Workers' Party.[12] But he was a reluctant recruit to the Democratic Left cause – not out of disenchantment with his colleagues, who had sought unsuccessfully to reconstitute the Workers' Party, but rather because the former student union activist and trade union official had already decided the future lay with the moderate, social democratic-leaning Labour Party. The latter move was still seven years away when Rabbitte, whose opinion was in the minority, sat down with other senior colleagues including Proinsias De Rossa, Eamon Gilmore, Tony Heffernan and Liz McManus. The objective of this grouping was to plot a political future beyond the ideological confusion and criminality allegations that had sundered the Workers' Party. Their conclusion was to form Democratic Left – a self-styled party of the radical Left.

THE IRISH LEFT

The party system in Ireland, as previously noted, has frequently been labelled the 'two and a half party system' given the traditional presence of two larger parties – Fianna Fáil and Fine Gael – alongside the smaller Labour Party. The failure of the Left to develop a major political presence in Ireland in a manner similar to other western European countries has been the subject of considerable discussion. According to Farrell: 'It is common in the comparative literature to refer to the Irish party system as unique, reflected in the weakness of the Left, the absence of class politics and the inherent similarity between the parties in terms of their policies and standpoints.'[13] This lack of relative electoral success is evident in Table 2.1, which records the outcomes of general elections in the Irish Republic from 1973 to 1997. This was the period in which the Workers' Party emerged as a political presence to the left of the Labour Party, and in which Democratic Left was formed and contested two general elections to Dáil Éireann.

This outcome led Mair to remark that, 'more than anything else, it is the relative weakness of the Left which has always marked the Irish party system out as an exception to the general patterns which prevailed

TABLE 2.1
DÁIL ÉIREANN ELECTION RESULTS, 1973–97

Year	WP/DL	F F	F G	Lab	PDs	Others
1973	1.1	46.2	35.1	13.7	-	3.9
1977	1.7	50.6	30.6	11.6	-	5.5
1981	1.7	45.3	36.5	9.9	-	6.6
1982 Feb.	2.2	47.3	37.3	9.1	-	4.1
1982 Nov.	3.3	45.2	39.2	9.4	-	2.9
1987	3.8	44.2	27.1	6.5	11.9	6.5
1989	5.0	44.2	29.3	9.5	5.5	6.5
1992	2.8	39.1	24.5	19.3	4.7	9.6
1997	2.5	39.3	27.9	10.4	4.7	14.7

Source: www.electionsireland.org

throughout the rest of western Europe.'[14] In an examination of the
various studies which have attempted to account for the marginalisation
of the Irish Left, Mair focused on four historical factors: the absence of
a substantial and politically self-conscious working class which denied
the Left a natural constituency; the strength of a clientelist culture
which stresses individual political relations over collective action; the
catch-all appeal of Fianna Fáil which has allowed the party to promote
welfarist policies (the salience of nationalist issues in the early years of
Irish politics meant that there was little scope for a party which
devoted itself almost exclusively to working-class socialist concerns);
and finally the decision of the Labour Party to stand aside from the 1918
Westminster general election when many voters casting their ballot for
the first time were influenced by the nationalist political agenda.

The Left in the post-1921 period was primarily represented by the
Labour Party, and although there were successes – for example, the party
achieved a record national vote in 1969 – there was no significant
realignment, with Fianna Fáil, Fine Gael and the Labour Party dominating the political landscape in that order of strength. Despite the longstanding 'two and a half party' label, the Irish party political landscape
became more crowded and complex in the 1980s and 1990s with the
emergence of several smaller parties including the Progressive Democrats
on the Right, and on the Left the Workers' Party/Democratic Left.
Nevertheless, the increased support for the Workers' Party in the 1980s
– as Table 2.1 illustrates – did not lead to a strengthened Left support

base as the party was, in effect, taking votes from the Labour Party. The Workers' Party did not have an opportunity to test its strategy of replacing the Labour Party as the largest force on the Irish Left as a series of pressures forced a split in its ranks in 1992.

Like other socialist and social democratic parties in western Europe – which were engaged in internal debate and analysis many years before the revolutions in 1989 – the Irish Workers' Party was not immune to internal soul-searching. The party emerged out of a split in the hardline Irish republican tradition in 1969/70 but it positioned itself on the radical Left in contrast to the moderate Labour Party. The party was never formally styled as a communist party, and there remains, among its former leading political figures, differing views as to its ideological classification. Eamon Gilmore was emphatic that the Workers' Party was never a communist party. 'It had within it people who were Marxists, people who were social democrats, people who were Left Labourites, if I can put it that way, you know, people who were socialists in a wide sense of the word.'[15] This broad definition is in sharp contrast to the view offered by Proinsias De Rossa. 'My clear understanding about the party was that it had evolved into what might nowadays be termed a communist party. It was much more like the communist party in Italy.'[16]

Despite these alternative opinions about the party's positioning on the Left political spectrum, the Workers' Party did in fact share many of the characteristics of the communist identity in western Europe. Martin Bull isolated three factors binding west European communist parties together:

- a privileged link with Moscow, which had replaced abject loyalty based on a shared recognition of the Russian Revolution and communist rule;

- a commitment to building a society different from the capitalist one;

- an internal organisation underpinned by democratic centralism.[17]

There is greater discussion about the history of the Workers' Party in Chapter 3 but at this stage it can be reasonably concluded that the party met the Bull criteria as it had links to the Soviet Union, a commitment to a post-capitalist future and an adherence to democratic centralism as a means of organisation. Moreover, the party was similar to many others on the socialist and communist Left in western Europe which felt obliged to create space to avoid being identified with the increasingly discredited Soviet Union. At a time when the Left in western Europe was in ideological questioning mode, Moscow's command economic management was failing to deliver sustained growth. The Soviet model was on the verge of crisis, while political suppression was ordered by Moscow to quell a desire for democratic governance in parts of eastern Europe. The response by many in the western European Left was to view the Soviet model in a more negative ideological light.

Dunphy placed the Irish Workers' Party into the reformist Eurocommunist category which emerged in the 1970s. Certainly taking the definition of Eurocommunism as parties committed to revolutionary goals, adhering to democratic socialism and defined by considerable membership uniformity, then the Workers' Party in the late 1970s and throughout 1980s, in effect, ticked the correct boxes. But, just like the communist model in the Soviet-controlled areas, Eurocommunism was inadequate as an ideological position. It was, as Kindersley noted, 'a good sales pitch'.[18] But it was also an inadequate sales pitch as it failed to give the Left a new voice. 'The 1980s thus opened with the Eurocommunist project effectively abandoned, although it was to be some time before this became apparent,' Dunphy concluded. While it is a conclusion that would not find universal acceptance, there is sufficient evidence to support the contention that the radical Left was on a trajectory towards convergence with the social democratic tradition.

Indeed, those to the left of mainstream Left parties in countries like Britain, Austria and Sweden – and including the Workers' Party in Ireland – were increasingly confronted with the reality that their positions, policies and outlooks were indistinguishable from the social democracy of many Left-wing parties. As Dunphy observed about the more radical Left in Spain, Denmark, Greece and Ireland (the Workers' Party), these parties were 'all relatively small organisations forced to define themselves in opposition to social democratic parties which seem to be post-socialist, never mind post-Marxist'.[19] As is discussed in subsequent chapters, one of the consistent outcomes from the various interviews undertaken for this study with Workers' Party/Democratic Left politicians was how they repeatedly defined their own outlook and ideological stance by reference to the Labour Party.

The Workers' Party adhered to democratic centralism as a means of organisation. This resulted in a highly authoritarian form of control and a culture that set very demanding criteria for party membership. Dunphy and Hopkins quoted Eric Byrne – a party representative in Dublin South Central – as saying that members were 'highly motivated and highly flexible people'.[20] They had no other choice – the same two authors recorded a story where applicants for membership were rejected because the potential members would not be available to sell the party paper on Sunday mornings. In 1982 the party agreed to expand its membership base. This exercise was not successful: 'The smallness of the party's membership had the effect of placing enormous demands on the existing members – and thus, ironically, deterring potential recruits from joining.'[21] There was undoubtedly internal tension over the matter as the parliamentary group led by Proinsias De Rossa increasingly questioned the relevance of a democratic centralist approach to party building.

As an activist in Cork and a national executive member, Kathleen Lynch was aware of the growing tensions within the party between a bloc including elected representatives based in Leinster House and another grouping involving activists and organisers in party head office:

> You had a very dynamic parliamentary party, not big by any means, but nevertheless I think all [small] parties gather very strong personalities because you don't have a core vote so you have to gather the vote yourself. And the parliamentary party was trying to assert itself ... and it was bound to clash with the sort of democratic centralist control within the party, and that more than anything else probably was the [reason for] friction, and that more than anything was probably what drove the party to split.[22]

The internal Workers' Party debate was undoubtedly given added impetus by developments in the Soviet Union where Gorbachev was opening up the possibility of an alternative definition of socialist democracy. As one writer observed, 'Democratic centralism's proven inability to allow the filtering of opinions up, as well as down, the hierarchy, eventually contributed to the downfall of the CPSU [Communist Party of the Soviet Union].'[23] Broadcaster Eoghan Harris was one of the leading reform figures in the Workers' Party. He heavily influenced a key speech delivered by Proinsias De Rossa in 1989 which Patterson acutely distilled:

> It strongly argued for an acceptance of the market economy and

the profit motive, criticised the 'dogmas' of traditional socialist economics, attacked welfare dependency and argued that enterprise and hard work should be rewarded. This was 'Blairism' ahead of its time and, written before the fall of the Berlin Wall, demonstrated Harris's acute sensitivity to those epochal changes that radically transform the basic contours and language of politics ...[24]

Harris's intervention hastened an internal debate among his colleagues but the collapse of the communist-controlled regimes in central and eastern Europe forced the Workers' Party to speed up the reconsideration of its ideological identity and organisational model. 'At stake were not merely organisational choices but also the party's political and ideological direction,' Dunphy and Hopkins noted.[25] Interestingly, there are different views among party members as to the importance of 1989 in bringing them to a point that forced a split in Workers' Party ranks, which in turn led to the formation of Democratic Left in 1992. There was some unease that senior members were clinging to the increasingly discredited ideology as represented by the Soviet-controlled states, as public representative Eric Byrne outlined:

> We were allegedly a sort of communist, Stalinist party in the mould of the Soviet Union. There would have been a very small ideological clique within the Workers' Party, and in fact they were an embarrassment to us. At annual conferences we would be most embarrassed when we'd see invitations ... bringing in people from North Korea and other weird communist countries ...[26]

Byrne's unease, however, does not sit well with the recollections of Seán Garland, a leading Workers' Party figure who did not join Democratic Left:

> It was never said, 'this is the problem'. It was never said openly what the problems were. I mean we had discussions and we had meetings about international relations. Nobody said we should halt this or stop these relations, or cut them off. We had many delegations from different countries at our Árd Fheis. You know it didn't come up until the end of the day [as] a stick to beat people with. I mean it was more of a general thing that was happening outside Ireland than what was happening in Ireland.[27]

Not unsurprisingly, another party veteran, Tomás MacGiolla, shared

Garland's assessment. Indeed, MacGiolla did not see the wider debate about the Left in Europe, and in eastern Europe in particular, as impacting on the Workers' Party. 'It never made the slightest difference; [it] was never raised by any of the branches. I was a total anti-communist and there were no Stalinists in the party. So it was never an issue [within the Workers' Party].'[28] But a more nuanced debate than MacGiolla acknowledged was well underway in party ranks. Others recognised the wider context. Proinsias De Rossa recalled:

> I remember making a speech where I pointed out that the fall of the Berlin Wall and what was happening in Russia was going to have far-reaching effects on the Left and on the Right, and that people didn't know quite yet what the outcome would be, how the political scene would pan out, and I think it's still being worked through.[29]

Few political parties positioned under the broad Left umbrella remained unchanged by the events of 1989 and the advance of economic globalisation. In that regard, the Workers' Party in Ireland was no different than its counterparts elsewhere in Europe. Notwithstanding the different perspectives offered in the previous discussion, there were other pressure points in the Workers' Party in the 1980s unique to the party's Irish experience and removed from the wider debate about European Left politics. As is discussed in greater detail in Chapter 3, the party was dogged by questions about the continued existence of the illegal Official Irish Republican Army (OIRA), an overlap in membership between the two organisations and the possibility that monies obtained by illegal means were funding legitimate political activities.

While the ideological debate had been developing throughout the 1980s, the question of members with links to criminal activities had been a recurring theme since the 1970s and eventually pushed the divisions to a stage where even reconstitution of the party was not going to overcome the deep internal tensions. For many of those who ultimately exited the Workers' Party, criminality was the main motivation for the split. 'For myself and almost everyone in our branch in Kildare the predominant issue that caused the split was criminality,' Catherine Murphy asserted.[30]

The Official IRA had called a ceasefire in May 1972 – and very much disappeared from the public sphere by 1975 – but questions about the organisation's continued existence lingered. The official line from all

leading Workers' Party figures for well over a decade had been that the
party was not associated with the OIRA nor was it funded from criminal
activity. But the negative publicity arising from media speculation about
the OIRA was a source of considerable frustration within the De Rossa
wing of the party. 'I think we tolerated too many excuses within the
North, special circumstances and conditions in which they lived ... We
didn't want any taint of illegality ... You couldn't be pretending this
and pretending that, and you couldn't be making excuses for people
...' Des Geraghty said.[31]

Ideological revisionism was already underway in the Workers' Party
by the late 1980s, signalled very clearly by Proinsias De Rossa when he
took over the leadership. There were differing perspectives about this
policy reorientation. It may well be that these clashes would have eventually led to a split in the party's ranks but the criminality allegations
undoubtedly forced the issue. For some associated with the De Rossa
grouping the changes in the Soviet Union were less significant, as
Rosheen Callender explained:

> A lot of us would have seen ourselves as a modernising party that
> was if anything ahead of what was happening in other parts of
> Europe ... so we wouldn't have been particularly split on those
> issues. I don't think the split was inevitable. I think it came
> because the people who thought we should be moving forward
> came to a point where they just felt that other people were dragging
> their heels just a bit too much, and it came to a head over issues
> that weren't really the central issue at all.[32]

Wicklow politician Liz McManus agreed with this argument. 'Obviously the things that were happening in Russia had an impact but I
don't think they were significant ... I didn't have the view that because
the [Berlin] Wall collapsed that suddenly all our policies were ripped
from under us.'[33] The latter viewpoint, however, underplays the ideological repositioning that the Workers' Party had already embarked
upon under De Rossa's leadership. According to Eamon Gilmore, who
was centrally involved in moves to reconstitute the party, the revision
of Left politics led to a revitalisation of the OIRA as part of the ongoing internal debate. In effect, those who were opposed to change sought
to protect the status quo by resorting to the practices of the past. In
that regard, Gilmore's analysis is worth considering in full:

The Workers' Party never had debates like a lot of parties on the Left in Europe had throughout the 1980s. And that debate came with the election of De Rossa as leader. Not reducing these things to a phrase but in his speech at the 1989 party conference after becoming leader, De Rossa effectively declared the Workers' Party to be a social democratic party. Some of us were absolutely delighted and weighed in very heavily behind De Rossa, and some of what you might call the old guard just took flight at this. And so what happened was [that] the debate took place in a very condensed period of time where a lot of things were happening – the 1989 general election where we did remarkably well, seven TDs, group status in the Dáil. [Then] De Rossa's spectacular election to the European parliament in 1989. Against what was happening in eastern Europe, and the whole change that was taking place over that period of time. And then, I think, what happened was there was an organisational attempt to regain the balance [of power]. In that organisational attempt it seems to me that a lot of people were brought back into the party who had dodgy connections, or dodgy pasts ... And we found ourselves in the situation in 1990 and 1991 where it was possible to finger people who were involved in petty criminal activity and somebody would say that person is a member of the Workers' Party. And, therefore, the Workers' Party was involved and so on and so on. Of course in a lot of these cases these were people who had been enrolled or re-enrolled as party members to get the numbers for the 1990 conference. Because there was a battle going on from the time of De Rossa's speech for control of the party. And the battle was between the social democratic political outlook, broadly speaking, and, I suppose, broadly speaking, a revolutionary or communist kind. That's really what happened.[34]

Gilmore's recollection summarises the background to the split from the perspective of those who ultimately founded Democratic Left. Like others on the 'radical Left' in west European politics in the late 1980s, they were forced to reconsider their core ideological beliefs. But room has to be made for the consideration of an additional factor that motivated change in the Workers' Party – criminality. In the end a combination of these two factors led the De Rossa grouping to form Democratic Left, and to join in the wider European search for a new Left identity in the 1990s.

POST-1989 POLITICAL IDENTITY

Discussions within Democratic Left from its formation in early 1992 always returned to the matter of where the party was positioned ideologically. As the analysis in subsequent chapters will show, the subject of the party's identity dominated internal debate. One example of this identity search is found in internal party executive minutes from July 1994: 'The very immediate task and objective of this party is to clearly establish and define itself as a democratic socialist party on the radical Left of the Irish political spectrum. This must be done in an unambiguous and unapologetic way.'[35] These sentiments were a variation of a theme repeated time and time again in internal party documents. The debate was largely unresolved when serious discussion turned to the question of a merger with the Labour Party after the 1997 general election. Democratic Left had not, however, been functioning in a political vacuum. In 2003, in a special issue of *Parliamentary Affairs* entitled 'What's Left? The Left in Europe Today', the editors opened their introduction by observing that 'one word which springs out from this review of western European socialist parties is "crisis".'[36]

For those involved in the Workers' Party there was an acceptance that internal reform, embraced by Proinsias De Rossa when he became party leader, was necessary. The formation of Democratic Left was, in part, a response to this situation. But at that time there was also a belief that a new form of Left politics would emerge, a politics more radical than social democracy. This 'New Revisionist' theme was addressed by Liz McManus, at the founding conference of Democratic Left:

> Never was there a greater need for a party like ours. An open democratic socialist party that is capable of facing up to the complexities of modern life and drawing out a framework for action from our daily experiences. No dead ideology of the past can match the task we set ourselves. The free market has made too many people unfree for us to abandon our commitment to the future. The collapse of eastern Europe has temporarily left capitalism without an opposition. But that fact does not make capitalism any more capable of creating a free and equal society. We know that the Soviet model was corrupt and dictatorial but its failure does not validate capitalism. Now is not the end of history. It is the beginning of a new phase in history and we are playing our part in it.

At the same conference Des Geraghty also attempted to place the formation of the new party in the post-1989 political context in Europe:

> We have defined our politics as democratic and socialist because we believe that the application of the socialist value system to the reality of a modern European democracy is the best way to bring about real change. We have rejected any utopian or elitist politics which seek to act on behalf of people but fails to involve the people in setting their political agenda for change.

The message could be distilled down to one that the new party was different from the old parties of the Left that had looked to the Soviet Union for guidance but it was also offering something different from social democratic parties such as the Irish Labour Party. Various contributions at the foundation conference were pointing towards a 'third way' debate underway in Left and liberal-leaning circles. The task was to find ideological expression in a post-Cold War world in which the old Left was bruised and lacking coherence. 'A very old Chinese leader said recently that it didn't matter to him whether a cat is black or white as long as it caught mice. I suggest we adopt the same pragmatism when it comes to our politics,' McManus said.

But, as noted previously, third way politics and new revisionism were somewhat ill-defined. Politicians like Proinsias De Rossa in Ireland were in the difficult role of trying to explain how their new positioning was different from the outlook held by their social democratic opponents. Those who departed the Irish Workers' Party in early 1992 were not yet prepared to make the leap into a new social democratic future. They were intent on finding – and maybe even creating – a new type of politics. Although his contribution came at the end of the conference proceedings, De Rossa posed some pertinent questions: 'some people ask – do we need a new party? And what is this new party? How does it differ?'

De Rossa could not avoid the subject, as elsewhere the issue of difference between the new undertaking and the Labour Party was being discussed. One media commentator, Dick Walsh, who had close links with the Workers' Party, noted, 'On most fronts, Labour and Democratic Left will find themselves in broad agreement, although they still differ on the North and ... may employ different tactics.'[37]

Ahead of the founding conference, Proinsias De Rossa received a letter of best wishes from Dick Spring, the leader of the Labour Party:

In the months ahead I look forward to continuing the co-operation that we have enjoyed in the Dáil on a wide range of issues. Given the increasingly right-wing stamp of the present Government ... it will be more important than ever that a strong and coherent Left-wing voice is heard leading the opposition.[38]

The good wishes were well received but De Rossa and his supporters wanted to offer a distinctive voice on the Left political spectrum. In response to his own questions about needing a new party, De Rossa said, 'The simple answer is that we are committed to breaking new ground, committed to new thinking on the Left. And what is on offer by Labour and the Workers' Party is a choice between modern social democracy and Leninism.' Both forms of ideological expression were linked, De Rossa argued. They represented visions of socialism that treated working-class people as passive objects while both had given socialism 'a statist and bureaucratic stamp which in part at least was responsible for the upsurge of the neo-liberalism of Thatcher and Reagan of the last decade'. De Rossa succinctly defined both ideological points available on the Left:

> Social democracy has, in its time, given comfort and security to millions who would otherwise have been denied even a minimum of human dignity. But it has run its course, and has in most cases degenerated into mere electoralism, has lost any resolve to be part of a wider strategy for the transformation of society, and has settled for a dull managerialism. Leninism, on the other hand, has collapsed everywhere as a model for the transformation of society and the development of a free and egalitarian society. It carries within it a fundamentally elitist and therefore antidemocratic premise – that the masses are too ignorant to comprehend the process of change and cannot be trusted to make the 'right' decisions if given the liberty to make them. It has sought to construct socialism from above and has failed.

By way of contrast, De Rossa was hoping to lead a new political party that would be 'an active democratic socialist party with a strong presence in parliament'. There is little doubt but that De Rossa's speech at the Democratic Left founding conference – and indeed the various documents approved by delegates – fitted with the Sassoon neo-revisionism thesis. De Rossa spoke of a party of activists that would promote 'the need for reform of politics, accountability of politicians, environment, peace, jobs, education ...' The new organisation, he asserted, would:

> ... not preach at people or talk in abstract terms about revolution and class struggle. Our concerns and practices will reflect the experience of people in their daily lives ... Ours will be a politics of empowerment, participation, analysis, and not just an electoral machine. We will be an activist party involved in a multiplicity of campaigns, bringing to each of them a broader and longer-term vision.

Yet that vision was never defined in a way that explained the party's distinctiveness nor was it made clear what policy instruments were to be used to implement the same vision. Democratic Left's search for ideological relevance became a recurring theme in the party's short life. In early 1992 the party and its leading members embarked upon a political journey in search of a middle ground, or third way, between a discredited communist/socialist/republican past and an unsatisfactory social democratic compromise. But Left politics – and in particular the type of ideology framed as more radical than social democratic thinking – struggled to find a coherent programme. Like its counterparts in countries like Italy and France, Democratic Left was confronted with the rejection of a Marxist past and its replacement with a variation of social democracy. David Arter has written how post-1989 politics led to 'the neo-liberalisation of social democracy, and the associated phenomenon of the social democratisation of the radical Left'.[39] Democratic Left's weakness was tied to its rejection of social democracy as a political and ideological programme. The party wanted a more radical prescription but struggled to create a new coherent ideological blueprint, especially in the economic arena.

Democratic Left was never an anti-establishment party. It sought the 'Radical Left' label and rejected the Blairist 'third way' model. But the party did not fit what March and Muddle described as 'Radical Left'. It would be incorrect to position Democratic Left in several of the radical Left categories discussed previously. The party was not pure communist, nor did it emerge (out of the Workers' Party) to seriously engage with the anti-system movement. There was also resistance to a transformation into a fully-fledged social democratic party, although this was in fact the direction in which Democratic Left would ultimately move. The

reform group within the Workers' Party was unwilling to contemplate
an immediate move into classic social democratic politics – including
joining the moderate Labour Party in 1992. Nevertheless, the speeches
at the founding conference of Democratic Left pointed to a desire to
forge a new Left politics. Those involved in the Democratic Left project
in Ireland could loosely be grouped under the 'democratic socialist'
heading which March and Muddle defined as those 'to the "Left" of
social democracy, [who] accept parliamentary democracy, but retain a
radical commitment to systemic transformation, usually through a commitment to grass-roots democracy and (especially) through a rejection
of capitalism'.[40]

The Democratic Left constitution approved at the party's founding
conference in 1992 is a document focused on a radical transformation of
Irish, and indeed world, society. The document described Democratic
Left as 'democratic, secular, socialist'. The first two objectives in the constitution were '(a) The development of a democratic, secular, socialist
society in Ireland [and] (b) To contribute to the development of
democratic socialism in Europe and throughout the world'. The latter
sentiments show that, in theory at least, it is possible to place the party
within the March and Muddle classification. Democratic Left's self-
positioning on the ideological spectrum was to the 'Left of social
democracy'. But the party was not 'Radical Left' in the wider European
sense, and certainly not in the view of, say, the Left Party in Sweden as
previously identified by Hudson who offered a hypothesis that as social
democratic and traditional conservative parties converge around a
neo-liberal agenda, a new Left wing would emerge to fight against such
convergence and win increased electoral support. The Democratic Left
policy platform was more centrist. The party was not rejecting capitalism,
rather it was seeking an accommodation of the market economy while
promoting social justice. The Democratic Left policy platform as
presented at its founding conference stated, 'Our idea of a successful
economy is one that can raise everybody's living standards, by creating
more wealth, distributing it more fairly and spending it more sanely.' The
Left Party in Sweden is one of the best examples to support Hudson's
hypothesis, along with smaller Left parties including the German PDS
and United Left in Spain. All of these parties survived on national electoral votes in the region of 10 per cent. It is arguable that there was
little space on the Irish political spectrum for a radical new Left party like

those mentioned previously. The identity crisis that engulfed Democratic Left was about seeking a radical Left positioning while increasingly adopting and following more moderate social democratic policies.

The former Democratic Left members interviewed for this study were all individually asked where they saw the new party positioned in ideological terms. The collection of answers was generally similar, with the word 'socialist' used repeatedly. 'We were Left wing and radical,' Kathleen Lynch stated.[41] Moreover, there was a tendency for respondents also (and unprovoked) to mention the Labour Party when defining Democratic Left. The problem in finding clear ideological space for Democratic Left undermined its ability to develop and, as is discussed below, the party and its members were constantly brought back to defining their ideological and political relevance by reference to the Labour Party. Eric Byrne's response is a good representation:

> We definitely would have seen the party as a mainstream socialist party to the Left, very much to the Left of the Labour Party. We would have seen ourselves as a party that was capable of attracting a greater political support base than the Labour Party. We would have seen the Labour Party as very much to right of centre. We would have been contemptuous of a lot of its former leaders [and] reactionary when coming to progressive issues – divorce, abortion. We would have seen it [the Labour Party] as a soft, yellow-bellied sort of party. So we would have seen ourselves as a party that was capable of replacing the Labour Party ... We were breaking away from an ideological, Stalinist type and becoming a more pure Left-wing socialist party.[42]

Those involved in Democratic Left, as subsequent chapters will show, were confronted by considerable challenges in building an organisation, raising resources, fighting elections and establishing a coherent identity. A combination of all these factors contributed to the failure of Democratic Left, although over the 1992–9 period the question of identity dominated internal party discussions. At the founding conference De Rossa pointed to the challenge the new party faced – not just in finding a successful electoral niche but also in formulating coherent political aspirations. 'We do not expect overnight success. We know that change is a complex process. But we also know that change must be worked for. That it will not happen simply because we want it to happen.' In an interview for this study De Rossa drew associations between the Workers' Party experience and that of the Communist Party in Italy, which respectively emerged in the 1990s as Democratic Left and the Democrats of the Left. There are difficulties with the comparison, not least the size issue and the long-time political and electoral impact of the Italian party vis-à-vis De Rossa's organisation. But the journey the two parties travelled in the 1990s is similar in its outcome: Democratic Left ceased to exist while the Democrats of the Left suffered dramatic decline.

The Italian Communists had once 'had the reputation of being the largest communist party in the west: its heir now [2003] has the distinction of being one of the smallest Left-wing parties in Europe.'[43] The crisis for the latter party, one writer observed, 'symbolised a failure over a decade to transform the former Communist Party into an effective non-communist reformist alternative in Italian politics'.[44] In a similar way, Democratic Left in Ireland existed without a clearly understood, reformist identity. Both parties participated in coalition governments in the mid-1990s which served to spark a crisis of identity. 'The outcome of that governing experience for the Democrats of the Left [a crushing electoral defeat] unleashed an unprecedented debate inside the party, which reached vitriolic proportions,' Bull asserted.[45] In the case of the Irish party, involvement in government led to less heated debate but rather a growing acceptance that there was little point in the already weak Irish Left essentially being represented by two social democratic parties. After its poor election performance in 1997, Democratic Left was faced with this reality. The differences between itself and the Labour Party were hard to discern – as most interviewees in this study testified. A merger, which could ideologically have happened in 1992, was therefore politically possible after 1997.

CONCLUSION

The changed global economy in the latter years of the twentieth century necessitated a revision in the tools of economic management. The preference of the Left for a demand management Keynesian policy prescription became more problematic. The role of state-sponsored interventionism – and its ability to have an impact on economic life – was thrown into question by the free movement of capital. This transformation in economic management was underway when the Soviet system collapsed, which added further uncertainty for the direction of Left political action. Against this background the theory and past practice of Left politics became harder to discern as the neo-liberal economic dogma reached an ascendancy, blurring the differences in the political orientation of many European governments. The credit crunch crisis and international recession which emerged in 2008 offered little evidence that the Left had an intellectual justification for interventionist government. Economics writer Larry Elliott in a bleak analysis of the then Labour government's response in the United Kingdom focused on the lack of a coherent strategy to create the Left's preferred society: 'The government is ideologically bereft as it tires to manage the crisis. Labour has control of the banks but wants to give it up as quickly as possible.'[46]

The discussion in this chapter shows that Democratic Left emerged during a period of political and ideological transition and that the party belonged to what may broadly be described as the New Left. Democratic Left did not meet the criteria to be classified as belonging to the Radical Left while a blurring of ideology between Left and Right made the New Left a broad social democratic church. At the time of its formation, many of the key participants in Democratic Left were unwilling to accept that they – like others on the Left across Europe – had arrived at a social democratic ideological position. Only personality and local political differences prevented those leaving the Workers' Party in 1992 from joining the Labour Party at that time. The eventual merger of the two parties in early 1999 should, therefore, not be seen as a surprising development but rather as natural evolution. In subsequent chapters the honest but ultimately futile and unsuccessful search for a 'third way' will be discussed in greater detail. But, as this chapter concludes, at the heart of the seven-year Democratic Left project was an inevitable movement towards the Labour Party.

NOTES

1. See P. Mair, 'The Party System', in J. Coakley and M. Gallagher (eds), *Politics in the Republic of Ireland* (Dublin: Folens, 1992), p.85.
2. B. Chubb, *The Government and Politics of Ireland* (London: Longman, 1992), p.91.
3. M. Manning, *Irish Political Parties: An Introduction* (Dublin: Gill & Macmillan, 1972), p.89.
4. Mair, 'The Party System', p.80.
5. C. Copus, A. Clark, H. Reynaert and K. Steyvers, 'Minor Party and Independent Politics Beyond the Mainstream: Fluctuating Fortunes but a Permanent Presence', *Parliamentary Affairs*, 62, 1 (2008), p.4.
6. See P. Mair 'The Electoral Universe of Small Parties', in F. Müller-Rommel and G. Pridham (eds), *Small Parties in Western Europe: Comparative and National Perspectives* (London: Sage, 1991). The political science literature generally uses the terms 'major' and 'minor' when describing

political parties. These descriptive terms are, however, confusing given their association with relevance – the term 'minor' generally carries certain meanings and can be confused with 'unimportant' or 'of lesser importance'. For this reason the terms 'larger' and 'smaller' are used in this study.

7. J. Coakley, 'The Rise and Fall of Minor Parties in Ireland', *Irish Political Studies*, 25, 4 (2010).
8. D. O'Malley, 'It is easier to set up a new party in Iraq than it is in Ireland', *The Irish Times*, 2 April 2010.
9. See S. McGraw, 'Managing Change: Party Competition in the New Ireland', *Irish Political Studies*, 23, 4 (December 2008), pp.627–48.
10. Ibid., p.630.
11. Interview with Pat Rabbitte, 9 January 2007.
12. Ibid.
13. D. Farrell, 'Ireland: A Party System Transformed?', in D. Broughton and M. Donovan (eds), *Changing Party Systems in Western Europe* (London: Pinter, 1999), p.32.
14. P. Mair, 'Fianna Fáil, Labour and the Irish Party System', in M. Gallagher and M. Laver, *How Ireland Voted, 1992* (Dublin: PSAI, 1993), p.165.
15. Interview with Eamon Gilmore, 11 September 2006.
16. Interview with Proinsias De Rossa, 7 September 2007.
17. M.J. Bull, 'The West European Communist Movement in the Late Twentieth Century', *West European Politics*, 18, 1 (1995), p.79.
18. R. Kindersley, 'In Lieu of a Conclusion: Eurocommunism and "the Crisis of Capitalism"', in R. Kindersley (ed.), *In Search of Eurocommunism* (London: Macmillan, 1981), p.186.
19. R. Dunphy, 'From Eurocommunism to Eurosocialism: The Search for a Post-Communist European Left', *University of Dundee Occasional Papers*, Series 1:7 (1993), p.29.
20. See S. Hopkins and R. Dunphy, 'The Organizational and Political Evolution of the Workers' Party of Ireland', *Journal of Communist Studies and Transition Politics*, 8, 2 (September 1992), p.98.
21. Ibid., p.106.
22. Interview with Kathleen Lynch, 10 October 2006.
23. D. Robertson, *Penguin Dictionary of Politics* (London: Penguin, 1993), p.131.
24. H. Patterson, *The Politics of Illusion: A Political History of the IRA* (London: Penguin, 1997), pp.257–8.
25. Hopkins and Dunphy, 'The Organizational and Political Evolution of the Workers' Party of Ireland', p.92.
26. Interview with Eric Byrne, 29 August 2006.
27. Interview with Seán Garland, 29 May 2006.
28. Interview with Tomás MacGiolla, 30 November 2006.
29. Interview with Proinsias De Rossa, 7 September 2007.
30. Interview with Catherine Murphy, 31 August 2006.
31. Interview with Des Geraghty, 9 May 2006.
32. Interview with Rosheen Callender, 12 September 2006.
33. Interview with Liz McManus, 18 October 2006.
34. Interview with Eamon Gilmore, 11 September 2006.
35. Youth Report to Executive, July 1994.
36. D. Bell and E. Shaw (eds), 'Introduction', in special issue on 'What's Left? The Left in Europe Today', *Parliamentary Affairs*, 56, 1 (2003), p.1.
37. D. Walsh, *The Irish Times*, 20 March 1992.
38. Correspondence from Dick Spring to Proinsias De Rossa, 27 March 1992.
39. D. Arter, 'Scandinavia: What's Left is the Social Democratic Consensus', *Parliamentary Affairs*, 36, 1 (2003), p.76.
40. L. Marsh and C. Muddle, 'What's Left of the Radical Left? The European Radical Left After 1989: Decline and Mutation', *Comparative European Politics*, vol. 3 (2005), p.34.
41. Interview with Kathleen Lynch, 10 October 2006.
42. Interview with Eric Byrne, 29 August 2006.
43. M.J. Bull, 'Italy: The Crisis of the Left', *Parliamentary Affairs*, 36, 1 (2003), p.5.
44. Ibid., p.65.
45. Ibid., p.68.
46. L. Elliott, in *The Guardian*, 22 December 2008.

3

The Republican Legacy

In the early 1960s the leadership of the republican movement in Ireland signalled a significant shift in direction. Defeated at the ballot box in the 1961 Dáil Éireann election coupled with the failure of the IRA's 1956–62 campaign against the Northern State – and lacking a real sense of direction – the republican movement was forced to reassess its political and military strategies. In February 1962 all IRA units were ordered to dump arms; the failed border campaign was formally declared over later that same month. The decision to end the armed campaign was very much recognition that, lacking popular support – coupled with a hardline governmental response – the IRA was not in a position to further its aims through violence.

One of those involved in the failed border campaign was Proinsias De Rossa, a future leader of the Workers' Party and also Democratic Left. De Rossa's political career moved from physical force republicanism in his teenage years to participation in the republican grouping which would eventually evolve into the Workers' Party. He played a singularly important role in the foundation of Democratic Left and was a leading figure in the party's membership of the 1994–7 Rainbow government. As such, the timeline of De Rossa's career neatly follows that of those in the 'Officials' who moved from military activism to political involvement.

De Rossa was born in Parnell Street in Dublin's north inner city in 1940. He was known to his family as Frank Ross, and was one of twelve children. 'It wasn't easy, but there were people around us who had nothing. My mother and father worked extremely hard. I don't know how they kept going, to keep us with shoes on our feet and clothes on our back. We weren't running around in rags or our bare feet.'[1] He had little interest in school, a feeling shaped by the atmosphere in the classroom. He recalled being beaten by his teachers, and on one occasion when the teacher hit him so hard with a ruler that it cut his hand his mother went to the school to complain.

De Rossa joined the IRA on his sixteenth birthday in 1956. The organisation was inactive at the time, depleted of resources and lacking public support, but plans were under discussion for a border campaign. The new recruit spent his time polishing what weapons the IRA had available and going on exercise runs in the Dublin mountains. At the time he said he felt 'appalled' when one senior republican said Irish freedom was not worth the shedding of one drop of blood. In an interview in 1998 he was asked was he prepared to kill people? 'I don't think I would have, to tell you the truth. At 16, I was very idealistic and, had an unreal view about what fighting for freedom was and of what the result would be in terms of mangled bodies.'[2]

De Rossa was arrested under the internment policy introduced by the Irish government following the start of the border campaign. He had been on a training hike in the Dublin mountains. This was the first time his family knew of his involvement in the IRA. In keeping with IRA policy he refused to recognise the court: 'I don't regret it. I think I was wrong in how I understood things then – I wasn't naïve, just wrong.'[3] He was sent to the Curragh internment camp. 'It didn't seem that much of a burden, except you would occasionally say, "When the fuck am I getting out of here?" I didn't suffer from depression. I kept my head together playing basketball, football, doing classes and I read a lot. But I saw some young fellas who were very badly depressed. There were people who wouldn't get out of bed from one end of the day to another, except perhaps to eat and then they'd go back to bed. One fella expressed the theory that the longer you were asleep, the less time you spent in prison.'[4] He described this period as 'my university days'. De Rossa was co-opted onto the Árd Comhairle of Sinn Féin in July 1962, although he refused a position four years later.[5] But he continued to be involved in republican politics and in later years emerged as a senior public figure for Sinn Féin The Workers' Party.[6]

De Rossa was an active member during the 1960s when new thinking was underway in republican circles. It appeared that the militant tendency in Irish republicanism had reached a final conclusion. But those who advocated republican traditionalism were not about to disappear. Only eight years later, republican leader Ruairí Ó Brádaigh reaffirmed the IRA/Sinn Féin inheritance: 'a republican today is one who rejects the partition statelets and gives his allegiance to and seeks to restore the 32-county republic of Easter Week.'[7] The eight years between the ending of the border campaign and the internal split, which signalled the start of the modern conflict, were marked by an attempt to fundamentally re-direct the energies of the republican movement. A new, younger leadership had emerged during the years of the border campaign, including Cathal Goulding, who was elected IRA chief of staff in 1962. Goulding – along with Tomás MacGiolla, who became Sinn Féin president – had an impeccable republican pedigree. He had been interned during the Second World War and served a prison sentence in England for his involvement in an arms raid on a British army training school in Essex in 1953. Goulding did not see republicans relinquishing the right to use armed action in pursuit of their aims. Indeed, military planning was authorised but the militarist front was to exist as an option within a wider republican strategic framework that included policy development in social, economic and cultural areas. But in reality the new leadership wanted to wean the republican movement off militarism. The task was to develop a policy platform beyond the traditional aspiration of removing the border, and to replace the conservative republican outlook with a Leftist socio-economic policy programme.

Sinn Féin adopted a new economic and social position at its 1964 Árd Fheis based on a self-sufficiency programme which ran contrary to the newly adopted strategy of the incumbent Fianna Fáil government, which focused on expansion of the country's weak industrial base through the attraction of foreign investment. Goulding questioned the value of foreign involvement in the Irish economy and was extremely doubtful about the merits of the Irish membership of the European Economic Community, the forerunner to the current-day European Union. The republican movement was being transformed into a protest movement. Republicans were encouraged to join organisations in which it was possible to propagate the new message of protest – credit unions, trade unions and housing associations. Activists and supporters became involved in groups in their communities campaigning on diverse issues such as non-nationals owning fishing rights on Irish rivers and population decline in the west of Ireland.

In addition to the policy of organisational infiltration, Republican Clubs were established where those with republican sympathies could meet to discuss politics and policies, while even more talking was done in the Wolfe Tone societies set up in Dublin and Belfast. There was also considerable republican representation in the civil rights campaigns that grew up in Northern Ireland from the mid-1960 onwards. Republicans were active in these organisations – and in the campaigns and protests – as individuals, never openly representing the IRA or Sinn Féin. Not that Sinn Féin offered much hope for political advancement – the Stormont government in 1964 once more proscribed the party in Northern Ireland.

A decision was taken to forgo electoral participation until such time as republicans had received adequate political training and Sinn Féin was sufficiently strong enough to successfully contest elections. The new leadership had seen the rise and collapse of the Sinn Féin vote in the 1955–61 period. They were not about to allow that pattern to be repeated. While this education process was underway, republicans withdrew from electoral politics. Indeed, Sinn Féin stopped contesting elections in the Republic after 1965 and the following year the party opted out of electoral involvement in Northern Ireland. The decision was also linked to an internal debate about the value of continuing with the traditional policy of parliamentary abstentionism. Goulding argued that Sinn Féin would never benefit from a new policy programme – or republican involvement in protests and campaigns – while abstentionism remained in place. Yet, despite the decision to, in effect, turn the republican movement into a radical Left-wing protest group, the long-standing policy of parliamentary abstentionism remained in place. There was discussion at the 1965 Sinn Féin Árd Fheis about changing the policy and allowing successful candidates to take their seats in Northern Ireland, the Irish Republic and even at Westminster. The proponents of change argued that the status quo abstentionist policy effectively equated a vote for Sinn Féin as a wasted vote. The Goulding group argued that in such an environment Sinn Féin was never going to advance as a political party.

Tomás MacGiolla forecast at the 1966 Árd Fheis that Sinn Féin would take seats in Leinster House if the party's representatives constituted a majority of the members of parliament. The Sinn Féin president offered the ambitious, but hugely unrealistic, forecast that within five years his party would have a majority in Dáil Éireann. There was considerable unease within the wider republican membership at the new direction. One of the opponents of the Goulding–MacGiolla strategy was Seán MacStíofáin, who, like Goulding, had received a prison term in England for involvement in an arms raid in 1953. MacStíofáin had a curious background. English-born, he had been a member of the Royal Air Force in Britain and only travelled to Ireland for the first time in 1959 after his release from prison. He was 31-years-old at the time. MacStíofáin argued that the Leftist policy drift risked turning the IRA into 'a paper army'.[8] He later wrote of the frustration of being a member of the Sinn Féin Árd Comhairle, where meetings were 'boring and a total waste of time. Numerous projects were discussed endlessly, but very few of them ever came to anything.'[9] There was some truth in this assessment because by the end of the 1960s the IRA and Sinn Féin were hardly active organisations. They had small, and largely inactive, memberships. Goulding admitted that 'by 1967 the Movement had become dormant. It wasn't active in any political sense or in any revolutionary sense. Membership was falling off. People had gone away. Units of the IRA and the cumainn of Sinn Féin had become almost non-existent.'[10]

With the outbreak of the contemporary conflict in Northern Ireland many believed that the IRA had failed to fulfil its traditional role as defenders of the nationalist population in Northern Ireland. The emerging conflict was the background to the split in the ranks of the IRA that occurred towards the end of 1969. Yet the sectarian violence on the streets in the North was not the principal reason for the split, which was provoked by a move to change the abstentionist policy. Plans were developed to end abstentionism and re-route republicans into a National Liberation Front (NLF) involving other Left-wing parties and groups. The 1968 Árd Fheis had mandated an internal party commission to examine the issues and report back to the membership at a subsequent Sinn Féin gathering. In fact, the matter was considered at an Army Convention of the IRA, which took place in December 1969. The move to lift the restriction on republicans participating in elections won support from a majority of those present. The following month, on 11 January 1970, delegates at a Sinn Féin Árd Fheis voted to abolish abstentionism. The Goulding leadership got their result, but the simple majority (153 to 104) was an inadequate outcome, as a two-thirds majority was needed to change the Sinn Féin constitution. Not for the first time since Arthur Griffith formed Sinn Féin in 1905 one of the offsprings of his party was facing a split.

MacStíofáin and his supporters had prevented the constitutional change but they were in a minority. They quickly exited to form a new organisation, described as the Provisionals, which would shortly come to represent the traditional republican doctrines as well as a majority of those within the militant republican constituency on the island. The grouping that pushed for change in late 1969 was associated with the Goulding–MacGiolla leadership. Known after the split as the Officials, this group also comprised a military wing – the Official IRA – and a political counterpart – Official Sinn Féin – that was known in North-ern Ireland as the Republican Clubs. The Provisionals pledged their 'allegiance to the 32-County Irish Republic proclaimed at Easter 1916, established by the first Dáil Éireann in 1919, overthrown by force of arms in 1922 and suppressed to this day by the existing British imposed Six-County and 26-County partition states'.[11] The decision to alter the abstentionist policy was repudiated. Those associated with the Provi-sionals quickly moved into the dominant position and, as Flackes and Elliott observed, 'All the indications ... were that PIRA [the Provisional IRA] rapidly outstripped the Officials in number.'[12]

In the aftermath of the split, the Official republican movement embarked upon an ideological transformation, moving from a physical force organisation to a party that emphasised socialist economic dogma alongside the question of partition. This was an ideological transformation – underpinned, as one writer noted, by 'contradictions and conflict'[13] – which was nothing less than, in English's words, 'a metamorphosis'.[14] The party was rebranded initially as Sinn Féin The Workers' Party, which in 1982 became the Workers' Party.

The Officials remained loyal to the agenda adopted by the republican movement in the 1960s. The leadership sought to expand a Left-wing view of the world with continued re-evaluation of the value of mili-tarism in achieving the ultimate republican goal of Irish reunification. Rooney described this strategy as a 'dual approach', with economic and political activism combining on equal terms with military action:

> Membership of the Republican Clubs became compulsory for Official IRA volunteers, and political agitation was incorporated into the training of IRA and Fianna volunteers ... There was also increased experimentation in community-based activity such as setting-up of local co-operatives and local advice centres.[15]

The Goulding–MacGiolla leadership espoused the objective of uniting the Catholic and Protestant working class to establish a socialist republic covering all of the island of Ireland. The task – as MacGiolla and his colleagues saw it – was to reach out to the Northern Protestant working class so as to unite them in common cause with their Catholic counterparts.

Interestingly, this desire to transcend traditional allegiances and move away from identity politics was maintained two decades later in Democratic Left's prescription for resolving the conflict in Northern Ireland. At the start of the 1970s, Goulding and his supporters wanted to transform the republican movement into a revolutionary party drawing support from people on all parts of the island of Ireland. This aim would be realised through a broadening of the scope of republican involvement in all facets of society, as Seán Garland noted: 'The struggle is everywhere, in the schools, the factories, in the fields, in the churches.'[16] The Officials did not, however, lose sight of the objective of creating a united Ireland, and all political policies and ideological positions were adopted with reference to the need to end partition. This aspiration would best be realised, according to the Officials, by reform of the Stormont regime, which would bring an end to the existing sectarian state in Northern Ireland.

While the Provisional IRA also wanted an end to Stormont, the Officials argued that the abolition of the Northern Ireland parliament would not seriously impact upon unionist political thinking. In September 1970 the question was posed in the Officials' newspaper, the *United Irishman*: 'Is not the real Unionist power base the determination of one million Protestant Irishmen not to enter a united Ireland?'[17] Moreover, direct rule was opposed because – the Officials argued – it would only strengthen Britain's grasp over Northern Ireland. The rationale behind this thinking was, however, difficult to sell. As Patterson observed: 'The strategy of pushing for the reform of the Stormont regime and opposing demands for its abolition was a difficult one to explain to many northern Officials, let alone to the Catholic communities in which they operated.'[18] Goulding and his colleagues did not view the situation in Northern Ireland from a traditional republican perspective – that role was left to the Provisionals – rather the Officials were set on building a popular mass movement. The difficulty with this positioning was the reality of politics and society in Northern Ireland in the period after the republican split.

The Provisional IRA adopted an aggressive military campaign – as they

portrayed it, to defend nationalist areas – while local Catholic sentiment towards the British was turning increasingly hostile. The atmosphere was heightened in the aftermath of events like the Lower Falls
curfew in Belfast, Bloody Sunday in Derry and the introduction of
internment. Against this background, the Officials found it difficult to
remain inactive. 'The dynamics of communal expectations and competition with the Provisionals drew the Officials into attacks on the British
Army and, after internment, even more indiscriminate violence,' Patterson noted.[19]

Richard English has explored the tension between the two IRAs based
on the Officials' declared Leftist outlook and the more conservative (and
Catholic) identity associated with the Provisionals: 'One Belfast [P]IRA
man was quoted in February 1971 as stating: "We could never come to
terms with the Goulding IRA which is now Marxist and socialist. We
were republicans and our notions of a free Ireland are based on Christian
principles and democracy."'[20] The Leftist ideological direction favoured
by the Officials drew some negative reaction in republican circles, as
Coogan recounted:

> There is a joke told in Belfast concerning an army haul from the
> Provisionals, the UVF [Ulster Volunteer Force] and the Officials.
> The Provisionals yielded some bombs, Armalites and machine guns,
> the UVF some rifles and revolvers, and the Officials 'five thousand
> copies of The Thoughts of Chairman Mao, five thousand copies of
> Das Kapital and a library of books on world revolution'.[21]

Republicanism was not known for its sophisticated ideological positioning. The Leftist thinking and talk of a National Liberation Front
was the source of some derision within republican circles. But as Coogan
admitted, '... it would be easy to dismiss them [the Officials] as preten-
tious and unreal rhetorians.'[22] Yet, for all of Goulding's attempts to push
the movement towards a more political direction, the Officials were still
involved in violence. In all, over 3,600 people lost their lives in the contemporary conflict in Northern Ireland. In a comprehensive catalogue
of the dead, McKittrick and his fellow authors attribute fifty-four of
those deaths to the actions of the OIRA, as Table 3.1 illustrates.

In December 1971 the OIRA shot dead unionist senator Jack Barnhill
and burnt down the home of the speaker of the Stormont Assembly. In
February 1972 seven people were killed in a bomb attack at the Aldershot

TABLE 3.1
OFFICIAL IRA RESPONSIBILITY FOR DEATHS

Year	Number Killed
1970	0
1971	9
1972	20
1973	2
1974	7
1975	9
1976	1
1977	4
1978	0
1979	1
1980	0
1981	0
1982	0
1983	1
1984 –	0
Total	54

Source: D. McKittrick et al., *Lost Lives: The Stories of the Men, Women and Children who Died as a Result of the Northern Ireland Troubles* (Edinburgh: Mainstream, 1999), p.1475.

(Hampshire) HQ of the Parachute Regiment. Among those who lost their lives in the OIRA attack were five female canteen workers, a gardener and the Catholic chaplain to the regiment. In the same month John Taylor, a minister in the Stormont government, was severely wounded in an assassination bid by the OIRA. Members of the OIRA were also killed in the emerging conflict. In April 1972 the Parachute Regiment shot dead Joe McCann, a leading figure in the Officials. Two years later Colman Rowntree was shot dead by the British army at a derelict farmhouse outside Newry. Rowntree was not only a member of the OIRA but the previous year he had contested local elections in Northern Ireland as a Republican Club candidate. The Officials did not wait long to avenge his death.

William Best, who was nineteen and from the Creggan estate in Derry, was attached to the Royal Irish Rangers in Germany. He had never served in Northern Ireland. On 15 May 1972 Ranger Best returned home to Northern Ireland on leave. The atmosphere in Derry – as across the North – had worsened considerably in the weeks since the events of Bloody Sunday in late January 1972. Six days after Best arrived home, his body was found on waste ground, shot in the head. A statement from the OIRA said: 'The ruthlessness shown by the British forces against the people of Free Derry could only be answered in similar terms. Regardless of calls for peace from slobbering moderates, while British gunmen remain on the streets of the Six Counties the [Official] IRA will take action against them.' Despite those strident sentiments, the shooting of William Best was to have serious repercussions for the future direction of the Officials. The attack provoked angry responses from women in the Creggan and Bogside areas, as is recounted in the book *Lost Lives*:

> Around 200 women ... marched on Official republican headquarters in Derry city to protest against the killing. One of them said of the Officials: 'They have brought themselves down to the level of the Paras on Bloody Sunday. We have been frightened in the past but not any more.' Another said: 'I do not mind them fighting for a free Ireland, but this is not a fight for a free Ireland. They are terrorising the people and we want them out.'[23]

The protest had an immediate impact. On 22 May 1972, the day after the shooting dead of William Best, the OIRA announced an end to all offensive shootings in Derry in accordance with the wishes of local people. Seven days later the Officials declared an indefinite ceasefire. Bishop and Mallie claimed that the Aldershot attack and the killing of William Best 'shook the already half-commitment of Goulding and the Official Army Council to violence ...'[24] Certainly the OIRA was left exposed. But it would be naive to underestimate the capacity of the organisation to maintain a military campaign, notwithstanding Coogan's comment that 'their [the OIRA] record of military operations is a litany of brutal bungling.'[25]

The May 1972 ceasefire was declared with one important condition – self-defence. An Official IRA statement read: 'The only exception to the general suspension of armed actions is the reservation of the right to defend any area under aggressive attack by the British military or by the sectarian forces of either side.' The OIRA guns did not remain totally silent. Of the fifty-four deaths attributed to the Officials, twenty-five took place in the aftermath of the May 1972 cessation. It should be stressed, however, that after the ceasefire was called the Officials 'ceased to pose a serious threat to the security forces' in Northern Ireland and its military actions were primarily associated with intra-republican feuds.[26]

The OIRA truce in May 1972 was not universally welcomed within the organisation. Many members were unhappy with the decision, although the leadership of the Officials was not moving to disband the organisation nor was there any possibility of OIRA weapons being decommissioned – issues which remained contentious for two decades and played a role in the formation of Democratic Left in 1992. The ceasefire was conditional on the OIRA reserving the right to take defensive and retaliatory actions. Rooney correctly concluded that there was 'no real evidence to suggest that it was anything other than a tactical ploy to take pressure off the Officials in the North'.[27]

Some OIRA members drifted into the PIRA while others eventually departed to the Irish National Liberation Army (INLA), a new group established in late 1974. These departures from the OIRA produced sporadic but bloody violence. As noted previously, many of the deaths from OIRA activity after its 1972 ceasefire were the result of intra-republican feuding. Throughout its history the OIRA was involved in several bloody feuds with competing republican organisations. Tensions with the Provisional IRA were evident right from the time of the split in late 1969. There were frequent gun battles between members of the two republican groups. In March 1971 PIRA member Charles Hughes was shot dead by the OIRA – the attack has been described as 'the first sign of the tension between the two IRA groups which would later spill into open conflict'.[28]

Once more, in late 1975 the rivalry between the Officials and the Provisionals turned bloody. A fistfight between members of the different groupings in mid-October 1975 was said to have started this latest feud. In response, the PIRA organised a series of attacks on the night of 29 October 1975. Up to ninety PIRA members were reported as being involved in the attacks on known OIRA members that left one man dead and another sixteen people wounded. The following day there was more violence. PIRA gunmen shot a 6-year-old girl dead in her home. They were firing at her father, who was described as 'a Republican Clubs sympathiser'.[29] The feud was ended some weeks later following the intervention of two Roman Catholic priests. By that time, eleven people were dead due to the feud, one member of the Provisionals, seven members of the Officials and three civilians. Earlier that same year, the Officials had been involved in another bloody feud, which left half a dozen people dead. That dispute had its origins in the formation of a new republican group that emerged largely from dissatisfaction with the OIRA ceasefire strategy and the decision to allow Workers' Party councillors to take the local government seats they had vacated in protest after the introduction of internment.

After his departure from the Official movement, Séamus Costello established the Irish Republican Socialist Party (IRSP) in December 1974. A military wing, the INLA, was set up around the same time. Costello had been active in the 1956–62 border campaign but opposed the 1972 OIRA ceasefire. He was suspicious of the direction which was being pursued by Goulding and had argued for a return to offensive OIRA action and even joint operations with the Provisionals. Relations between Costello and the Goulding leadership deteriorated to such an extent that the former was expelled from the Officials in late 1974. Costello's new Left-wing republican group attracted into its ranks disaffected Officials and also members of the PIRA who were unhappy with the Provisionals' 1975 ceasefire strategy. Tension was inevitable given the history between the Officials and the breakaway group, which Goulding described as 'a few misguided and confused malcontents'.[30] Bishop and Mallie, however, are among a number of writers who suggest more substantial defections from the OIRA to the IRSP/INLA:

> In Belfast, one third of the Officials' remaining strength defected to the IRSP, including some of the more impressive members ... The Official IRA could see history repeating itself. Once again the organisation in the city was going to be reduced to insignificance by the birth of a more militant and ruthless rival and it was not going to make the same mistake twice. A decision was taken to strangle the IRSP at birth.[31]

In February 1975 the Officials shot dead Hugh Ferguson, the chairman of the IRSP who had previously been a member of the OIRA. Costello named Ferguson's killer as leading OIRA member Christopher John Fox. Five days later Fox was shot dead. The chain of shootings continued: 'It was reported that John Fox was shot by Danny Loughran, who himself was killed over a month later by the Officials.'[32] Shootings and counter-shootings marked the feud, with leading figures on both sides targeted. In March 1975 Seán Garland was injured in a shooting attack in Dublin while Costello survived an assassination attempt in Waterford. The intra-republican conflict took on an added dimension when the INLA shot dead Billy McMillen in Belfast in April 1975. McMillen was an influential figure in republican circles in Belfast who has been described as 'one of the most senior republicans to side with the Officials'.[33] In 1973 McMillen had warned about impatience with the organisation's ceasefire strategy. 'Be patient, for it is as important to know when not to fight as it is to know when to fight.'[34]

McMillen had been, according to Rooney, 'a central figure in defining both the ideology and actions of the Movement ...' in Northern Ireland as well as being the 'original architect of the dual approach'.[35] He did not favour a strategy whereby the political wing would move into the dominant position in the Official movement. However, with his death that was the very situation that developed. The senior figures in the movement were now primarily based in Dublin and they favoured a more political approach. The militants were increasingly sidelined, although the OIRA was still an active organisation. In October 1977 Costello was shot dead in Dublin. His death was believed to have been a reprisal killing for the shooting dead of McMillen. Costello – who was chairman of the IRSP, the political wing of the INLA – was also a member of Bray Urban District Council and Wicklow County Council. Despite the ongoing denials, the OIRA obviously still existed and elements within the Official movement were involved in criminal activity at a time when a process of ideological transformation was very much underway. The original Goulding strategy was to develop the political wing of the republican movement as the dominant element with the military wing playing a less prominent role, and possibly eventually fading away altogether.

THE WORKERS' PARTY

The decision to adopt the name Sinn Féin The Workers' Party was taken in January 1977 in part to differentiate the party in the public's mind from Provisional Sinn Féin. The renaming exercise also stressed the Left orientation of the organisation and the constituency from which it hoped to garner votes. There was still considerable misunderstanding about the 'two Sinn Féins', which was not unsurprising given their recent genesis and the limited public and media attention the parties attracted.

In the period from the mid-1970s the Dublin-based leadership effectively rewrote the party's mission statement to such an extent that Rooney, writing in 1984, pointed out a potential difficulty for the

Workers' Party as a self-styled 'revolutionary party' with 'the increasingly social democratic nature of its politics, and the fact that these tend to be confined to an internal debate within rather than against capitalism ...'[36] The type of ideological transition in European Left politics discussed in Chapter 1 was underway. The party promoted a policy agenda with heavy state involvement in all facets of socio-economic life, including nationalisation of the banking sector and the creation of a national health service. In the economically depressed 1980s this alternative to the agenda of the main parties won a significant audience in the Irish Republic. Progress was also helped by the participation of the Labour Party in an unpopular coalition government with Fine Gael.

The statist-type underpinning of domestic policies was coupled with a foreign policy that backed the communist leadership in the USSR. From the mid-1970s there was vocal support for Soviet foreign policy even in the face of the USSR's military interventions in Afghanistan and Poland. There were some internal doubts about this strategy but ideological purity and membership discipline necessitated that the debate was shut down. The fall of the Berlin Wall in 1989 came as a relief to many on the reformist wing of the party as it provided strong justification for quickening the pace of ideological reform. 'The Berlin Wall fell, which as far as I and a lot of people were concerned was a godsend. Here we were relieved of all this baggage,' Proinsias De Rossa admitted.[37] During this period of transformation the party also fundamentally altered its approach to Northern Ireland where hostility to traditional republicanism was considerable: 'The party's fixation with distancing itself from its own past as well as from the Provisionals and the IRSP has helped to push it towards what is in effect a pro-establishment line.'[38]

The party was organised on an all-Ireland basis. In Northern Ireland it had contested elections to the Sunningdale Assembly in 1973 but on an abstentionist platform. This policy remained in place until internment ended and the emergency powers were dropped. The party's ten candidates in 1973 polled poorly, receiving less than 2 per cent of the overall first-preference vote across Northern Ireland. In local district elections in May 1977 six Official candidates were elected, with the party taking 2.6 per cent of the overall vote. But three of those seats were lost in 1981 as the party's overall vote slipped back to 1.8 per cent. There was a slight recovery four years later but throughout this period, as their colleagues in the Irish Republic were making decent electoral gains, the party in Northern Ireland failed to make an electoral breakthrough of any note.

The first evidence of progress in the Irish Republic came in June 1981 with the election to Dáil Éireann of Joe Sherlock in Cork East. The party would make strong electoral gains at national and local elections in the Irish Republic over the following decade. Dunphy and Hopkins wrote that the Workers' Party 'was almost alone amongst West European communist and workers' parties in having experienced steady, if modest, electoral growth throughout the 1980s'.[39] But electoral success brought its own internal tensions. Garland observed in 1984 that:

> Whilst elections are not the sole extent of our struggle, they are an integral and primary part of our development. They are stepping stones and the way to state power and every effort must be made to ensure our approach is wholehearted and professional at all times.[40]

The full-time officers were confronted by a new leadership grouping – namely elected representatives. The motivation for the eventual split in the party was a combination of ideology and criminality allegations, and both were set in the context of a nascent power struggle between party officials and elected representatives. Moreover, electoral success in the Republic was not matched by positive results in Northern Ireland. This relative difference in performance only served to increase the tension between different factions. Ideological uncertainties increased as the problems associated with electoral success combined to create internal difficulties, with different priorities and ambitions emerging between the full-time party officers and the parliamentary grouping. Personality differences and political ambitions undoubtedly also played a part in the divisions that surfaced in the late 1980s which led to an eventual split in 1992 and to the formation of Democratic Left.

TYPE OF PARTY

From the early 1970s the Workers' Party structured its organisation on a Marxist–Leninist model organised along democratic centralist lines. The party was similar to other Left groupings in Europe which looked to the Soviet model for inspiration and guidance. Democratic centralism, generally regarded as an element of Leninism, is considered a model for organising a revolutionary workers' party. The model is considered democratic in that all party members discuss and debate policy and strategy while the model is centralist in that once the debate has concluded, all members are expected to totally endorse the decision that has been reached. Lenin described democratic centralism as the 'freedom of discussion and criticism, unity of action'.

An internal party commission on organisational restructuring reported in early 1973. In truth, its brief was to determine what was to happen to the OIRA as the Officials developed as a political movement. The Officials were to be transformed into a Left-wing revolutionary party adhering to a Marxist philosophy and Leninist organisational principles. A resolution was passed at Official Sinn Féin's 1973 Árd Fheis, opening the way for closer links with countries ruled along Leninist lines. The Officials were represented at the World Congress of Peace Forces in Moscow in late 1973. As Patterson wrote:

> In the 1970s Marxism was increasingly attractive to leading Officials as a way of justifying in 'revolutionary' terms their policies of demilitarisation and gradualism in Northern Ireland. Marxism's emphasis on the central role of the organised working class in revolutions in capitalist countries could be used as an antidote to the frantic and fevered claims that 'armed struggle' in the North had a revolutionary significance.[41]

The transformation of the party involved changes in its organisational structure, political identity and policy platform. Dunphy and Hopkins identify two primary requirements that were pursued to build this Marxist party:

> First, a firm commitment to party discipline and self-sacrifice, consistent with the principle of democratic centralism expressed as unanimity and a strict subservience of the membership to the leadership; and second, a commitment to 'proletarian internationalism', and a world view that saw the Bolshevik revolution as the harbinger of a new era of progress, the USSR as an essentially benevolent force on the world stage, and solidarity with Third World liberation struggles as a touchstone of political good faith.[42]

In the Republic the Officials emerged in the economically depressed mid-1970s as a radical Left-wing voice, a position undoubtedly helped by the Labour Party's membership of a coalition government with Fine Gael between 1973 and 1977. There was a respective audience, particularly in urban areas, for a policy agenda that argued for the protection of the public sector and the expansion of state ownership as a recipe for the Republic's economic ills.

> The state sector is the greatest enemy confronting capitalism in Ireland today. The strategic importance of the state sector was first identified by the party at its Árd Fheis in 1976 … Beyond monopoly capital the future belongs to the state sector and to the Irish working class.[43]

Alongside this adoption of the state sector as the engine for economic growth, the Officials revised their attitude towards the role of multinational investment in the Irish economy. The party also softened its attitude towards the farming community. The influential Research Section of the party's Economic Affairs Department in Dublin was the main engine in this policy evolution, indeed policy revolution. Two forceful personalities within the party, Éamonn Smullen and Eoghan Harris, were among those most associated with the Research Section. Smullen had been involved in the republican movement and fringe Left-wing politics since the 1940s. While living in England he joined the British Communist Party and in 1969 was convicted of conspiracy to buy arms illegally. After his release from prison he returned to Ireland and Goulding recruited him to run the party's Research Section. Smullen and Harris, an award-winning television producer from County Cork, were responsible for most of the party's policy statements and official publications. Harris recalled:

> We had a commanding influence in the party. In a way we were the proletarian guard; the élite, the advanced guard. And everyone knew we worked every hour God gave us. We had policies on everything, published pamphlets, and we gave great credibility to the party. Our plan was to hold the balance of power [in parliament] … We wanted anti-nationalist socialism to be the norm of Irish thinking.[44]

Membership of the Research Section was tightly controlled, while its method of operation was secretive and its members were unknown to the vast majority of the wider party membership; in fact the Research Section existed like an 'independent republic' within the organisation.

But having an influential and controlling élite was not unsurprising given the Marxist–Leninist model of democratic centralism adhered to by the Workers' Party.

The advancement of a Left-wing political agenda was evident in a number of policies published by the Economic Affairs Department. For example, in September 1974 the party published a case study of the natural resource sector in Ireland, which highlighted the role of foreign multinational companies in maintaining imperialism. The party advocated nationalisation of multinationals without the payment of compensation. As Tomás MacGiolla wrote in *The Great Oil and Gas Robbery*:

> The sell-out of the gombeen class is not confined to oil and gas. It permeates Irish industry, commerce and agriculture. It began in 1922. It was boosted by the Whitaker plan of 1958, the Anglo-Irish Free Trade Agreement of 1965 and by the seduction of Ireland by the Common Marketeers in 1972 ... This work furthermore shows that imperialism is now the dominant force in Ireland.[45]

A number of policy documents including the *Irish Industrial Revolution* in early 1977 sought to marry Left-wing thinking with the work of revisionist historians. The outcome was a major re-evaluation of Irish republicanism as well as a reassessment of many key events in Irish history. The thesis eliminated the role of 'British imperialism' in causing Irish economic backwardness with blame instead attributed to the Irish Catholic bourgeoisie for 'refusing' to create an industrial revolution.[46]

The new thinking provided a framework for the Officials to continue the transition from a political-military movement into an organisation with a primary focus on political activism. As one writer concluded, 'Despite the inaccuracies, naiveté and theoretical confusion contained in the Irish Industrial Revolution, its strength lies in the simple, logical revolutionary strategy which emerges.'[47] The document followed on from the decision earlier in 1977 to add the title 'The Workers' Party' to Sinn Féin and the Republican Clubs. Until this stage the political wing was organised as the Republican Clubs in Northern Ireland and Official Sinn Féin in the Irish Republic. It was not until 1982 that the political movement adopted the shortened label, The Workers' Party. The 1977 decision had been taken to end what Rooney had classified as 'the dual approach'. The use of 'militarism and terrorism' in

Ireland was rejected as the organisation sought to move into the mainstream of Irish political life.

The Officials in their new guise may still have had anti-system tendencies – and, ideologically, they wanted to transform the capitalist system in Ireland to create a socialist republic – but now, increasingly, there was public acknowledgement that such objectives would have to be achieved within the existing system. The party was aiming to win over the working class to its cause, which would bring electoral success, and with a majority in parliament the socialist republic could then be created democratically. The plausibility of this ideological position may be questioned, but from a very low electoral base the party began to enjoy some success, particularly south of the border.

The adherence to democratic centralism as an organisational structure resulted in a highly authoritarian form of control and a culture that set very demanding criteria for party membership. Eric Byrne described members as 'highly motivated and highly flexible people'.[48] The party was not easy to join, as very strong emphasis was placed on membership quality over membership quantity. A six-month probationary period had to be served before a membership application was accepted. One party member writing in 1977 warned:

> We know from experience that by throwing our party open to all comers, we will destroy our party and do a disservice to the Irish people ... It is extremely important in this respect that the rules for party membership, and the minimum education programme and the probationary period be strictly adhered to.[49]

This hardline attitude was reflected in the constitution of the Workers' Party. The clauses on membership give a very clear outline of the attitude held by many in the party – inactive or undisciplined members were not welcome:

> Before being admitted to membership each applicant shall be required to satisfy the Party of their suitability. They shall have attended new members' classes. They shall have worked in the Party for a period of not less than 6 months. (Article 2)

> Refusal to accept the direction of central leadership is tantamount to refusing to remain in the Party, it is tantamount to disrupting the Party. (Article 4)

> ... the existence of factions or individuals that oppose or refrain
> from engaging in activities decided upon by the Party shall not be
> allowed. (Article 5)

In 1982 the party agreed to expand its membership base but this exercise
was not successful. The small size of the party's membership placed
considerable demands on members – and this commitment discouraged
some potential members from joining. There was undoubtedly internal
tension over the matter as the parliamentary group questioned the relevance of a democratic centralist approach to party building. This debate
was given added impetus by developments in the Soviet Union where
Mikhail Gorbachev was opening up the possibility of an alternative definition of communist democracy, and in the process allowing ideas and
opinions to emerge from the grassroots as well as from leadership
levels.'[50]

Alongside the view that party membership was for the ideologically
pure, there was the matter of 'secret' membership of the Workers' Party.
The recruitment of Smullen as a party officer in 1973 coincided with the
development of 'secret' branches within the party. From the early 1970s
the Workers' Party leadership paid particular attention to building links
with the trade union movement. Moreover, its policy stances helped
the party to expand its position in the pubic sector unions. This development was also helped by the inflow into the party of a new
generation of talented and energetic members in the Irish Republic.
Activists like Pat Rabbitte, Eamon Gilmore and Des Geraghty were
attracted to the radical agenda on offer and one which, they saw, as in
stark contrast to the moderate stance of the Labour Party which in the
1973–7 period was participating in an unpopular coalition government
with Fine Gael. The party focused on the development of 'secret'
branches in two trade unions, the Irish Transport and General Workers'
Union (ITGWU) and the Workers' Union of Ireland (WUI). Smullen
was the main link between the 'secret' branches and the party leadership. The approach was characterised by what Patterson described as 'a
secretive and conspirational style of work'.[51] He added:

> Throughout this period of Dublin expansion in the mid-1970s the
> movement retained the secretive and conspiratorial side that was a
> legacy of its history. The input of intellectuals was organised through
> two secret branches distinct from the ordinary, geographically based

one. Members of these branches were not open members of the organisation and had little if anything to do with the activities of its ordinary members. Justified by reference to the possible victimisation of individuals who had jobs in the media and the civil service, the secret branches tended to restrict serious discussion of major revisions of party policy by the bulk of the membership.[52]

From the mid-1970s onwards the Officials were active politically both in Northern Ireland and the Irish Republic. New members joined; these individuals were concerned with political involvement, a fact that also assisted in the transformation from a political-military body to a purely political movement. Smullen was increasingly influential, as was Eoghan Harris, who has been described as 'the principal ideologue for the party since 1973'.[53] Moreover, it has been noted that '... certainly the input of Harris was immense, as was the input of those he brought into the Industrial Section of the party with him. These were mainly colleagues from RTÉ.'[54]

In a *Magill* magazine series on the Workers' Party, it was alleged that there was bias in certain current affairs programming in the national broadcaster. In particular, journalist Vincent Browne claimed that on RTÉ's current affairs programme 'Today Tonight', 'treatment of the party was bordering on the deferential', noting also that six of the sixteen editorial staff associated with the programme held political views very similar to Workers' Party position. Moreover, Browne observed: 'There has perhaps been a curious incidence of programmes on topics dear to the heart of The Workers' Party – tax evasion, lead poisoning, the meat industry, etc – but these were valid topics in themselves and deserved treatment.'[55]

As 'Today Tonight' was the main current affairs outlet on RTÉ television, the allegations made in *Magill* – and debated privately within RTÉ – were taken seriously by station management. The most serious allegation concerned coverage of Northern Ireland. Browne claimed there was 'slanted editorial treatment' on 'Today Tonight'. 'The bias has been most evident on programmes on Northern Ireland, where the virulent antipathy to the Provisionals has expressed itself at times in terms of a general antinational bias.'[56] The period in question was among the most bitter in the history of the contemporary conflict in Northern Ireland with the 1980/1 hunger strikes by republican prisoners pushing even further apart the already divided nationalist and unionist communities. There is no doubt that Harris – and others sympathetic to the Workers' Party – fulfilled the role envisaged by Smullen's tactical ambition to infiltrated organisations to promote the agenda espoused by the party. Harris has long rejected the allegation of bias – and he was not directly involved in 'Today Tonight' – but in an interview in 1997 he provided a revealing insight into just how a particular view could be propagated:

> There was a lot of debate going on, but basically it broke down into supporters of the Provos and supporters of the Conor Cruise O'Brien line. There is a retrospective air of manipulation because I was a WP [Workers' Party] supporter ... [but] each case had to be won by debate. And we were better and brighter than the rest, so we got the best jobs. And, if there was a last seat to be filled on the panel debate I'd put on John A. Murphy rather than Tim Pat Coogan, and if it was for a news insert and I wanted someone to interpret a baton charge for me then I wouldn't pick someone who would sound a tribal tone. But if I broke the broadcasting restrictions I never did it in an underhand way ... I've seen my personnel file in RTÉ and there's a report in it by Michael Garvey where he said that I just wasn't capable of producing an unbalanced programme.[57]

Browne's assertions about programme bias were, however, met with some backing within RTÉ. One senior member of the editorial staff in the RTÉ newsroom observed, 'within RTE the area within which the Workers' Party exercised most control was the Workers' Union of Ireland, of which Eoghan Harris and a lot of people involved in the television current affairs production were involved, and that's the level at which the Workers' Party had most influence.'[58]

Caution about this apparent Workers' Party influence in the national broadcaster – and also in the trade union movement through 'secret' members – has been raised by John Horgan. In a historical assessment of RTÉ's news and current affairs output, he wrote, 'The supposed secrecy of the whole operation was, however, to some extent compromised by the high visibility of some of its members, notably (in the case of RTÉ) Eoghan Harris and (in the case of the ITGWU) Des Geraghty ...'[59] The high level of activity was, however, causing internal difficulties within the Workers' Party. The electoral success in the 1980s attracted new members into the party ranks. Many of these individuals had no connection with the Northern Ireland issue and were motivated by challenging the political status quo. The Workers' Party was seen as a more radical option than the Labour Party which, due to its involvement in a coalition government with Fine Gael, was perceived as another establishment party. Catherine Murphy was one of these new members. 'The group including myself in Kildare joined around the time of the water charges campaign. There were issues of taxation, equality and all of that,' she recalled.[60] Murphy, who was elected to the party's Árd Comhairle in 1988, was aware that key decisions were being taken elsewhere:

> There was a political committee that was headhunted or selected. There were particular key people on it. And that was where a lot of the more serious stuff went on ... It was almost like the equivalent of an army council. And I remember Árd Comhairle meetings and people who wouldn't have been on the political committee constantly asking questions about where money came from, you know. And then RTÉ did a television programme and essentially it more or less captured a lot of what was going on.[61]

The influx of new members changed the internal dynamic within the party and, coupled with external pressures, eventually brought the growing internal tensions to a point of no return. MacGiolla had led the Workers' Party and its predecessor party for over a quarter of a century. By 1988 he was marking his twenty-sixth year as party leader. He was approaching his sixty-fifth birthday when he announced his decision to stand aside as leader while continuing as a public representative:

> I had been there since 1962. Most people I knew died in their sixties and I was going to be 65 in 1988 and if you saw my diary ... There were other things I wanted to do so I decided to go in 1988. Nobody suggested to me that there'd be any problem with De Rossa when he was elected ... I was handing over a very successful party with seven Dáil deputies, a party that was growing and would continue to grow. If I had any idea of the problems [in subsequent years] I wouldn't have stood down.[62]

De Rossa and Joe Sherlock from County Cork contested the leadership vacancy at the 1988 Árd Fheis, although there was never any doubt about who would succeed MacGiolla. The breakdown of the vote was not announced, though it is understood that De Rossa's margin of victory was ten to one. The first sign of new thinking from the new party president emerged with De Rossa's Árd Fheis address in 1989. It was the opening gambit in the battle that would rage in the party until early in 1992. Eoghan Harris was a key player in the background at this stage. As Patterson observed, 'It would be Harris who would be a major stimulus to the profound internal crisis which wracked the party for two years from 1990 and out of which Democratic Left emerged.'[63] Harris argued for a reassessment of the socialist model adopted by the Workers' Party. He was heavily influence by the Gorbachev revolution in the Soviet Bloc as well as the new approaches adopted by the Italian Communists, among others. There were significant changes underway in Left politics – Sassoon's New Revisionism – but the signalling of a convergence in ideological positions still surprised many in the Workers' Party. 'I saw a structural crisis in socialism, and I didn't believe it could be contained in eastern Europe,' Harris stated.[64] According to long-time member Tony Heffernan, De Rossa's speech 'shocked lots of people in the party [as] it raised questions about a whole series of assumptions that people had'.[65] He added, 'For a lot of people the use of the words "revolutionary party" was a pure thing about a revolutionary transformation of society, but for others it was a sort of code, saying that well, you didn't have to mind too much about the law and the legalities and so on.'[66]

Harris expanded this thesis in his document *The Necessity of Social Democracy*, which for many in the party was a transformation too far. Hanley and Miller describe the document as 'an incendiary thesis' which was 'a disjointed but savage attack on "Left" politics and a demand that they be discarded in favour of what he [Harris] called "Social Democracy", which, according to Harris, had been the actual intention of Marx and other early communist writers'.[67] An internal debate about publishing the document continued for some time, which ultimately led to Harris's resignation in 1990 – and Smullen's expulsion. But even these departures, which reduced the influence of the Research Section, could not prevent the head-on collision between the two factions that were by then vying for control of the party. Patterson has credited Harris with leading the debate: '… by highlighting the profound inadequacy of the party's existing ideology, strategy and organisation for dealing with even a limited amount of electoral success, Harris accelerated a growing conflict between the traditional party leadership of full-time functionaries and the new power centre of the party's TDs and most of its local councillors and aspirant public representatives.'[68]

Patterson's thesis is supported by Seán Garland, who attributed responsibility for the deepening divisions to the newly enlarged group of Dáil deputies linked to De Rossa:

> Most of what happened extended from the parliament. They had to look away from head office to establish constituency organisations which were independent of head office, whereas we were always for a centralised structure and that [was] through the Árd Comhairle officer board. Then you see there was less contact or communications with members in the Dáil. MacGiolla was the only one who more or less retained those connections, loyalty.[69]

This nascent battle for control of the party was given further impetus by two other factors. First, with the collapse of the communist-controlled regimes in central and eastern Europe the Workers' Party – like other Left parties – was forced to reconsider its ideological identity and organisational model. Second, the party was dogged by questions about the continued existence of the OIRA, an overlap in membership between the two organisations and the possibility that illegal monies were funding legitimate political activities. A combination of these elements contributed to the split in the Workers' Party ranks, which in turn led to the formation of Democratic Left in 1992. While the ideological debate had been developing over several years, the question of members with links to criminal activities eventually pushed the divisions to a stage where even reconstitution of the party was unlikely to overcome the deep internal tensions.

CRIMINALITY

In February 1992 at the height of the debate within the Workers' Party about its future direction – and only weeks before the eventual split that gave birth to Democratic Left – the question of links with the Official IRA was put to Eamon Gilmore during the course of a radio interview on RTÉ's 'Morning Ireland' programme. Gilmore repeated the official party line that all leading Workers' Party figures had made for well over a decade, that the party was not associated with the Official IRA nor was it funded from criminal activity. The fact that leading Workers' Party figures continued to be confronted with the past from which their party had evolved was one of the contributing factors in the formation of Democratic Left. The Official IRA may have called a 'ceasefire' in May 1972 – and very much disappeared from the public view at the end of its feuds with other republican groups in 1975 and 1977 – but questions about the organisation's continued existence lingered. The situation was unsustainable for those who wanted to see further electoral development.

Many who held leadership positions in what became the Workers' Party after 1982 had emerged from the militant republican tradition, including MacGiolla and De Rossa. In the 1970s there was undoubtedly membership overlap between the OIRA and its political wings in Northern Ireland and the Irish Republic. This membership overlap was highlighted with the killing of Gerard Gilmore in north Belfast in July 1976. Gilmore, who was nineteen and armed at the time of his death, was shot dead by loyalist paramilitaries. He was not only a member of the political wing of the movement but also active in the Official IRA. The organisation placed a death notice in the *Irish News* describing Gilmore as a volunteer in I company, 1st battalion, Belfast command.[70] At the 1976 Official Sinn Féin Árd Fheis, MacGiolla issued a strong warning to those who saw value in military action, either alongside or as   an alternative to political activism. His message was that there was no room in the newly named Sinn Féin The Workers' Party for militants; the OIRA was being left behind. But for some in the Official movement there was a gradual disassociation from violence, as Ó Murchú observed: 'the occasional aberration is to be expected in an organisation with such a history.'[71] In 1984 Rooney noted of the Workers' Party:

> Although their *ideology* has been de-militarised and the military structure has been significantly run-down, the Movement itself has never been fully de-militarised … [The OIRA] is primarily concerned now with providing back-up services to the electoral campaign, such as fund-raising and the organisation especially in the North.[72]

The fact that no OIRA arms were ever decommissioned certainly helped to fuel interest in the continued existence of the organisation and also its possible links to the Workers' Party. Moreover, there was renewed interest in the matter with the electoral breakthrough of the Workers' Party in the Irish Republic in 1981. The party increasingly found it difficult to discard its own past but persisted with a policy that 'it had no knowledge of the Official IRA's existence, and the party showed an increasingly marked reluctance to acknowledge that it had ever existed.'[73]

The two-part series in the monthly current affairs publication *Magill* in early 1982 alleged that 'the Official IRA is alive and active and that almost all its operators are members of SFWP.' The magazine went on to claim that the OIRA was involved in robberies, murders, kneecapping, intimidation and racketeering, all activities that continued up to 1982. The magazine also alleged that the equivalent of €3 million had been generated over the previous decade from robberies organised by the OIRA. The articles raised questions about the finances of the Workers' Party: 'The Workers' Party is probably the wealthiest party in the country, bar none. This is especially surprising given the small membership of the party – we estimate less than 1,000 throughout the entire country.'[74] The same article listed properties owned by the Workers' Party, identified twenty full-time employees and provided an outline of the range of party publications. The writer noted: 'several former members of the party estimate that the net costs of running the party is in the region of IR£3,000 [approx. €3,800] per week – i.e. IR£150,000 [approx. €190,000] per annum and this would not include the repayment of any mortgages on premises.'[75]

The implication was that the Workers' Party was being bankrolled by illegal activities. There were claims that the party funded its political operations from monies generated from bank robberies. The *Magill* series in the spring of 1982 touched upon this issue in an article under the headline 'Bank Levies SFWP Style'. The magazine noted that 'Sinn Féin, the Workers' Party, strenuously denies that any of its finances come from robberies. In spite of these denials however we have identified the following robberies as having been carried out by members of the Official IRA since 1975.'[76] The list of robberies which the magazine linked to the OIRA included a IR£150,000 (approx. €190,000) raid on a CIÉ wages office in Dublin. 'We have been informed by several sources connected with the movement [the OIRA] that this robbery was conducted by the Official IRA to provided finance for Sinn Féin, the Workers' Party,' the magazine article stated.[77]

Having to deal repeatedly with such controversial allegations was undoubtedly embarrassing for those who sought to broaden the party's electoral base. In March 1982 after the first of two Dáil Éireann elections in that year, Tomás MacGiolla was questioned on RTÉ radio about the existence of the OIRA and any relationship between that military grouping and the Workers' Party. MacGiolla's response in 1982 would be repeated again and again over the following decade when questions about the OIRA arose:

> I certainly have no knowledge of them. All I know is that I am convinced and I am aware that there is no question of any military organisation in any way associated with us at the present ... I have no reason to think that it [the OIRA] still exists. Certainly it doesn't exist in any way down here. There was for some years a suggestion that it may have existed in the North and I pursued that there for quite a number of years to see any evidence of its existence and I am satisfied that it certainly doesn't exist in any association with us.[78]

It remains unclear how the OIRA 'went out of business' and what exactly happened to the arms and weapons which the organisation had at its disposal. There is considerable variation in the assessments about the activity of the OIRA after its 1972 ceasefire. As described previously, the organisation was active in Northern Ireland in the mid-1970s. The diversion of some former members into criminal activity was an undeniable reality. 'After the demise of Joe McCann and the announcement of the ceasefire, the Officials had sunk into gangsterism,' was one conclusion.[79]

Faced with the criminality allegations and confronted by ideological upheaval, an internal commission was established – headed by Eamon Gilmore – to assess the party's future direction. The body was a final attempt to finally deal with the 'leftovers' from the early days of the Workers' Party. The controversial issue was a serious negative in terms of future development, especially in the Irish Republic. The OIRA was also a stick with which to beat the party as opponents made opportunistic political capital from the obvious discomfort of leading Workers' Party figures over their organisation's historical associations.

Despite the party's electoral growth in the Republic in the 1980s – and its increased political presence at national and local level – the allegations lingered, and attacks on the Workers' Party using the OIRA had become part of political discourse. Two ministers in the 1982–7 Fine Gael–Labour coalition government claimed the OIRA was still active. In May 1983 Michael Noonan, who was justice minister, said he could confirm the OIRA was still in existence, a claim supported by the RUC in Northern Ireland. In December 1985, Ruairi Quinn of the Labour Party claimed not only that OIRA still existed but also that the organisation had links with the Workers' Party. Quinn had previously said his party had to act to prevent the Workers' Party becoming the party of the radical Left in the Irish Republic.[80] Tomás MacGiolla rejected the allegations, describing Quinn's claim as a 'smear tactic'.[81]

But the allegations would not disappear and they remained an obvious source of acute embarrassment for senior party figures. This was especially so in the Irish Republic where the party was on an upward growth curve. Most of the damaging allegations were derived from the party's past involvement in Northern Ireland where there had been little electoral advancement. This situation was an increasing source of tension between elements in the party on either side of the border, and among those who had firmly cut their ties, or had no associations, with the organisation as it existed in the 1970s. 'Quite honestly, some of the allegations weren't terribly serious but they were enough to be embarrassing for the party,' Tony Heffernan admitted.[82]

An example of the embarrassing legacy arose in June 1991 when Séamus Lynch was elected to the chair of the Belfast City Council's community services committee. Lynch secured the position with the help of votes from the Democratic Unionist Party (DUP) and two independent unionist councillors including Elizabeth Seawright, wife of the late George Seawright, a hardline unionist politician. One of the two DUP councillors to back the Workers' Party member was Rhonda Paisley, daughter of party leader Ian Paisley. This unusual voting combination ensured that Lynch became the first non-unionist to ever hold the chairmanship of any of Belfast City Council's standing committees. In Dublin, De Rossa heralded the election as a great breakthrough for the party but in Belfast there was a somewhat more muted reaction. One independent unionist councillor, Nelson McCausland, remarked: 'The Workers' Party is the current name of Official Sinn Féin which was the political wing of the IRA. It is a republican socialist party which seeks a united Ireland.'[83] McCausland spoke of the link to the OIRA in the past tense but only a few days later another Workers' Party member featured on 'Spotlight', the BBC Northern Ireland current affairs programme, denying any contemporary involvement with the OIRA.

De Rossa had labelled the Lynch election a 'breakthrough' but the BBC 'Spotlight' programme titled 'Sticking to their Guns' confronted the party with its own uncomfortable evolution. According to Paul Larkin, the producer on the programme, 'the point of the "Spotlight" film was to show the links (criminal and "military") between the Workers' Party and the supposedly deceased Official IRA.'[84] Moreover, Larkin added, the documentary 'meant that no party member could any longer claim that they were unaware of the secret army in their midst'.[85] The BBC programme made a number of very damaging claims, including that not only was the OIRA still in existence (in 1991) but also that several convicted OIRA men also held membership of the Workers' Party.

The programme provided several examples to substantiate its central thesis. Affidavits were obtained from people in Belfast who alleged they had been shot at by members of the Official IRA in a standoff with the Provisional IRA at a social club in the city in 1990. In addition, the four social clubs run by the Workers' Party in Belfast were, according to Larkin and his colleagues,

> ... described in police anti-racketeering documents, to which 'Spotlight' gained access, as central venues for the organisation of crime and funding of Workers' Party activities. Indeed, the membership rolls and lists of committee members of these social clubs were a perfect cross section of elements of the Official IRA and elements from the Workers' Party.[86]

The BBC programme also gave details of a number of incidents involving violent acts and racketeering in Belfast which it claimed involved the OIRA. More damaging for the credibility of the Workers' Party itself, the programme focused on four men and their connections to the OIRA and the Workers' Party, including the case of John Anthony Crossan who had signed nomination papers for John Lowry in the Lagan Valley constituency in the 1987 Westminster elections. According to Larkin, 'Crossan had been prosecuted and convicted of having ammunition with intent to endanger life whilst being a member of the

Official IRA.'[87] There was also the case of Billie Holden, convicted of stealing money in 1986, who was pictured at the 1991 Workers' Party Árd Fheis. Larkin alleged that 'the Workers' Party's northern delegation to its annual Árd Fheis ... included Official IRA members, who were well known to have convictions for paramilitary offences.'[88]

As well as these examples, the BBC programme also quoted sources in the Irish and British governments who said the OIRA was still active. Moreover, as Larkin noted, 'The "Spotlight" film showed the former Soviet and Stalinist states were also used as a refuge by Official IRA figures who were on the run from the authorities. Brian Lynch from Cork, for example, fled the country to East Germany in 1982 after Gardaí discovered a huge sum of counterfeit dollars in a raid on a Workers' Party printing press.'[89] The BBC had refused to allow the Workers' Party view the programme before it responded to the allegations. John Lowry was nominated as a party spokesman and he was interviewed as part of the programme. Lowry denied all the allegations made by the programme-makers: 'The Workers' Party has no connection whatsoever with any paramilitary organisation and unambiguously rejects paramilitarism of any form.'[90]

The BBC programme was broadcast on 27 June 1991, the same day as polling in the local elections in the Irish Republic. A much stronger response than that offered by Lowry followed the transmission of the programme. In a statement the party 'emphatically rejected' the allegations contained in the 'Spotlight' programme, claiming the material was 'totally spurious' and 'old hat' and had been 'conceived in hostility and in collaboration with people bitterly opposed to the Workers' Party'. The programme was described as a 'kangaroo court' which denied the party a chance to defend itself.

The allegations were taken up by the then Fianna Fáil minister for justice in the Republic. Ray Burke, whose own political career would end in ignominy over the taking of bribes, demanded that the Workers' Party answer the questions raised in the BBC programme. De Rossa repeated the denial about a link between his party and the OIRA. He also claimed one of those interviewed by the BBC had been discredited and that several members of the Workers' Party had issued libel proceeding over the broadcast.[91] Pat Rabbitte also claimed that libel proceedings would follow from the allegations in the programme. Writing thirteen years later, however, the programme's producer observed that he was 'not aware of any writ ever having been served on the BBC as a result of the "Sticking to their Guns" film'.[92]

The 1991 local election results were a huge disappointment for the Workers' Party, especially as pre-poll opinion surveys had been pointing to significant gains in the Dublin region. 'I remember confidently writing a statement saying how we were about to overtake Fine Gael as the second largest party in the capital city, and four days later it all fell flat and we ended up behind Fine Gael and Labour in Dublin, and we actually lost seats,' Tony Heffernan recalled.[93] While the programme was only broadcast on the eve of polling, Heffernan said that 'BBC Northern Ireland kept running this trailer all through the election campaign, all these sinister looking guys in balaclavas and so on. That was what, I think, brought things to a head.'[94] The disappointing local election results, according to Kathleen Lynch, advanced the party towards a split, with many members finally convinced that issues around criminality and ideology had to be addressed. 'The 1991 local elections were significant and probably drove the split as I think that's what made people in the Workers' Party a little bit jittery and contributed to the split,' Lynch said.[95]

The negative publicity arising from media speculation about the OIRA was a source of considerable frustration within the De Rossa wing of the party. 'I think we tolerated too many excuses within the North, special circumstances and conditions in which they lived ... we didn't want any taint of illegality ... You couldn't be pretending this and pretending that, and you couldn't be making excuses for people' Des Geraghty said.[96]

As tensions increased in the organisation in the 1991–2 period the matter of the OIRA was raised increasingly in both private and public. As Patterson explained, a body previously thought to be defunct by many had re-emerged as part of the party's power struggle:

> This was the context in which it appears that the hitherto largely moribund Official IRA was reinvigorated as part of the struggle for control of the party. It was seen as a means of mobilising a base for the traditionalists whose support was significantly greater in the North than in the Republic. The unintended effects of this, media speculation about the IRA's role in the party and embarrassing court appearances of members, pushed the conflict to the point of no return by the end of 1991.[97]

The different recollections of the motivations behind the split were evident in Tomás MacGiolla's reaction to the views of Des Geraghty and others who went on to form Democratic Left:

> Things in the North? There weren't things in the North. There was stuff in the papers, media stuff … If there was any truth in those stories – the Official IRA being better armed than the Provos – all that was rubbish. If there was any sense about the North it is that none of them had any great interest in the North. They were glad to be rid of the North.[98]

Despite MacGiolla's views, the criminality allegations were an increasing source of embarrassment for those firmly committed to democratic political activism. 'The people who were taking the flack for the carry on up the North, and whatever Garland and others were involved in, were essentially the people who had no involvement in it,' Catherine Murphy observed.[99] Tension was mounting between the different factions. Eric Byrne believed one particular episode over the recruitment of an assistant press officer in Leinster House eventually pushed the conflict to breaking point:

> One guy was shortlisted and he got the job. He was a former IRA prisoner. I remember De Rossa had extreme difficulty in having this guy get security clearance to work in Leinster House. The Gardaí obviously process all employees. De Rossa played a very honourable position. He had taken this man on the basis that he had been interviewed. Now Garland would have been involved in the interview and the interview would have happened in party headquarters. De Rossa took the decision as a democratic decision that this lad had been duly appointed. He had a terrible job in getting him security clearance. He had to go to Haughey, who was taoiseach at the time. Haughey swung it for him and he got his clearance. What broke De Rossa was that he got a report some months later that there had been fishy activity engaged in by elements attached to the Workers' Party, and this guy's name had come up.[100]

There were allegations of paramilitary activity, and De Rossa felt obliged to act. The new press officer was sacked.

That provoked an immediate ripple effect within the party. Looking

back in retrospect, Garland obviously needed or felt he needed –
he couldn't trust the parliamentarians – this man, an IRA activist
under his control, in parliament. That was the one issue that I am
absolutely convinced that broke the camel's back.[101]

In the opinion of Eric Byrne this issue brought the two pressures within
the party – developments in the communist bloc and criminality – to a
point where action was necessary. 'They were co-determinant issues and
both of them were [happening] simultaneously, and it happened that the
guy De Rossa was sacking also represented the Stalinist side of the
party.'[102]

CONCLUSION

The developments in central and eastern Europe caused internal tension
in the Workers' Party but the organisation had continued without an obvious split after De Rossa started the process of clarifying – and
reorientating – the party's political positioning. There were also obvious
differences between those associated with head office and the Leinster
House parliamentarians. Criminality was, however, the ingredient that
drew together the ideological questioning and organisational clashes which
eventually forced the split. For many who ultimately left the Workers'
Party criminality was the main motivation for the eventual split. 'For
myself and almost everyone in our branch in Kildare the predominant
issue that caused the split was criminality,' Catherine Murphy asserted.[103]

The criminality allegations caused different reactions from party
figures. 'I would have been generally politically happy with the direction
of the party, and thought that everyone was going to go that road, but
then discovered that this wasn't true,' Des Geraghty admitted.[104] This
view was widely shared among those close to De Rossa. Senior party
member Paul Sweeney said the media coverage 'showed an attitude that
I didn't share because the Official IRA was certainly dead in the South'.[105]
But 'the remnants of the old republican movement' – as Pat Rabbitte
described those causing the embarrassment – continued to surface. A
point of no return seemed to have been reached: 'it was a piece of
chewing gum, and if you pulled it long enough, it would break.'[106]
Proinsias De Rossa was centrally involved in the changes in the party,
and he was able to see the various pressure points which combined to
force a decision on future political direction:

There were still people in the Workers' Party who clearly were Leninist in terms of our organisation. But once the party had become involved in parliamentary politics that was going to influence the way the party evolved in terms of its understanding of society and how socialism could be developed in Ireland ... However, there was also a sense that the party wasn't going to go much further unless the broader image, how the party was perceived, was reformed. There was the overhang of the Official IRA and so on, which needed to be dealt with; there was the need to reform the finances of the party. When the Berlin Wall fell we were relieved of a lot of baggage. But there were a few people in the party who didn't want to take the next step to reform the party. And out of that turmoil, if you like intellectual turmoil, theoretical turmoil, came the crisis in the Workers' Party, and out of that came the DL [Democratic Left].[107]

An impasse was reached which forced people to decide about their political future. The type of organisational model and membership structure discussed previously was unsustainable in a party that was in the process of ending its reliance on democratic centralism. Under the De Rossa leadership, ideological reorientation had been brought to the fore. But any reconstitution of the party necessitated dealing with the continuing criminality allegations. Leading figures in the party were divided on the importance of engaging in the type of debate underway in other Left parties in Europe. They were also split about the significance of the Official IRA. As Catherine Murphy noted, the division was as much 'about culture as much as it was about the organisation'.[108] The leading figures in the Workers' Party were moving in opposite directions. In an accurate description of the situation at the end of 1991 Catherine Murphy concluded that 'there really were two parties at that stage, coexisting within one party.'[109] This uneasy existence was untenable. The scene was set for a battle over the future of the Workers' Party at a special conference in early 1992.

NOTES

1. *Ireland on Sunday*, 6 September 1998.
2. Ibid.
3. Interview with Proinsias De Rossa, 7 September 2007.
4. *Ireland on Sunday*, 6 September 1998.
5. S. Swan, *Official Irish Republicanism, 1962–82* (Belfast: Lulu, 2008), p.166.

6. Ibid., p.185.
7. *Irish Independent*, 9 December 1970.
8. S. MacStíofáin, *Memoirs of a Revolutionary* (Edinburgh: Gordon Cremonesi, 1975), p.104.
9. Ibid.
10. RTÉ Radio 1, 'This Week', 31 July 1970.
11. *An Phoblacht*, February 1970.
12. W.D. Flackes and S. Elliott, *Northern Ireland: A Political Directory, 1968–88* (Belfast: Blackstaff, 1989), p.206. The new provisional leadership turned their attention to the military campaign against the British presence in Northern Ireland. There was little time for political activity. During the decade that followed, Provisional Sinn Féin acted as a mouthpiece for the Provisional IRA and functioned as a fringe anti-system protest organisation. It was more a support body than a fully-fledged political party, and it certainly was not independent of its dominant militant partner. Under the leadership of Gerry Adams, the party's political activism increased in the 1980s and it was centrally involved in the Irish peace process. The Provisional IRA called a ceasefire in August 1994, while Provisional Sinn Féin was a participant in the talks with led to the Good Friday Agreement in 1998 and in July 2005 the military leadership ordered its members to 'dump arms' and back a political future. In May 2007 the leadership of Provisional Sinn Féin entered into a power-sharing administration with the SDLP and the two largest unionist parties in Northern Ireland.
13. E. Rooney, 'From Republican Movement to Workers' Party: An Ideological Analysis', in C. Curtin, M. Kelly and L. O'Dowd (eds), *Culture and Ideology in Ireland* (Galway: Officina Typographica, 1984), pp.79–80.
14. R. English, *Armed Struggle: The History of the IRA* (Oxford: Oxford University Press, 2003), pp.176–7.
15. Rooney, 'From Republican Movement to Workers' Party', p.82.
16. Quoted in H. Patterson, *The Politics of Illusion: A Political History of the IRA* (London: Penguin, 1997), p.148.
17. Ibid.
18. Ibid., p.147.
19. Ibid., p.152.
20. English, *Armed Struggle*, p.131.
21. T.P. Coogan, *The IRA* (London: Harper Collins, 1995 edition), p.459.
22. Ibid.
23. D. McKittrick, S. Kelters, B. Feeney, C. Thornton and D. McVea, *Lost Lives: The Stories of the Men, Women and Children who Died as a Result of the Northern Ireland Troubles* (Edinburgh: Mainstream, 1999), pp.190–1.
24. Bishop and Mallie, 1987, p.199
25. Coogan, *The IRA*, p.459.
26. P. Bishop and E. Mallie, *Provisional IRA* (London: Heinemann, 1987), p.223.
27. Rooney, 'From Republican Movement to Workers' Party', p.82.
28. McKittrick et al., *Lost Lives*, pp.69–70.
29. Ibid., p.560.
30. Flackes and Elliott, *Northern Ireland: A Political Directory, 1968–88*, p.161.
31. Bishop and Mallie, *Provisional IRA*, p.280
32. McKittrick et al., *Lost Lives*, p.520.
33. Ibid., p.538.
34. McKittrick et al., *Lost Lives*, p.538.
35. Rooney, 'From Republican Movement to Workers' Party', p.90.
36. Ibid., p.96.
37. Interview with Proinsias De Rossa, 7 September 2007.
38. Rooney, 'From Republican Movement to Workers' Party', p.95.
39. R. Dunphy and S. Hopkins, 'The Organisational and Political Evolution of the Workers' Party of Ireland', *Journal of Communist Studies*, 8, 3 (1992), p.91.
40. Quoted in ibid., pp.104–5.
41. Patterson, *The Politics of Illusion*, p.171.

42. Dunphy and Hopkins, 'The Organisational and Political Evolution of the Workers' Party of Ireland', p.97.
43. Sinn Féin The Workers' Party, *The Irish Industrial Revolution* (Dublin: SFWP, 1977), p.59.
44. Interview with Eoghan Harris, 28 April 2009.
45. Sinn Féin The Workers' Party, *The Great Irish Oil and Gas Robbery: A Case Study of Monopoly Capital* (Dublin: Repsol, 1977).
46. Patterson, *The Politics of Illusion*, p.169.
47. Rooney, 'From Republican Movement to Workers' Party', p.86.
48. See Dunphy and Hopkins, 'The Organisational and Political Evolution of the Workers' Party of Ireland', p.98.
49. *Teoiric: Theoretical Journal of the Republican Movement* (winter 1977/8), pp.3–16.
50. D. Robertson, *Penguin Dictionary of Politics* (London: Penguin, 1993), p.131.
51. Patterson, *The Politics of Illusion*, p.168.
52. Ibid., p.173
53. *Magill*, May 1982, p.12.
54. Ibid., p.8.
55. Ibid., p.53.
56. Ibid.
57. See *Magill*, November 1997.
58. RTÉ ref. no. BP20/8821/7008.
59. J. Horgan, *Broadcasting and Public Life: RTÉ News and Current Affairs, 1926–1997* (Dublin: Four Courts Press, 2004), p.164.
60. Interview with Catherine Murphy, 31 August 2006.
61. Ibid.
62. Interview with Tomás MacGiolla, 30 November 2006.
63. Patterson, *The Politics of Illusion*, p.257.
64. Interview with Eoghan Harris, 28 April 2009.
65. Interview with Tony Heffernan, 13 September 2006.
66. Ibid.
67. B. Hanley and S. Millar, *The Lost Revolution: The Story of the Official IRA and the Workers' Party* (Dublin: Penguin, 2009), pp.549–50.
68. Patterson, *The Politics of Illusion*, p.258.
69. Interview with Seán Garland, 29 May 2006.
70. McKittrick et al., *Lost Lives*, p.662.
71. E. Ó Murchú, 'The Workers' Party: Its Evolution and its Future', *Irish Socialist Review* (September 1982), p.22.
72. Rooney, 'From Republican Movement to Workers' Party', p.96.
73. Hanley and Millar, *The Lost Revolution*, p.375.
74. *Magill*, May 1982, p.9.
75. Ibid.
76. *Magill*, April 1982, p.12.
77. Ibid.
78. RTÉ Radio 1, 'Day by Day', 8 March 1982.
79. Bishop and Mallie, *Provisional IRA*, p.280.
80. RTÉ, *Day by Day*, 8 March 1982.
81. RTÉ Radio 1, *News at One Thirty*, 19 December 1985.
82. Interview with Tony Heffernan, 13 September 2006.
83. *The Irish Times*, 25 June 1991.
84. P. Larkin, 'Sticking to their Guns', in *A Very British Jihad: Collusion, Conspiracy and Cover-Up in Northern Ireland* (Belfast: Beyond the Pale, 2004), p.80.
85. Ibid., p.81.
86. Ibid., p.83.
87. Ibid., p.84.
88. Ibid.
89. Ibid., p.82.

90. BBC Northern Ireland, 'Spotlight', 27 June 1991.
91. RTÉ Radio News, 17 October 1991.
92. Larkin, 'Sticking to their Guns', p.87.
93. Interview with Tony Heffernan, 13 September 2006.
94. Ibid.
95. Interview with Kathleen Lynch, 10 October 2006.
96. Interview with Des Geraghty, 9 May 2006.
97. Patterson, *The Politics of Illusion*, p.258.
98. Interview with Tomás MacGiolla, 30 November 2006.
99. Interview with Catherine Murphy, 31 August 2006.
100. Interview with Eric Byrne, 29 August 2006.
101. Ibid.
102. Ibid.
103. Interview with Catherine Murphy, 31 August 2006.
104. Interview with Des Geraghty, 9 May 2006.
105. Interview with Paul Sweeney, 6 September 2006.
106. Interview with Pat Rabbitte, 9 January 2007.
107. Interview with Proinsias De Rossa, 7 September 2007.
108. Interview with Catherine Murphy, 31 August 2006.
109. Ibid.

4

Division and Departure:
A New Party is Born

INTRODUCTION

The crisis in the Workers' Party had been building for several years. In the latter half of 1991 talk within the De Rossa group turned to the possibility of forming a new political party. Such a move would immediately remove the burden of the history and ideology dogging the Workers' Party. Before this next step could be taken a decision was reached to make one final effort to find an accommodation within the Workers' Party. An attempt to reconstitute the existing party was undertaken at a special conference in February 1992. Over the preceding weeks the two sides had clashed at a number of meetings, including an Árd Comhairle meeting at which it was agreed that all members would 'stand down' and then 're-register' to remove individuals with divided loyalties from the political organisation. At the February conference the scene was set for a final public confrontation between the various internal fractions over ideological relevance and criminal allegations. The outcome of the conference, however, only increased the likelihood of the formation of a new party. 'People have to understand the type of organisation the Workers' Party was and how it evolved. It came from a conspiratorial background. A lot of us worked very hard to transcend that legacy. There was an element there that would not give up that legacy. Most of us then decided there was nothing more we could do and we left,' De Rossa admitted.[1]

THE 1992 SPLIT

Proinsias De Rossa and his supporters failed by the narrowest of margins in their efforts to secure change within the Workers' Party at the one-day conference on 15 February 1992. They needed a two-thirds majority of attending delegates to support the proposal to reconstitute the party as an independent, democratic, socialist and secular party. Some 374 delegates voted on the crucial conference motion and, in the end, with 133 delegates backing the status quo, the De Rossa group with 241 delegates was a mere nine votes short of the required threshold for change. 'You have your decision. I honestly believe it is a bad decision, but you have made it,' De Rossa told delegates after the result was announced.

Eamon Gilmore did not see the split as an 'inevitable' outcome of the conference: 'nine votes was the difference between the Workers' Party being reconstituted and those of us who left with De Rossa.'[2] Several different scenarios were recalled as leading to the eventual conference result. 'There were certainly views at the time that a number of people who basically supported what was being done voted against the motion on a tactical basis because they thought the Workers' Party was unreformable,' Tony Heffernan said.[3] Catherine Murphy agreed with this assessment: 'People were astonished by the vote. I think there were people on the [De Rossa] side that wanted the split and there was some electoral engineering that went on in my opinion to make sure that the outcome wasn't to reconstitute.'[4]

There was some surprise among those backing the changes at the direction in which events moved. 'I was one of the last to come to the conclusion that we weren't going to convince everyone. I was of the view that we would bring everyone with us,' Des Geraghty admitted.[5] Prior to the vote, De Rossa also believed that the required majority would be achieved. He attributed the outcome to the presence of many old guard members. 'They managed to bring in a large number of people from Northern Ireland who had not been active for donkey's years and swung the vote to have a sufficient minority to defeat the proposal.'[6] There was a certain amount of 'packing' of votes by both sides. Yet, according to Kathleen Lynch, the vote nearly swung in De Rossa's direction. 'A branch from Cork had decided to go for a drink at lunch time, and on the way back [they] couldn't find one of their members. He was still in the toilet and never voted. If they had found this man, the split would never have taken place. I'm not going to name the branch now because they stayed with the Workers' Party, but I could name them and I could name the guy who was stuck in the toilet. And [with this vote for De Rossa] there would have been no split. So that's how close it was.'[7] In any event, Kathleen Lynch believed the vote at the Dún Laoghaire conference was most likely immaterial to the future of the Workers' Party. 'The force of personalities was such that it might have delayed it [the split] to a great extent. There were things said that were very hurtful … It might just have delayed the inevitable.'[8]

The conference proceedings attracted considerable media comment. 'It was a frustrating end to a day of intense debate in which Marxist rhetoric and talk of revolution competed with a vision more in tune with the realities of modern Ireland …' was how *The Irish Times* summarised the outcome in an editorial devoted to the one-day conference.[9] In a separate report the same newspaper speculated on the next course of action: 'If supporters of Mr De Rossa indicate their backing for a move to establish a separate party it is generally believed that the seven TDs will move en masse and take most of the membership with them.'[10]

On the day of the conference in Dún Laoghaire, De Rossa was still interested in preserving the organisation he led. Caution about leaving to form a new party was urged on him by one long-time colleague: 'After the vote I bumped into Tomás MacGiolla and he was pretty down, and he said, "Don't make any sort of decisions."'[11] The two sides were, however, moving in the direction of separation, with their futures in different organisations. In media interviews in the days after the conference decision, De Rossa admitted that setting up a new party was one of the options available to those who had failed to secure change within the Workers' Party. Seán Garland was not surprised by the direction in which events moved. 'They had their agenda for some considerable time … They didn't want to keep the party together,' he remarked, adding 'the split was inevitable because the people pushing it were going to have it. They wanted a loosely based organisation which could adapt to any situation, particularly elections, the question of Northern Ireland, the question of international relations. These were all points but at the end of the day there was no basic fundamental principle in what they were at.'[12]

The idea of a new party had, in fact, been under active consideration by De Rossa and some of his closest advisors since the latter stages of 1991. Tony Heffernan was involved in those discussions. 'We had a series of Sunday morning meetings in Des [Geraghty] and Rosheen's [Callender] house in Blackrock coming up towards the end of 1991 … [about what] … we were going to do … And for a lot of people including myself who had been involved since 1968... [a new party] ... was essentially saying well, effectively, you're writing that off. That was quite big. It was a huge decision to take and something that was very difficult and not something that you lightly arrived at.'[13]

At these meetings in the latter half of 1991 there had been different views about forming a new party. 'I was one of the ones who was the least optimistic about the chances for a new party,' Heffernan recalled.[14] There was, however, a genuine sense of optimism among those involved. 'We thought we would do really well with a new party that wasn't tied down with baggage and that had all the talent of the Workers' Party,' Paul Sweeney admitted.[15]

The seven Workers' Party Dáil deputies met on 17 February 1992 in Leinster House to review the options open to them following the divisive conference. Discussions were also undertaken with leading figures in key constituencies but all the indications pointed to a break. Along with sharp ideological differences, the baggage of Official IRA associations had been aired enough times at the special conference to convince sufficient members, and elected representatives, of the necessity in establishing a new party. Eamon Gilmore's reaction summarised the stance of many of his colleagues:

> Obviously from the work in the Workers' Party, we were aware of the challenge and the difficulty of operating a small political party. But in some respects some of it didn't appear as daunting as it was. First of all the Workers' Party was always broke so nothing was going to change from that point of view. Secondly, we didn't have a choice. I mean we were leaving the Workers' Party and we had to maintain our political organisation. Thirdly, we did think there was scope for building a wider party ... We felt there was scope for a wider brief than the Workers' Party because the Workers' Party was carrying a certain amount of historical handicap and if that wasn't there, it was possible for people to join.[16]

Discussions got underway in several key constituencies, including Cork city, the base of Kathleen Lynch. The decision to leave the Workers' Party was not taken lightly. According to Seán Garland, Lynch had divided loyalties on what was happening in the party. 'Kathleen Lynch was all in favour of the Workers' Party but then she went off. De Rossa persuaded them [Lynch and her supporters] to side with him,' Garland said.[17] The difficulties faced by party activists are clearly illustrated in Lynch's case. 'I suppose it took about a week and a half. Every individual had to sit down and decide what they were going to do. We decided to go with Proinsias. We felt that it was the only way forward. The Workers' Party at that stage had been so exposed ... And whether it was true or not the exposure was very damaging. But the decisions were made with great difficulty.'[18]

A meeting of the Workers' Party Árd Comhairle was called for 22 February 1992. Reconciliation between the two sides was by this date an unlikely outcome. 'The question now is not if but when the formal break in the Workers' Party takes place,' one newspaper editorial observed.[19] Indeed, many on the De Rossa side were already preparing for the formation of a new party. It was reported that a majority of the forty-six members of the Workers' Party Árd Comhairle had indicated a preference to join a new political entity, as had over half of the party's local public representatives.[20] Various political figures were dropping broad hints about how they saw matters progressing. Eamon Gilmore said he would 'act in concert with his parliamentary colleagues'.[21] Joe Sherlock was more explicit about the political landscape after the planned meeting: 'I won't be Workers' Party, that is for sure.'[22] Pat Rabbitte was already talking openly about a new party: 'There is a broad constituency that has never been captured by the Left. The new political formation will be seeking to give expression to those groups.'[23] Rabbitte had his own personal view on the correct direction forward but he was in a small minority at that time.

> My preference was that the reformers would have joined the Labour Party, and I had discussions with Dick Spring around that time, at his request. As he saw it, although there was no evidence of this in the polls at the time, he felt six – we thought seven – deputies merging with Labour would have been a tremendous boost and added a dynamic for the ensuing [electoral] contest. As it turned out he was more right than he or I thought. But it was a step too far for most of my colleagues.[24]

De Rossa did not give serious consideration to the Labour Party option. But neither was he prepared to allow the minority who had succeeded at the Dún Laoghaire conference to force him out of political life. 'I felt a responsibility to the people in the Workers' Party – do I walk away from them and say, "well that's it, goodbye, find your own way around them [the old guard]." But I needed to provide some vehicle for our politics which was very progressive politics.' [25]

The objective of taking most of the leading figures in the Workers' Party into a new formation met with a serious stumbling block. All attempts to get Tomás MacGiolla to join his other parliamentary colleagues in a separate organisation proved unsuccessful. 'I am not joining any new party. That is my view and that is what I'm doing,' MacGiolla announced on 20 February 1992.[26] Shortly after the Dún Laoghaire conference, Liz McManus had sought to convince him to change his mind. 'I even wrote to Tomás MacGiolla at the time saying, "Look, we need you, come with us." He never replied to it and in hindsight he wasn't going to buy into it.'[27]

Considerable pressure was placed on the former Workers' Party leader to join with his parliamentary colleagues. 'The surprise to me when it came to the actual crunch was that MacGiolla went with the Workers' Party ... I was disappointed. I thought MacGiolla would have come but there was an umbilical cord there that he couldn't break,' Des Geraghty admitted.[28] Eamon Gilmore took a different view: 'I don't think there were any circumstances in which Tomás MacGiolla was going to leave the Workers' Party. But if he had supported De Rossa's motion at the Dún Laoghaire conference the party would not have split.'[29] In the days after the reconstitution conference party figures were engaged in an endless series of meetings about their future direction and MacGiolla's future. Eric Byrne was one of those who met with the former party president:

> Everybody had a session with him. He was just stonewalling. He didn't try to defend anything. He was just caught in his old republican loyalty to the boys, you know. I personally thought he was committing political suicide. The tide was moving our way, the tide had moved. The intellectual progressive activists were to become Democratic Left, leaving behind the republican rump. And it was going nowhere and he couldn't see it, which was kind of sad. We were talking to him at length in the members' restaurant [in Leinster House], trying to explain to him but there was no budging him at all which, in a sense, indicated the incredible negative loyalty that republicans have to each other. It was one of those political tragedies ...[30]

In an interview for this book MacGiolla, who died in February 2010, said he was taken aback at the direction in which events moved in the aftermath of the Dún Laoghaire conference.

> They all came to me. They said, 'we should act together' but I replied, 'You'll finish the party and you'll finish yourselves.' I had built this fucking party. I was there [as party president] for twenty-seven years and I had no inkling whatsoever that anyone had a problem and that something like this was going to happen. To me De Rossa's decision was a big shock; I thought I knew him inside out. I was shocked at him and also Des Geraghty – not with Rabbitte – but without the other two it could not have happened. There was no political reason that I could see [to form Democratic Left]. I still can't see the purpose. I think it was a career move. There was a great phrase in the Dáil – 'come in from the cold'. But when it was said to me I told people, 'But I don't feel cold.' I think they were coming in from the cold believing lots of things would open up for them ... I think they betrayed me.[31]

De Rossa recognised that the decision would end a long-time relationship between the two men which went back to the 1950s:

> I knew Tomás MacGiolla since I was 17. We were in The Curragh. We knocked around together from when he was leader of Sinn Féin. He lived a short distance from where I lived before I got married. We'd been friends right through, and I assumed that he wanted reform in the way that I did. It eventually transpired that he in fact didn't want this reform. Now maybe he didn't want the reform the way it was done. Maybe he didn't trust some of the people who were promoting the reform [and] that he felt there was another agenda. He was always distrustful of Pat Rabbitte, which I thought was extremely unfair. He [Rabbitte] certainly wasn't in their mould in terms of politics, but he was clearly committed to the basic ideas of the Workers' Party in terms of fairness and justice. So there was that element in it [but] I think once MacGiolla took the position he did at the special conference in Dún Laoghaire then he would not come to a new party. It was a pity.[32]

MacGiolla's decision was, nevertheless, a blow to the De Rossa group, which would have preferred to have departed the Workers' Party as a single unit and, by taking all seven TDs, they would have left the party with little, if any, national profile. As it was, MacGiolla's decision would cause certain parliamentary difficulties for the new party in terms of Oireachtas recognition and related parliamentary rights and funding.

The decision to confirm the split was not easy for any of those involved. Indeed, the strength of feelings involved clearly illustrates the importance of personal relationships in the internal dynamic of a political party. Long-time colleagues and friends found themselves on difference sides, as Des Geraghty discovered: 'I lost very good friends – a lot of people I would have been very close friends with for years. It was very bitter. People would pass you in the street. I think it takes time but it was really bitter, you know, it probably goes with a lot of those splits anyway.'[33] Liz McManus described the split as 'emotional'.[34] For those involved with the party in Cork the split was particularly difficult. 'We were very close and very loyal to one another ... the people in Cork were our friends for twenty-five years. You know if there was a christening they were at it. If there was a wedding, they were at it, birthday parties, anything, and you were walking away from that,' Kathleen Lynch remarked.[35]

The bitterness remained, and in many cases never eased. 'I remember the day we wrapped up the anti-apartheid movement at the Mansion House. MacGiolla was the lord mayor, and he was really resentful after the split, and he wouldn't talk to us,' Paul Sweeney recalled.[36] Eric Byrne shared this experience. 'The antagonism continues to this day,' he admitted.[37] The latter view was clearly evident from Seán Garland's recollection of his former colleagues:

> History will demonstrate that they were opportunists who saw a way in which they could carve out a space for themselves and a career in politics. They had no justification for what they did. I've always said if someone wants to leave a party, then leave it. But you do not undermine and destroy the party, which was of the working class, that was a betrayal.[38]

The option of forming a new political party had been discussed prior to the outcome of the Dún Laoghaire conference. The conference result meant there was really only one road for De Rossa and his colleagues, irrespective of MacGiolla's stance.

PRIVILEGES, FUNDING AND RECRUITS

The first steps towards the formation of the party that was eventually named Democratic Left were taken on Saturday 22 February 1992 with the formal departure of six of the Workers' Party TDs from its ranks. Interestingly, it was reported in the media that 'By Tuesday, the six TDs and possibly also the Labour Party TD, Mr Emmet Stagg, will have registered a new political party and found a new name. Within the next few months the group will seek a new direction, recruit and organise its first conference and, its leaders hope, constitute itself as a new organisation to the left of the Labour Party.'[39]

The parliamentary status of the six now former Workers' Party TDs was unclear. The Ministers and Parliamentary Secretaries Act, 1960 stipulated that the leader of a registered political party with seven or more deputies was entitled to funding from the party leaders' allowance scheme. The Standing Orders of Dáil Éireann stated that such groups were entitled to certain defined benefits including speaking rights, the ability to table priority questions, allocated private member's time and membership of the Committee on Procedure and Privileges.

Following the 1989 general election the seven-strong Workers' Party group in Dáil Éireann enjoyed these defined parliamentary entitlements. With Tomás MacGiolla opting to remain with the Workers' Party, the breakaway grouping was one TD short of the entitlement threshold. The matter was important for the De Rossa group, as recognised political groups, as well as enjoying parliamentary privileges, also received annual state funding from the party leaders' allowance scheme. The fund was worth almost IR£100,000 (approx. €127,000) to the Workers' Party in 1992.

One solution to the MacGiolla absence opened up with speculation that Emmet Stagg, a Labour Party TD, would join the new grouping. Stagg was on the Left of the Labour Party and, throughout the 1980s, had found himself in a continuous battle with the more moderate party leadership. Intriguingly, he resigned the Labour whip in the days before the Workers' Party split. Publicly, he justified his decision as a response to the failure of the Labour leadership not to rule out coalition with what he called Right-wing parties. There was, however, considerable speculation that the Kildare TD was about to change party allegiance. 'If the Workers' Party TDs form a new party, I see it as a positive development. I am not saying whether I will join it. I am keeping my options open,' Stagg said.[40]

De Rossa was surprised that Stagg was prepared to join the new party as he considered his internal difficulties as not insurmountable. But he was keen to attract the Labour Party deputy. 'There were serious discussions and it looked quite close, and we thought he was on board, and then within twenty-four hours suddenly he was gone. I still don't know why he changed his mind. Perhaps Dick Spring spoke to him and said, "look lets work out our differences and so on" but I don't know.'[41] Eamon Gilmore was convinced about the seriousness of Stagg's intentions. 'I believe he changed his mind when he talked to members in his constituency and some people probably had some serious words with him.'[42] Stagg did not join Democratic Left, and in any event his arrival probably would not have had any benefit in terms of securing parliamentary privileges or state funding for the new party. The standing orders of Dáil Éireann, in early 1992, stated that a parliamentary group must have a membership of at least seven TDs who were elected as a party at the previous general election. The rules made no provision for a situation where seven or more TDs might establish a new political party or parliamentary group in the period between elections.

The Committee on Procedure and Privileges – which has cross-party membership – agreed on 26 February 1992 to examine the matter should it arise, although it was not clear that the other political parties would actually have backed a change. 'It was made clear at the meeting that even if the six former Workers' Party deputies succeeded in attracting a seventh member … this would not mean they would automatically win group privileges,' *The Irish Times* reported.[43] The committee did, however, agree to change the rules on the definition of a political party in the standing orders of Dáil Éireann so that MacGiolla, as the sole remaining Workers' Party TD, did not continue to receive group privileges.[44]

While changing internal Dáil Éireann rules on parliamentary privileges was one issue, it was a different matter entirely in relation to qualification for the party leaders' allowance scheme. This funding was dependent on legislation and there seemed to be little political interest in changing the law to assist the new party.[45] The result was that the new party was deprived of a vital source of funding. The failure to attract Emmet Stagg, however, went beyond money, as Eamon Gilmore explained:

What we ended up with was six former Workers' Party TDs, and therefore there was, if you like, a perception that this was the Workers' Party under a different name. But if we had got a number of people, and some of those who spoke to us and committed themselves to us, it [Democratic Left] would have widened and it would have been much more possible to promote a separate, new political party.[46]

Along with Stagg, there was speculation that Michael D. Higgins, another well-known figure in the Labour Party, was considering his political future. The failure to secure either politician was a blow, as Tony Heffernan (in agreement with Eamon Gilmore) recalled. 'The big disappointment was that we didn't get any sort of figure in the Dáil, or any substantial public figure from outside the Workers' Party, to join. People had hopes about Michael D. Higgins, and particularly about Emmet Stagg.'[47] The lack of success in landing either Stagg or Higgins was, according to Heffernan, 'the big failure' – adding: 'Emmet Stagg came very close and I think he would have joined but his organisation in Kildare just made it clear that they weren't going anywhere and that understandably caused him to review the situation. I think Michael D. would have been too engrained in the history and the traditions of the Labour Party to have ever jumped.'[48]

Interestingly, in early 1995 there was speculation that Democratic Left was about to be joined by Brendan Ryan. Based in Cork, Ryan had been an independent member of Seanad Éireann – elected on the National University of Ireland panel – from 1981 until 1993 when he lost his seat. Ryan said he was keen to contest the subsequent general election and was interested in talking with Democratic Left. The idea received the backing of the party's only Cork TD, Kathleen Lynch. 'I have made no secret of the fact that I feel closer to Brendan Ryan than anybody else outside of Democratic Left,' Lynch said.[49] The discussions, however, never came to anything, and some years later Ryan joined the Labour Party.

Beyond big political names, the new party also had hopes of attracting into its ranks unaligned supporters of Left-wing politics. Eamon Gilmore explained the thinking: 'We all knew there were people for a pile of reasons who were on the Left of Irish politics and would always tells us, "No, no. We'll never join the Workers' Party; you know if you're doing something else we would become part of that." There were people in the Labour Party who told us the same things.'[50] The history of

Democratic Left, however, showed that few big names found their way into its ranks. The party suffered from an over-reliance on a core group of members who shouldered a considerable workload which was one of the factors prompting moves to eventually merge with the Labour Party. These organisational weaknesses are discussed in greater detail in Chapter 8.

FROM 'NEW AGENDA' TO DEMOCRATIC LEFT

The financial and organisational challenges involved in setting up a new party were not underestimated by those involved. The task was complicated by the fact that the De Rossa grouping were not just setting up a new party, they also had to manage the split from their former comrades. 'It's not that easy to form a political party, believe it or not, especially when you're dealing with the existing party that's splitting and you have to see how many you can attract away,' Eric Byrne said.[51] A temporary steering committee was established to work on setting up the new party. It would be, De Rossa predicted, 'a new and fresh party which will offer a clear alternative to the existing parties'.[52]

The scale of the undertaking was evident in correspondence sent to potential members on 9 March 1992 ahead of a foundation conference which was set for 28 March 1992. The correspondence was headed 'Launch of New Party' and was signed on behalf of the steering committee by Des Geraghty. A number of 'urgent tasks' were set out for members, supporters and friends of the new party. These tasks included establishing branches, affiliating branches, convening meetings to discuss conference items, publicising the conference and party locally – organising advance publicity to ensure maximum attendance at the conference and raising money. With such an imposing list of 'things-to-do' it was little wonder that Dermot Boucher, a founder of the Socialist Labour Party, wrote in one assessment of the prospects for the De Rossa undertaking, 'The precedents are not generally encouraging.'[53] There were, however, some positives arising from the split, as Liz McManus recalled. 'In the Constitution Room in the Shelbourne Hotel when we announced the new party ... I would say I was confident, I think partly naive, and you know the great thing about going through an experience like that is, it does put iron in your soul. That was the great strength of Democratic Left, we all got through it, the cauldron of fire, and came out the other side.'[54]

The steering committee commissioned a number of working papers – circulated prior to the founding conference – divided into four areas: the Economy; Northern Ireland; Health/Education/Women; and Culture/Civil Liberties/International Affairs/Youth. They were fortunate in being able to draw support and assistance from a group of sympathetic supporters from academic and professional backgrounds. The foundation conference had twin objectives, as the leading participants informed potential members:

> In addition to launching the new party the conference will have to decide on a framework which will make clear the political direction of the new party and allow it to function effectively while detailed policies and structures are worked out, without in any way inhibiting the process of discussion and debate that must get underway once we are up and running.[55]

Five tasks were identified which had to be completed at the founding conference:

1. Agree procedure/standing orders for the meeting itself;
2. Agree a set of interim rules so that the meeting can proceed to elect a leader, officers and functioning executive to carry the new party through to its first full conference;
3. Agree a name for the party;
4. Agree an outline constitution, based on the principles set out in our preliminary leaflet and an outline political programme;
5. Establish policy committees to develop detailed policies ahead of a policy conference in the autumn.[56]

Those involved were taking on a considerable workload. A decision was taken to allow the membership to select the name of the new political entity. The ultimate decision was to be made at the founding conference. An information letter was circulated as part of the pre-conference consultation process. 'Your assistance in deciding upon the name of the party would be very welcome,' members were informed. 'Our title should signal that we are an open democratic, socialist party (without <u>necessarily</u> using those words). That we are a new type of party as outlined in our founding principles, that we are creative, inclusive and professional in our approach.'[57]

At a media conference on 2 March 1992, the name 'New Agenda' was announced as a 'working title' for the new party. A corresponding slogan – Working Towards A New Agenda – was also adopted by the steering committee which was busy organising the party's foundation conference scheduled for the RDS in Dublin on 28 March 1992. 'New Agenda', De Rossa predicted, would be an alternative political movement 'for all who feel disenfranchised; for those who know that the old agenda does not recognise their grievances. We want to set a new agenda in Irish politics.'[58] The lack of certainty over the new party's name remains a source of differing opinion among those involved with what eventually emerged as Democratic Left. Des Geraghty was one of those taken with the 'working title':

> I thought New Agenda was reasonably good. But it was an exercise that we could have done without. If we'd got the thing right from the start it would have been easier. But trying to convince the public of two name changes ... I think we should have put a bit more thought into it.[59]

Liz McManus did not favour retaining the 'New Agenda' name. 'You need to have huge resources to sell the name and a lot of luck ... I don't think New Agenda would have worked. It was an awful name ...'[60] Eric Byrne was even blunter: 'The naming was a bit of a mess when you look back at it. New Agenda filled a gap [but] it's a nonsensical name for a political party.'[61] The naming decision was ultimately taken by the new party membership. A questionnaire was circulated on 19 March 1992. Two questions were posed:

> Part I: Should any of the following words or their variations be used in our title? Draw a line through those you don't want: DEMOCRACY; SOCIALIST; NEW; AGENDA; PEOPLE; ALLIANCE; PARTY; PROGRESS; CITIZEN; LEFT.

> Part II: Which of the following titles (listed alphabetically) would you prefer? Mark 1,2,3, etc. in order of your choice:
> Democratic Left
> New Agenda
> New Democracy
> New Left
> People's Party
> People's Progress Party

Socialist Party
Socialist People's Party.

Those in receipt of the correspondence were also asked if they had any alternative suggestions for the name of the new party. Arising out of this pre-conference consultation process, four names were eventually put to the conference. The vote on the name of the new party – along with the election to the party's executive – was held under the qualified majority system of proportional representation. People voted in the order of their preference but higher votes were given additional weighting. For example, on the vote on the party's name, with four choices available, a number 1 vote was given four points, a number 2 was given three points, and so on. 'This system is simpler to count than the transferable vote, but is equally fair,' the steering committee concluded.[62] The names voted upon by delegates attracted the following levels of support – Democratic Left (1,039), New Agenda (1,010), People's Party (660) and Socialist Party (665). It was interesting that the two options that sounded most socialist, in a traditional sense – People's Party and Socialist Party – were relegated to lower-preference positions. In light of the ideological turbulence in the European Left after the collapse of the Soviet system this was not an unsurprising result, as was discussed in Chapter 1. The choice of name revealed a conscious decision by the conference delegates to depart from old ground.

The transition from Workers' Party to 'New Agenda' to Democratic Left in a matter of weeks became a source of considerable derision from political opponents. 'We wanted to select the name democratically but we had to have a holding name and a lot of people didn't understand that and sort of mocked the fact that we had this name, New Agenda, and then we changed it to Democratic Left,' Rosheen Callender recalled.[63] Proinsias De Rossa agreed with the latter point:

> Democratic Left wasn't a bad name but maybe we should have stuck with New Agenda. For some reason the media seemed to think that there was the Workers' Party then New Agenda and then DL when in fact New Agenda was just an interim name. I think that's one of the things we made a mistake about.[64]

FOUNDING CONFERENCE, 28 MARCH 1992

The conference began its proceedings at 10.30 a.m. on Saturday 28 March 1992. Following the adoption of standing orders and other procedural matters, Liz McManus delivered the opening address at 10.50 a.m.[65] Between 11.00 a.m. and 12.15 p.m. time was allocated for debate on the party name, the draft constitution and the political principles of the new party. Voting on the party name as well as any amendments to the constitution and principles was set from 12.15 p.m. to 12.30 p.m. A debate on the draft interim rules – followed by votes on any amendments to those rules – was due to run from 12.30 p.m. until 1.20 p.m. Following a fifty-minute lunch break, the conference timetable allowed for an hour and forty-five minutes on policy. After a fifteen-minute allocation for announcements and an introductory speech, Proinsias De Rossa was scheduled to deliver his keynote address at 4.15 p.m. The conference was set to conclude at 5.00 p.m. There was a pre-conference dispute with RTÉ about the level of airtime the national broadcaster was planning to allocate to the weekend gathering. It was an early indication of the uphill battle those involved would have to fight to ensure their rights were guaranteed in various areas, from parliamentary privileges to television coverage.

The press release headline on Proinsias De Rossa's keynote address stated that the speech was given 'at the meeting to transform a new agenda into a political party'.[66] One of those involved, Kathleen Lynch, recalled an atmosphere that was 'upbeat and very energising but I still think that the split took a little bit of the gloss off what should have been a good experience'.[67] A party spokesman was reported as saying that between 600 and 1,000 members would attend the conference.[68] Many of the objectives in the party's founding documents were referenced in set-piece speeches. The keynote speakers had a number of objectives – to put distance between themselves and the Workers' Party, to position themselves ideologically in the post-Berlin Wall world and to explain why their new undertaking was different from the Labour Party. Liz McManus in the opening address of the conference said the day was 'a historic occasion' with the prospect of 'a new kind of politics'. Like many other speakers she did not directly mention her previous political home but the message was clearly understood.

In this party there are no longstanding members and no raw recruits.

As equals we are starting out to forge a new kind of politics – one that is built from the ground up ... We are without any tradition of organisation. We are not weighted down by history or the burden of outdated rules. We can make of this party anything we like ... We are challenging the existing parties not just in their politics, but in their ways of operating, the power structures and their prejudices.[69]

Many of those attending the founding conference stuck with the new party for almost seven years. But ultimately they were confronted with the practical and conceptual uncertainties at the core of their undertaking. These issues are examined in later chapters but in early 1992 there was a genuine sense of embarking upon what could best be described as a new political adventure. There was recognition that a single day would limit the scope for discussion. The steering committee sought to ease any concerns: 'The business on the agenda today is the minimum necessary to get us up and running as a political party. It is not the end of the process, but the beginning. Matters decided today, whether it is the constitution rules or policy matters, can all be amended at future conferences if they are found to be in any way defective.'[70]

Over sixty amendments were received in relation to the constitution, interim rules, politics of the new party and the political practices of the new party. These amendments were among the issues debated by those who attended the conference. The draft interim constitution was divided into four sections – general, objectives, means, and principles of organisation – and is reproduced in Appendix II.

The sentiments expressed in the draft interim constitution showed that the new party was intent on positioning itself on the Left. But there was little in the objectives to differentiate Democratic Left from most social democratic parties including the Irish Labour Party. Democratic Left was not positioned on the 'Radical Left' as defined by Kate Hudson, who offered a hypothesis that as social democratic and traditional conservative parties converged around a neo-liberal agenda, a new Left would emerge to fight against such convergence. But Democratic Left's policy platform did not contain a rejection of capitalism. The party had accepted an accommodation of the market economy with the objective of social justice. The conference also debated a document entitled 'The Politics of the New Party' which in tandem with the proposed constitution in effect laid down a very clear sense of the ethos and philosophical outlook of the new organisation. The new party was defined as a:

> ... democratic, socialist party. We believe that the idea of social-
> ism coupled with the practice of democracy provides the basis for
> the radical transformation of Irish society. We aim to be a feminist
> party. An environmental party. A party of the unemployed and the
> low-paid. A champion of personal freedom. A friend and ally of
> the Third World. An integral part of the European Left.

There were twenty-seven amendments tabled to the draft constitution, fifteen of which were carried at the founding conference. Many of these amendments introduced subtle changes of emphasis into the wording of the constitution; for example, in Article 2.1(j) it was agreed to sub-stitute the phrase 'third world' with 'developing countries'. A number of amendments from the Dún Laoghaire constituency were obviously intended to stress the ideological outlook of the new party while ensur-ing that the language used provided no reason for criticism from their political opponents. In that regard, the conference backed the Dún Laoghaire proposal in Article 1.2 to delete the word 'secular' while the same word was also deleted from Article 2.1(a) and replaced by the apparently more politically sensitive word 'pluralist'.

Pragmatism was also evident in the decision to reject an amendment from Dublin South East to fundamentally change the priority of Article 2.1(g) by replacing the proposed wording with 'To see the protection of the environment from planet to locality as paramount and as super-seding any economic interests.' Once again, this latter decision can be seen as evidence of political realism among those involved in the new undertaking. The party was not going to be marginalised from main-stream public opinion. Many of the other amendments were of a minor technical nature, dealing with internal party elections and voting systems. Some amendments were framed in the context of the new party's difficult birth and previous associations with the Workers' Party. For example, Article 4.4 was amended to include the additional wording 'that public representatives of the party be equally accountable to the membership'.

The draft interim rules – which were agreed with some amendments – were also influenced by the events of the previous few months. The rules dealt with membership, branches, constituency councils, elections and public representatives, annual delegate conference, executive, central council, president, general secretary, trustees, joint treasurer/finances, disputes and rule changes. Probably of most significance was the importance placed on the position of members within the new organisation that was described as 'a member-centred Party'. Membership was set at IR£5 (approx. €6.35) with a pledge that 'the Party at every level shall endeavour to enable all members participate fully in decision-making and in Party activities.' Eamon Gilmore proposed the new rules for endorsement by the conference delegates.

> These rules are for a party which will be governed by its members. The policy and major decisions of this party will not be made by any select group – not by the TDs, not by some ideological élite, not by some backroom media handlers, but by the members through the structures provided for in these rules. This will be a members' party.

Gilmore was one of several speakers who highlighted the fact that the new party was incorporating 'full gender equality' into its rules – a first for an Irish political party. Interestingly, an amendment to the rules proposed by the Dungannon branch did not make it onto the conference agenda. The proposal – 'That a no-smoking rule shall apply in all meeting rooms before, during and after party meetings' – was obviously still somewhat ahead of its time. The founders of this new party were very keen to put distance between themselves and the organisation they had left behind. The 'politics' of the new party was very much about defining a distinct brand of socialism, and every effort was made to expand and explain the ideological background. There was, however, little in the 'politics of the new party' that a social democratic party could find objectionable.

> Our socialism is rooted in the great democratic principles of 'liberty, equality, fraternity'. For us there can be no socialism without liberty and democracy. We see democracy as the full and active participation of all citizens in decision-making and in controlling their own lives. Socialism for us is the political, economic and social development of society to achieve personal freedom, economic and social rights, equality of citizenship, equitable distribution of wealth and social solidarity within that democracy.

The document outlining the 'politics of the new party' was divided into sixteen sections, all of which were to become familiar themes associated with Democratic Left, including solidarity with the exploited, the unemployed and PAYE workers; criticism of the profoundly unequal distribution of power and resources, deeply embedded in a remarkably rigid class structure; the expansion of democratic control of the economy; gender equality; an end to corruption in public life; a clear separation of church and state; an end to the Republic's territorial claim on Northern Ireland; an end to global military blocs and support for a more account-able European Union. Delegates also decided on what was called 'the political practice of the new party'. The objectives of the new organi-sation were clearly elaborated upon in this section of its rules. Members were committed to replacing 'alienation from politics with active participation; to be the voice of those who have been excluded from influencing our society'. Once more the impact of the departure from the Workers' Party was clearly evident – 'we want to be a party of the people and not simply a party for the people.' Clientelism, whereby national politicians attempted to curry favour with voters by promising local services, was going to be challenged, while the party would endeavour to be a place of vibrant debate: 'it must never be simply an electoral machine.' Democratic Left was going to be 'a campaigning party' with considerable membership involvement. 'We are about changing society and fundamental change cannot be constructed at the parliamentary level alone.'

The end result of this type of political activity was seen as revitalising politics on the Left in Ireland. 'We will work for the continued realign-ment of Irish politics. We seek to offer clear, democratic politics on the Left. A Left government is an achievable goal which has the capacity to offer a real alternative in the short-term. Our strategy will be to seek the widest possible co-operation on the Left. We see no role for our party as a partner in a right-wing government.' The only significant amendment to the 'political practice' of the new party was the addition of a new clause which noted that 'In keeping with our objective for an open, democratic society that we enable our members to play the fullest possible part in the party through training and personal development.'[71]

Liz McManus urged caution with a sober warning about the daunt-ing task of setting up a new political party. 'Today we are putting together the bones of a party. It will take time to put all the flesh on those bones.' Rosheen Callender, at the start of the conference session on policy statements, made a similar point. 'Indeed the statements are intentionally lacking in detail. What they are intended to do is to provide a broad outline of the general policy direction of a new party determined to open new doors, develop new ideas and step boldly in a new direction as we see fit.' Many of the party's policies are examined in subsequent chapters but it is worth noting here that there were some omissions. Callender mentioned transport, communications and tourism while the statement on the environment was only added to the agenda after delegates had been circulated with their conference material. It was decided that policy development committees would meet over subsequent weeks and months to formulate proposals in areas omitted from discussion at the foundation conference. The omissions were somewhat understandable given the pace of events over the previous few weeks. But this could also be viewed as further evidence of the uncertainty about the 'New Left' agenda that Democratic Left was attempting to launch in 1992. Proinsias De Rossa admitted as much about the economy – what should have been the core policy around which all others pivoted.

> It would be true to say that the economic dimension of the party was not that well developed. I think we would have been looking around to see what were the issues that we needed to connect with. We were strong on public services and the idea that people benefited from the economy in ways wider than simply gaining a better salary or wages … But it wasn't any clearer than that in my view.[72]

De Rossa's statement is clear evidence that the Left had failed to find an alternative economic model for the new global world. The Left in Europe had neither the vocabulary nor the principles to replace the traditional Keynesian model. The New Right championed the agenda of free markets and reduced state interventionism, and political parties like Democratic Left came to articulate their ideology within the economic parameters of this new globalised world.

CONCLUSION

The split in the Workers' Party in February 1992 nearly did not happen.

With a handful of additional votes at the reconstitution conference, Proinsias De Rossa would have continued as party president. His supporters would have remained within the organisation, and the party would have retained a presence in national politics. But the divisions between the factions were irreconcilable. Even if De Rossa had secured the required two-thirds majority, the internal differences would ultimately have required confrontation. If De Rossa had succeeded at Dún Laoghaire his opponents might well have departed to form a new political entity. But such speculation ignores the energy-sapping battles which would have continued before such a point in time was reached. Moreover, there is the matter of the damage these debates would have done to the Workers' Party brand with the wider public. The formation of Democratic Left may ultimately have been the best possible scenario for De Rossa and his supporters.

Many of those who attended the 1992 conference that gave birth to Democratic Left gave the project considerable energy and time over the following seven years. But ultimately these individuals were confronted by the practical and conceptual uncertainties at the core of their undertaking. These organisational challenges alongside restrictive financial constraints are discussed in subsequent chapters. They were matched by the hugely daunting task of carving out a distinctive political identity for the new party. The Left in European politics was convulsed in the late 1980s and many transition parties post-1989 were unable to find a distinctive ideological niche. New Revisionism, as Democratic Left discovered, was not easy, especially in the absence of a distinct and coherent economic platform to challenge the New Right consensus.

The Democratic Left project had at its core a flawed identity – the party sought to be on the 'radical Left' but the contents of the debate at its founding conference, and the sentiments in the documents approved at that same conference, were largely social democratic in their ideological orientation. As far as De Rossa was concerned, the new party was 'in a sense anti-establishment and it wasn't part of the mainstream'.[73] This view may be correct in terms of the Irish political spectrum. But in terms of Left politics Democratic Left in 1992 was very much positioned as Left establishment and in the mainstream of the post-Berlin Wall Left. The biggest challenge the party faced at its founding conference was finding a distinctive identity. But as the discussion in subsequent chapters will show, those involved in Democratic Left were unsuccessful in finding a political space to the Left of social democracy.

NOTES

1. *Irish Press*, 19 November 1992.
2. Interview with Eamon Gilmore, 11 September 2006.
3. Interview with Tony Heffernan, 13 September 2006.
4. Interview with Catherine Murphy, 31 August 2006.
5. Interview with Des Geraghty, 9 May 2006.
6. Interview with Proinsias De Rossa, 7 September 2007.
7. Interview with Kathleen Lynch, 10 October 2006.
8. Interview with Kathleen Lynch, 10 October 2006.
9. *The Irish Times*, 17 March 1992.
10. Ibid.
11. Interview with Proinsias De Rossa, 7 September 2007.
12. Interview with Seán Garland, 29 May 2006.
13. Interview with Tony Heffernan, 13 September 2006.
14. Ibid.
15. Interview with Paul Sweeney, 6 September 2006.
16. Interview with Eamon Gilmore, 11 May 2006.
17. Interview with Seán Garland, 29 May 2006.
18. Interview with Kathleen Lynch, 10 October 2006.
19. *The Irish Times*, 21 February 1992.
20. Indeed, by 29 February 1992, Tony Heffernan was able to issue a media notice stating that ten constituency organisations of the Workers' Party had voted to dissolve and back a new party structure.
21. *The Irish Times*, 19 February 1992.
22. Ibid.
23. *The Irish Times*, 22 February 1992.
24. Interview with Pat Rabbitte, 9 January 2007.
25. Interview with Proinsias De Rossa, 7 September 2007.
26. *The Irish Times*, 21 February 1992.
27. Interview with Liz McManus, 18 October 2006.
28. Interview with Eamon Gilmore, 11 September 2006.
29. Interview with Eamon Gilmore, 11 September 2006
30. Interview with Eric Byrne, 29 August 2006.
31. Interview with Tomás MacGiolla, 30 November 2006.
32. Interview with Proinsias De Rossa, 7 September 2007.
33. Interview with Des Geraghty, 9 May 2006.
34. Interview with Liz McManus, 18 October 2006.
35. Interview with Kathleen Lynch, 10 October 2006.
36. Interview with Paul Sweeney, 6 September 2006.
37. Interview with Eric Byrne, 29 August 2006.
38. Interview with Seán Garland, 29 May 2006.
39. *The Irish Times*, 22 February 1992.
40. Ibid.
41. Interview with Proinsias De Rossa, 7 September 2007.
42. Interview with Eamon Gilmore, 11 September 2006.
43. *The Irish Times*, 27 February 1992.
44. Ibid.
45. See Charlie Flanagan, Fine Gael party whip in *The Irish Times*, 26 February 1992.
46. Interview with Eamon Gilmore, 11 September 2006.

47. Interview with Tony Heffernan, 13 September 2006.
48. Ibid.
49. *Cork Examiner*, 3 January 1995.
50. Interview with Eamon Gilmore, 12 September 2006.
51. Interview with Eric Byrne, 29 August 2006.
52. *The Irish Times*, 25 February 1992. The members of the steering committee included De Rossa, Des Geraghty, Liz McManus, Catherine Murphy, Séamus Lynch, Michael Enright and Triona Dooley.
53. Dermot Boucher, *The Irish Times*, 2 March 1992.
54. Interview with Liz McManus, 18 October 2006.
55. Letter from Leinster House Press Office to members, 19 March 1992.
56. Ibid.
57. Ibid.
58. *The Irish Times*, 3 March 1992.
59. Interview with Des Geraghty, 9 May 2006.
60. Interview with Liz McManus, 18 October 2006.
61. Interview with Eric Byrne, 29 August 2006.
62. Steering Committee document, undated, in possession of author.
63. Interview with Rosheen Callender, 12 September 2006.
64. Interview with Proinsias De Rossa, 7 September 2007.
65. All conference speeches quoted in this section are in the possession of the author, unless otherwise stated.
66. Proinsias De Rossa speech, 28 March 1992.
67. Interview with Kathleen Lynch, 10 October 2006.
68. *The Irish Times*, 27 March 1992.
69. All quotations in this section are from conference speeches in the possession of the author, unless otherwise stated.
70. Steering Committee document, undated.
71. Amendment proposed by Wicklow constituency.
72. Interview with Proinsias De Rossa, 7 September 2007.
73. Ibid.

PART 2
Life

5

History Through the Ballot Box

INTRODUCTION

In its short history, Democratic Left contested two general elections, one European Parliament election, one set of elections to local town councils, one election to Seanad Éireann and a series of by-elections to Dáil Éireann. The party was also involved in Adi Roche's unsuccessful bid for the presidency in 1997 as well as actively participating in a series of constitutional referendums between 1992 and 1998 and a number of elections in Northern Ireland. The discussion in this chapter focuses on the party's history through an examination of its performance in these electoral contests. The analysis illustrates the organisational and ideological weaknesses which combined to prevent Democratic Left achieving a sustainable electoral position to remain a viable presence on the political landscape. The issues which emerge from this examination of the party's electoral history are discussed in depth in subsequent chapters. These issues include political identity, party organisation and access to resources. Another significant factor which emerges from the discussion of the electoral contests is the considerable rivalry that existed between the Labour Party and Democratic Left, a rivalry that previously existed with the Workers' Party prior to 1992. The competition between the two parties is examined below, although it must be stressed that the competition, while often intense, did not lead to an increase in electoral support for the Left in Ireland which remained over a sustained period well below 20 per cent of the national vote.

ELECTORAL HISTORY, 1992–9

An outline of the electoral record of Democratic Left in the period between 1992 and 1997 is provided in Table 5.1. The party's performance can best be described as poor, with a singular failure to make a substantial electoral breakthrough most particularly in the general elections in 1992 and 1997. Democratic Left never achieved an 'electoral spectacular' akin to that of the Workers' Party when Proinsias De Rossa was elected to the European Parliament in 1989.

TABLE 5.1
DEMOCRATIC LEFT, ELECTORAL HISTORY

Election		Candidates	Seats won*	First Preferences (%)
General,	1992	20	4	47,945 (2.78)
Council,	1995	22	11	6,264 (2.52)
European,	1994	2	-	39,706 (3.49)
General,	1997	13	4	44,901 (2.51)

Source: www.electionsireland.org
*Joe Sherlock successfully contested the 1992 Seanad Éireann election.

An analysis of the party's performance in a series of opinion polls in the 1992 to 1997 period – see Table 5.2 – further illustrates the failure to make a significant national impact.

TABLE 5.2
DEMOCRATIC LEFT, OPINION POLL HISTORY, 1992–7

Year	Percentage
November 1992	2.8
February 1994	2
May 1994	6
August 1994	1
November 1995	2
June 1996	2
September 1996	2
December 1996	2
January 1997	2
March 1997	2
May 1997	2

Source: MRBI

Table 5.3 provides an overview of the voter appeal of candidates over three Dáil elections – in 1989, 1992 and 1997. Two points are worth observing. First, there was a failure by the new party in 1992 and again in 1997 to seriously expand and develop beyond the number of constituencies where the Workers' Party had previously enjoyed success.

TABLE 5.3
GENERAL ELECTION RESULTS, 1989–97 (BOLD INDICATES CANDIDATE WAS ELECTED)

Constituency	Candidate	1989 WP First Pref. (%)	1992 DL First Pref. (%)	1997 DL First Pref. (%)
Cork East	Joe Sherlock	**7,414 (18.08)**	5,351 (12.90)	4,622 (10.73)
Cork North Central	John Kelleher	3,395 (8.23)	1,795 (4.00)	Did not run
	Kathleen Lynch	See Cork South Central	See Cork South Central	3,146 (7.15%
Cork South Central	Kathleen Lynch	4,457 (8.31)	2,539 (4.74)	See Cork North Central
Donegal South West	Seamus Rogers	2,768 (9.59)	1,825 (6.12)	No candidate
Dublin Central	Mike Jennings	1,827 (4.42)	467(1.28)	No candidate
Dublin North Central	Helen Lahert	No candidate	1,376 (3.0%)	1,194 (2.77)
Dublin North East	Pat McCartan	**5,968 (16.95)**	3,743 (9.36)	Did not run
	Anthony Creevy	Did not run	Did not run	1,381 (3.7)
Dublin North West	Proinsias De Rossa	**7,976 (26.65)**	4,562 (12.19)	**3,701 (10.08)**
Dublin South	Marian White	No candidate	640 (1.07)	No candidate
Dublin South Central	Eric Byrne	**6,849(14.86)**	2,990 (7.43)	4,586 (11.30)
Dublin South East	Jim Allen	No candidate	874 (2.17)	No candidate
Dublin South West	Pat Rabbitte	**7,166 (18.37)**	3,743 (8.78)	**5,094 (12.17)**
Dún Laoghaire	Eamon Gilmore	**6,723 (12.82)**	**7,045 (11.87)**	**7,534 (13.89)**
Galway West	Jacqueline O'Dowd	No candidate	392 (0.78)	No candidate
Kildare	Catherine Murphy	1,520 (2.99)	1,613 (3.20)	2,762 (8.80)
Limerick East	John Ryan	No candidate	835 (1.73)	3,403 (6.85)
Meath	Christy Gorman	No candidate	809 (1.58)	798 (1.41)
Waterford	Paddy Gallagher	4,570 (11.06)	1,039(2.42)	No candidate
Wexford	Michael Enright	1,049 (2.04)	797 (1.53)	1,454 (2.61)
Wicklow	Dermot Tobin	2,049 (4.83)	Did not run	Did not run
	Liz McManus	Did not run	**5,510 (10.62)**	**5,226 (9.90)**

Source: *Nealon's Guides* to 26th, 27th and 28th Dáil, www.electionsireland.org

The election of Liz McManus in Wicklow was the only new constituency opened up by Democratic Left (although reference must be made to Kathleen Lynch's brief representation in Cork North Central). Second, there was a failure to attract new names to stand for the party. The personnel pool from which Democratic Left selected candidates was very much the one formerly associated with the Workers' Party.

GENERAL ELECTION, 1992

The November 1992 general election came too early for Democratic Left. The newly formed party had had little time to develop an organisational base, it lacked money and had few policies prepared for public consumption. Its reported membership was in the region of 2,000 individuals, many of whom were 'teenagers, by the party's own account'.[1] The accuracy of this estimate is, however, open to question given that the number of members at the time of the merger with the Labour Party was less than 900. Democratic Left also faced the problem of name recognition, having had little time to break the public's association of its leading members with the Workers' Party. Despite an initial bounce in the opinion polls in May 1992, the party's ratings quickly returned to 'margin-of-error' territory.

Some preparatory work on electoral strategy had commenced in the aftermath of the March 1992 founding conference. A national election committee was established – chaired by Pat Rabbitte – with a brief to study the Dáil constituencies. The magic figure was seven TDs, the number which would guarantee the party formal recognition as a Dáil group with the corresponding financial and non-financial benefits that such recognition would bring. Pat Rabbitte summarised the challenge in a memorandum on electoral strategy prepared in August 1992. 'A poor performance could literally mean terminal problems; seven seats or better means a new beginning and – perhaps with Labour in Government – prospects for real progress and development. Seven seats seems an achievable bottom line.'[2] In an earlier memo, also on electoral strategy, Rabbitte noted that the party would 'be relying on local constituency organisations and the ability to translate perceived Dáil performance to local level'.[3] He added:

We would seem to have a greater or lesser capacity to contest about 25 constituencies – all eleven in Dublin and Wicklow, Kildare, Meath, Waterford, Wexford, Cork East and the two Cork Cities, Limerick, Galway, Donegal NW, Carlow/Kilkenny and perhaps the two Tipperaries. Strategically it is necessary to contest the widest spread possible consistent with an assessment of reasonable prospects in order to get the national vote over 5%.[4]

It was an ambitious list, although it dealt with constituencies where Democratic Left had the capacity to simply nominate an election candidate, as Rabbitte acknowledged. 'Within resource constraints, this will involve at the same time acknowledging that there will have to be priority constituencies in terms both of winning seats and showing a national spread.'[5] The party nominated twenty candidates as it ventured into six constituencies not contested by the Workers' Party at the 1989 general election – Dublin North Central, Dublin South, Dublin South East, Galway West, Limerick East and Meath. Liz McManus in Wicklow was the only new name to emerge, although she was a candidate in a constituency previously contested by the Workers' Party. Her husband, John McManus, had stood unsuccessfully in five previous general elections in Wicklow. In a pre-election analysis, Rabbitte noted that the possibility of 'head-hunting high-profile candidates' had been raised. Yet he was unconvinced about the idea, which had in any event come unstuck some months previously with Emmet Stagg: 'For a Socialist Party this tends to remain in the realm of aspiration. Specifically we are not of the view that selection conventions should be deferred in the hope of a suitable high-profile candidate falling out of the sky.'[6]

The term of the incumbent Fianna Fáil–Progressive Democrat coalition could have run to late 1994. But relations between the two government parties had become increasingly strained after Albert Reynolds succeeded Charles Haughey as Fianna Fáil leader and taoiseach. Difficulties over statements given to a judicial tribunal inquiring into the operation of the beef industry precipitated a crisis in the coalition. Nevertheless, the view in Democratic Left circles by late August 1992 was that a contest would not take place until the spring or summer of the following year:

For an election to be called this autumn it would require still improbable accidents (to provide the excuse) and/or miscalculation by Reynolds (in an attempt to capitalise on the opportunity). For Democratic Left the immediate task is no different either way, since a later date merely allows more time to do more of what needs to be done, starting now.[7]

The time available, however, was relatively short. The government eventually collapsed and a general election was called in November 1992. Eight months after its formation Democratic Left was involved in its first electoral test. The calling of the election was for Democratic Left – as one writer put it – 'a battle for survival'.[8] With so many obvious handicaps Democratic Left could only hope that the voters would be willing to back the party on the basis of the legislative and constituency record of its six Dáil deputies since the 1989 general election. The party was putting strong hope on candidate name recognition but not its own. Brian Girvin noted that the new party published a 'comprehensive manifesto' with strong emphasis on industrial development, job creation and state intervention in the economy, although he observed that the party 'remained coy about the circumstances for state action'.[9]

> Our objective is to harness market forces on behalf of ordinary people – workers and consumers – and use them for the greater good of society. This also requires social ownership, in various forms, of many of society's resources, as an alternative to the concentration of wealth, power and privilege in the hands of a small élite.

Alongside the formal manifesto, Democratic Left also published a ten-point programme to address the high rate of unemployment. Entitled *301,000 Reasons for Change*, the document also stressed the need for greater state involvement in Irish economic life. The ideological conundrum that followed Democratic Left during its short life was evident in these early policy proposals. In a post-election assessment Girvin wrote: 'Whatever intrinsic merits these policies might have had, the problem for the party was that it entered the election without a clear identity after the split, and had yet to define its purpose in relation to the Labour Party and to the older Workers' Party.'[10]

Despite the ambition signalled by nominating candidates in several new areas, Democratic Left was really targeting ten constituencies in November 1992. These included the six areas where the party had outgoing TDs along with constituencies where an existing local representative had a decent public profile. The latter areas were Waterford, Wicklow, Cork South Central and Cork East. Some party activists had hopes that gains could be made in other constituencies, including Dublin North Central and Dublin South East. The combined Democratic Left vote in those two constituencies, however, totalled a mere 2,250 first-preference votes. This was an indication of the unrealistic expectations held by some Democratic Left members about the party's appeal to voters. In fact, the results of the November 1992 general election were very disappointing for the new party as it failed to make a significant impact. Eamon Gilmore, however, believed there was a slight change in his voter appeal in his Dún Laoghaire constituency. 'There were people who voted for me as a Democratic Left candidate who would never have voted for me as a Workers' Party member.'[11]

Gilmore may have been correct but the reality was that there were not enough voters, new or old, backing the party. The 1992 general election belonged to the Labour Party as it attained historic high levels of support and returned a record number of TDs. Democratic Left was squeezed out, the reasons for which are discussed in detail below. The election results were deeply disappointing, as Tony Heffernan explained:

> The party came within a thread of being wiped out. At one stage watching the results coming in, it looked like Liz McManus was going to be the only Democratic Left TD elected, and she would have been a new, first-time TD. Rabbitte, De Rossa and Gilmore all came very close to losing, and Sherlock and McCartan did lose.[12]

As the votes were counted, potential newcomer Liz McManus was aware of the possibility of being the party's sole TD. 'I do remember getting absolutely the heebie-jeebies when at one point it looked like I was the only Democratic Left person to be elected.'[13] The fledgling party lost three of its outgoing TDs – Sherlock, McCartan and Byrne – while it won only one new seat with McManus in Wicklow. De Rossa, Rabbitte and Gilmore all held their seats, leaving Democratic Left with four seats in the new Dáil. At the previous general election in 1989 the Workers' Party won seven seats, while Democratic Left went into the 1992 contest with six seats. The new party did not contest the Dublin

West constituency where Workers' Party leader Tomás MacGiolla lost his seat.

The combined vote for the Workers' Party and Democratic Left in November 1992 was 1.5 per cent behind the vote for the Workers' Party in 1989. This outcome led Richard Sinnott to conclude that 'Labour's recovery plus the split in the Workers' Party put paid to the run of successive increases chalked up by the Workers' Party in its various guises over a series of seven elections since 1973.'[14] Michael Gallagher added: '... the WP's achievement in outpolling Labour in Dublin in 1989 now seems a distant memory.'[15] Moreover, the fraught relationship between Democratic Left and Labour was evident in the voting behaviour of Labour Party supporters. Post-election analysis indicated that more Labour Party transfers passed to Fine Gael candidates than to Democratic Left candidates in the thirteen cases where those two parties were still available to receive terminal Labour Party transfers.

As noted previously, Democratic Left nominated twenty candidates at the 1992 general election – thirteen of those individuals had contested the 1989 contest under the Workers' Party banner. Of those thirteen candidates, eleven saw their first preference decline between 1989 and 1992. Some of the individual performances provide an indication of just how poorly the results were for Democratic Left. (These figures are shown in Table 5.3 page 117) A number of examples illustrate this point. In Cork East, Joe Sherlock saw his vote fall by over 2,000 first preferences from 18.08 per cent to 12.9 per cent while in Dublin South Central Eric Byrne's vote declined by over 4,000 first preferences from 14.86 per cent to 11.3 per cent. Despite this decrease, Byrne narrowly missed out in the constituency where, after a marathon count, Ben Briscoe of Fianna Fáil held off the Democratic Left candidate by a mere five votes. Transfers from an anti-abortion candidate, representing the Christian Centrist Party (CCP), ultimately determined the destination of the final seat. After the elimination of the CCP candidate, Briscoe received 152 votes while Byrne only got 39 additional votes. This transfer pattern helped to preserve the seat for Fianna Fáil.

Insufficient transfers may have decided the final result but Byrne's fate was ultimately sealed by a lack of first-preference votes. His vote in 1992 was his lowest general election first-preference result since June 1981, a period during which there had been five general elections. It was a similar experience for Proinsias De Rossa and Joe Sherlock. Pat Rabbitte received his lowest vote since his first electoral outing in November 1982 as his vote collapsed from 7,166 in 1989 (18.37 per cent) to 3,743 (8.78 per cent) in 1992. Moreover, Paddy Gallagher, who had first run for the Dáil in Waterford in 1977 – winning a seat in February 1982 – received his lowest ever first-preference vote in a general election.

There were two exceptions to this downward trend. Eamon Gilmore in Dún Laoghaire and Catherine Murphy in Kildare recorded small increases in their first-preference votes between 1989 and 1992. As previously noted, new candidate Liz McManus was the big electoral success for Democratic Left in 1992. She received 5,510 (10.62 per cent) first preferences as a Democratic Left candidate compared to the 2,049 (4.83 per cent) first preferences secured in 1989 by Dermot Tobin, who contested as a Workers' Party candidate. It was also a better performance than that of her husband, John McManus, who contested each general election from 1977 to 1987 inclusive for the Workers' Party, failing each time to get elected. Liz McManus was undoubtedly helped in 1992 by a decision to increase the size of the Wicklow constituency from a four-seat constituency to a five-seater. That constituency revision in itself was, however, no guarantee that she would take the additional seat. Interestingly, in a post-election essay describing her experiences during the 1992 campaign McManus made no reference to the split in the Workers' Party or recognition for the new party, Democratic Left, as an issue in her constituency. A county councillor since 1985 – having been re-elected in 1991 – she stressed her local track record as the main contributing factor in her success:

> My campaign began three and a half years before the November 1992 election. At the time I was selected as a candidate for the then Wicklow Constituency. Already a member of Wicklow County Council and Bray Urban District Council for a number of years, I had good local experience and a grounding in public representation which was invaluable. Generally the move into national politics was seen as a natural progression ... I acted as a county-wide politician, running advice clinics on par with a TD.[16]

While local factors have always to be considered in any Dáil election performance, one possible lesson that Democratic Left could have taken from the McManus performance was the inability to attract new names to run in constituencies where the party inherited a political and electoral base from the Workers' Party. It may have been to the advantage of the new party to have fielded more new candidates in its target constituencies. A counter argument, however, may be made that such a policy might have generated considerable organisational and personality clashes in individual constituencies. Insufficient time to organise lessened the ability to engage in strategic decision-making over candidate selection. One other notable feature of the 1992 general election campaign was the attacks from the Workers' Party. This was not unsurprising given the acrimonious split earlier in the year which had stripped the Workers' Party of all but one of its TDs and most of its active membership. Tomás MacGiolla was critical of Democratic Left for its emphasis on market forces and for what he perceived as a lack of clarity about its attitude to Northern Ireland.

The tension and rivalries between Democratic Left and the Workers' Party were most prevalent in the small number of constituencies contested by candidates from both parties. The Workers' Party nominated two candidates to run in Dublin North West where Proinsias De Rossa was an outgoing TD. This move led to claims that the Workers' Party was attempting to undermine Democratic Left, a claim the former party dismissed. As well as fighting old colleagues, the new party struck up new alliances in 1992. Disregarding ideological differences, a successful electoral pact was agreed with the Progressive Democrats and the Green Party prior to the 1993 Seanad Éireann elections. The exchange of second preferences assisted the Progressive Democrats and Democratic Left in winning Seanad seats that otherwise they could not have had any realistic chance of securing. The Progressive Democrats won two seats, Democratic Left took a single seat (Joe Sherlock) while the Green Party candidate polled well but ultimately failed to get elected.[17]

LOCAL AND EUROPEAN ELECTIONS, 1994

On 9 June 1994 elections were held to the European Parliament and sub-county local authorities in several areas in Ireland. Two Dáil by-elections were also held on that date to fill vacancies that had occurred in Dublin South Central and Mayo West. Democratic Left nominated candidates in several of these different contests. The European Parliament and local elections are examined in this section. The two by-election contests are discussed later in this chapter. Elections to the European Parliament take place at regular five-yearly intervals. In 1994 there were fifteen seats allocated to the Republic of Ireland, divided into four separate constituencies. This was a similar situation to the previous election in 1989 when Proinsias De Rossa achieved the notable distinction of winning a seat in the four-seat Dublin constituency.

De Rossa was the newly elected leader of the Workers' Party when he was nominated to contest the 1989 European elections. He first won a Dáil seat in February 1982 in Dublin North West and held that seat at the two subsequent general elections. He had a high media profile, which influenced the decision to nominate him for the 1989 European Parliament contest. The situation was, however, complicated by the decision of the incumbent taoiseach Charles Haughey to call an early general election, the date of which would coincide with the scheduled European Parliament contest. Haughey's government had been elected in 1987 and although only having a minority of seats in parliament it could conceivably have remained in office until 1992. Political opportunism, however, pushed Haughey to go to the country in an attempt to win an overall parliamentary majority. Two election contests on the same day put huge pressure on De Rossa, who sought not only to win a European Parliament seat but also defend his Dáil seat in Dublin North West. Whatever about the demands of the dual campaign on the candidate and his party, the additional profile served to assist De Rossa as he topped the poll in his Dáil constituency and was comfortably elected to the European Parliament. De Rossa received 15.84 per cent of the first-preference vote in the Dublin constituency, which amounted to 71,041 votes.

The period from the 1989 election to the next European Parliament contest in 1994 was marked by several significant developments, most particularly the split in the Workers' Party in 1992 that led to the formation of Democratic Left. De Rossa operated a dual mandate for a period after the 1989 European and Dáil elections. He stood down as an MEP in early 1992 to concentrate on his career in Dáil Éireann and party leadership role. He was replaced by Des Geraghty, a trade union official and long-time senior party member. Name recognition was a big issue for all the political parties as they considered the European Parliament elections scheduled for June 1994. The geographical size of the constituencies ruled out candidates personally meeting significant numbers of voters. Selecting someone who was already well known was therefore considered an important strategic factor. In that regard, Fianna Fáil convinced the director of the Dublin Rape Crisis Centre, Olive Braiden, to run in Dublin; Fine Gael made room for the former Farmers' Association leader Alan Gillis on the party ticket in Leinster while the Labour Party selected broadcast journalist Orla Guerin in Dublin. In each of these cases, however, the inclusion of a high-profile name – who had no previous ties to the party – was the source of some internal disquiet. This was most obvious in the Labour Party, where the party leadership had decided the outgoing MEP Bernie Malone was not a sufficiently strong candidate to retain the party's Dublin seat.

There was no indication that Democratic Left was about to select anyone in Dublin but the party's sitting MEP, Des Geraghty. Indeed, a succession of media reports in early 1994 indicated that Geraghty would be the Democratic Left candidate in the Dublin constituency. On 26 January 1994 *The Irish Times* confidently reported that Geraghty 'will be standing in his own right as a Democratic Left candidate in June'.[18] Several leading party figures were, however, privately unconvinced about Geraghty's ability to hold the Dublin seat won by Proinsias De Rossa as a Workers' Party candidate in 1989. He was seen as effective and hardworking but lacking in the necessary profile to attract sufficient support to win one of the four seats in the Dublin constituency. Geraghty's failure to make an impact with the public was confirmed by the results of private market research, news of which was circulating in political circles in early 1994. Eamon Gilmore explained how this research impacted on thinking in the party:

> The 1994 European election was quite a difficult experience for us. We had opinion poll evidence which showed Des wasn't registering. We decided, I mean at the end of the day Des decided himself, but there was a lot of discussion about it, you know, that he wouldn't run.[19]

A Democratic Left selection convention for the Dublin constituency was scheduled for 27 March 1994. In the days before this convention news emerged for the first time about the private concerns within Democratic Left about Geraghty's candidacy. Geraghty had, in fact, been approached ahead of the selection convention. He later said he was not asked to stand down but the idea of another candidate emerging presented the sitting MEP with a difficult proposition. On 26 March 1994 several newspapers reported that Pat Rabbitte would also seek a nomination in the Dublin constituency. Political journalist Maol Muire Tynan noted: 'It is expected that only one Democratic Left candidate will actually contest the election in Dublin but the convention could decide to place two people on the ticket.'[20] Such an outcome was, however, unlikely as a two-candidate strategy would have split the Democratic Left vote and endangered the party's chances of winning a seat. Significantly for the Democratic Left strategy in Dublin, Tynan also reported that:

> Concerns have been growing in the party for some time that Mr Geraghty faces a formidable task in holding onto their only Strasbourg seat. The decision by some members to ask Mr Rabbitte to run in Dublin is seen by observers as an attempt to place a high-profile candidate in the field.[21]

Geraghty made no comment ahead of the party convention on 27 March 1994 at which he announced his decision not to seek a nomination. Newspaper reports speculated that the decision was taken so as to 'avoid a split in Democratic Left'.[22] It was reported that Geraghty told the convention delegates that the decision 'was his and his alone and, while taken with great regret, it was based on careful consideration of all the factors affecting this particular election'.[23] The decision was not made without some internal disquiet. It was reported that Geraghty's 'unexpected decision was greeted with shock by some delegates and a number of them did not applaud when asked by the convention chairwoman, Ms Liz McManus, to indicate their approval of the proposal for the sole nominee, Mr Pat Rabbitte'.[24] Further unease at the decision was expressed at a closed session of the convention in the absence of the media. An indication of Geraghty's unhappiness was evident in that it was later confirmed that he was not putting his name forward as a substitute candidate on the Democratic Left ticket. Nevertheless, the decision to select Rabbitte was achieved by Democratic Left without the type of public rancour that featured in other parties over candidate selection, most particularly in the Labour Party.

In explaining the rationale for the decision, Tony Heffernan spoke to the media – and it was reported that he made 'comparison with the former Fine Gael MEP, Mr Chris O'Malley, who was, he said, a good representative who also made it as a replacement and had a low profile. Despite his work in Brussels and Strasbourg, he failed to get elected. Mr Geraghty could have been in a similar position.'[25] Pat Rabbitte immediately met with sharp criticism for his decision to contest the European election. 'Is he really taking on a third job with the Dáil and county council or merely ensuring one for party colleague and sitting Euro-MEP, Des Geraghty?' one political rival queried.[26] The uncertainty over Rabbitte's intentions – whether his future was in national or European politics – undoubtedly hurt his campaign. 'Nobody believed he was going to Europe. People saw what we were doing. They said, "this guy is not going to Europe. This is just for twelve months and then there'll be a switch over,"' Eamon Gilmore said.[27]

Despite this uncertainty, Democratic Left campaigned to win the European seat. De Rossa openly appealed to disaffected Labour Party voters to switch allegiance. He said the party's candidate in Dublin would 'draw a lot of people who would vote for Labour' as they passed judgement on the incumbent Fianna Fáil/Labour coalition.[28] The elections to the European Parliament took place on 9 June 1994. Five years previously, the Workers' Party had candidates contesting in each of the four European Parliament constituencies as well as in Northern Ireland. Only De Rossa was elected in 1989 while several of the other Workers' Party candidates polled poorly. There was a more focused – and realistic – approach from Democratic Left in 1994 as the party

TABLE 5.4
EUROPEAN PARLIAMENT ELECTION RESULTS, 1989 AND 1994

Constituency	1989 Candidates	1989 Results	1994 Candidates	1994 Results
Dublin	De Rossa (WP)	71,041(15.84%)	Rabbitte (DL)	24,133 (8.69%)
			MacGiolla (WP)	15,830 (5.70%)
Munster	Sherlock (WP)	26,828 (5.43%)	Lynch (DL)	15,573 (4.27%)
			O'Regan (WP)	6,270 (1.72%)

Source: www.electionsireland.org

only nominated two candidates: Rabbitte in Dublin and Kathleen Lynch in Munster. A comparison of the election outcomes in these two constituencies in both 1989 and 1994 is shown in Table 5.4.

The results of the 1994 European Parliament elections were disappointing for Democratic Left. Despite replacing Geraghty with Rabbitte – in an attempt to capitalise on the latter's apparent higher profile – the party still lost its seat in Dublin. In fact, compared to the performance of De Rossa in 1989, Rabbitte polled poorly. Even allowing for the presence on the ballot paper of Tomás MacGiolla of the Workers' Party, the combined Democratic Left–WP vote was down substantially on that won in 1989. 'We thought Rabbitte would win. He didn't and that was a setback,' Eamon Gilmore admitted.[29]

The performance of Kathleen Lynch in Munster did, however, offer a glimmer of hope. The result in itself was down on the 1989 outcome but as Lynch was relatively unknown, the campaign had allowed her to improve her public profile, especially in her electoral base in Cork. She had been unsuccessful in the three previous general elections in Cork South Central but later in 1994 she won a by-election contest in Cork North Central. The European election campaign undoubtedly helped her performance in the Dáil by-election.

Alongside the Dáil by-elections and the elections to the European Parliament in June 1994, there were also elections to sub-county local authorities. Members were elected to eighty authorities comprising five borough councils, forty-nine urban district councils and twenty-six town commissions. There was no requirement at that stage for local government elections to take place at regular intervals. Governments had legislative powers to postpone local contests. Elections to all local authorities had last taken place in 1985. Six years later elections were held for county councils and county borough corporations but not the sub-level bodies pending an overhaul of the powers and responsibilities of the entire local government system.

The 1994 local elections were limited in their scope. It was the first time that elections to borough councils, urban district councils and town commissions had taken place on their own, unaccompanied by elections to county councils and county borough corporations. Once more, the rationale for postponing the latter contests was justified due to the ongoing reform process. Elections to all local government units were scheduled for June 1998 but eventually took place twelve months

TABLE 5.5
LOCAL GOVERNMENT ELECTIONS, 1994

Council Type	Electoral Area	No. of candidates	No. elected	Candidate Name (Successful candidates in bold)
Borough				
	Kilkenny	1	-	Joe Butler
	Wexford	2	1	**Michael Enright**
				David Hynes
Urban District				
	Bray	5	4	**Anne Egan**
				John McManus
				Liz McManus
				Dermot Tobin
				Joseph Bolland Jnr
	Cobh	1	-	Leo Owens
	Dungarvan	2	1	Christy Power
				Tony Wright
	Mallow	2	2	**Joe Sherlock**
				Kathleen Scuffins
	Navan	1	1	**Christy Gorman**
	Tipperary	1	-	Peadar O'Donnell
Town Commission				
	Ballyshannon	1	-	Dessie Doyle
	Newbridge	1	-	Jimmy Kelly
	Greystones	2	-	Michael McGrath
				Margaret O'Callaghan
	Leixlip	3	2	**Catherine Murphy**
				Seán Purcell
				Gerry McDonagh

Source: Department of the Environment, 1995.

later. The law was also changed to allow for regular five-year intervals between local elections from 1999 onwards. Democratic Left nominated a small number of candidates to the local authority elections in 1994, as shown in Table 5.5. As noted previously, these authorities are one component of the local government system in Ireland. They cover a limited geographical area and have few powers.

Several candidates who contested the 1992 general elections for Democratic Left were nominated for the 1994 local elections. A number of those who were successful in the local elections subsequently contested the 1997 general election. Of the individuals in that category, Michael Enright in Wexford and Catherine Murphy in Kildare registered increases in their vote between the two general elections although neither was close to securing a Dáil seat. Christy Gorman in Meath, Joe Sherlock in Cork East and Liz McManus in Wicklow were also elected in the 1994 local elections but all three saw their respective Dáil vote decline between 1992 and 1997. In the case of McManus this reduced vote was marginal and did not prevent her holding her Dáil seat.

The results of the 1994 local elections were too limited to provide a significant boost to the electoral fortunes of Democratic Left. The party was probably unfortunate that there were no elections to the more significant element of the local government system – county councils and county borough corporations – in the period between 1992 and 1997. These bodies are nationwide and also cover urban areas where Democratic Left would have been confident in getting candidates established for subsequent Dáil contests. In fact, the failure to call elections to these bodies between 1991 and 1999 resulted in Democratic Left attaining the distinction of never having contested elections to the mainstream institutions of the local government system.

GENERAL ELECTION, 1997

In its short history Democratic Left contested two general elections, although the circumstances in which the party entered both elections could not have been more different. In November 1992 Democratic Left was a new political entity ill-prepared for a national election in the aftermath of a divisive and difficult birth. Five years later, Democratic Left faced the electorate having spent the previous two and a half years as a participant in the three-party Rainbow coalition.

The John Bruton-led coalition was formed without a general election after the collapse of the Fianna Fáil–Labour government in late 1994. The events from this period are discussed in detail in Chapter 6. Fine Gael was the largest party in the coalition arrangement that included the Labour Party and Democratic Left. The three-party arrangement came into office in December 1994, and remained in power until May 1997 when a general election was called. The experience in government was considered to have been a positive one by the Democratic Left TDs. There was a view that they had played a significant role in government. For that reason the party was happy to campaign on a joint platform with Fine Gael and the Labour Party to seek a direct mandate for the re-election of the Rainbow coalition. So when the outgoing coalition government put itself to the electorate for re-election one advisor – no party affiliation was identified – told one newspaper: 'We are going into the election as a team and we are determined to present ourselves to the public as such.'[30]

Aside from their individual party manifestos – which obviously stressed particular priorities – the three parties published a common programme which set out agreed principles and '21 goals for the 21st century'. Democratic Left advisor Paul Sweeney was involved in drafting the aspirational programme that was intended to 'illustrate the concept of cohesion'.[31] The document was presented to the three party leaders on 10 April 1997 and published when Dáil Éireann was dissolved on 15 May 1997. In the days leading up to the formal start of the election campaign, one newspaper made reference to this 'choreographed three-party campaign'.[32] The united front was most obvious when the three party leaders held a press conference together. Indeed, there was considerable background co-operation between the three parties before and throughout the campaign. An ad hoc committee involving senior figures in each party met every Wednesday in Leinster House prior to the election. John Gallagher and Tony Heffernan represented Democratic Left. This group also met during the election campaign and there was constant telephone contact. The parties sought to co-ordinate the diaries of their leading figures. Occasional meetings and photo opportunities were organised to show the public the good relations between the parties. In his review of the 1997 campaign, Michael Holmes observed: 'there was a certain degree of strategic co-ordination among the parties with, in essence, Fine Gael concentrating on dealing with Fianna Fáil while the Labour Party and Democratic Left were to look after the Progressive Democrats ... However this strategy came about more by chance than intent and proved a bad approach for the two smaller parties.'[33]

There were some practical advantages for the Democratic Left campaign arising from its involvement in the electoral alliance with Fine Gael and the Labour Party. Both larger parties had the resources to commission opinion polls in various constituencies, something Democratic Left with its limited budget was not in a position to do. Where there was no serious constituency competition between the parties the findings of these opinion polls were shared. In Dublin South Central, where Fine Gael was not in contention for a second seat, the party was willing to share its poll finding with the Labour Party and Democratic Left. The opposite was, however, the case in Cork East where Fine Gael believed there was a prospect of a seat gain, most likely at Labour's expense. Joe Sherlock was also seeking to regain his seat in Cork East and with such intense and complicated competition on the ground involving candidates from the three Rainbow partners there was little for Fine Gael to gain by sharing private poll findings.

Aside from the common programme with its coalition partners, Democratic Left also published its own policy manifesto. The mechanics of preparing the document differed from previously in that an advisory committee was established with a membership drawn from inside and outside the party. Pat Brady, a senior party figure who was close to Pat Rabbitte, later noted that 'the whole process had become excessively consultative.'[34] This process had actually commenced with the preparation two years previously of a detailed and comprehensive eighty-page document. There was internal agreement that this document needed to be shorter and more focused on particular policies associated with the party. In the end the Democratic Left manifesto in 1997 was actually shorter than that produced in 1992, a feat not achieved by any other political party with Dáil representation.

It was decided that the material in the manifesto not only had to represent the ideological position of the party but also had to be accessible and attractively presented. Acknowledging the public popularity of its leader, a photograph of De Rossa was placed on the front cover of the manifesto while professional advice on writing presentation was received from a senior media figure. Democratic Left officials believed that by playing on De Rossa's appeal and a positive spin-off from the experience in government the party would strengthen its electoral performance. But this was not to be the case.

The 1997 general election was a disappointment for Democratic Left. The party won four seats in 1992 but had added another two TDs to its ranks with successful by-election results during the life of the twenty-seventh Dáil. But the two by-election winners – Eric Byrne and Kathleen Lynch – failed to hold their seats in the subsequent general election. Moreover, in Dublin North West party leader Proinsias De Rossa only held off the threat of Fine Gael's Brendan Brady by 100 votes. The thirteen constituencies contested by Democratic Left in 1997 as well as the candidates nominated by the party and their election performances are shown in Table 5.3. The party contested seven fewer constituencies than at the 1992 general election, which is surprising given the contrasting positions at the two contests. After all, going into the 1992 elections Democratic Left was a new party not quite ready for a national election, but five years later it went to the polls having enjoyed almost two and a half years in government. The latter experience – alongside the benefit of time to put roots down – appears to have had no impact on the party's ability to secure attractive election candidates.

Democratic Left failed to nominate candidates in seven constituencies where it had contested five years previously. These were Cork South Central, Dublin Central, Dublin South, Dublin South East, Galway West and Waterford. Only one new candidate featured for the party against the list of names nominated back in 1992. Pat McCartan, who lost his Dáil seat at the 1992 general election, had been appointed a judge, a role that required his departure from active political involvement. McCartan was replaced on Dublin City Council by Anthony Creevy. But securing the local authority position was little help to Creevy when it came to attempting to win back the McCartan seat in Dublin North East at the 1997 general election. Creevy won less than 4 per cent of the first-preference vote and was eliminated early in the counting process. (He later joined Fianna Fáil.)

Taking all thirteen constituencies contested by Democratic Left in both 1992 and in 1997, the fortunes of the party produced mixed results. In seven constituencies the party's share of the vote increased between the two elections while in the other six it actually declined. As noted, two outgoing Democratic Left TDs failed to hold their seats – Byrne and Lynch – while De Rossa, Rabbitte, Gilmore and McManus were successfully returned to Dáil Éireann. The latter four individuals had held ministerial office of either junior or senior rank in the outgoing administration. But the high profile associated with their governmental positions did not automatically translate into increased first preference votes. In fact, De Rossa's vote actually declined on his 1992 performance and – as indicated in Table 5.3 – his share of the first-preference vote at marginally over 10 per cent was down substantially on the 26 per cent he received as a Workers' Party candidate at the 1989 general election. Rabbitte's vote recovered between 1992 and 1997 but he was still some 2,000 votes below his 1989 performance. The first-preference vote received by McManus was down marginally on her result in 1992 while Gilmore once more increased his share of the vote in Dún Laoghaire.

The absence of countrywide local government elections in the period between the two general elections may have hampered the development of Democratic Left. The party was unable to 'blood' new candidates in local areas, although as already noted Democratic Left had a poor record of attracting new candidates even in the limited number of elections the party contested. The limited local election contests in 1994 – discussed previously – allowed several potential Dáil candidates to gain or consolidate a local government foothold, and this ground-level representation is very often the first step to an eventual move into national politics.

Several successful candidates in the 1994 local elections went on to contest the 1997 general election for Democratic Left. Among those in this category – and who saw their performance improve between the 1992 and 1997 general elections – were Michael Enright in Wexford and Catherine Murphy in Kildare. Local election success did not, however, automatically guarantee a better Dáil outcome – Joe Sherlock in Cork East, Liz McManus in Wicklow and Christy Gorman in Meath all saw their share of the vote decline between the 1992 and 1997 general elections despite being elected at the 1994 local elections.

The results of the 1997 general election left Democratic Left in a weakened state – its four TDs returned to the opposition benches with considerable uncertainty about their future direction. 'Throughout its existence Democratic Left remained heavily dependent on the appeal and calibre of its individual candidates, as a party it seemed almost invisible to the voters,' Michael Gallagher accurately observed.[35] Survival was possible in government but the outcome of the 1997 general election was clear evidence that the Democratic Left brand had still not connected with the voters.

DÁIL ÉIREANN BY-ELECTIONS

There were eleven by-elections for vacancies in Dáil constituencies in the period between 1992 and 1999. Members dying or resigning their seats caused these vacancies. Democratic Left contested five of the eleven

TABLE 5.6
DÁIL ÉIREANN BY-ELECTIONS, 1992–9 (BOLD INDICATES CANDIDATE WAS ELECTED)

By-election date	Constituency	Candidate	First Preference (%)
9 Jun 1994	Dublin South Central	**Eric Byrne**	7,445 (25.56)
9 Jun 1994	Mayo West	No DL candidate	-
10 Nov 1994	Cork North Central	**Kathleen Lynch**	9,843 (26.35)
10 Nov 1994	Cork South Central	No DL candidate	-
29 Jun 1995	Wicklow	John McManus	2,841 (9.76)
2 Apr 1996	Donegal North East	No DL candidate	-
2 Apr 1996	Dublin West	No DL candidate	-
11 Mar 1998	Dublin North	Joe Holohan	225 (0.68)
11 Mar 1998	Limerick East	John Ryan	3,868 (9.01)
23 Oct 1998	Cork South Central	No DL candidate	-

Source: www.electionsireland.org

by-elections, as indicated in Table 5.6. The party enjoyed two considerable successes.

A by-election was called in Dublin South Central in June 1994 following the resignation of John O'Connell of Fianna Fáil the previous February. Democratic Left nominated Eric Byrne as its candidate. Byrne had a long track record in the constituency going back to the 1981 general election. He had served as a Dáil deputy for Dublin South Central from 1989 to 1992. The vacant seat in the 1994 by-election was taken by Byrne, who topped the poll with 7,445 first preferences – just over 25 per cent of the vote. A second by-election victory for Democratic Left followed later in 1994 when two by-elections were held in Cork constituencies. A decision was taken to nominate Kathleen Lynch in Cork North Central. She had previously run unsuccessfully in the neighbouring Cork South Central constituency where a by-election was also scheduled for the same day in November 1994.

Lynch was considered as having a better chance of success in Cork North Central, where the by-election had been caused by the death of a Labour Party TD, than in Cork South Central, where the vacancy arose due to the resignation of Pat Cox, who had been elected for the Progressive Democrats before going Independent. The strategy proved successful as Lynch took the seat. A mistake may have been made, however, in not contesting the Cork South Central constituency and using the opportunity to field a new candidate with an eye on subsequent elections. The party had, after all, taken 2,539 first preferences in that constituency in the 1992 general election. No Democratic Left candidate contested the 1994 by-election or the 1997 general election in Cork South Central. The two 1994 by-election successes facilitated the formation of the Rainbow government later that year as the results changed the parliamentary arithmetic which John Bruton capitalised upon following the collapse of the Albert Reynolds-led Fianna Fáil–Labour administration. 'The by-election wins were a remarkable achievement,' Eamon Gilmore said, adding, 'I don't know of any other country where a party of our size won two by-elections. I think the party hadn't been credited for that as a big political achievement.'[36]

In several other by-elections, however, there was little to be gained by nominating a Democratic Left candidate, as was the case of Mayo West in 1994 where the party had neither an organisation nor a natural constituency. A similar reason may be put forward for the decision not to contest in Donegal North East in 1996. In other cases the rationale for not contesting was less obvious and only served to illustrate the failure to establish Democratic Left as a viable political force. The fact that Democratic Left was unable to challenge in Dublin West in 1996 confirmed this lack of organisational dynamism combined with an inability to overcome established Left-wing groupings on the ground. Dublin West should have been fertile ground for Democratic Left but the party never challenged the Workers' Party, Labour or Socialist Party dominance in this constituency.

In March 1998 a by-election was called in Limerick East following the death of the Labour Party TD, Jim Kemmy. Democratic Left had a strong local base in the constituency with John Ryan, who had been a local councillor since 1991. Ryan had contested the 1992 and 1997 general elections and, while unsuccessful, his first-preference vote had grown from 835 (1.73 per cent) to 3,403 (6.85 per cent). Ryan was considered one of the favourites to take the Kemmy seat and was seen as vying with Labour's Jan O'Sullivan to win the by-election. In fact, Ryan had a dreadful result, securing only 3,868 first preferences (9.06 per cent), a marginal increase on his performance in the previous general election. The Democratic Left candidate was way off taking the seat, which was won by O'Sullivan with a first-preference vote of 24.87 per cent or 10,619 votes.

The Limerick East result left many in Democratic Left shell-shocked and was, according to several senior figures, a major factor in the decision to progress the idea of a merger with the Labour Party. This subject is discussed in detail in Chapters 11 and 12. The mood in early

1998 cannot have been helped by the fact that as the disappointing performance in Limerick East was assessed the result in the Dublin North by-election produced the lowest ever first-preference vote for any Democratic Left candidate in a Dáil constituency election. The party had deliberated for several months about contesting the Dublin North by-election. 'For Dublin North the aim of the campaign is to build a wider base of support in the constituency, which has not been contested by the party in any previous Dáil election,' the Democratic Left members' newsletter explained.[37] The party was facing a difficult choice about its future direction. The reality should not have been a surprise to leading party figures. They had grappled with questions about their identity for several years while also battling a poor organisational base. Indeed, in the months prior to the 1998 by-elections the weakened state of the party's local organisation was evident when the National Executive heard that 'a number of constituencies have failed to respond to a letter from Eamon Gilmore on local election issues.'[38] The party had reached a crossroads and ultimately the decision taken about its future direction meant that the two by-election campaigns were the last electoral contests fought by Democratic Left.

ELECTORAL COMPETITION

The discussion so far in this chapter has shown the performance of Democratic Left in a number of different electoral settings. In many cases – local, national and European – it becomes clear that the relationship between Democratic Left and the Labour Party is central to the history of the former party. The competition, and the resulting tensions, between the two parties can be traced back to the electoral growth of the Workers' Party in the 1980s. The information in Table 5.7 shows the competition in terms of Dáil Éireann seats, with continued movement between the two groupings – Labour and Workers' Party/Democratic Left – prevailing over the entire 1981 to 1997 period. This competition was manifest in seat gains and losses between the two groupings.

While the Labour Party struggled in bleak economic times as part of a coalition government with Fine Gael in the 1982 to 1987 period, the Workers' Party had had free reign to articulate a Left alternative.

TABLE 5.7
SEAT VOLATILITY – WORKERS' PARTY 1981–9; DEMOCRATIC LEFT 1992–7

Name	Area	Year	Result	Details
Joe Sherlock	Cork East	1981	GAIN	New constituency. No LB seat.
		1982 Nov.	LOSS	To FF. No LB seat.
		1987	GAIN	From FG. No LB seat.
		1992	LOSS	LB take DL seat.
Paddy Gallagher	Waterford	1982 Feb.	GAIN	From FF. No LB seat.
		1982 Nov.	LOSS	To FF. No LB seat.
Proinsias De Rossa	Dublin North West	1982 Feb.	GAIN	From FG. No LB seat.
Tomás MacGiolla	Dublin West	1982 Nov.	GAIN	From FG. No LB seat.
		1992	LOSS	Constituency reduced to four seats. WP & FG lose. LB gain.
Pat McCartan	Dublin North East	1987	GAIN	From FG. No LB seat.
		1992	LOSS	To LB.
Pat Rabbitte	Dublin South West	1989	GAIN	From FF. One LB seat.
Eamon Gilmore	Dún Laoghaire	1989	GAIN	WP & FF gain. LB & PD lose. No LB seat.
Eric Byrne	Dublin South Central	1989	GAIN	From LB. No LB seat.
		1992	LOSS	Constituency reduced to four seats. DL & FG lose. LB gain.
		1994*	GAIN	From FF
		1997	LOSS	To FF
Liz McManus	Wicklow	1992	GAIN	Constituency increased to five seats. DL & Ind. Gain. FF loss.
Kathleen Lynch	Cork South Central	1994*	GAIN	From LB
		1997	LOSS	To FF. No LB seat.

*Dáil Éireann by-elections

During this time the party was able to function as an alternative-voting outlet for disgruntled supporters of the Labour Party. For the first time, the Workers' Party won more first-preference votes than the Labour Party at the 1985 local elections. The smaller party built on the 1985 performance as it took full advantage of Labour's negative appeal arising from its involvement in government with Fine Gael. Relations were poor, as Dick Spring recalled: 'It was bloody rough. We were fighting for the same territory.'[39]

The Labour Party's share of the first-preference vote had declined at each general election since 1969. Almost running parallel to this Labour decline was the electoral rise of the Workers' Party, particularly in Dublin constituencies. There is some limited evidence that the competition between the two parties contributed to a slight increase in over-all Left support. Even before the emergence of Democratic Left there had been a 'slow but steady rise in the rate of transfers between the two Left parties during the 1980s, though this still falls short of the degree of solidarity between Fine Gael and the PDs, and indeed between Labour and Fine Gael before 1987'.[40]

The Labour Party rejected overtures for a transfer pact at the 1987 general election, a fact which, Brian Girvin concluded, 'reflected the threat Labour felt'.[41] The Workers' Party was on the move, while the Labour Party was in trouble. The former organisation won seats in Dublin South Central and Dún Laoghaire – both from Labour – and in Dublin South West from Fianna Fáil. After the 1987 contest there were six Workers' Party deputies in the Dublin region compared to three Labour Party TDs. Political scientist Michael Gallagher, however, pointed out a salient weakness in the Workers' Party position – an inability to match Labour's claim to be a national party: 'Although the Workers' Party now overshadows Labour in Dublin, its problem is that it has only one seat, Joe Sherlock's personal creation, outside Dublin.'[42] There were obvious benefits from this intense inter-party competition. Gallagher noted: 'The battle between the two parties will continue and if it expresses itself in intensive constituency activity and policy development rather than mutual public attacks, this may work to the overall benefit of the left.'[43]

The rivalry continued after the formation of Democratic Left in 1992 and manifested itself in several areas, most particularly in inter-party constituency electoral battles and poor transfer patterns between the two groups. Eric Byrne recalled: 'We were always looking at the Labour Party as the natural enemy.'[44] Labour Party general secretary Ray Kavanagh commented upon 'a history of intense rivalry verging almost on hatred on the ground'.[45]

There were very mixed views in the Labour Party about Democratic Left. There were obvious suspicions about the origins of the party related back to its Workers' Party roots and the legacy of the official republican movement. There was also the natural antipathy between two parties seeking to draw support from a similar electoral base. Moreover, there was intense competition between individual party members in a variety of constituencies. Yet, coupled with the negative Labour Party responses, there was also private – and often begrudging – respect for the work ethic and strong Oireachtas performances of the Democratic Left TDs. Labour Party advisor Fergus Finlay described the differing views about their rivals as:

> ... ranging from envy for their discipline and coherence to outright hatred, arising from individual incidents in the past. They were at their most dangerous when we were in government – constantly sniping at anything we tried to do ... As a party they were viewed with the utmost suspicion. But individual members of the party had managed to transcend that, and were universally regarded as among the brightest of Dáil performers.[46]

In the aftermath of the 1991 local elections the general assessment within the Labour Party was that the Workers' Party 'had run out of steam'.[47] Labour strategists believed there was a possibility that some Workers' Party TDs could be attracted into joining them. There was considerable speculation that Pat McCartan would defect to Labour but after private discussions he 'declined the offer'.[48] As was discussed previously, there was also a hope within the De Rossa grouping in 1992 that some Labour Party figures would join Democratic Left although, as with McCartan, no allegiance changes were undertaken. It was against this background that relations between the Labour Party and the newly formed Democratic Left must be seen. Moreover, the issue of the new party's individual identity was closely linked with the Irish Labour Party. In early April 1992 Pat Rabbitte addressed inter-party relations at a public meeting in Dungarvan in County Waterford. 'I agree there is a good deal of convergence between ourselves and the

Labour Party and I certainly would look forward to maximum co-operation between our parties, but I think that there is a space in our
society, to the left of the Labour Party, and it is important that that
space is filled,' Rabbitte said.[49]

Nevertheless, it is again worth noting that the question of a merger
with the Labour Party was informally on the agenda at the time of the
split in the Workers' Party in early 1992. There was, however, little
support among the De Rossa group for joining the Labour Party – on
an individual basis or en masse – at that time. 'A merger between us
and Labour is not a runner. There are similarities but there are other
important issues on which there is no agreement,' De Rossa later said.[50]
At that time he singled out policy on Northern Ireland as an area of
significant difference between the two parties. In an interview for this
study, he said of the Labour Party option in 1992: 'Some would have
been happy enough to do it but I don't think the vast majority would
have joined. I certainly didn't want to join the Labour Party at that
time.'[51]

Des Geraghty described the Labour Party option in 1992 as 'a passing thought' but one that many people would have seen as 'unprinci-
pled' and 'opportunistic'.[52] Paul Sweeney expressed a similar view.
'There was never anyone who I knew with the intention of joining the
Labour Party,' he said.[53] Tony Heffernan said a post-Workers' Party
move into Labour Party ranks would have caused much deeper
division than that which actually occurred. 'It was certainly an idea that
was canvassed but there were very few takers for it. There was a view
that it might be right in theory, "but I'm not bloody well doing that",
you know,' Heffernan admitted, and added:

> If it happened at that time you would have had a split within a
> split ... the people who went to Democratic Left wouldn't have
> done; some might, but you would probably have had a three-way
> split then – the Workers' Party, a new party and a smaller group
> who would have went to the Labour Party.[54]

Having remained in the Workers' Party, Seán Garland was also unconvinced that his departing colleagues would join the Labour Party. 'It
would have been too soon for them in 1992 to suddenly join Labour.
It would have been less credible [than setting up a new party]. But they
[only] put off what was inevitable.'[55]

Pat Rabbitte was the only senior party figure to give serious consideration to the Labour Party option in 1992. For many in what became Democratic Left, opinions were influenced by the poor relations between the two groupings. But there were other issues involved, as Rosheen Callender observed: 'We felt that the Labour Party was very staid and not that open to change, the sort of radical change that we were discussing. There would have been not just personality differences as much as the perception that we were very different types of people. We felt that Labour was hostile to us and, generally speaking, they were ...'[56] Callender's view is shared by many of her former colleagues in Democratic Left, including Catherine Murphy, who saw even more fundamental differences between the two parties.

> We felt that the Labour Party would sell their souls. Most of us saw them as the real enemy because essentially they were seen as the impediment to building a decent Left-wing party. I personally thought the difference between Democratic Left and the Labour Party was a cultural difference. And when people are looking for policy differences – and very often it's the same with Fianna Fáil and Fine Gael – they may not find a gigantic policy difference but there's a cultural and historical difference. The cultural difference is, I think, critically important.[57]

For Murphy this 'cultural difference' was evident in the involvement and activity levels of the members of the respective members.

> The culture of people who have a feeling of equality of membership as opposed to head office sending out dictates. Culturally the Labour Party had card-carrying members, not real members. One Workers' Party member was worth twenty Labour Party members ... Less so in Democratic Left, but certainly we would have had more active members than the Labour Party.[58]

Despite these strongly argued points from Callender and Murphy, others believed the differences between the two parties were driven more by personality and individual political ambition than political ideology. 'Very often relations were defined by what relations were like in the constituencies,' Eamon Gilmore admitted.[59] For Gilmore, the ultimately unsuccessful talks about government formation in late 1992 helped to overcome many personal difficulties at leadership level in the two parties. 'I must say that the discussions between Labour and Demo-cratic Left in that post-1992 election period, that's what really brought about the subsequent merger. We had the same objectives.'[60] Despite the strong rejectionist strand advocated by many interviewees in this study, Gilmore provided a more nuanced view about the Labour Party option.

> Even in the discussions when we were still in the Workers' Party, some believed that we needed to do business with the Labour Party. I know that Dick Spring was very open to that. We had worked with the Labour Party in the [Mary] Robinson campaign [in 1990]. But we wouldn't have brought the organisation with us at that time. There were a lot of people in Democratic Left because it wasn't the Labour Party. So therefore there was a degree of hostility amongst some people in Democratic Left, which wasn't necessarily shared by the parliamentary people. So yes, the idea [joining Labour] was certainly around. Our options post-the Dún Laoghaire conference were: do we stay in the organisation, which was not possible because of all that had happened beforehand; do we leave the Workers' Party and form a new party; or do we leave the Workers' Party and join the Labour Party? Not all of the TDs would have joined the Labour Party [and] certainly not all of the members would have ... and these things very often come down to constituency considerations.[61]

Interestingly, in light of the tensions between the new party and the Labour Party, there was a warmer welcome from their comrades in Britain. Late in 1992 Des Geraghty briefed his colleagues on contacts with the British Labour Party. An internal party memo summarised Geraghty's contribution as 'invited Democratic Left, refused entry to WP. Attended by Proinsias De Rossa and Séamus Lynch. Meeting held with John Smith.'[62]

It seems that there was a growing acceptability for the Democratic Left politicians in their new roles, although relations with the Irish Labour Party remained at best strained. In an interview with journalist Liam Fay in *Hot Press* magazine during the 1992 general election campaign, De Rossa was openly hostile to Spring's party. The exchange is worth repeating to illustrate the negativity between the two sides at that time:

Fay: There's obviously considerable rivalry at ground level on the campaign trail between canvassers for both Labour and Democratic Left. Isn't this likely to develop into bitter feuds in some areas?

De Rossa: Not that I'm aware of. Certainly, nothing like that has been reported to me. But I know for a fact that Labour's strategy is to see us off, completely. They have made no secret of the fact, privately, that's their strategy.

Fay: Surely, that puts a strain on your personal relationship with Dick Spring?

De Rossa: I don't have a relationship with Dick Spring so there is no strain … We're not allies. The nature of the work in the Dáil is that I have a job to do for Democratic Left and he has a job to do for the Labour Party. We both operate separate, independent parties. I would rarely see him. He's over the far side of Leinster House. I'm over in Kildare Street. His constituency is in Kerry, mine is in Dublin North West.[63]

Several months later, in early 1993, De Rossa gave a far more favourable assessment of the Labour Party–Democratic Left relationship. 'Relations are good and have been since the end of the election campaign,' De Rossa told one newspaper.[64] The dynamic between the two parties after the November 1992 general election was significantly changed following discussions in the aftermath of the electoral contest. The Labour Party and Democratic Left held talks on the possibility of agreeing a shared policy platform. 'We went into the negotiating process with the aim of maximising the influence we could have on the policies of the new government. We were also interested in discussing the prospect of a centre left government based on the sort of arithmetic there would be if Fine Gael, Labour and ourselves were involved,' De Rossa explained.[65] Many in Democratic Left identify the thawing of relations between the two parties as starting with the talks on possible government formation, which took place at the end of 1992.

CONCLUSION

Democratic Left's electoral performance ranged from modest to poor.

The by-election successes in 1994 were a remarkable achievement for a small political party but they must be considered against the failure to hold the party's European Parliament seat in 1994 and also the poor general election results in 1992 and again in 1997. The discussion in this chapter has shown that a small pool of candidates gave the party some success but there was a failure to attract new candidates and an inability to grow the party in new electoral areas. Given the long-established progression route to national politics offered by membership of a local authority, the electoral development of Democratic Left was significantly hampered by the failure to hold nationwide local elections in the 1992 to 1997 period. But it is debatable if even greater access to local governing bodies would have been sufficient to develop the party. In the absence of an organisational overhaul, an influx of new members and more financial resources, Democratic Left faced an ongoing challenge to remain relevant. The period in government between 1994 and 1997 only paused the inevitable issue, which was forced back on the agenda by poor by-election results in Limerick East and Dublin North – many who had previously discounted the merger route with the Labour Party had to think again. Having examined Democratic Left's electoral history, the various weaknesses in the party – organisational, financial and ideological – will now be discussed in the next two chapters.

NOTES

1. B. Farrell, 'The Formation of the Partnership Government', in M. Gallagher and M. Laver, *How Ireland Voted, 1992* (Dublin: Political Studies Association of Ireland (PSAI), 1993), p.27.
2. Pat Rabbitte, Memorandum to National Council Members Re Electoral Strategy, 26 August 1992.
3. Pat Rabbitte, Memo to council meeting, General Election Strategy, 26 June 1992
4. Ibid.
5. Ibid.
6. Ibid.
7. Pat Rabbitte, Memorandum to National Council Members, Re Electoral Strategy, 26 August 1992
8. Farrell, 'The Formation of the Partnership Government', p.27.
9. B. Girvin, 'The Road to the Election', in M. Gallagher and M. Laver, *How Ireland Voted, 1992* (Dublin: PSAI, 1993), p.14.
10. Ibid., p.15.
11. Interview with Eamon Gilmore, 11 September 2006.
12. Interview with Tony Heffernan, 13 September 2006.

13. Interview with Liz McManus, 18 October 2006.
14. R. Sinnott, *Irish Voters Decide: Voting Behaviour in Elections and Referendums Since 1918* (Manchester: Manchester University Press, 1995), p.108.
15. M. Gallagher, 'The Election of the 27th Dáil', in Gallagher and Laver, *How Ireland Voted, 1992*, p.66.
16. L. McManus, 'On the Campaign Trail', in Gallagher and Laver, *How Ireland Voted, 1992*, p.52.
17. Sherlock unsuccessfully contested the 1997 Seanad Éireann elections having failed to win a Dáil seat in Cork East in the general election in the same year.
18. *The Irish Times*, 26 January 1994, p.13.
19. Interview with Eamon Gilmore, 11 September 2006.
20. *The Irish Times*, 26 March 1994.
21. Ibid.
22. *The Irish Times*, 28 March 1994.
23. Ibid.
24. Ibid.
25. *The Irish Times*, 4 May 1994.
26. Bernie Malone quoted in *The Irish Times*, 29 March 1994.
27. Interview with Eamon Gilmore, 11 September 2006.
28. *The Irish Times*, 10 May 1994, p.3.
29. Interview with Eamon Gilmore, 11 September 2006.
30. *Sunday Tribune*, 13 April 1997, p.13.
31. *The Irish Times*, 11 April 1997, p.6.
32. *The Irish Times*, 10 May 1997, p.5.
33. M. Holmes, 'Organisational Preparation and Political Marketing', in M. Marsh and P. Mitchell (eds), *How Ireland Voted, 1997* (Oxford: Westview Press, 1999), p.42.
34. J. Garry and L. Mansergh, 'Irish Party Manifestos', in M. Marsh and P. Mitchell (eds), *How Ireland Voted, 1997* (Dublin: PSAI/Westview, 1999), p.86.
35. M. Gallagher, 'The Results Analysed', in M. Marsh and P. Mitchell, *How Ireland Voted, 1997* (Dublin: PSAI, 1999), p.134.
36. Interview with Eamon Gilmore, 11 September 2006.
37. Democratic Left Members Newsletter, February 1998.
38. Democratic Left National Executive minutes, 29 November 1997.
39. *Examiner*, 6 November 1997.
40. M. Gallagher, 'The Election Results and the New Dáil', in M. Gallagher and R. Sinnott, *How Ireland Voted, 1989* (Galway: PSAI Press, 1990), p.80.
41. B. Girvin, 'The Campaign', in Gallagher and Sinnott, *How Ireland Voted, 1989*, p.32.
42. Gallagher, 'The Election Results and the New Dáil', p.77.
43. Ibid.
44. Interview with Eric Byrne, 29 August 2006.
45. R. Kavanagh, *Spring, Summer and Fall: The Rise and Fall of the Labour Party, 1986–1999* (Dublin: Blackwater Press, 2001), p.214.
46. F. Finlay, *Snakes and Ladders* (Dublin: New Island, 1999), p.129.
47. Kavanagh, *Spring, Summer and Fall*, p.90.
48. Ibid.
49. *Dungarvan Observer*, 4 April 1992, p.8.
50. *Sunday Business Post*, 3 January 1993.
51. Interview with Proinsias De Rossa, 7 September 2007.
52. Interview with Des Geraghty, 9 May 2006.
53. Interview with Paul Sweeney, 6 September 2006.
54. Interview with Tony Heffernan, 13 September 2006.
55. Interview with Seán Garland, 29 May 2006.
56. Interview with Rosheen Callender, 12 September 2006.

57. Interview with Catherine Murphy, 31 August 2006.
58. Ibid.
59. Interview with Eamon Gilmore, 11 September 2006.
60. Ibid.
61. Ibid.
62. Des Geraghty, Issues Report to Council Meeting, 3 October 1992.
63. *Hot Press*, November 1992.
64. *Sunday Business Post*, 3 January 1993.
65. Ibid.

6

Government Talks:
Unsuccessful and Unexpected

INTRODUCTION

The opportunity for Democratic Left to enter government arose in an unexpected way late in 1994. The outcome of the 1992 general election led to the formation of a Fianna Fáil–Labour administration. The two-party coalition had a substantial parliamentary majority. The arrangement, however, was not without internal tension and eventually came undone in the latter stages of 1994. The negotiations that led to the formation of the self-styled Rainbow coalition involving Fine Gael, the Labour Party and Democratic Left are discussed below. This anaysis focuses upon some of the main issues faced by the new administration, including the priorities for Democratic Left, as well as the areas which caused internal contention and the stresses and strains placed on a political organisation arising from its participation in a coalition arrangement. What emerges from the analysis, in particular, is the importance of the strength of the unlikely relationship which developed between Proinsias De Rossa and John Bruton.

GOVERNMENT TALKS, 1992

The possibility of entering a government with the Labour Party was under discussion in senior Democratic Left circles during the summer of 1992. As regards the attitude towards Labour, Pat Rabbitte had a straightforward suggestion for his colleagues – 'it is recommended that we ignore them.' He added:

> We will campaign as an Independent Left/Party acknowledging

that if the Labour Party is more modest, it has a great deal to be more modest about. If confronted with a national request for a transfer pact then we will study that situation. Local Constituencies in close co-ordination with the Party centre should decide how to respond to local transfer requests.[1]

The subject of electoral strategy was discussed in some detail by senior figures in the party. In a paper prepared for the Executive Council on 2 October 1992, Rabbitte developed his thoughts on how Democratic Left would deal publicly with the Labour Party:

> We should plan now to avoid our relations with the Labour Party or our attitude to participating in Government dominating part of the actual Election Campaign. It is suggested for approval that we fight the Election as an Independent Left Party with no pacts or agreements with other parties. We should avoid getting into horse-trading on vote pacts with the Labour Party on the basis that automatically many of our voters will transfer to other Left candidates including the Labour Party just like we assume that many Labour voters will transfer to us. We must avoid being seen as the junior partner in a Left Alliance whilst at the same time not alienating the electorate by allowing ourselves to be drawn into a bickering contest with the Labour Party. The ground to be laid for this tactical approach by a major political speech on a suitable occasion by the Party Leader. Politically we should set out our own stall. We will not participate in any conservative dominated Coalition Government. Our objective is to represent our own voters and force realignment in Irish politics. Subject to agreement on policy, we can see ourselves participating in a Left Majority Government. We do not envisage circumstances in which we would support a minority Conservative Government.[2]

There were other views about how the new party should treat Labour. An internal document from August 1992 bluntly advised that 'Democratic Left should engage Labour in a confrontational way. We should publicly criticise Labour for the role it has played and continues to play as an establishment party.'[3] Despite this hostility, the parliamentary arithmetic after the November 1992 general election meant the two parties started discussions about participating in a coalition arrangement led by Fine Gael. The talks were aimed at arriving at a joint policy agreement to be adopted in subsequent negotiations with Fine Gael. As discussed in the previous chapter, the election was a disappointment for Democratic Left, which failed to make a significant impact in seat terms. But the numbers game in Leinster House left open the real possibility that the party might be needed to form an anti-Fianna Fáil coalition. Previous talk about a Left-led coalition and avoiding a conservative-led government were set aside. The talks with the Labour Party were discussed at a special General Council meeting on 5 December 1992. The minutes of that meeting record that:

> Proinsias De Rossa outlined three choices on the talks which should be addressed: to endorse the work to date and continue the process with the aim of achieving government; to continue the process with the aim of finding a way out at an opportune time, or to state that having examined the options it was clear to the party that it was not possible to put a government together.[4]

Despite some limited dissent, the meeting agreed to continue the discussions with the Labour Party with a view 'to strengthening a Left input to the formation of any new government'.[5] The Labour Party had emerged as the main winner from the 1992 general election. The first meeting of the newly enlarged parliamentary party took place on 1 December 1992. The discussion on Labour's strategy in forming a new government dealt with the possible role of Democratic Left. According to one account of the meeting, eleven of the TDs who made contributions spoke about involving Democratic Left in any government arrangement. There were several arguments for pursuing this option.

The general secretary of the Labour Party, Ray Kavanagh, recorded, 'Many in Labour believed this to be the right thing to do ideologically, but also the right thing to do from an opportunistic point of view. As a left-wing party, it would be dangerous to leave DL in opposition; it would revive its fortunes at Labour's expense.'[6] Kavanagh speculated that two differing views about Labour existed within Democratic Left, with the four Democratic Left Dáil deputies evenly divided in their opinions. De Rossa and McManus were – according to Kavanagh – 'bitterly opposed to Labour' while Gilmore and Rabbitte were 'more pragmatic and craved a role in government'.[7] Another advisor, Fergus Finlay, confirmed this Labour Party view. He recalled that Pat Rabbitte admitted to him that the idea of participating in government with Labour was not fully supported in Democratic Left, although this view would not have been shared by Labour's parliamentary party members. As part of the talks process, Finlay and Brendan Howlin met with Rabbitte and Des Geraghty. 'They were somewhat suspicious of our intentions,' Finlay recorded.[8]

Despite the hostility on both sides, if a different conclusion had emerged from the prolonged re-count in Dublin South Central to fill the final seat in the general election, a three-party coalition would have been a real possibility. 'By lunchtime that day, with Dick Spring's agreement, I had arranged a private meeting with Pat Rabbitte. And by the end of that meeting, I knew that he too desperately wanted to see the potential realised. The hatchet was capable of being buried,' Finlay later wrote.[9]

A document agreeing a joint programme between the two parties was finalised on Wednesday 9 December 1992. But Fine Gael – the largest party in the proposed arrangement – was less keen about involving Democratic Left. Their objections to Democratic Left were ideological and practical. The ideological issue was derived from the new party's roots and concerns over the criminality allegations which had dogged the Workers' Party, as well as a view of its Left-wing positioning on policy matters including state interventionism, and capital and corporation taxation.

It was also reported that Fine Gael had concerns about parliamentary arithmetic. A government comprising Fine Gael, Labour and Democratic Left would have had, at best, 82 of the 166 seats in Dáil Éireann, in effect a minority coalition administration (83 if Democratic Left won Dublin South Central). The alternative option of Fine Gael, Labour and the Progressive Democrats would have had a combined voting bloc of 88 seats. Aside from the stability issue offered by the latter option, Fine Gael would have had more in common with the Progressive Democrats, thus ensuring that their ideological outlook commanded a clear majority within the three-party government. John Bruton had in any event taken a decision about a Fine Gael–Labour arrangement with Democratic Left during the general election campaign. 'It wasn't about any negativity towards the Democratic Left but in terms of my own appreciation of what I thought the Fine Gael base could take at that time. I didn't think they were ready for Fine Gael coalescing with the Democratic Left at that time.'[10]

The final seat in the 1992 general election in Dublin South Central took several days to be allocated. A handful of votes separated Eric Byrne of Democratic Left and Ben Briscoe of Fianna Fáil. Victory for Byrne would have reduced concern about the parliamentary arithmetic of a Fine Gael–Labour–Democratic Left administration. However, the conclusion of the Dublin South Central count in favour of the Fianna Fáil candidate lessened the likelihood of a Rainbow government, although it would still have been feasible for Fine Gael, Labour and Democratic Left to have formed a minority coalition. 'If Labour had held its nerve it would have been a fascinating situation. A government of Labour, Democratic Left and Fine Gael would have stuck together,' Pat Rabbitte recalled.[11] Instead, Spring and his colleagues moved to form a coalition administration with Fianna Fáil. 'We agreed a joint policy programme with Labour but other events intervened which put a halt to that. But if the discussions between Labour and Fianna Fáil break up without an agreement being reached, we would still be interested in talking about a centre left government,' De Rossa said, adding that 'in the meantime, Labour is maintaining regular contact with us.'[12]

A progress report was delivered at a National Executive meeting on 12 December 1992. But with the parliamentary numbers providing Labour with a far more stable arrangement with Fianna Fáil, the alternative option involving Fine Gael and Democratic Left was not seriously pursued by Spring's party. There was, in any event, another potential impediment that may have emerged to prevent the formation of a so-called Rainbow coalition: resistance within De Rossa's party to the government option. Tony Heffernan explained:

> It would have been very difficult to get that through a Democratic Left conference at that stage. I think most people would have regarded it as being too early to go into government. We'd only been in existence for a little over six months and going into government would have been a very, very high risk. Who knows if, for instance, there was no other government capable of being formed ... it might have been passed by a conference but I suspect it mightn't ...[13]

Kathleen Lynch provided a similar assessment of the views of party members: 'They'd probably have said "yes" but with a series of demands that were probably undeliverable.'[14] Interestingly, Eric Byrne – whose defeat in Dublin South Central, when it was eventually confirmed, killed off the government idea – was not keen on serving in a coalition arrangement:

> In that particular period, I think, there was a consensus that you didn't go into government. There was never great enthusiasm in Democratic Left for government. There was a very interesting

internal debate [after 1992] and Rabbitte would have been very much to the fore, and De Rossa slowly getting around to the idea that, you know, we must break from this sort of anti-establishment position ... But [in 1992] we couldn't see our viability in the long term in being a government party.[15]

However, one of those involved in the 1992 discussions with Labour – Rosheen Callender – was open to the idea of participation in the proposed coalition arrangement at that time.

I remember drawing up a document and I was strongly in favour of getting into serious discussions on a whole range of policy issues, and in fact we did have discussions with them but Fine Gael put their foot down in the end. And Labour actually took quite a lot of our policies from those discussions and implemented some of them. The famous one being the May Day holiday and [also] integrating tax and social welfare ...[16]

With the Labour Party eventually agreeing a programme for government with Fianna Fáil, Des Geraghty saw the benefits to remaining outside a coalition arrangement: 'Maybe because I wasn't a parliamentarian, I would have preferred to get breathing space rather than being in government. Can you imagine the problem of trying to develop political ideas [and] then develop the public awareness of them [while] being in government?'[17]

A blunt assessment of the talks with the Labour Party was provided in a memo circulated in the names of two party members in early January 1993.

The negotiations themselves were hardly a public relations success for DL. Labour's programme contained no redistributive element (unlike Kinnock's and Clinton's). Why wasn't this said? Are Articles 2 and 3 the only issue on which we disagree with Labour? The failure to emphasise our distinctive radicalism helped to suggest that there were darker reasons for our unacceptability.[18]

The two authors proposed the establishment of a Strategy Sub-Committee to examine the way forward in terms of organisation and policy. 'We believe that the failures of the campaign and the subsequent Labour/DL negotiations highlight the need for broadening the consultation and decision-making process on strategic issues in the party'. The idea was accepted, and not long afterwards a task force was established to re-evaluate the party and help develop the best route forward.

GOVERNMENT NEGOTIATIONS, 1994

The collapse of the Fianna Fáil/Labour coalition in late 1994 created a novel political scenario in Ireland. For the first time since the foundation of the state a government was formed without recourse to a general election. Democratic Left's by-election successes in Dublin South Central and Cork North Central had helped to tilt the parliamentary arithmetic in favour of an alternative coalition combination involving Democratic Left, Labour and Fine Gael. This three-party arrangement had a Dáil majority so President Mary Robinson used her constitutional authority to facilitate the formation of a new government to replace the troubled Albert Reynolds-led coalition without a general election. The new government was, however, made possible by more than just a favourable total of seats in parliament. Since the general election in late 1992 John Bruton had co-operated more closely on the opposition benches with Proinsias De Rossa. Whereas previously there was suspicion from the Fine Gael leader, now he displayed respect for his Democratic Left counterpart. Des Geraghty detected this new attitude from Fine Gael: 'I think there was less suspicion about our motives as time went on,' he said.[19]

Discussions were in fact held between the leaders of the three main opposition parties – Fine Gael, the Progressive Democrats and Democratic Left – and the leader of the Labour Party. 'I conversed with Proinsias individually and we had meetings of the four party leaders. I think there were at least two meetings where all of us were present,' John Bruton recalled.[20] The Fine Gael leader favoured a four-party arrangement – Fine Gael, Labour, PDs and Democratic Left – which would have, in his own view, created a centrist administration – but his preference found little support: 'None of them really wanted a four-party government because the smaller parties recognised that one of them would be sort of surplus to requirements. There was a preference on the part of the Labour Party for the Democratic Left to be in government.'[21]

When the Fianna Fáil–Labour coalition collapsed in November 1994 attempts to form an alternative government moved very fast, as Democratic Left's general secretary, John Gallagher, recalled:

A very quick decision was needed. We were asking, what are we

going to do? If we don't do it, are we able for another general
election? And if we do go into government, could we make it
work? We quickly came around to the idea. It all happened so
quickly. One of my tasks was to phone around reassuring people
and getting their perspective on us going into government.[22]

There was a minority within the party's ranks who questioned the wisdom
of entering government. But the overwhelming majority of members –
and all those associated with the parliamentary party – were supportive of commencing serious negotiations with Fine Gael and the Labour
Party. Catherine Murphy recalled a few voices opposing the decision to
start government formation talks.

> There was a discussion about whether it was the right thing or
> not. There was a selling job done by the TDs and, you know, I can
> well understand capable people wanting to be in positions where
> they can deliver. We had become, if you like, a traditional politi-
> cal party at that stage ... And it was a question then if you didn't
> take this opportunity to go into government – or go to the coun-
> try not knowing how you would come back – well, you know, in
> two and a half years we can do something ...[23]

Liz McManus also recalled the internal party discussions. 'I remember
we had a bit of a debate about it. Proinsias was very clear. He said,
"What is the point of being in this game if we pass up on a chance
to actually deliver?"'[24] As chairperson of Democratic Left's National
Executive, Catherine Murphy was aware of this argument. 'The view
was that if you were anyway politically mature, you'd have to look at
this as an opportunity. There's no point in shouting and roaring about
stuff that you need, and then when you get an opportunity not delivering on it.'[25] The majority view was to participate in John Bruton's three-
party coalition. A list of priorities for government was easily agreed
within the party, as Eamon Gilmore recalled:

> I was involved in the negotiation of that programme for govern-
> ment. We knew that our priorities were the employment issue
> [and] we wanted to do the divorce referendum. We wanted to get
> something on the environment, the legal challenge to Sellafield, to
> get that moving. But, the big project was, I suppose, to get people
> working, to get the economy going.[26]

The 1992 negotiations between Democratic Left and the Labour Party assisted with the process two years later. 'The experience in 1992 was useful when it came around again in 1994,' Tony Heffernan admitted.[27] Proinsias De Rossa, who had been prepared to enter government in 1992, acknowledged the benefit of the talks even if they had been unsuccessful. 'They were important from the point of view of maturing the party. There is no doubt that involvement in discussions helps you to clarify what are the differences between us [Democratic Left and the Labour Party],' De Rossa said.[28]

A broad policy agenda had already been agreed between the two parties. 'There was an agenda but it didn't differ dramatically [from 1992]. We clicked a bit with the Labour Party,' Eamon Gilmore said.[29] 'We'd hammered out a lot of stuff then [in 1992] and we didn't basically have that many major policy disagreements,' Rosheen Callender added.[30] Paul Sweeney, another member of the Democratic Left negotiation team, noted:

> I was sent with Rabbitte and Gilmore up to Fine Gael headquarters [in Upper Mount Street in Dublin] which was embarrassing being on television going into [the building]. I did the negotiations on the technical side and, by God, that was real politics where we traded. We were totally against free [third level] fees as they were utterly regressive – and I still believe that to this day – but we traded that for the abolishment of water charges. I got a note from Rabbitte [during the meeting] telling me to drop the free fees ...[31]

The issue of ending fees for third-level tuition was not just supported by Fine Gael but also by the Labour Party. It was not an argument that Democratic Left was going to win. The talks were an early lesson about the compromises necessary in a coalition government, as Rosheen Callender explained:

> We had very detailed, extensive discussions with Fine Gael and Labour, sort of tri-partite discussions, and we really hammered out a lot of major policy issues before putting together the programme for government. We felt afterwards that each party, in the end, had one mad policy issue that the other two parties wouldn't agree with, and we had one of those, and we just agreed to differ and said, 'Ok, you have yours' and we just accepted that each of us were going to have our own. DL's was social welfare arrears for married women ...

Labour's was the free [third level] fees. I can't think off hand [about Fine Gael's]. Was it something to do with taxing farmers, or not taxing them [laughs]. I can't remember ...[32]

There was more substance in the talks with the Labour Party than with Fine Gael, according to Paul Sweeney.

> The real talks were between us and Labour. Fine Gael sat there and the only thing I remember was one day Ruairi Quinn said to me, 'what would you say to a proposal from Fine Gael that every Principal Office or Assistant Principal Office and above' – I can't remember the details – 'would have to reapply for their job every two years?' I said that would lead to a lot of industrial relations problems and it would be very hard to get anything done. It was the only thing they proposed that I was to hear ...[33]

The talks also focused on some key areas of concern for Democratic Left. Rosheen Callender was involved in the negotiations on tax and social welfare – these were areas where the party required tangible pledges in order to convince its membership of the merits of joining a coalition government.

> We had a very major discussion which went on for days and days about child benefit. The Labour Party and ourselves managed to get Fine Gael around to our view that child benefit is a very good payment to address child poverty, and we got agreement that we would put as much resources as possible into improving child benefit ...[34]

While the negotiations took place between nominated representatives of the three parties, the final draft document required the agreement of the three party leaders. Interestingly, John Bruton had little difficulty with the Democratic Left policy demands. 'There wasn't a big long shopping list. What the Democratic Left was looking for were reasonable things. They were worried about local charges [and] the tax treatment of the lower paid. That was not something I had any problems with.'[35] From a Democratic Left perspective, Catherine Murphy also argued that possibly more could have been achieved on the policy front. 'The concern was that we didn't push a hard enough bargain, and there was a bit of inexperience. Now, I think, looking back on it that probably was the case.'[36]

It may well be that Democratic Left could have been more ambitious in the party's demands for involvement in the proposed coalition. The talks commenced with all involved knowing that the Labour Party had a strong preference for Democratic Left rather than the Progressive Democrats being the third element in the arrangement. Democratic Left may have been able to set a higher price for its support of a government the formation of which ultimately prevented the calling of a general election.

A GOVERNMENT OF RENEWAL, 1994–7

John Bruton was elected taoiseach on 15 December 1994. As mentioned previously, it was the first time since the foundation of the Irish state that a new government had been formed during the life of a parliament without a general election being called. The policy priorities of the new three-party coalition were set out in the document *A Government for Renewal*. The opening section stated that:

> ... the principles of this Government include reform of national and local institutions to provide accountability, transparency and freedom of information; completion of progress towards peace in Northern Ireland, a commitment to the employment needs of people, an innovative, enterprising economy, reform of the tax system to benefit the low paid and families; quality social services; and integration of environmental considerations in policy development.[37]

During the final negotiations between Bruton, Spring and De Rossa, Democratic Left sought two full cabinet posts, arguing strongly that without a second party member at cabinet their leader risked being isolated among fourteen ministers drawn from the Labour Party and Fine Gael. But neither Spring nor Bruton was willing to reduce their own representation. The Labour leader was conscious that his party had had six others in the outgoing arrangement with Fianna Fáil so dropping one of his ministerial colleagues would have been problematic, while Bruton needed numbers at cabinet to reflect the status of his party as the largest participant in the coalition.

On the eve of the Dáil meeting to elect a new government the content of the policy agreement had been finalised between the three parties. But there was still no deal on ministerial allocations. With only hours to the Dáil vote on the new government, a compromise was presented with a proposal to create the position of a 'super junior' minister. Bruton and Spring were offering Democratic Left a single seat out of the fifteen at the cabinet table along with two minister of state positions, and one of these junior ministers – the 'super junior' – would be allowed to attend cabinet meetings although in a non-voting capacity.

The proposal was not sufficient for De Rossa and his colleagues. Having been denied two full cabinet positions they were not prepared to sign-up to the deal on offer. The Democratic Left parliamentary party was based in the Kildare House building opposite Leinster House, and on 15 December 1994 as the party's TDs crossed the road to attend the Dáil meeting to elect a new government they were convinced they would only be offering external support. They were committed to supporting Bruton on the vote for taoiseach but Democratic Left would not participate in what was now going to be a minority Fine Gael–Labour Party coalition. Negotiations, however, continued on the floor of the Dáil chamber with intensive discussions led by Gilmore and Michael Lowry of Fine Gael. Democratic Left was eventually offered another – a third – minister of state position along with the chair of a new Oireachtas committee on Northern Ireland.

The three ministers of state positions for Democratic Left included the 'super junior' post. In the most dramatic of circumstances – and with only minutes to the nomination of a new government – the compromise allowed the Rainbow government to be formed. But the stand-off left a sour note, although not one that ultimately impacted on working relations between the coalition partners. Pat Rabbitte was the one to lose out as he would have filled a second full cabinet role available to his party.

> It came about because I was shafted at Dick Spring's insistence that Labour would retain six ministers [as they had in the Fianna Fáil–Labour coalition]. Dick Spring was confronted with the situation where, having crossed the floor, was he going to sack one of his colleagues? So, in the circumstances, the three leaders obviously came up with the formula which subsequently operated.[38]

The failure to secure Rabbitte's full status at cabinet was lessened by Bruton's determination as taoiseach to oversee a cabinet built on consensus. During the lifetime of the Rainbow coalition Bruton chaired a cabinet at which no decision was taken by way of a vote of ministers. Officials and ministers considered all policy differences between the three parties before they reached the cabinet. The three party leaders had the final say on contentious issues, as Bruton recalled:

> On the mathematics, Democratic Left was only entitled to one cabinet post. So we came up with the idea of a super junior minister for Pat Rabbitte so Pat would be at cabinet meetings but he wouldn't be a voting member. I took the view that one should be more generous to the smaller parties.[39]

It was not the ideal outcome for Democratic Left, but the 'super junior' role was an important concession. De Rossa was aware of the importance of having a party colleague at the cabinet table.

> I'd never been inside a cabinet room before so I had no idea how often things went to votes. Now I know Pat didn't have a vote but [it was] important for the party to have two people in the cabinet … the importance of somebody being able to be there all the time. So if I couldn't be there Pat was there, that was important. And when there were sub-committees of the cabinet being set up I couldn't be on all the sub-committees. Also the fact that each of us had a colleague so that we wouldn't be on our own.[40]

Alongside De Rossa as minister for social welfare, three other Democratic Left politicians held ministerial rank. The four ministerial positions – one senior and three juniors – was an excellent return for a party of only six TDs. Pat Rabbitte was minister of state to the government and minister of state at the Department of Enterprise, Trade and Employment. He had responsibility for Commerce, Science and Technology. Eamon Gilmore was minister of state at the Department of the Marine. Liz McManus was minister of state at the Department of the Environment. She had responsibility for housing and urban renewal.

Despite past controversies and its history, the arrival of Democratic Left into government apparently met with little resistance from the civil service. The four Democratic Left ministers all mentioned the professionalism of the officials who worked in their respective departments. There were some minor incidents when the history of the new party in government was explained abroad, as Eamon Gilmore humorously recounted. 'I remember doing St Patrick's Day events in the United States, and the embassy decided that they would have to tell their hosts what party I belonged to. So the consulate very politely said in my ear, "we've told them you represent the democratic party. I hope that's alright, minister."'[41] There were, however, some exceptions. A former civil servant, Eamon Delaney, recalled hostility from some of his colleagues in the Department of Foreign Affairs. Delaney wrote of one official:

> He was speaking of DL and WP in the same breath, still a common confusion. By now, of course, DL had become partners in the Rainbow Coalition and we had the ridiculous situation of one Counsellor ... questioning whether to give a Brief (or a copy of the Box) to one of the DL Ministers! 'You know, that fellow ... he's not sound at all,' he said ruefully, and he painted a subversive picture of left-wing anti-nationalists.[42]

Such views were, however, in a minority, although there were other sensitive issues for Democratic Left arising from its participation in government. The party was embroiled in controversy when De Rossa advertised for five assistants to work in his office in the Department of Social Welfare in an internal party publication. This issue prompted calls of 'jobs for the boys' and was an early warning about how important perception and the role of the media is in modern politics.

The evolution of Democratic Left's thinking in relation to three key policy areas – Northern Ireland, the liberal/social agenda and economic matters – is assessed in Chapter 7. The discussion here deals with the party's impact on the agenda of the Rainbow coalition and also the impact that governmental participation had on Democratic Left. The economy was the main item on the political agenda at the start of 1995, with unemployment the top priority against a backdrop of improving but still limited public finances. The programme for government of the new coalition stated: 'The Government is committed to keeping a firm control of the public finances, maintaining a stable exchange rate, giving first priority to long-term unemployment, and providing substantial tax relief targeted to the lower paid and families.'

The document arose from the compromises agreed between the three participating parties in their government formation negotiations at the end of 1994. There was some resistance within Democratic Left. 'I think we have to be wary, and be careful not to lose our policy platform,' John Ryan from Limerick East warned.[43] Leading party figures were, however, aware of the compromises required from participation in a multi-party coalition. 'It is more difficult to maintain the allegiance of idealistically minded people if you have to deal with the greasy till and the compromises of government,' Pat Rabbitte accepted.[44] At the party's annual conference in 1995, De Rossa addressed the reality of being the smallest party in a multi-party coalition: 'Clearly in a coalition government with two other parties, we cannot expect to achieve all of our policy objectives, but nobody can dispute our substantial input into the programme for government or the impressive achievements of our first few months in office.'

In terms of the *A Government of Renewal* document, there were elements in the deal that diverged significantly from Democratic Left's policy, including acceptance of the Maastricht Treaty's public borrowing and expenditure limits, a reversal of the 1994 extension of the residential property tax and a pledge to sell state assets (although only minority stakes, which indicates a compromise between the three parties). There was also fudge on abortion, where Fine Gael and Democratic Left had different policies. The section on the so-called substantive issue was left sufficiently non-specific: 'Legislation on abortion information will be introduced shortly and work on the substantive issue by the "X-case" will continue,' the 1994 document stated. John Bruton, however, subsequently said he did not support legislating for the controversial 'X-case' judgement.[45] Numerous pledges in the document, however, coincided with Democratic Left policy, including a commitment to worker enterprise participation, the revitalisation of public enterprise, pressing for an EU industrial policy, holding a divorce referendum, as well as Ireland not becoming a member of a military alliance. Democratic Left was also happy with the inclusion of a pledge to promote the idea of a third banking force, extended family planning services and plans for freedom of information legislation. A confidential Democratic Left memo dated 30 January 1995 is revealing about the party's assessment of the priority commitments they had managed to get included in the programme for government. The memo stated: 'There is [sic] a number of areas where the DL's "hand" is clearly identifiable: (a) Equality Payments – in hand at social welfare, (b) Child Benefit, and Supplement – ditto, (c) Service Charges – tax allowance a budgetary matter …'[46]

When the Rainbow coalition was agreed, Proinsias De Rossa opted to become Minister for Social Welfare. The portfolio allowed him to target several key priorities which his party had stressed since its foundation and which Democratic Left members had also argued for inclusion in the programme for government. The main social welfare

elements in the programme for government document included a
pledge to restructure the child benefit system with increased payments
and the introduction of a child benefit supplement for all social welfare
recipients as well as low and middle-income families. Other social welfare commitments included enhanced unemployment and disability benefit payments and the integration of tax and social welfare systems. De
Rossa's choice of Social Welfare did not receive universal internal approval. 'Not everyone in Democratic Left was pleased with my choice.
They thought it presented us as a social welfare party ...' De Rossa later
admitted.[47] In an interview for this study, he explained the rationale behind his portfolio choice:

> Social welfare was the one I wanted. First of all it spent something
> like one third of the government budget, so it had enormous
> economic clout with potential for reform. And I felt that if DL
> had a role it was to demonstrate that you could in fact deliver a
> quality of life for people who were not at the top of the pile. So I
> felt there was a good role there for us.[48]

The intention was to re-focus the department's agenda increasingly
towards employment creation for those who had been out of work and
to target increases in child benefit payments. Long-time Democratic
Left member Rosheen Callender worked as an advisor with De Rossa
during the lifetime of the Rainbow government.

> We raised the status of the social agenda. We had a lot of dealings
> with Richard Bruton who was in [the Department of] Enterprise
> and Employment. There would have been much less contact
> before between those two departments [Bruton's and De Rossa's]
> but we saw them as two departments that should be working
> much more closely together in terms of various job creation
> schemes to get people off social welfare and into work. I think
> that was quite a major contribution ... and we brought that to
> government in a way that hadn't been done before.[49]

The new coalition delivered its first budget in February 1995. There
was sharp opposition criticism at the decision to target resources to
increase child benefit over other areas in the social welfare brief. Fianna Fáil tabled a private members motion criticising the government
for 'its uncaring attitude towards social welfare recipients, especially

the old'. Democratic Left hit back, pointing out that the public reaction to the budget in an *Irish Times* opinion poll had been positive. The budget measure, regarded as most positive (by 25 per cent), was the increased child benefit payment, 'the cornerstone of Proinsias De Rossa's social welfare proposals'.[50] Moreover, 54 per cent of those surveyed expressed satisfaction with the Democratic Left leader's performance, albeit after only three months in office.

When asked to identify the achievements of Democratic Left in government, all of those interviewed for this study mentioned the first national anti-poverty strategy which aimed to 'reduce, or ideally eliminate (consistent) poverty' by 2007.[51] Catherine Murphy's assessment was typical. 'I think we made a difference in terms of putting poverty on the agenda.'[52] Proinsias De Rossa recalled this aspect of his tenure as a government minister:

> One of the things I am proudest of was the national anti-poverty strategy which obliged each department to take into account the impact of their policies and decisions on people who were on the margins. We had to introduce it at quite a low level in order to get it through, and one of my regrets is that the government was not re-elected to build on that.[53]

Democratic Left figures were clear about what they wanted from the strategy but they had to convince others in the coalition about the merits of the plan. 'I remember when we were on a plane to Copenhagen that John Bruton was on and [he asked] "what's this anti-poverty strategy?" He was still trying to get his head around it, you know,' Rosheen Callender recalled.[54] Proinsias De Rossa remembered a similar experience with the taoiseach during the Irish presidency of the European Union in the second six months of 1996.

> We were negotiating a new language in the [EU] treaties to allow for poverty programmes and anti-discrimination. We had been sort of battering Bruton's head about poverty and social inclusion and how important they were, and how you couldn't have a modern economy without dealing with them and so forth. And Bruton's going, 'tell me again about this social exclusion?'[55]

There was strong praise for Bruton's willingness to engage with the Democratic Left agenda and for his ability to change his stance if convinced of the merits of a particular policy proposal. 'There was a sort of meeting of minds, not in terms of agreeing but of thinking through, and looking at what works and what doesn't work,' De Rossa said.[56] The new government also promised to make outstanding social welfare payments to married women over a four-year period. The issue had been championed by Democratic Left for several years so there was a certain satisfaction that the party brought resolution with the payment of the outstanding monies.

As mentioned previously, Bruton as taoiseach headed a cabinet which he sought to lead on a consensus basis. But that did not mean there were no differences between the three government parties. There were strains surrounding the separate resignations in controversy of two senior Fine Gael ministers, Hugh Coveney and Michael Lowry. There were also policy disputes involving Democratic Left and the Labour Party over how to deal with long-term unemployment and over an exemption of denominational schools from employment equality legislation. Tensions arose on occasions as there was considerable external pressure on each of the parties to deliver to their respective constituencies. For example, as the first anniversary of the coalition's formation approached in November 1995, Democratic Left's headquarters was occupied by students from the Dublin Institute of Technology protesting about a failure to deal with third level issues. 'Why is Democratic Left, the party that promised us the most, doing the least?' one student leader asked.[57]

The challenges of government confront all political parties irrespective of their ideological positioning. This reality is particularly evident in a coalition government, as an agreed political programme has to be reached before entering office. The parties in a coalition are from the beginning of their term in government confronted with the necessity of compromise and concession. Democratic Left was in this position. As a result, De Rossa and his colleagues had to judge whether or not certain issues were, in effect, 'issues of principle' and, if they were, were they important enough to cause the party to leave office.

Democratic Left had to deal with a number of contentious issues while in government, including water charges and residential property tax. When the Rainbow coalition was formed in late 1994 there was a growing controversy over local government service charges. The new coalition pledged to reform the local service charge system through the introduction of a new tax allowance and an end to the practice of cutting off water supply to those who did not pay the charge. The reforms were planned in conjunction with a review of the funding of the local government system.

Democratic Left was not initially to the fore of the anti-service charge campaign. There was no reference to the subject in the 1992 general election manifesto that, interestingly in light of the subsequent development of the 'green' agenda, included a proposal for an energy tax to promote environmental conservation. The party also published a policy paper on local government in 1994, again with no mention of the service charges issue.[58] John Bruton associated the water charges issue with his Labour Party colleagues in the three-party government:

> My sense was that this narrowed the tax base and I never really favoured narrowing the tax base. I'm in favour of a wide tax base with low rates rather than narrowing it. But it [abolition] seemed inevitable ... the Labour Party in particular wanted it done. They felt that in some way or other that it was important to holding their seats in places like Dublin West, which didn't prove to be the case. I know the DL was in favour of that too but I didn't associate the pressure so much with them ...[59]

Anti-water charges campaigners organised protests outside Democratic Left's annual conferences in 1996 and 1997. Different views in the party about how to address the increasingly controversial issue were heard at these conferences. Ultimately, however, the party joined the lobby seeking an end to service charges. The government eventually brought the controversy to a close by ending the charges in tandem with the abolition of residential property tax, and the introduction of reforms to the local government system.

From a Democratic Left perspective, the two most contentious policy decisions concerned third level fees and corporation taxation. Both issues caused considerable debate within the party. Working in the party's head office – and with exposure to the wider constituency organisation personnel – John Gallagher was conscious of internal feelings:

> It took a couple of months to bed into government and for people to become aware that we could deliver results to people rather than just whinge. As we went on, there were arguments about the need for a separate identity and that we should stand aside from government and take up what I would call Left-wing initiatives,

really that [which] would have been undertaken in an opposition context. To me that was a nonsense, and there would have been meetings when I would have had to deal with those arguments between people who felt 'we are now in government and we implement as much policy as is practical with the agreement', and those who would say, 'we're not the government, we're Democratic Left'.[60]

Despite accepting the wishes of Fine Gael and Labour in the programme for government negotiations, Democratic Left remained unconvinced about the abolition of university/third level fees: 'It can't be done in terms of robbing other areas that need it. Certainly not in relation to areas like health or social welfare or other areas of education,' De Rossa said in early 1995.[61] The party argued that free tuition fees would not increase the numbers from lower socio-economic groups getting into third level education. The preference was for higher maintenance grants for students but the two other parties in the Rainbow coalition did not share this view. Despite Fine Gael backing the Labour Party position, John Bruton was also sceptical of the benefits of the policy proposal: 'The free fees decision was one that was pushed by the Labour Party. I don't think it was a good decision myself.'[62] The free fees issue is a good example of how in a coalition governmental arrangement compromises are necessary if the preferences of different parties are to be accommodated. Proinsias De Rossa explained the necessity of compromise:

> University fees I lived with mainly because it was a Labour Party proposal and it is like a lot of things in life – when you're in a group or an organisation, you accept something because the others are going to have to accept something from you that they don't want. So there was that kind of give and take. I still think I was right and that the money would have been far better spent and it would have been far better to lower the [qualification] threshold for [third level] grants and to pump a lot of money into primary education.[63]

Along with the free fees issue, a proposal to reduce the corporation tax rate was the other problematic policy which caused serious internal problems within Democratic Left. The idea of introducing a single 12.5 per cent corporation tax rate had won the backing of Fine Gael and Labour. Democratic Left ministers were prepared to back the move, as De Rossa recalled:

It seemed to me having listened to the arguments that there wasn't an issue of principle involved. There was no proposal to do away with corporation tax. In fact as far as I was concerned it was a proposal which would bring in more tax, applied in a more strict way, with less exclusions and so on. So it seemed to me to make more sense.[64]

But some senior Democratic Left figures had reservations. Paul Sweeney argued very strongly against the change. He believed the proposal came as close as any other subject to threatening the stability of the Rainbow government.

The big issue where we nearly pulled out was on corporation tax. They told us they were going to reduce corporation tax. I was livid. I remember an executive meeting at party headquarters in Abbey Street. It was very tense. Bad language was used. I was personally abused, quite strongly. I just couldn't believe that they pulled this out of the hat. I knew that if I pushed it I would have had the majority but I was assured that they would keep the 25 per cent rate for the banks [but] I didn't think they would ...[65]

The 12.5 per cent rate was eventually agreed by the government. Rosheen Callender was fully aware of the difficulties the issue had created.

It caused angst for some people. Some of my very close union colleagues were very annoyed with us for going along with that but on balance we were persuaded that this would be, overall, beneficial to the economy and rightly or wrongly went along with it. Fine Gael were very anxious about it, and obviously I did a lot of thinking and toing and froing with other advisors, and in the end my advice was different to some of the other economists in the party.[66]

The debate on corporation tax rates raises relevant issues about the distinctiveness of the Democratic Left policy agenda. The party was by that stage in 1996 far removed from the type of radical Left party described in Chapter 1, and a drift towards the moderate centre was possibly inevitable. The term in government also produced a dramatic change in Democratic Left's policy on foreign affairs. When the party was founded in 1992 the position was very firm: 'radical review of global security is urgently required. Ireland must develop a "positive neutrality" as distinct from traditional neutrality to promote a global collective security system, nuclear disarmament, outlawing of chemical and biological weapons and dissolution of military blocks such as NATO.'

The end of the Cold War and the conflict in the former Yugoslavia renewed the debate among European Union member states about collective foreign policy and military alliances. A government white paper on foreign policy published in 1995 reaffirmed a commitment to Irish neutrality, but there was a new willingness to participate in international peacekeeping. Democratic Left was open to the idea of collective security under the authority of the United Nations. 'Neither I nor Democratic Left are opposed to the principle of a shared European policy on foreign affairs and security, based on mutual respect and political co-operation,' Des Geraghty argued.[67] The alternative, described by Democratic Left as a 'European Peace Making Policy', would have been built on mediation, humanitarian aid and an early warning system to prevent conflicts escalating.

The party's policy was, however, fundamentally changed at the 1997 annual conference. De Rossa reasserted opposition to Irish membership of military alliances such as NATO or the West European Union. He also rejected participation in the NATO-led Partnership for Peace grouping. 'Our party position is that it is only under the auspices of the UN that Ireland ought to commit her military forces in the causes of peacekeeping,' De Rossa stated. But in agreeing a policy backed by Fine Gael and the Labour Party, De Rossa also said Irish troops should participate in a UN-backed peace-keeping mission in Bosnia under NATO command: 'This is a test for us as a Party. We can dodge the issue or grasp the nettle.' A newspaper report noted, 'There was scattered applause for Mr De Rossa's appeal.'[68]

Keeping members applauding has long been a difficulty for political parties in power. Government is a challenge for all political parties, especially in maintaining the link with party members and party structures as the demands of office consumes ministers and their advisors. Democratic Left was not unique in this regard, but as a small party the constraints and pressures were obviously increased. Rosheen Callender acknowledged these pressures.

> When you take something to government, it's a government decision. It's not a DL, or a Fine Gael or a Labour decision. So in a sense that was a downside for us as a party ... A lot of good ideas

were coming from us but we didn't get credit for them. There was a certain etiquette about these things that you just have to conform to, and you can't go around disclaiming things you didn't like – claiming all the good stuff was yours. That certainly was a problem relating back the party. There would be a lot of difficulty just physically finding the time to report back after every cabinet meeting, or even explaining in great detail why you'd gone along with this or that. It was very, very difficult to handle that side of things.[69]

On the subject of internal communications, Tony Heffernan observed: 'You can't go with every single cabinet decision to the [party] executive, or anything like that.' He argued that, compared to the open divisions which existed previously within the Labour Party over its role in government, Democratic Left did well:

There was a fair degree of reporting back and liaison. Inevitably at party conferences there was a certain amount of complaint but there was never any challenge to the principle that we should be in government or never any demand to get out of government in the way you would have had at every Labour Party conference, say, during the 1980s.[70]

Internal party discipline was strong – perhaps a legacy of the old Workers' Party's organisational approach. Like Heffernan, Eamon Gilmore also offered a similar recollection of how the party coped with the demands of government.

We never had a problem at a party executive meeting or party conference where there was a rebellion about some major issue. And we didn't have, to my recollection, party councillors or party activists coming out attacking the party. It was done in government and by and large we had very loyal support from the party membership.[71]

Another challenge faced by Democratic Left was maintaining contact between its elected representatives. Government is a busy place, with ministers confronted with heavy work schedules and full diaries. 'One thing I instituted was that we would have a ministers' lunch once a month, just the four of us, because we were so disconnected,' Liz McManus recalled.[72] Ironically, the relative smallness of the party only augmented the problems which were even more difficult for the party's two TDs who were not office-holders. 'I must say being a backbencher in government is difficult,' Byrne admitted.[73] Across those interviewed for this study there was universal acknowledgement of the particular challenges faced by Eric Byrne and Kathleen Lynch. Both politicians were not only newly elected deputies, having been successful in by-elections held just prior to the coalition being formed, but they were also the only backbenchers among the six TDs in the party.

Efforts were made to maintain communication channels between party colleagues but there were difficulties between ministers and backbenchers. At the party's 1995 annual conference, De Rossa acknowledged the role which his two backbench colleagues were playing in the governmental arrangement: 'Eric and Kathleen ensure that the sharpness of Democratic Left politics is kept honed.' As part of the Democratic Left strategy to create some space between party and coalition, Byrne and Lynch were often used as public spokespersons on contentious governmental issues. Kathleen Lynch recalled one episode concerning controversial legislation, proposed by the equality and law reform minister, Mervyn Taylor of the Labour Party. The anti-discrimination legislation left open the possibility that religious organisations controlling educational institutions would be able to discriminate against certain groups, including unmarried women.

> I went into the [Oireachtas] committee and I sat there, and you know the way the Minister comes in and introduces the bill, and then the chair goes around looking for speakers. I put my hand up and I said, 'Chair, I am very sorry to have to tell you that we will not be supporting this Bill.' I mean here we are, the party is in government, the government is producing this Bill and I'm in there telling them that we won't be supporting the Bill, and here are the reasons why. I will never forget the look of shock on the man's face. He was totally and completely gobsmacked. And, of course, everything was withdrawn ...[74]

There were also internal party tensions. 'There were rows between Kathleen Lynch and De Rossa. We were bringing in a 3.5 per cent increase in social welfare payments. It was very low. A lot of stuff was embarrassing for us. It was very hard to take the negative criticism when you know that the criticism was essentially right. It was a miserable old increase,' Eric Byrne said.[75] For her part, Kathleen Lynch recalled meeting her ministerial colleagues when, 'we had terrible rows ... Not that we did not actually agree because we did all think along the same lines.

[But] the rows were rows about presentation, never rows about core issues.'[76] Lynch also accepted that 'it's difficult for ministers in government to publicly promote the party, so myself and Eric became spokespersons on everything. We had to cover every committee meeting.'[77]

THE DE ROSSA–BRUTON RELATIONSHIP

Proinsias De Rossa's transition from republican activist and anti-establishment politician to government minister was best exemplified by his relationship with Fine Gael leader John Bruton during the 1994–7 Rainbow coalition. There had been difficulties in Fine Gael in 1992 when the Labour Party suggested the idea of a coalition involving Democratic Left. The arrangement was not successful at that time but once the Fianna Fáil–Labour Party coalition was formed Bruton initiated regular lunch meetings with De Rossa (and with Mary Harney, the new leader of the Progressive Democrats).

> It was principally for relationship building, and it worked really very well in so far as it broke down the sort of barriers that might have existed, at least in the minds of the leaders about the other people involved, and in particular, I came to trust Proinsias De Rossa very much.[78]

The collapse of the Fianna Fáil–Labour coalition in late 1994 coupled with by-election results that same year meant Bruton was presented with an opportunity to form an alternative government. Despite the shift in Bruton's stance, there was still some resistance within Fine Gael to sharing power with De Rossa and his colleagues. The Democratic Left leader was aware that his past made him unappealing to some in Fine Gael.

> Pat Rabbitte probably did a job of persuading Bruton in terms of coming on board because inevitably going into government with people he perceived to be IRA men must have caused some [unease], and I am sure there were people in Fine Gael who were saying, you know, 'they're unclean, don't touch them.'[79]

De Rossa may have been conscious of his past involvement, especially as he had seen how the subject had been raised in 1992, but it seemed that such views were a minority in Fine Gael by late 1994. Moreover, Bruton saw differences from two years previously:

I didn't think it was a problem as this was not a proposed pre-election alliance. This was a coming together of three parties to solve a political problem that had arisen due to the collapse of a government less than half way through a Dáil in circumstances where people didn't want another general election. And in those circumstances, Fine Gael was willing to be more practical ...[80]

In a confused political environment arising from the collapse of the Fianna Fáil–Labour government, each of the three parties moving to form an alternative coalition had a vested interest in agreeing a deal and then working to make the government succeed, as De Rossa explained:

There were consequences of the way in which Labour had pulled out of the government with Fianna Fáil. Labour had previously pulled out of a Fine Gael [led] government. So Labour needed to prove that it could take a government to full term. The DL needed to prove that it was capable of being in government and, I think as Rabbitte said, of being able to hold their knives and forks at the table. He was always a good man for the phrase but it was real ... Bruton also needed to prove that he could keep a government together.[81]

There were very different relationships between the three party leaders. Bruton and Spring had served in the 1982–7 Garret FitzGerald-led coalition. Set against a depressed economic backdrop with Bruton favouring significant expenditure cutbacks, the experience had not been a good one, and poor relations existed between the two men. Relations were also somewhat tense between De Rossa and Spring. The fact that they led competing parties was an obvious source of friction. De Rossa admitted that Spring had a 'particularly spiky personality' – but there were other reasons for a none too close relationship:

As a minister I'm far more likely to have a relationship with the taoiseach than with the tánaiste in terms of day-to-day business. I had a much more working relationship with Ruairi Quinn as minister for finance than with Dick Spring who was minister for foreign affairs. So it was a different kind of relationship. By dint of his job he spent a lot of time out of the country. So it wasn't a personal thing.[82]

The strong, positive relationship between the leaders of Fine Gael and Democratic Left was obvious to Ruairi Quinn of the Labour Party:

'Bruton and De Rossa were very comfortable with each other. Spring was still suspicious and still reserved.'[83] Pat Rabbitte was surprised at the good relationship. 'It was very odd, a rancher from County Meath who previously had shown a very conservative disposition, and an inner city radical. It was very peculiar.'[84] There are differing views to explain the good relations between the two men. 'Bruton certainly trusted De Rossa as a straight player, and that made an awful lot of difference ...' was Des Geraghty's assessment.[85] Pat Rabbitte added:

> I think their like-mindedness on Northern Ireland was probably a factor. And Bruton changed his views as he progressed in life and in politics. By the time he finished in that government he was quite a convinced social democrat and he had come from a very conservative position. I think he found De Rossa honourable in that dealings entered into were kept.[86]

De Rossa saw the Fine Gael leader as a conservative politician but admitted, 'for all of Bruton's instincts as a big farmer he is a highly intelligent man.' There was strong respect at play:

> We did have a good working relationship because we treated each other as equals – not that I was equal to the taoiseach – but he was a party leader and I was a party leader. I was a key part of the government even though we weren't large in numbers but the government couldn't have existed without us. So, you know, John Bruton made it clear from day one that he wanted the government to work, and he would do whatever within reason needed to make it work, and I made exactly the same point. I said [to Bruton], 'Look I intend to stay here until the end of the term. If this government breaks up it is going to break up because we, the three of us [party leaders] agree it is going to.'[87]

From an initial position of personal distance and political antagonism Bruton came to admire and respect his Democratic Left counterpart:

> I remember having lots of conversations with Proinsias De Rossa. Of course there were things on which we profoundly disagreed like abortion but I found his method of discussion was one that was very easy for me to enter into. I knew if I said something to Proinsias he mightn't answer me there and then, but he would go away and think about it.[88]

Notwithstanding their respective personal relationships, the three party leaders quickly agreed orderly working rules to progress the agenda of the coalition government. De Rossa recalled: 'We put in place a system of managers [advisors] and also a system of Bruton, Spring and myself meeting to iron out issues and difficulties.'[89] Bruton explained the working structure:

> Contentious issues didn't reach the cabinet table. There was a meeting of the three party leaders an hour before the cabinet meeting and we looked at the agenda, and if we thought that one of those issues was going to be problematic, basically we decided that we wouldn't take the issue. And I would announce at the beginning of the meeting that the item was not being discussed today as we're not ready. It took the heat out of cabinet meetings. It meant that we worked managerially rather than politically ...[90]

The relationship between the three party leaders in the government, and, in particular, the unlikely alliance between Bruton and De Rossa, did cause some resentment, as Pat Rabbitte explained.

> There was the extraordinarily, unexpected good personal relationship between De Rossa and Bruton. It was a catalyst for conflict resolution ... I would have often complained privately that the pre-cabinet meetings between the three party leaders was sometimes not all that desirable because they would come into cabinet, and when you would pick up the file, that some awkward problem had been resolved and you as a member around the cabinet table didn't know exactly on what basis it was resolved but you were expected to go along with it.[91]

De Rossa, however, rejected this viewpoint. He saw the cross-government programme manager advisorial system as central to progressing the agreed programme of government and meetings of the three-party leader as a forum for resolving problems.

> I disagree [with Pat Rabbitte] because first of all Spring and Bruton had the experience of the 1980s where issues were brought to cabinet meetings and they spent weeks debating them. There was no way I was going to get involved in a process like that, which would be crazy. The idea of the programme managers and

political advisors was that each party and each minister would have an input into discussion through their political advisors on every issue. Not just on the issues that related to their own department. One presumed that the programme managers were tick-tacking with their bosses. Those discussions could go on for weeks, even months, and when they came to a point where they could be presented to cabinet, where there was a consensus, then they came to cabinet. There still might be issues that people wanted to clarify [and] that could be done at cabinet. But where there were obstacles, where there were points which they couldn't reach agreement it would be kicked up to myself, Spring and Bruton to find a solution. And sometimes we did and sometimes we didn't.[92]

An important lesson De Rossa learnt from his participation in the Rainbow coalition is worthy of comment, especially as it reflects on the role of the smaller party in coalition arrangements. Bruton as taoiseach was based in Government Buildings in Merrion Street in Dublin. Spring as minister for foreign affairs was based in his department's offices in Iveagh House on St Stephen's Green. But Spring also had offices and staff based in Government Buildings in what was described as the Office of the Tánaiste which had been created by the Fianna Fáil–Labour coalition in 1992. Spring's presence in Government Buildings was maintained after the three-party Rainbow coalition was agreed in 1994. De Rossa as minister for social welfare had his department offices at Hawkins House on the other side of the Liffey river. That was where his political and advisorial staff were located. The Democratic Left leader had no physical presence in Government Buildings.

I think in retrospect I should have had. I talked to the people in the department about moving but there was no great desire for that. I probably should have found a solution but I didn't. Proximity is extremely important. In order for me to meet Bruton I would have to ring up and make an appointment, and then go over. Whereas if I had had an office on the same floor or whatever [in Government Buildings] there would have been no problem to just nip down and have a coffee. Also there was no [television] feed from the Dáil to my offices [Hawkins House] so you had to go to the offices in Leinster House to see what was going on. So you're out of the loop. And Spring and Bruton were in Government Buildings, passing each other in the corridor, which is important, and also bumping into civil servants, which is also important.[93]

RECORD IN GOVERNMENT

There was inevitably a learning curve for Democratic Left in terms of participation in government. After all, its leading figures had spent all of their political lives on the opposition benches. Given how the government had been formed mid-way through the life of a Dáil term, the party was also faced with a truncated period in office. Catherine Murphy identified a certain lack of experience as undermining the party's impact:

> In retrospect, we should have been a little bit more pragmatic about getting stuff delivered. For example, I remember De Rossa was very keen to tackle the issue of child poverty and to get the whole national anti-poverty strategy put in place. But people didn't understand that detail. There would have been a sizable increase in child benefit but it was at the expense of other things, and it left us open ... If you had five years you could have done it ...[94]

At the party's 1997 annual conference – only weeks before that year's general election – De Rossa focused on the achievements from being in power:

> In government, Democratic Left did what we always said it was possible to do. We achieved economic growth and unprecedented job creation. We welcomed emigrants home and created work for our young people. At the same time we improved social protection, reformed the public service and made a real impact on poverty and in the battle against drug abuse and crime.[95]

Under the heading 'Democratic Left in Government' in the same speech, De Rossa listed the party's achievements as including:

- Unemployment at its lowest level in six years;
- Nearly IR£600m (approx. €762m) in extra support for pensioners, children, families and the unemployed;
- Publication of the National Anti-Poverty Strategy;
- Equality arrears of IR£260m (approx. €330m) paid to 70,000 married women.

He also mentioned the introduction of divorce, the anti-drugs strategy and tax reform. A party document produced for the 1997 general election campaign identified achievements in government as putting priority on long-term unemployment and poverty, the payments of the equality arrears, making all social welfare schemes more work-friendly, ending water charges and increased resources for programmes to reduce illegal drug demands.[96] The party had to accept some policies that they did not favour, including the aforementioned ending of third level fees. Ironically, despite opposing what the party considered an incorrect policy decision, in the 1997 general election Democratic Left listed the removal of university tuition fees as an achievement from its period in office.

Among those interviewed for this study, including the four Democratic Left ministerial holders, there remains a strong sense of achievement from their term in office, although there was acceptance of the downside of participation in government for a small political party. Tony Heffernan observed, 'We were lucky that the people we had in the four office holders were people of exceptional ability who attracted a certain amount of good publicity, and to tell you the truth we used Kathleen Lynch and Eric Byrne to go out and moan when we wanted to moan and so on.'[97] He added, 'We certainly delivered on a number of things that we said we would such as the abolition of water charges and the social welfare arrears.'[98] Rosheen Callender also spoke of a sense of accomplishment at what Democratic Left had achieved.

> The contribution of policies that were fairly sharp and clear on the North, on social policy issues, on taxation, the national anti-poverty ... [but] what comes out of one particular government, a coalition government, you can't say, 'well, this was ours and that was ours'. But I would flag those as the main achievements ...[99]

Liz McManus said she had two priorities as a minister of state:

> One was homelessness and we developed a homelessness initiative. The other was legislation relating to travellers and unfortunately we didn't stay long enough in government to see it [passed into law] but Bobby Molloy [PD politician] came in and fair dues to him he introduced it.[100]

According to McManus, the party's role in government was marked out by 'the fact that a radical Left party came into government [and] had a pretty effective influence in government which far outweighed its size'.[101] This view was shared by other party members despite the downsides that government ultimately had for Democratic Left itself. 'We did a good deal for the size of the party ... We achieved a lot and that is why I believe it was the right thing to go into government. But in a way it was burying ourselves as well because we became indistinguishable from the other two parties,' Paul Sweeney concluded.[102]

This blurring of difference was discussed at the 1996 annual conference when a motion was tabled to commit the party to campaign solely on its own policy programme at the following year's general election. The motion from the Dublin South Central organisation was supported by the constituency's TD Eric Byrne who said while people had heard of Democratic Left, 'the problem, we feel, is that we have not yet managed to convey to the larger electorate our programme of a radical, distinctive socialist party.' Eamon Gilmore was among those opposing the motion, which was amended to give the national executive the authority to make 'tactical decisions' about electoral pacts in consultation with local constituencies.[103]

The three coalition partners ultimately agreed to contest the 1997 general election on a joint programme, although each party also produced a separate policy manifesto. 'Democratic Left is part of a good Government that has worked. So why change a winning team. Help us to continue that good work over the full five years of the next Dáil,' a Democratic Left document stated.[104] As is discussed below, going into the 1997 general election the party moderated some of its policies to account for the views of its coalition partners. A list of ten policy priorities was prepared. They included job creation, tackling crime, tax reductions aimed at the lower paid, introduction of a minimum wage, free health care for the young and the old, education resources targeted at pre-school and primary level, a green audit of key industries and a focus on urban traffic congestion.

'We're confident going into this election that DL will increase its representation in the Dáil. And we're equally confident that the Government will be returned to office on its record of achievements since 1994,' Tony Heffernan predicted ahead of the election campaign.[105] There were reasons for confidence. The Irish economy had improved significantly. The party's election manifesto noted that 'Ireland has become the Celtic Tiger Economy, with the best economic performance of any European country and much better than virtually any country in the world since Democratic Left went into government in late 1994.' The economic environment had strengthened sufficiently to lead Eamon Gilmore to believe that electoral success was achievable.

> We thought the government would be re-elected. And the opinion polls showed that that was a very popular government. The approval rating of the government was very, very high right through the campaign. In fact, there was a perception that Fianna Fáil was very poor in opposition and that Bertie Ahern wasn't performing as leader of the opposition.[106]

On the back of this strong economic situation, the early months of 1997 also saw a positive media assessment of Democratic Left's performance. 'By any objective standard, Proinsias De Rossa has done a fine job, prompting some to describe him as the best Social Welfare Minister this country has ever had,' one commentator concluded.[107] The general election, however, saw the three Rainbow parties returned to the opposition benches in Leinster House. The electoral outcome has been discussed previously but, in summary, rather than gaining credit for its role in government, Democratic Left lost seats. The outcome of the 1997 general election raises two questions – why was the Rainbow government not re-elected, and why did Democratic Left not benefit from its period in office? In seeking reasons why the electorate turned against a government presiding over a booming economy, Rosheen Callender referred back to the budget earlier in 1997.

> We met with Ruairi Quinn [minister for finance] and we argued that we needed to go for a big tax break for the lower paid, big increases in the tax-free allowances … it just didn't happen. That last budget was a very cautious budget in my view on the tax side. There were a few good things done on the social welfare side, but it wasn't enough. It wasn't an election budget in the way that Fianna Fáil would have done it.[108]

This opinion is widely held among those associated with the Rainbow coalition, as remarks by John Gallagher exemplify: 'I often wonder if the government and Democratic Left had taken a more ambitious and expansive economic approach, we might have been re-elected.'[109] Pat Rabbitte identified two further issues as contributing to the government's failure to secure re-election, including the timing of the election itself. 'We made a right balls of it in the sense that we could have won the election, I have no doubt about it. The call, as I observed it, was mainly Dick Spring's. I think he had a certain fatalism in his approach. He felt that they [the voters] were waiting for him in the long grass, and he wanted to get it over that summer … but the timing was wrong.'[110] Rabbitte also pointed to the pressure on ministers from the European Union presidency which was held by Ireland from June to December 1996. 'It's an enormous burden on a small country. I would be in Brussels three days a week, be at Baldonnel [Aerodrome] at six in the morning and, you know, come back at midnight … I think that by the time Christmas [of 1996] came the ministers were exhausted.'[111]

The considerable workload associated with the EU presidency undoubtedly placed additional pressure on the government, although going into the campaign itself there was little in the opinion polls to separate the two competing coalition alternatives. But having failed to deliver a populist pre-election budget, the Rainbow parties struggled during the campaign to win voters with their taxation policies. Fianna Fáil and the Progressive Democrats were judged to have won the taxation debate during the election campaign. The two opposition parties were considered in media comment to have had more easily understood policies of cutting tax rates set against the Rainbow's more complicated preference for increases in tax allowances and credits. A combination of these factors led to the parliamentary arithmetic which allowed Fianna Fáil and the Progressive Democrats to form a minority coalition administration with the support of a number of like-minded independent TDs.

CONCLUSION

There is some truth in the cliché about 'events' playing a role in political developments. The collapse of the Fianna Fáil–Labour Party coalition unexpectedly allowed Democratic Left to participate in a multi-party government formed without a general election. The unexpected government negotiations in late 1994 provided an opportunity for Democratic Left to pursue some of its key policies in office. The success or otherwise of the party in getting sufficient elements of its agenda into the programme for government has been examined. As the previous discussion has also shown, the relationship between Proinsias De Rossa and John Bruton was vitally important in maintaining stability in the three-party arrangement. Notwithstanding the internal Democratic Left tensions over corporation taxation in particular, there is little evidence that the smallest party in the government introduced an element of instability into the coalition. If anything, the opposite was the case, with Democratic Left intent on having lasting achievements in defined areas, most particularly in its sole senior ministry in social welfare. The biggest weakness, as Catherine Murphy testified to, may have been to have operated like a government with a full parliamentary term when in fact a general election was required within less than three years.

Small parties face considerable challenges in preserving internal cohesion in a coalition arrangement while preventing their identity being lost in the shadows of larger government partners. In the case of Democratic Left, involvement in government allowed the party a political lifeline in the context of the internal debate about its relevance and future which was underway in 1994. In many respects that initial debate was effectively paused from the time the Rainbow coalition was formed until the outcome of the 1997 general election was known.

Writing in 1995, Richard Sinnott observed that the potential benefits of sharing government with Fine Gael and Labour were twofold for Democratic Left: 'it represented the final step in the incorporation of the onetime revolutionary party into normal democratic politics and, at a more basic level, presented an opportunity to establish the new party's name and image in the minds of the voters.'[112] It could also be argued that participating in a coalition government, particularly one involving the Labour Party, was a signal that Democratic Left was moving a further step closer to its eventual demise. A failure to find a clearly understood political agenda meant the smaller party was struggling – and now in the spotlight of government – to show the electorate a distinctive ideological message that was radically different from that of one of its new coalition partners, the larger Labour Party.

The founders of Democratic Left had been seeking a 'third way' as a radical Left party. By 1997, however, the party was in a bind, still looking in a radical direction but willingly accommodating itself to the reality of coalition politics. 'Democratic Left appears to have made the difficult transition from being an opposition-style party to one of

government: where rhetoric has to be abandoned in favour of realpolitik,'
an editorial in *The Irish Times* observed.[113]

The problem with this transition, however, was the dilution effect it
had on the party's identity. The first draft of the party's 1997 general election manifesto was entitled *The Next Steps: Your Vote for the Socialists in
Government*. By the third draft the wording had been changed to *The
Next Steps: You Can Vote to Make the Future Work*. The party was, in effect, moderating its message. There was also a move to capture a more
middle-class voter. In a memo on the draft manifesto one party advisor
wrote:

> SOME POINTS ON DRAFT NO.7
> Page 1, Introduction
> 'We speak for those who are poor, down on their luck, struggling
> to improve themselves ...' This is very narrow and certainly does
> not reflect the composition of our voters. Should we not say that we
> represent the interests of the great majority of people, but promote
> in particular the interests of those who are poor ... etc.[114]

Alongside these observations, Paul Sweeney's previous point about a
blurring of difference with its coalition partners is strengthened in its
relevance. In agreeing to participate in the Rainbow coalition, Democratic Left was obliged to accept many policies that it would have railed
against from the opposition benches. This was a natural outcome for a
small party involved in a multi-party governmental arrangement. Yet it
only compounded the already uncertain internal view about Democratic Left's own political identity and ideological stance.

NOTES

1. Pat Rabbitte, Memorandum to National Council Members, Re Electoral Strategy, 26 August
   1992.
2. Ibid.
3. 'Democratic Left and Political Strategy', 28 August 1992. Internal DL document, no author
   given.
4. General Council meeting minutes, 5 December 1992.
5. Ibid.
6. R. Kavanagh, *Spring, Summer and Fall: The Rise and Fall of the Labour Party, 1986–1999*
   (Dublin: Blackwater Press, 2001), pp.120–1.
7. Ibid., p.121.
8. F. Finlay, *Snakes and Ladders* (Dublin: New Island, 1999), p.131.
9. *The Sunday Times*, 9 August 1998.
10. Interview with John Bruton, 28 March 2008.
11. Interview with Pat Rabbitte, 9 January 2007.
12. *Sunday Business Post*, 3 January 1993.

13. Interview with Tony Heffernan, 13 September 2006.
14. Interview with Kathleen Lynch, 10 October 2006.
15. Interview with Eric Byrne, 29 August 2006.
16. Interview with Rosheen Callender, 12 September 2006.
17. Interview with Des Geraghty, 9 May 2006.
18. Peter McDermott and Gerard O'Quigley, Proposal for a Strategy Sub-Committee, 4 January 1993.
19. Interview with Des Geraghty, 9 May 2006.
20. Interview with John Bruton, 28 March 2008.
21. Ibid.
22. Interview with John Gallagher, 15 June 2007.
23. Interview with Catherine Murphy, 31 August 2006.
24. Interview with Liz McManus, 18 October 2006.
25. Interview with Catherine Murphy, 31 August 2006.
26. Interview with Eamon Gilmore, 11 September 2006.
27. Interview with Tony Heffernan, 13 September 2006.
28. Interview with Proinsias De Rossa, 7 September 2007.
29. Interview with Eamon Gilmore, 11 September 2006.
30. Interview with Rosheen Callender, 12 September 2006.
31. Interview with Paul Sweeney, 6 September 2006.
32. Interview with Rosheen Callender, 12 September 2006.
33. Interview with Paul Sweeney, 6 September 2006.
34. Interview with Rosheen Callender, 12 September 2006.
35. Interview with John Bruton, 28 March 2008.
36. Interview with Catherine Murphy, 31 August 2006.
37. 'A Government of Renewal, Agreed Programme for Government between Fine Gael, the Labour Party and Democratic Left', December 1994.
38. Interview with Pat Rabbitte, 9 January 2007.
39. Interview with John Bruton, 28 March 2008.
40. Interview with Proinsias De Rossa, 7 September 2007.
41. Interview with Eamon Gilmore, 11 September 2006.
42. E. Delaney, *Accidental Diplomat: My Years in the Irish Foreign Service, 1987–1995* (Dublin: New Island, 2001), p.372.
43. *The Irish Times*, 28 April 1997.
44. Interview with Pat Rabbitte, 9 January 2007.
45. *The Irish Times*, 20 May 1997.
46. Democratic Left memorandum, 'A Government of Renewal: Discussion Notes on DL Priorities', 30 January 1995.
47. *Sunday Tribune*, 19 February 1995.
48. Interview with Proinsias De Rossa, 7 September 2007.
49. Interview with Rosheen Callender, 12 September 2006.
50. Government Information Service, *Public Opinion and the Budget*, 28 February 1995.
51. See http://www.eapn.ie/policy/141 (accessed 9 June 2007).
52. Interview with Catherine Murphy, 31 August 2006.
53. Interview with Proinsias De Rossa, 7 September 2007.
54. Interview with Rosheen Callender, 12 September 2006.
55. Interview with Proinsias De Rossa, 7 September 2007.
56. Ibid.
57. *The Irish Times*, 21 November 1995.
58. Democratic Left, *Local Government Democracy and Development*, 1994.
59. Interview with John Bruton, 28 March 2008.
60. Interview with John Gallagher, 15 June 2007.
61. *Sunday Tribune*, 19 February 1995.
62. Interview with John Bruton, 28 March 2008.
63. Interview with Proinsias De Rossa, 7 September 2007.
64. Ibid.

65. Interview with Paul Sweeney, 6 September 2006.
66. Interview with Rosheen Callender, 12 September 2006.
67. D. Geraghty, 'A Peace Policy for Europe: Constructing a New Model of Security', *Work in Progress: Discussion Journal of Democratic Left* (Dublin: Democratic Left, 1993), p.18.
68. *The Irish Times*, 28 April 1997.
69. Interview with Rosheen Callender, 12 September 2006.
70. Interview with Tony Heffernan, 13 September 2006.
71. Interview with Eamon Gilmore, 11 September 2006.
72. Interview with Liz McManus, 18 October 2006.
73. Interview with Eric Byrne, 29 August 2006.
74. Interview with Kathleen Lynch, 10 September 2006.
75. Interview with Eric Byrne, 29 August 2006.
76. Interview with Kathleen Lynch, 10 October 2006.
77. Ibid.
78. Interview with John Bruton, 28 March 2008.
79. Interview with Proinsias De Rossa, 7 September 2007.
80. Interview with John Bruton, 28 March 2008.
81. Interview with Proinsias De Rossa, 7 September 2007.
82. Ibid.
83. Interview with Ruairi Quinn, 6 February 2008.
84. Interview with Pat Rabbitte, 9 January 2007.
85. Interview with Des Geraghty, 9 May 2006.
86. Interview with Pat Rabbitte, 9 January 2007.
87. Interview with Proinsias De Rossa, 7 September 2007.
88. Interview with John Bruton, 28 March 2008.
89. Interview with Proinsias De Rossa, 7 September 2007.
90. Interview with John Bruton, 28 March 2008.
91. Interview with Pat Rabbitte, 9 January 2007.
92. Interview with Proinsias De Rossa, 7 September 2007.
93. Ibid.
94. Interview with Catherine Murphy, 31 August 2006.
95. Democratic Left, Proinsias De Rossa's party leader's speech, Annual Conference, 26 April 1997.
96. Democratic Left, *Make the Future Work: Achievements in Government, 1994–97*, May 1997.
97. Interview with Tony Heffernan, 13 September 2006.
98. Ibid.
99. Interview with Rosheen Callender, 12 September 2006.
100. Interview with Liz McManus, 18 October 2006.
101. Ibid.
102. Interview with Paul Sweeney, 6 September 2006.
103. *The Irish Times*, 13 May 1996.
104. Democratic Left, *Stick With a Winning Team*, draft party document, April 1997.
105. *Sunday World*, 29 March 1997.
106. Interview with Eamon Gilmore, 11 September 2006.
107. *Sunday World*, 29 March 1997.
108. Interview with Rosheen Callender, 12 September 2006.
109. Interview with John Gallagher, 15 June 2007.
110. Interview with Pat Rabbitte, 9 January 2007.
111. Ibid.
112. R. Sinnott, *Irish Voters Decide: Voting Behaviour in Elections and Referendums Since 1918* (Manchester: Manchester University Press, 1995), p.60.
113. *The Irish Times*, 28 April 1997.
114. Memo from Pat Brady to Tony Heffernan, undated but most likely May 1997.

7

Policy Positions and Party Agenda

INTRODUCTION

In the aftermath of the 1992 general election Democratic Left established an internal task force to review the party's politics, strategy and organisation. The task force committee recommended that the party 'adopt a set of specific, identifiable "flagship policies"'. It stated that these 'flagship policies' 'would symbolise DL's broader political perspective. They would not in themselves be detailed policy documents but would clearly be backed up by them. To be effective these flagships 'should be imaginatively and aggressively marketed – as a Charter, perhaps – and clearly identify a left agenda'.[1]

The uncertainty about what was understood as the Left in a post-Berlin Wall political world had been an issue for Democratic Left from its foundation. The task force exercise was an attempt to resolve the apparent inability to define clearly what was the Left in the early 1990s. The discussion about 'flagships' is evidence how the party was searching for a new agenda. As has been discussed elsewhere in this study, the challenge was not unique to Democratic Left in Ireland. The convergence of Left and Right in the post-Berlin Wall period posed considerable challenges for parties of the Left, which had seen their ideology overturned and many of their core policy instruments disappear.

Several labels, including Third Way and New Revisionist, have been used to describe this process of ideological transition. The aspiration was to overcome the post-Berlin challenge and to deal with the agenda of economic globalisation so as to offer a coherent policy prescription that was distinctive, and certainly different from social democracy. The fact that social democracy itself was in a state of transformation did not help matters. An early draft of the 1993 Democratic Left task force report recommended that the 'flagship policies' be drawn from a list which included a statutory right to work, basic income, separation of church and state, full employment and a political settlement in Northern Ireland. The idea of 'flagside policies' had a certain attraction, and was seen as having worked for their political opponents. One submission to the task force observed that the Progressive Democrats 'didn't burst on the scene with a plethora of policies. They sold their image on primarily three policies – 25% standard tax rate, privatisation and abolition of the Senate. These three policies put across their anti-social, pro-market populist anti-bureaucratism.'[2]

In the discussion in this chapter the success or otherwise of Democratic Left in carving out a unique political space is examined by grouping some of the 'flagship policies' under three separate headings. These headings are Northern Ireland, the liberal agenda (or social and moral values) and economic policy. These three policy areas have been chosen because they encompass the areas where Democratic Left adopted key stances in the 1992–9 period. Moreover, the main political debates in Irish society in the 1990s were driven by Northern Ireland, the economy and the liberal agenda. The general background to each area is examined, following which the position of the main political parties is outlined. Each separate section concludes with an assessment of the impact made by Democratic Left, and a discussion about what difference the party contributed to policy on Northern Ireland, the liberal agenda and the economy.

PARTY POLICY POSITIONS

The long-term electoral dominance of Fianna Fáil (from 1932 to 2011) was underpinned by that party's cross-class appeal. Fine Gael traditionally had a more middle-class appeal while the Labour Party has in recent times witnessed a blurring of its support base between its traditional working-class voters and newer middle-class voters. Nevertheless, it was still possible in the 1980s to conclude that there was a class base in the support for the Labour Party and the Workers' Party, and – as one study concluded – this was '… especially true of the Workers' Party, whose support among the unskilled working class substantially exceeds its support elsewhere'.[3] Moreover, the Labour Party lost ground to the Workers' Party among working-class voters in the 1980s.

The Labour Party's support in 1992 was equal among middle-class, skilled working-class and unskilled working-class voters.[4] A similar pattern – although at a lower level – was evident in the support for Democratic Left in 1992. The party experienced a significant drop in the support received by the Workers' Party in 1989 from unskilled working voters. The Workers' Party gained its highest vote share at the 1989 general election, but even then that vote was only five per cent of the total poll. The 1989 election results appeared to indicate a shift to the Left but one study concluded that this apparent ideological movement was not 'the result of any upsurge of socialist sentiment ... it was a vote of protest against the general economic situation rather than a demand for fundamentally different policies.'[5]

Peter Mair speculated about the impact the newly strengthened party would have on the Irish political scene. He wrote: '... the presence of the Workers' Party in the Dáil ... constitutes one of the most important new elements in Irish party politics in recent years', as the formation of any non-Fianna Fáil coalition government would in the future be 'very difficult to realise' – in Mair's view – without the involvement of the Workers' Party.[6] There was solid evidence to support Mair's conclusion. The traditional partners in an anti-Fianna Fáil government were Fine Gael and Labour. Their combined parliamentary representation after the 1989 general election totalled seventy seats [FG, 55; Lab, 15], a figure which was fourteen seats short of a clear Dáil majority. The electoral growth of the Workers' Party clearly opened up the possibility that its membership would be needed in a future three-party coalition government involving Fine Gael and Labour.

The reason why voters in Ireland tended to vote across class has traditionally been explained in terms of the lack of difference between the main political parties. Conclusions about the relative sameness of Irish parties may, however, be too simplistic. Several studies were undertaken in the period after the 1987 general election that allow for comment on the ideological positioning of both the Workers' Party and Democratic Left relative to the other parties. These studies show that differences did, in fact, exist between Irish political parties. The Workers' Party certainly stood out from the other parties in Dáil Éireann in that it was more secular, more anti-nationalist and anti-irredentist. It also had past associations that its opponents were not afraid to use for political and electoral gain. Democratic Left obviously emerged from this tradition but the party had a less rigid political and ideological

TABLE 7.1
ESTIMATED POSITION ON KEY POLICY AREAS, 1992 AND 1997

	DL		Labour		FF		FG	
	1992	1997	1992	1997	1992	1997	1992	1997
Economic	4.93	5.47	7.50	7.77	12.29	12.07	14.29	12.30
N. Ireland	11.80	11.81	8.44	8.73	4.71	5.53	10.20	11.03
Social	3.79	4.97	6.79	6.57	16.21	13.55	12.59	10.82
Foreign	n/a	6.62	n/a	10.20	n/a	11.60	n/a	15.47
European	9.43	10.78	14.29	14.53	16.36	14.60	17.96	16.97
FOI	n/a	7.00	n/a	7.90	n/a	13.72	n/a	12.34
Environment	10.59	11.18	10.66	10.97	14.96	13.50	13.52	13.03
Decentralisation	10.81	10.19	9.54	10.32	14.32	13.89	12.39	12.96

	Green		SF		PD	
	1992	1997	1992	1997	1992	1997
Economic	5.96	6.07	4.24	5.56	16.89	17.27
N. Ireland	8.71	9.08	1.04	1.07	10.81	12.29
Social	6.65	6.79	8.39	10.12	3.77	6.93
Foreign	n/a	3.17	n/a	3.83	n/a	15.73
European	7.20	5.97	4.29	6.61	17.89	15.17
FOI	n/a	4.11	n/a	7.17	n/a	7.48
Environment	1.22	1.70	9.83	9.85	12.56	12.97
Decentralisation	3.73	3.79	7.67	8.84	10.69	10.78

Source: M. Laver, 'Party Policy in Ireland, 1997: Results from an Expert Survey', *Irish Political Studies*, vol. 13 (1998).

approach to political life. A series of academic studies located the Workers' Party firmly to the Left of all the other parties. For example, Mair's analysis of the party positions in 1989 – in Sinnott's words – 'portrays the main dimension of party competition as a straightforward left/right socio-economic dimension, with the Workers' Party on one end, the Progressive Democrats on the other, Fine Gael in the centre, Labour left of centre and Fianna Fáil right of centre'.[7]

One approach used to determine what differences exist between the political parties drew on expert assessment where academics and other experts were invited to plot the differences between the parties. The results of expert surveys in 1992 and 1997 provide a useful assessment of Democratic Left's positioning in a number of key policy areas. Experts were asked to use their judgement to position the main parties on each of eight policy scales. Six of the policy scales were used in 1992 and again in 1997: tax cuts versus public services; policy on abortion and homosexuality; environmental policy; the decentralisation of decision-making; policy on Northern Ireland; and policy on the European Union. The 1997 scale included a new heading, namely public access to information. The results displayed in Table 7.1 are based on the average of the scores given by the respondents to the two expert surveys. The data shows the substantive positions that each party was judged to have on each policy dimension according to the expert responses in 1992 and 1997.

Taking each of the main policy areas, the following can be recorded about Democratic Left in the expert studies in which participants were asked to rank parties on a scale of 1 to 20 against the statements given under each heading, where 1 is extreme Left and 20 is extreme Right.

1. Taxes/Economy:
Scale Text: Increase level of public services even if this means increasing taxes (low ranking) *versus* Cut taxes even if this means cutting level of public services (high ranking). Democratic Left scored 4.93 in 1992 and 5.47 in 1997.

Overall, as Michael Laver observed, 'In relation to economic policy, these figures document very well the conventional wisdom of a policy spectrum that runs from the PDs, clearly to the right, through Fianna Fáil and Fine Gael in the centre … through the centre-left position of Labour, to DL, the Greens and Sinn Féin to the Left.'[8] Democratic Left was to the Left of the Labour Party in 1992 and also in 1997, although the margin of difference in the scale result was not significant in either study. Moreover, the results indicate that for Democratic Left there was a slight drift to the Right in the 1992–7 period. This may be attributed to the party's term in government but it cannot be the sole reason as other parties – which were in opposition in this period – including the Green Party and Sinn Féin also moved slightly rightwards. The outcome is not unsurprising given the discussion in Chapter 1 about the emergence of the New Right economic agenda in the 1990s coupled with the uncertainties about what was defined as Left politics. Democratic Left was following a pattern also experienced by other Left parties at that time.

2. Foreign Policy and European Policy:
Scale Text: Promote more distant relationship with North Atlantic Treaty Organisation (NATO) and West European Union (WEU) (low) *versus* Promote closer relationship with NATO and WEU (high). Democratic Left scored 6.62 in 1997.

Scale Text: Oppose more integration with European Union (low) *versus* Promote more integration with European Union (high). Democratic Left scored 10.78 in 1997 and 9.43 in 1992.

The results gave the party a greater anti-establishment foreign policy position than the Labour Party (10.20) but less radical than Sinn Féin (3.83) and the Green Party (3.17). While there are no comparable figures in the 1992 expert survey for foreign policy, the 1997 results came after a period in which the former Workers' Party members steered their new formation in the direction of a more positive attitude to the European Union while maintaining their traditional view of international military alliances. The results indicate that a more benign attitude towards the European Union developed between 1992 and 1997. Democratic Left was still some way behind the Labour Party (14.53 in 1997) in its attitude to the EU but there was a clear distance from the stance of the Green Party (5.97 in 1997) and Sinn Féin (6.61 in 1997). The latter figures led Laver to assert that 'European and foreign policy essentially put all of the establishment parties against Sinn Féin and the Greens.'[9] The fact that Laver included Democratic Left with the three main parties in Dáil Éireann is indicative of a view about the leaning of De Rossa's party at that time. This conclusion fits with the previous discussion about the lack of a 'radical' nature to Democratic Left's politics.

3. Environment, Decentralisation and Freedom of Information:
Scale Text: Promote environmental protection, even if this slows economic growth (low) *versus* Promote economic growth, even if it damages the environment (high). Democratic Left scored 10.59 in 1992 and 11.18 in 1997.

Scale Text: Promote decentralisation of all decision-making (low) *versus* Oppose decentralisation of all decision-making (high). Democratic Left scored 10.81 in 1992 and 10.19 in 1997.

Scale Text: Promote policies increasing public access to information (low) *versus* Oppose policies increasing public access to information (high). Democratic Left scored 7.00 in 1997 with no comparable data generated in the 1992 expert survey.

In examining the data, Laver observed that 'Sinn Féin, DL, Labour and the PDs all have very similar centrist positions on these issues.'[10] The Green Party clearly emerged with a distinctive policy position on environmental matters, which is probably not unsurprising. In the case of Democratic Left, however – given the inclusion of ecological values as a priority in the party's constitution in 1992 – there should have been some disappointment that its recorded score (11.18 in 1997) did not show any distinctiveness from the other main parties. Indeed the main parties were bunched with relatively similar centrist results on environmental policy, and, once more, Democratic Left was seen to have failed to create an individual niche. The party's estimated policy position on decentralisation in 1997 was very similar to that of the Labour Party (10.19 against 10.32), while on freedom of information there was also little difference in 1997 (7.00 against 7.90). These results are interesting in light of the debate in Democratic Left about its political future, which deepened after the 1997 general election and which is discussed in subsequent chapters.

4. Social Values:
Scale text: Promote more liberal policies on abortion and homosexuality (low) *versus* Promote more restrictive policies on abortion and homosexuality (high). Democratic Left recorded 3.79 in 1992 and 4.97 in 1997.

Democratic Left emerged with a distinctive policy position on social/moral issues in both expert studies. However, the ability of the party to capitalise on this liberal stance lessened in the 1990s, as Laver explained: 'in the wake of the string of controversial referendums on moral issues that culminated in the 1995 divorce referendum, not only is the social and moral dimension declining in importance, according to the expert survey, but it is polarising Irish parties less than it once did.'[11] As the discussion which follows argues, in seeking to create a distinctive public position Democratic Left was in a way unfortunate that its main point of difference – social and moral issues – was increasingly resolved in the 1990s. The party could claim some credit for this achievement – its policy statements at the 1992 founding conference were distinctively liberal, while it was in government for the successful 1996 divorce referendum. But the party failed to stress other areas of distinctive policy difference such as grabbing hold of the emerging environmental agenda or identifying more clearly with 'new' issues such as freedom of information.

5. Northern Ireland:
Scale Text: Oppose permanent British presence in Northern Ireland (low) *versus* Defend British presence in Northern Ireland (high). Democratic Left 11.80 in 1992 and 11.81 in 1997.

Policy on Northern Ireland provided wide variation in estimated party positions according to the respondents in the two studies, with Sinn Féin holding a strong anti-British stance. Democratic Left recorded the result with the highest pro-British score and on this policy area there was a significant gap with the Labour Party (11.81 against 8.73, both in 1997).

These expert studies placed Democratic Left on the opposite end of the spectrum to the Progressive Democrats on public services and reductions in taxation while showing the party positioned at the polar extreme to Sinn Féin on policy on Northern Ireland as well as being the most liberal party on social issues like abortion and homosexuality. Overall, there is evidence of a general stability in the party's policy positions between 1992 and 1997, although there was slight movement towards more 'establishment' positions. This latter fact was, however, true of nearly all the parties in this period. Compared to the Labour Party, Democratic Left took a harder line on foreign and EU matters, was more pro-British, more-liberal and more Left-leaning on economic matters. But – and this is an important conclusion in light of decisions taken about the party's future post-the 1997 general election – the differences were not so great as to conclude that there were distinctive policy positions between Democratic Left and the Labour Party. Once more, the analysis is brought back to the failure of Democratic Left to define itself in clearly understood policy terms on the Left and the possibility that there was no real room on the political spectrum for the party. These issues are treated in greater detail in subsequent discussions in terms of Northern Ireland, the economy and liberal/social issues.

NORTHERN IRELAND, 1992–9

The modern conflict in Northern Ireland was into its third decade when Democratic Left was formed in 1992. The death toll had by the end of 1991 reached 3,271 with many thousands more injured. The Provisional IRA had, as discussed previously, been formed out of a split in the republican movement which also gave birth to the Officials, the group from which Democratic Left eventually emerged. In 1992 there was little public evidence that the Provisional IRA was considering an end to its campaign, or that an accommodation could be reached between the communities in Northern Ireland.

Set against this backdrop of ongoing paramilitary violence, there was little room for confidence about the situation in Northern Ireland. The official policy of the British and Irish governments – as well as all the main political parties in both jurisdictions – was one of marginalisation of the political representatives of the republican movement. Sinn Féin politicians were denied access to the airwaves in Ireland and the UK while the party was excluded from all initiatives seeking to establish a normal society in Northern Ireland. In the three years before Democratic Left was founded, talks had been ongoing between politicians from Northern Ireland's four constitutional parties and representatives of the British and Irish governments. Those talks were divided into the three strands that would continue as the framework for later discussions – strand one concerned the internal affairs of Northern Ireland; strand two the relationship between Northern Ireland and the Irish Republic; and strand three British–Irish relations.

The talks – sponsored by Northern Ireland secretary Peter Brooke and his successor, Patrick Mayhew – ended without success in November 1992. 'After two years and at a cost of IR£5m [approx. €6.35m], the talks have served only to emphasise the seemingly irreconcilable differences between nationalism and unionism,' Bew and Gillespie concluded.[12] Sinn Féin had not been invited to participate in the talks process in the absence of an IRA ceasefire. There were, however, hints at possible movement. A close associate of Gerry Adams – Jim Gibney – told a republican gathering in June 1992: 'We know and accept that the British government's departure [from Ireland] must be preceded by a sustained period of peace and will arise out of negotiations [involving] the different shades of Irish nationalism and Irish unionism.'[13] Bew and Gillespie observed that the Gibney statement 'encourages the belief in some quarters that Sinn Féin and the IRA might be moving towards calling off the campaign of violence'.[14]

There were also indications of the possibilities which could emerge if IRA violence was ended. Northern Ireland secretary Patrick Mayhew admitted in December 1992 that Sinn Féin could be included in future talks if the IRA ended its campaign and that British troops could be withdrawn from the streets of Northern Ireland.[15] Those positive sentiments had, however, to be considered against the security situation in Northern Ireland. In 1992 – the year in which Democratic Left was formed – there were 85 deaths arising from the conflict and 207 casualties due to paramilitary activity. But the main participants had, in fact, started the process of engagement. It was not known in 1992 that the British and Irish government had opened up separate, secret communication channels with the republican movement.

There were also contacts between the SDLP and Sinn Féin. John Hume and Gerry Adams met for talks in April 1993 which marked the first official discussions between the two parties in two years. In a joint statement issued in April 1993 they agreed that 'the Irish people as a whole have a right to national self-determination. This is the view shared by the majority of people on this island, though not by all its people. The exercise of self-determination is a matter for agreement between the people of Ireland.'

Hume was hopeful about the benefits from his engagement with Adams. In October 1993 he said the talks provided 'the most hopeful dialogue and the most hopeful chance of lasting peace that I have seen in twenty years'.[16] The SDLP leader received considerable criticism for his talks with Adams. But the situation was altered somewhat in November 1993 when it emerged that the British government had had a secret communication channel with the republican movement over the previous three years. The election of Albert Reynolds as Fianna Fáil leader and as taoiseach in February 1992 also significantly changed the dynamic of what would come to be known as the Irish peace process. Reynolds immediately sanctioned direct confidential face-to-face contacts between Martin Mansergh, his most senior advisor, and republican representatives.

There was a tangible sign of progress when the British and Irish governments published the Downing Street Declaration in December 1993. In the document the two governments pledged to work towards a new political framework in Northern Ireland based on the principle of consent. The British government confirmed that it had no selfish strategic or economic interest in Northern Ireland and accepted that a united Ireland was one of the future options which the people on the island could endorse.

Bew and Gillespie described the Downing Street Declaration as 'a document of considerable originality and sophistication'.[17] It came at the end of 1993 and set up what would be a hugely dramatic period in the history of Northern Ireland. The IRA campaign continued but there was greater engagement between the various participants even if, in public at least, the media was the main platform for communication. There were a number of significant events in the early part of 1994, including the Fianna Fáil–Labour Party coalition ending the broadcasting ban on Sinn Féin representatives in January of that year. In the same month United States president Bill Clinton backed a visa for Gerry Adams against advice from the British government and the US State Department. Speculation about an IRA ceasefire intensified, and on 31 August 1994 the IRA issued a statement that there would be 'a complete cessation of military operations'. The announcement met with very different reactions. Unionist politicians and the British government noted the absence of the word 'permanent'. The Irish government adopted a more positive stance and within days Gerry Adams was invited to meet Albert Reynolds and John Hume at Government Buildings in Dublin. The meeting was public evidence of the so-called 'pan-nationalist front', which annoyed unionist opinion but showed the priority of the Irish government at that time to pull republicans into the democratic system.

The government in Dublin changed before the end of 1994 – and as discussed previously in this study the Fianna Fáil–Labour coalition was replaced by a government involving Fine Gael, Labour and Democratic Left. The significance of this change is explored below in the context of an examination of the policies of the different political parties. The months that followed the August 1994 ceasefire were dominated by discussion about the word 'permanent' and a debate about the timing of decommissioning of the IRA's arsenal of weapons. The British and Irish governments published the Framework Documents in February 1995. The documents contained proposals for the future governance of Northern Ireland and the relationship between Northern Ireland and the Irish Republic. The Irish government pledged to change its constitutional claim over Northern Ireland to reflect the principle of consent. The proposals met with mixed responses from the parties in Northern Ireland. As the months passed the impasse over decommissioning continued, with differing views held about when the issue should be addressed in terms of the opening of all-party talks on the future of Northern Ireland. Sinn Féin repeated its position that the decommissioning of IRA weapons as a precondition to negotiations was not an option. There were obviously different views on the British and unionist sides.

Despite the continuing stalemate, in April 1995 the British government announced that its ministers would open exploratory dialogue with Sinn Féin. An international commission on decommissioning was eventually established to help resolve the issue. In a submission to the arms body Sinn Féin asserted that the IRA might agree to the disposal of weaponry after a political settlement had been agreed and in the context of overall demilitarisation in Northern Ireland. The decommissioning body reported on 24 January 1996. The body – chaired by former US senator George Mitchell – said the paramilitary organisations were committed to decommissioning but not before the start of all-party talks. The report suggested that there might be some decommissioning during the talks process. There were some positive signs in this period, including Sinn Féin and Ulster Unionist politicians appearing together for the first time on the same radio and television programmes. But the situation took a dramatic turn on 9 February 1996 when the IRA issued a statement ending its ceasefire. On the same evening a bomb exploded in Canary Wharf in London killing two men, injuring hundreds and causing almost stg£100 million (approx. €117 million) worth of damage. There was universal condemnation of the action. But significantly the Irish government, in which Democratic Left was a member, kept open contacts with Sinn Féin, with officials continuing to meet Gerry Adams and his colleagues to see how the IRA ceasefire could be restored.

With the renewed IRA campaign focusing on commercial targets in Britain – with numerous bombings in London during 1996 – relations between Sinn Féin and the two governments deteriorated amid accusations and recriminations. The talks process with George Mitchell in the chair commenced in June 1996 without Sinn Féin's involvement. A renewal of the IRA ceasefire was seen by all sides as the minimum requirement for Sinn Féin's participation in the negotiations. The decommissioning issue also remained an obstacle to progress. There was some hope that the impasse could be broken with elections at Westminster in May 1997 and for Dáil Éireann in June 1997. Sinn Féin polled a record 16.1 per cent in the Westminster contest, gaining two extra seats, while the party won its first Dáil seat in modern times in the Irish general election. There was a view in some quarters that the IRA had decided that its ceasefire would not be renewed until the results of the two sets of elections were known. According to one media observer of the process:

> The renewal of the IRA campaign was meant to give a short, sharp shock to the British leading to a rapid restoration of the ceasefire and Sinn Féin's entry to talks, but that was not the way things worked out. It eventually got to the stage where the conditions for restoring the ceasefire included the return of Fianna Fáil to power in Dublin and a Labour victory in Britain.[18]

With the election of Tony Blair as prime minister in London and Bertie Ahern as taoiseach in Dublin the process was given a new injection of optimism. (Democratic Left returned to the opposition benches in Leinster House along with Fine Gael and the Labour Party as Ahern's Fianna Fáil–Progressive Democrat coalition took office.) The new governments published proposals in June 1997 which suggested that decommissioning could take place in parallel with all-party talks. Sinn Féin was informed that a renewal of the IRA ceasefire would see party representatives invited to the talks table within a matter of weeks. On 18 July 1997 the British government published the text of a letter sent to Sinn Féin which stated that the party could participate in the talks process without any IRA decommissioning. The following day the IRA announced the restoration of its ceasefire from midday on 20 July 1997. Sinn Féin then joined the talks process. But when the party arrived at Castle Buildings at Stormont, the Democratic Unionist Party and the UK Unionist Party withdrew in protest. The multi-party talks process formally commenced on 15 September 1997, with all the main political parties in Northern Ireland – with the exception of the Democratic Unionist Party – accepting invitations to attend. The negotiations continued until the early part of 1998 based on the three-stranded structure referred to previously.

The parties eventually reached a deal, and the Belfast Agreement was published on 10 April 1998. The document included plans for a 108-member assembly in Northern Ireland to which power would be devolved over certain policy areas. The new power-sharing institutions would operate on a cross-community basis with checks and balances built into the operation of both the assembly and executive. Cross-border co-operation would operate via a North–South Ministerial Council covering a number of listed areas. A new British–Irish Council was also to be established. The agreement also included provision for measures such as a prisoner release programme, decommissioning of paramilitary arms and policing reforms. The Irish government pledged to amend Articles 2 and 3 of the Irish Constitution. The deal was endorsed by referenda held in Northern Ireland and the Irish Republic on the same day in May 1998. Subsequent developments in the Northern Ireland peace process fall outside the scope of this study as by the end of 1998 Democratic Left had concluded a merger deal with the Labour Party.

Democratic Left inherited its policy on Northern Ireland from the Workers' Party. Not unsurprisingly given its past, this was one area where the Workers' Party had a substantial and nuanced set of policy proposals. 'The positions that the Workers' Party had developed on Northern Ireland were quite progressive,' De Rossa said.[19] The Workers' Party had moved a considerable distance from its origins at the start of the contemporary conflict in Northern Ireland. The policy position was aptly described by Coakley as meaning that 'by the 1980s the Workers' Party rejection of traditional nationalism had become so clear that it was no longer possible to place it on the same category as the other nationalist parties.'[20] This policy formulation – defined by anti-sectarianism and anti-nationalism – was maintained by De Rossa and his supporters after the split. As discussed previously, Democratic Left recorded the result with the highest pro-British score in the expert analysis studies of Irish political parties in 1992 and 1997.

At the Democratic Left founding conference in 1992 there was a detailed explanation of the new party's attitude to Northern Ireland in Section 12 of the adopted constitution. The new party said it stood against the 'rot of fossilised attitudes, political stalemate and a violence that clearly is designed to prevent political or economic progress'. As well as condemnation of violence there was backing for the police force and a call for a Bill of Rights to underpin a new political settlement. The main Northern Ireland elements in the 1992 party constitution were:

- Rejection of those 'who by maintaining the inflexible absolutist politics of nationalism and unionism are making it impossible to create the conditions in which terrorism can be marginalised and defeated'.

- Support for 'the deletion of Articles 2 & 3 ... and to have it replaced by an aspiration to unity only by consent'.

- Call for 'the replacement of the Anglo-Irish Agreement with an accord between Dublin, London and the Northern Ireland parties which takes account of deep-seated unionist fears about the present agreement'.

- Proposal for 'the devolution of substantial powers to new democratic institutions within Northern Ireland'.

These policies were the bedrock of all proposals on Northern Ireland from Democratic Left over the following number of years. Party members were conscious that their stance on Northern Ireland set them apart from the other political parties in the Irish Republic. Liz McManus explained:

> The area that I think we would have had the most radical views, earlier than everybody else, was in relation with Northern Ireland. I think that's really where there was very interesting thinking. We were way ahead and we were there having gone through a lot of shite ourselves so it wasn't as if we didn't know. We had members in Northern Ireland who would have to stand by their beliefs. It was something that was engrained in us.[21]

The three main political parties supported the aspiration of Irish unity and they had varying attitudes to any revision of Articles 2 and 3 of the Irish Constitution. Despite Fianna Fáil's strong attachment, along with Fine Gael and the Labour Party, it was prepared to see amendment as part of an overall settlement. Democratic Left, on the other hand, was willing to see earlier constitutional change, independent of a final settlement. During a Dáil Éireann debate on cross-border co-operation in 1992, De Rossa stated:

It seems to me that so long as we maintain hard-nosed attitudes in relation to Articles 2 and 3 it will be difficult to convince the people of Northern Ireland that there is no hidden agenda ... That issue has to be addressed seriously before we will be able to make substantial progress on cross-Border co-operation.[22]

Democratic Left was very clear about its position. The party's 1992 general election manifesto said that Articles 2 and 3 should be replaced by an aspiration to unity by consent. But the party was not an advocate for Irish unity.

De Valera's nationalism has nothing to offer the Catholic population of Northern Ireland. Their identity and rights can best be effectively ensured through structures of government in which their political representatives participate. It would be much easier to build these structures if parties like Fianna Fáil and the SDLP dropped their emphasis on the need for some grander 32-county 'solution'. Any settlement in Northern Ireland will entail the agreement of the government of this state, and new and imaginative forms of co-operation between the two states are more necessary than ever in a common European context.[23]

In a Dáil speech on Northern Ireland in April 1993 De Rossa attacked those who he claimed were living in the past:

It is a pretence that the removal of the political Border on this island is either feasible or even desirable ... We will never have peace until we accept the reality that the political Border on this island represents a real divide between the people of this island. That divide can only be bridged by tolerant pluralist democratic politics.[24]

In his leader's address at the party's 1993 annual conference, De Rossa called for 'the recognition that Northern Ireland has a right to continue to exist within the United Kingdom'. Four years later, as a government minister he stated, 'We look to new political structures that will permanently free the people of Northern Ireland from the grip of inter-communal division and recurring violence. These structures will not be found in a united Ireland ...'[25] The party's policy was driven by a belief that Northern Ireland was not divided along religious, race or ethnic lines but rather the divisions were based on conflicting national identities.

The core principle underpinning Democratic Left's policy was the belief in the need for equal treatment for nationalist and unionist identities. But Democratic Left – like the Workers' Party – sought to move beyond traditional identity politics. In a parliamentary contribution in 1993, De Rossa asked:

> Is it not time we got away from the sloppy thinking which presumes that every Catholic is a nationalist thirsting for unification with this State? The consistent findings of the Annual Social Studies Attitudes Surveys is that about half of the Catholics in Northern Ireland would not describe themselves as Nationalists.[26]

Democratic Left argued that the emergence of a 'third strand' – neither unionist nor nationalist – could help set a new political agenda. At the publication of a party policy document in September 1994 De Rossa argued that his party belonged to this 'third strand'.[27] The party's stance was consistent during the 1990s:

> Democratic Left's concern is to assist in reaching an accommodation between Ulster unionism and Northern nationalism. At the same time, we also seek the basis for the political expression of other identities and allegiances. Those whose primary allegiance is not defined by national identity – the Third Strand – have a crucial role to play in the development of pluralist political culture.[28]

The party was not convinced that the Anglo-Irish Agreement offered a meaningful contribution as the Irish government's involvement was based on it being the representative of the nationalist community. The 1992 general election manifesto was explicit on this matter:

> We should stop participating in the structures of the Anglo-Irish Agreement as defenders solely of the interests of northern Catholics. This is a sectarian approach and only confirms unionist suspicions of north–south links. Our commitment should be neither Catholic nor Protestant but to doing all we can to foster peace and a democratic political culture. The people of Northern Ireland must decide their own future democratically, free of coercion.[29]

Interestingly, in the negotiating document which Democratic Left sent to the Labour Party after the 1992 general election the language on this matter was toned down somewhat, with a pledge to 'participate in the structures of the Anglo-Irish Agreement in the interests of the whole community ...'[30] Democratic Left approached the nascent Irish peace process with a number of distinct positions. The party criticised the Hume–Adams talks which were made public in 1993. De Rossa expressed his concern that the talks could lead to 'a strengthening of the Provisionals, with a consequent augmentation of the loyalist paramilitaries ...'[31] He had previously been strongly outspoken about Hume. At the Workers' Party Árd Fheis in April 1989 he said, 'We the Workers' Party can assist the South in its slow and shocked reappraisal of John Hume who once had the status of a Saint in the South but is now exposed as another tribal leader whose main asset is that he says tribal things very slowly and very quietly.'[32] As Democratic Left leader, De Rossa accused Hume of a 'monumental error of judgment' and urged him not to have talks with Adams until Sinn Féin unequivocally rejected the IRA's military campaign.[33] In Belfast in May 1993, De Rossa argued:

> I would have hoped that all democrats would accept that it is not possible to achieve political arrangements on Northern Ireland over the heads of one million Unionists and that any attempt to by-pass them is simply a recipe for disaster. Unfortunately, this lesson seems to be lost on John Hume.[34]

Sections of the media were heavily critical of Hume, but no other political party offered such a damning critique of the SDLP leader than Democratic Left. In 1993 De Rossa was also unconvinced about Adams' intentions or his ability to deliver a ceasefire without splitting the republican movement. 'Unless he declares that violence has no place in the republican scheme of things ... then there is little point in hoping against hope.'[35] Some time later he told the Dáil, 'On the basis of my own experience, I suggest that a split in the Republican movement is almost inevitable if any section of them decides that they want a cessation of violence.'[36]

But the Democratic Left leader acknowledged the possibility of change as the situation unfolded in 1994: 'Nobody quite knew where we were going – and I still had reservations about whether the Provos could pull off a ceasefire, prevent a major split and so forth. But nevertheless it was a process that needed to be engaged with.'[37] His own past experience in the republican movement obviously impacted on De Rossa's assessment of the internal dynamic in the leadership group surrounding

Adams. Democratic Left welcomed the IRA ceasefire in August 1994. The party, unlike others, was less hung up on the absence of the word 'permanent' from the IRA ceasefire statement, believing there were reasonable grounds for concluding that that was the intention.

Around this time there was evidence of Democratic Left being imaginative in its response to developments in Northern Ireland. Ahead of the other parties, Democratic Left had at its 1993 conference backed the idea of an early prisoner release programme, an amnesty for those who abandoned military activity and a reduction in the security force presence, including a withdrawal to barracks of British Army troops in areas where a ceasefire existed. De Rossa had also pre-empted the decommissioning debate when, at his party's 1993 annual conference, he proposed 'a 24-hour "free period" initiated without prior publicity in which individuals holding weapons could surrender them without penalty'. He went further in a Dáil debate on the Downing Street Declaration in December 1993:

> We should avoid at the same time setting preconditions about arms or amnesties. The bottom line must be an acceptance by the IRA and Sinn Féin of the Declaration and an unequivocal rejection of violence. There can be no negotiation on this, but if and when that is agreed, other matters can then become a matter for discussion and consultation. It is clear that the question of surrender of weapons will constitute a major problem should a ceasefire be forthcoming. At no stage in Irish history has the IRA ever voluntarily surrendered its arms, yet without the handover of weapons and explosives the prospects of real peace would be remote indeed. There is particular fear in Northern Ireland that in the event of an IRA ceasefire without the surrender of arms, much of these might find their way into the hands of criminal gangs in Belfast and other areas. The prospect of surrendering their arms to the British army or the RUC may constitute an insurmountable barrier for the Provos. In that context it may well be worth offering the IRA the facility to voluntarily surrender arms in the Republic.[38]

These views on decommissioning provide evidence of considerable pragmatism in Democratic Left's thinking about the mechanics of the peace process. The party had also diverged from the other opposition parties early in 1994 in supporting the Fianna Fáil–Labour Party coalition's

decision to end the Section 31 broadcasting ban. Fine Gael and the Progressive Democrats proposed a rolling two-monthly review, which
Democratic Left opposed. 'I appreciate the concerns expressed by the
Progressive Democrats and Fine Gael about the dangers of allowing
those who espouse violence access to the airwaves, but I think they are
wrong to seek the reimposition of the order without first seeing how
the new situation works,' De Rossa told the Dáil.[39] Only weeks after the
IRA's August 1994 ceasefire announcement Democratic Left came
to join Fine Gael and the Labour Party in a coalition government. The
relationship between the republican movement and the Rainbow coalition was not as good as had existed when the Albert Reynolds-led government was in office. John Bruton was sympathetic to the British
government's demand for an early start to paramilitary decommissioning, but even more significantly, the new administration was less
attached to the maintenance of the so-called pan-nationalist alliance as
a key element of the peace process. Democratic Left supported the shift
in emphasis, as explained by John Bruton:

> It was essential to bring the unionist viewpoint to the table and to
> show unionists in Northern Ireland that public opinion in the
> Republic was interested in their welfare too ... So I was very
> determined that unionism would be taken into account, and Sinn
> Féin had a bit of difficulty with the idea ...[40]

From the opposition benches there was strong criticism from Fianna
Fáil, while Gerry Adams saw difficulties with the Rainbow coalition's
approach. 'That stability and leadership [from the Reynolds govern-
ment] had been crucial to persuading the IRA that the peace process,
and the nationalist consensus that had created it, was a viable alternative
to armed struggle. Now this important element is gone,' Adams
argued.[41] De Rossa obviously had a different view.

> I thought we handled the Northern Ireland brief well. I know that
> John Bruton came in for a lot of criticism but a lot of it is knee-
> jerk kind of anti-Fine Gael stuff. The Shinners were much more
> comfortable with Fianna Fáil and John Hume – that old-style
> nationalist reading. But given that and given the position Bruton
> came from – and [the position] I came from, the relationship was
> reasonably workmanlike.[42]

Nevertheless, De Rossa did have a more open relationship with union-ist politicians than with their nationalist or republican counterparts. This was not unsurprising given the positions adopted by Democratic Left on identity politics and the party's outright hostility to the IRA and the idea of the Irish government 'representing' the nationalist com-munity in Northern Ireland. As Tony Heffernan explained, 'the com-bination of Fine Gael and Democratic Left meant that there was probably more consideration given to unionist attitudes and concerns than might otherwise have been the case, particularly say if there had just been Fianna Fáil and Labour in government.'[43]

Given his own personal experiences and the transition in his political career, it was not unsurprising that De Rossa was so hostile to the repub-lican movement. By the time he became a government minister he had in fact a better relationship with members of the unionist community. De Rossa was the first Irish politician David Trimble met following his elec-tion as Ulster Unionist Party (UUP) leader in 1995. The meeting actu-ally happened by chance when De Rossa was in Belfast for a Democratic Left function. 'When Trimble learned that De Rossa was visiting Belfast, he immediately invited him to visit Unionist headquar-ters: had any other Irish Cabinet minister been visiting he would not have moved as he did,' Dean Godson recounted in his biography of Trimble.[44] The thirty-minute meeting was largely symbolic, although it caused some unease in Dublin where senior Department of Foreign Af-fairs officials were concerned Trimble was attempting to sideline Dick Spring. De Rossa recalled: 'I got hassle over it; though Democratic Left loved it.'[45] Trimble would probably have shared Godson's view that Democratic Left as 'previously pro-Moscow Marxists were arguably the most anti-nationalist political force on both sides of the border ...'[46] After the meeting, Trimble drew parallels between the political evolu-tion of individuals like De Rossa and the path still to be travelled by Gerry Adams and his colleagues.

> Some unionists at the moment would have difficulty envisaging Gerry Adams coming to Glengall Street, but that's because they see Adams as he is today. But here we have a situation where people have proven a commitment to exclusively peaceful methods and have shown that they abide by the democratic process, that will put them in the same position as Proinsias De Rossa is today.[47]

Trimble's welcome for De Rossa was matched by feelings held by his own party members. In a vox pop undertaken by *The Sunday Times* at the November 1995 Ulster Unionist annual conference De Rossa emerged as the Irish politician most trusted by UUP members.[48] There was much greater tension with republicans. In truth, the Democratic Left leader had little time for Gerry Adams: 'He's so patronising and pompous. You know he really gets on my nerves.'[49] When the Rainbow coalition was formed in late 1994, the two men met as part of the peace process: 'The first thing I said to him was, "Look I detest everything you stand for" but I'm going to work with you to make this work.'[50]

The difficult relationship between De Rossa and Adams was acknowledged by Rosheen Callender: 'With Proinsias, his history and background enabled him to give very good advice on the North, and then to keep back a bit from the direct [laughs] involvement. You know, himself and Adams would have never got on all that well, for obvious reasons.'[51] Relations, however, deteriorated not just between the republican movement and the Irish government but also between republicans and the British side. The IRA ceasefire ended with the bombing in Canary Wharf early in 1996. De Rossa condemned the action in a subsequent Dáil debate:

> On one occasion when I opposed attempts by Sinn Féin and the IRA to take control of my constituency of Dublin North West through the so-called Concerned Parents Against Drugs I was threatened by an armed man at a public meeting. I did not back down then and I will not do so now in terms of my total political opposition to every-thing Sinn Féin and the IRA stand for. I oppose and abominate every-thing they stand for ... Certainly, there have been difficulties. When differences arise, the onus is on democratic politicians to persevere with negotiations. We do not need or want IRA bombs to concen-trate our minds. The best thing the Army Council of the IRA ever did was to call the ceasefire in August 1994. The next best thing it can do is to restore the ceasefire now. You cannot have half a ceasefire, and you cannot be half a democrat; the Irish Government will not be deflected in its search for a just and lasting settlement, based on the principles of agreement and consent.[52]

Despite the efforts of all involved, there was no further political move-ment until after the British and Irish general elections in 1997. 'The history has yet to be written as to why they set those bombs off in Canary Wharf at that time. Was it that they were trying to bring the government down?' De Rossa queried.[53] John Bruton posed similar questions when asked if the Canary Wharf decision was an attempt to destabilise his administration:

> I don't honestly know. I have no evidence of that. I think it might be more interesting to inquire in the delaying of the ceasefire [restoration] which occurred after Bertie Ahern came into office. Was the IRA ready to have a ceasefire before that? That might be worth looking into but I don't want to say any more.[54]

From the opposition benches Democratic Left welcomed the Good Friday Agreement in 1998 which included the party's long-called-for changes to Articles 2 and 3 and a devolved assembly in Northern Ireland. De Rossa was generous in his praise for the deal: 'The Agreement is a painstakingly constructed accommodation between Nationalism and Unionism, which is in itself a great achievement.'[55] Democratic Left had, however, reservations about the mechanics of the proposed institutional arrangements. For several years, Democratic Left had warned about basing a settlement deal along the lines of community allegiances in Northern Ireland. A 1994 party document clearly spelt out those concerns:

> Since institutionalised power-sharing would freeze politics along present lines in perpetuity and make very difficult the emergence of normal democratic politics, we should not support the institutionalised power-sharing solution. All elected bodies should operate on the basis of weighted majorities to make sure of cross-community support for all important decisions. This would protect minority communities while allowing for the development of normal politics.[56]

De Rossa raised these reservations in the Dáil in April 1998.

> If there is one area of concern I would have about the Good Friday Agreement it would be the arrangements for the Assembly set out under Strand One where elected members will be required to register as Nationalist, Unionist or other. This, clearly, carries the danger of institutionalising sectarianism … There are many people in Northern Ireland who do not define themselves exclusively as Nationalist or Unionist. I would count myself among the

third strand. Members of my party, Democratic Left, in Northern Ireland would classify themselves as 'other'. Indeed, there are very many other people to whom we also need to give space and a share in the power which is being given to the assembly.[57]

Despite these concerns, Democratic Left joined with the other parties in Leinster House in endorsing the Belfast Agreement as the template for a peace settlement in Northern Ireland. The Belfast Agreement came at a time when there were discussions among leading figures in Democratic Left about the party's future. The referenda result – the party concluded – removed 'the National question as a legitimate source of division' and created 'the space for the development of post-nationalist politics'.[58] Within a matter of months Democratic Left and the Labour Party had concluded a merger agreement.

During the 1992–9 period Democratic Left had a limited party political presence in Northern Ireland arising from its origins in the Workers' Party, which was organised north of the border, and had local government representation in a number of electoral areas. The split in the Workers' Party in early 1992 had caused some uncertainty for party members from Northern Ireland who backed De Rossa. A number of different models for an all-Ireland organisation were discussed at a meeting in March 1992 attended by four members from Northern Ireland, including Séamus Lynch. The models all included a separate Northern Ireland executive elected by the party's local membership which produce policies for Northern Ireland. 'The nearest thing to DL in terms of its relationship with the community in Northern Ireland was the Alliance Party, although they were sort of UK liberals,' De Rossa said.[59] About 50 people attended a conference in Northern Ireland in June 1992.[60] But an undated party memo – most likely from late 1992 – painted a bleak picture of Democratic Left's organisation in the North.

> The party membership in Northern Ireland is relatively small. At the most we have members in North South and West Belfast while outside of Belfast members are located in Dungannon Omagh Antrim Town and Downpatrick … Progress of Democratic Left in N.I. has been slow for a number of reasons these include the lack of finance no Party Office with Admin facilities which are essential for the running of a modern Political Organisation.[61]

The question of how best to organise in Northern Ireland was discussed at a national executive meeting in July 1993. In correspondence, De Rossa observed: 'Our members have a very difficult task in Northern Ireland ...'[62] A seminar on organisational options was arranged, but the party continued to have a limited presence north of the border. 'We had very little public representation so it was largely a media kind of presence that we had,' De Rossa admitted.[63] Democratic Left's anti-sectarian and anti-nationalist message found few backers. The party also found operating in two jurisdictions virtually impossible. De Rossa concluded: 'I don't think you can seriously engage in the politics of Northern Ireland at an elected level, and in the Republic at an elected level, and not have constant conflicts of interest. They are two distinct entities, politically and economically.'[64] Seán Garland – one of the senior Workers' Party figures who opposed the De Rossa strategy in 1992 – was critical of his former colleagues for their views on Northern Ireland. 'I think some of those who eventually became DL had little feeling for the involvement in Northern Ireland,' Garland said. This assessment was, however, not borne out by the evidence of the 1992 to 1999 period.

Democratic Left articulated a distinctive set of policies for the future of Northern Ireland. The party was very critical of the Provisional IRA and its campaign of violence. It offered a nuanced assessment of the role of national identity and attempted to find support for a post-nationalist and a post-unionist future. There was, however, little endorsement of this viewpoint from the entrenched communities in Northern Ireland. Moreover, south of the border the issue of Northern Ireland was not a political priority for the electorate when casting their votes. In the latter regard Democratic Left received little ballot box credit for offering imaginative responses to the conflict. In addition, as the peace process developed in the 1990s many of the party's stances were either incorporated into mainstream policy or simply made redundant as events unfolded. With the electorate's endorsement of the Belfast Agreement in May 1998 the policies offered by the various Leinster House parties largely converged. It was in this environment that De Rossa accepted that changes north of the border should be matched by a realignment of Left activism in the Irish Republic.

VALUES AND SOCIAL CHANGE, 1992–9

Irish society had undergone dramatic changes in the three decades lead-ing up to the formation of Democratic Left in 1992. The nature of the family, the role of women and the position of the Catholic Church were just some of the areas subjected to radical change. Many writers start their analysis of this process of change in the 1960s and 1970s as – according to Girvin – 'the primary reason for this was the recognition that it is the period when most observers locate their origins of change and crisis in Ireland's recent past.'[65] Many of these controversial issues consumed public attention in the 1980s – a decade marked by bitter battles over divorce, abortion and, to a lesser degree, contraception. Writing in 1992, Chubb captured the transformation that was under way: 'In the second half of the century, the traditional, stable attitudes associated with nationalism and with the lingering pre-industrial society, together with the values and life style inculcated by an austere and authoritarian church, began to be eroded. Changed circumstances and new influences increasingly undermined these three foundation pillars on which that stable society had rested.'[66]

When Proinsias De Rossa addressed the Democratic Left founding conference there were two significant blocs in Irish society, represent-ing the liberal and conservative positions. The traditional lobby's in-fluence was waning but it still held significant sway. De Rossa was speaking about an Ireland where a constitutional ban on divorce was still in place, abortion was illegal, homosexuality was a criminal offence and contraception availability was limited. But in 1992 Ireland was on the cusp of considerable societal change. Whereas there was still a distinctive conservative appearance to Irish society in 1992, within a few years evidence of greater liberalism was to become clearly avail-able. Many factors aided this transformation of Ireland into a far more liberal and secular society.

There had been a dramatic shift in Irish demography over the preceding decades. The marriage rate had declined, while marital fertility had fallen, with a rise in non-marital births. The number of non-marital births moved from 3 per cent of all births in the mid-1960s to 19.5 per cent in 1993. Membership of the European Union helped to push equality up the domestic legislative agenda as the number of married women in the labour force increased significantly. These changes must also be considered in the context of a transformation in the position of the Catholic Church in Ireland. Church attendance was in decline – during the 1980s the numbers attending church/mass more than weekly declined by one-fifth. Whelan's analysis of value survey data indicates that attendance was in decline in all but the oldest age group.[67] Moreover, the authority of the Catholic Church was significantly damaged in the 1990s following a series of controversies involving clerical child abuse and high-profile clerics being exposed as having fathered children.

Evidence of more independent thinking can be seen in the debates about contraception, abortion and divorce. The liberalisation of contraception legislation was a gradual process from the 1970s onwards. Initial limited reforms – as is discussed below – caused some political controversy. The importation and sale of contraceptives was prohibited until 1979. The legislation in this area lagged public opinion, but by the early 1990s political attitudes to contraception had changed. In general, there was less strident argument about contraception, possibly because the conservative lobby was more concerned with abortion and divorce, two more important topics from their perspective.

A legislative ban on abortion had been in place since the foundation of the Irish state. It was further entrenched with public backing for a 1983 constitutional amendment which was described as 'pro-life'. But as Whelan and Fahey observed, 'in 1992 this consensus was thrown into turmoil by the details of the "X" case, which came before the Supreme Court early in that year. The court ruled that a fourteen-year-old girl – the victim of an alleged rape – had a constitutional right to an abortion on the grounds that her life was threatened by the suicidal tendencies arising from her pregnancy.'[68]

The Supreme Court judgement in the 'X' case led to a three-part referendum in 1992, with the electorate backing the right to travel abroad to have an abortion and to provide information in Ireland on legal abortion services abroad. A more restrictive wording to replace the 1983 anti-abortion clause was rejected by voters. The results were interpreted as offering evidence of 'a significant shift in a liberal direction'.[69]

The abortion issue was not the only subject to generate heated constitutional debate at this time as the issue of a divorce referendum had returned to the national agenda. The 1937 Irish Constitution contained a clause stating that no law could be enacted providing for the granting of dissolution of marriage. Divorce was prohibited and, while marital breakdown was a reality for very many people, 'there was no coherent body of family law to deal with the consequences of marriage break-down.'[70] The campaign for a referendum removing the constitutional ban on divorce pushed the issue onto the political agenda in the early 1980s. In April 1986 the Fine Gael–Labour coalition backed the idea of a referendum on divorce. After a heated, and bitter, campaign the referendum was rejected in June 1986 with over 63 per cent of voters opposing the proposal.

In the aftermath of the referendum result, new family law legislation was passed to ease the legal position of those whose marriages had ended. But the right to remarry was still prohibited. The legal reforms prepared the way for a second constitutional referendum. A white paper on marital breakdown in 1992 estimated that the number of separated couples had doubled since 1986. A number of options to amend the constitution were proposed, along with a draft of the legislation which would be introduced if the divorce ban was removed.

The conservative and liberal constituencies mobilised for the 1995 referendum, which was captured by the emotive slogan of one opposing group, *Hello Divorce, Goodbye Daddy*. 'Highly organised and effective fear campaigns were again mounted by anti divorce campaign groups in the lead up to the 1995 referendum. The concerns relating to the consequences of divorce including money, children, property inheritance and the Irish way of life were again a feature of the anti divorce campaign ...'[71] Democratic Left was strongly supportive of a 'yes' vote: 'The amendment proposed by the Government is about choice, pluralism and the development of an open, tolerant society.'[72]

Over one million voters decided in favour of lifting the ban on divorce in the November 1995 referendum. The numbers voting 'yes' corresponded to 50.28 per cent of those casting their ballot. The margin of victory was less than 1 per cent. On the numbers alone an argument could be made that the liberal agenda was being introduced in a sharply divided society. Indeed, as has been noted, 'the proposal to introduce divorce was vociferously opposed by more than two thirds of the population in the 1986 referendum and by almost half in 1995.'[73] But societal values were changing rapidly. In the space of seven years in the 1990s there was resolution (in favour of the liberal agenda) in many contentious areas. By 1999, when Democratic Left was dissolved, divorce was legal, contraception freely available, homosexuality decriminalised and while the status of the abortion laws was lacking in clarity it was far from the entrenched 'pro-life' position the backers of the 1983 referendum had envisaged.

The policy positions adopted by the membership of Democratic Left at the party's founding conference in April 1992 placed the new political entity in a very different space to the other parties with Oireachtas representation. The party's constitution, and subsequently published policy documents, used words such as 'secular' and 'pluralist' which in 1992 were not part of the vocabulary of Fianna Fáil or of considerable sections of Fine Gael or the Labour Party. The party openly backed the separation of church and state and supported a non-denominational curriculum in state-funded schools. There was also very strong support for women's rights. At the founding conference, endorsement was given to a document which stated: 'a socialist feminist perspective is an integral part of the party's policies, structures and organisation.'

The 1992 conference also backed the introduction of divorce legislation, a comprehensive family planning service, sex education in schools and the right to an abortion in Ireland where the life of the mother was threatened along with the deletion of the 1983 anti-abortion clause in the constitution. The party also supported the decriminalisation of homosexuality and the lowering of the age of consent to 16 years of age. As was discussed previously, Democratic Left emerged with a distinctive policy position on social/moral issues in the 1992 and 1997 expert studies. The party was also led by someone who was unmistakably a liberal politician. 'Proinsias is a very strong feminist and secularist and would have driven that message home,' Liz McManus said.[74] Rosheen Callender agreed: 'Proinsias to this day is one of a few party leaders who would get up at a meeting and unequivocally say that, you know, I believe there should be abortion available, divorce and all the rest of it …'[75]

During a 1993 Dáil debate on the status of women in Irish society, De Rossa declared: 'I regard myself as a feminist.'[76] It was not the kind of remark uttered by the other party leaders at that time. Some months earlier, the Democratic Left leader had been very clear about his party's agenda for women.

> What we need now is a more comprehensive programme of reform to deal with the medical, social and economic issues which arise directly from the unique biological function of women. This must include legislation specifying the circumstances in which

abortion will be permissible; a comprehensive national family planning service; a wider programme of education on sex in our schools; a community-based childcare service; longer maternity leave and the introduction of paternity leave; and a reform of the social welfare system to provide an adequate independent income for all women not in paid employment.[77]

Democratic Left was very clearly a liberal party, and De Rossa had no hesitation in actively pursuing a liberal agenda, as was evident during his contribution to a 1992 debate on family planning legislation:

> It is time the State was finally and unceremoniously evicted from the bedroom. This is the third family planning Bill within a period of 13 years and it is the third botched attempt. Important issues have been ignored and fundamental questions dodged.[78]

In the context where Ireland was positioned in 1992, and the stances of the other parties described previously, Democratic Left was offering a very different policy agenda. 'That type of radical politics, at a time when you didn't have radical politics, was very important,' Kathleen Lynch remarked.[79] Eamon Gilmore stressed the importance to the political system generally in having a party pursuing a liberal agenda:

> We said things that maybe a larger party might have been reluctant to say. I remember I was one of the first TDs to say that in certain circumstances we should legalise abortion. We took a very prominent role in all the abortion referendums. So I think we probably made a contribution in bringing the final chapter of the liberal agenda ... I think it would be an exaggeration to say Democratic Left per se left a legacy but where it made its contribution was in the liberalisation of our laws ...[80]

Democratic Left did not always get its own way even as a partner in the 1994–7 Rainbow coalition which oversaw the second divorce referendum, as Liz McManus explained in the Dáil debate on the proposal:

> The amendment drafted by the Government represents a compromise, not only between the partners in Government but also between the various strands of society. In an ideal world Democratic Left would have favoured a simple deletion but we do not live in an ideal world and the amendment before the House is the

best possible option. The terms of the amendment will reassure those who are concerned that we could open the door to the regime adopted in other jurisdictions where so called 'quickie' divorces are the norm rather than the exception. This is the best proposition that we can put and is in tune with the concerns of Irish people. It reaffirms values and it can only be altered by the people.[81]

In the same debate McManus also defended the liberal tradition in Irish politics:

Those harbingers of doom who prophesied Armageddon follow-ing the passage of the Abortion Information Bill and who are engaging in a campaign of misinformation in the run up to the divorce referendum are unable to accept that we can exist in the modern world without losing our values and our common decency. They appear to view the modern world as a bacillus to which Ireland is peculiarly susceptible. As an Irishwoman living in that world, I find that notion deeply offensive.[82]

The difficulty faced by Democratic Left was the eventual resolution of many high-profile and tangible issues which drove the liberal/moral debate. Many controversial issues mentioned at the party's founding conference in 1992 were dealt with over the following years, including divorce, family planning and decriminalisation of homosexuality. In effect, the other parties caught up with the liberal agenda as a majority of public opinion generally moved in a more liberal direction. By the late 1990s the big liberal–conservative battle was effectively ended in terms of the change agenda which had been pursued over the previous two decades. As with the situation in relation to policy on Northern Ireland, Democratic Left's distinctive message was no longer unique nor, as issues were resolved, was it relevant. That is not to say that other issues on the so-called liberal agenda, including abortion, sex educa-tion and the separation of church and state, had become irrelevant. But they failed to capture the public attention like the issues in previous debates and, perhaps also, Democratic Left failed to identify more strongly with these issues so as to generate public debate and create distinctive political space.

ECONOMIC POLICIES, 1992–9

In the summer of 1992, the Irish national broadcaster RTÉ commissioned a radio series of thirteen lectures from leading academics, economists and commentators. The series, entitled 'The Jobs Crisis', said much about the state of the Irish economy at the start of the 1990s. The radio series editor, Colm Keane, observed:

> Irish unemployment statistics make for disturbing reading. Current Irish unemployment rates are the worst in the history of the State, the worst in the EC and almost twice the EC average. More than 125,000 people are long-term unemployed and over 90,000 people under 25 are without work.[83]

The lack of jobs was the dominant item on the political agenda. The opening sentences of the 1992 budget speech noted that 'the increasing numbers looking for work demand a truly exceptional employment performance – right through to the end of this decade. The overriding concern must, therefore, be to safeguard existing jobs and encourage the creation of new ones.'[84] The Irish economy was undergoing a period of fiscal retrenchment as the government sought to address the difficulties that had plagued the economy throughout the 1980s. 'We have, after a period of intensive and very successful correction of our public finances, reached a point where our annual borrowing has been reduced to levels well in line with our Community partners. The size of our national debt, however, continues to be a problem,' finance minister Bertie Ahern said in his budget speech.[85]

TABLE 7.2
IRELAND'S ECONOMIC PERFORMANCE

	1993	1994	1995	1996	1997	1998
GNP	2.6	6.3	8.0	7.2	9.0	8.1
GDP	2.6	5.8	9.5	7.7	10.7	8.9
Unemployment (% labour force)	15.5	14.1	12.1	11.5	9.8	7.4
Employment (% change)	1.9	3.6	4.6	3.7	4.6	5.7
Employment (000s)	22	43	57	48	62	82
General Gov. Balance (% GDP)	-2.2	-1.7	-2.1	-0.2	1.0	2.5
General Gov. Debt (% GDP)	93	86	78	69	60	49
Fixed Investment	-4.1	12.0	22.9	15.9	18.9	16.7
Exports	9.1	14.7	19.6	11.8	17.0	20.5

Source: Department of Finance, *Budget 2000*, http://www.budget.gov.ie/2000

The various economic indicators in Table 7.2 show the difficult situation Ireland faced in the early 1990s. The economy was marked by high unemployment and declining but continued emigration. Economic growth was low and, as mentioned, the public finances were restricted while high rates of taxation stifled innovation.

When Democratic Left was formed no one was predicting the economic transformation that would take place in Ireland in the 1990s. The scale of development was such, however, that at the end of the decade the Department of Finance – not an organisation known for hyperbole – observed:

> Ireland's economic progress in the 1990s has been outstanding. GNP grew in real terms by an average of 7.6% per annum between 1994 and 1999. This growth has led to a significant increase in employment with the numbers employed increasing by over 30%. The unemployment rate has fallen from over 15% in 1993 to around 5¼ % today [2000].[86]

In a few short years Ireland became the fastest growing economy in Europe. The economy doubled in size between 1990 and 2000. Indeed, income per capita measured on both average GDP and GNP indicators converged and started to surpass the EU average by 2000. Employment increased from just over 1 million in 1994 to 1.7 million in 2001, while emigration was replaced by immigration as the main feature of discussions on Irish demography patterns.

The economic principles agreed at the Democratic Left founding conference underpinned a desire to see the party positioned on the Left of the political spectrum. Equality and fairness were stressed in the party's founding policy principles: 'Our idea of a successful economy is one that can raise everybody's living standards, by creating more wealth, distributing it more fairly and spending it more sanely.' The economic environment in the early 1990s shaped initial thinking in Democratic Left and the type of priorities the party stressed. Employment creation was top of the agenda in 1992 while there was also emphasis on tax reform and protecting the more vulnerable in society through the social welfare system and, where possible, getting people on the live register back to work.

The party's policy was explained in the traditional language of the Left but the positions adopted were far less rigid than, for example, espoused by the Workers' Party in the 1980s, and they now included caveats in many important respects. For example, the party's belief in the state sector was outlined in its constitution: 'We do not believe that essential public services should be subject to market forces.' But Democratic Left was prepared to accept a role for the private sector: 'Where market forces *are* appropriate, these should be harnessed on behalf of ordinary people – workers and consumers – and used for the greater good of society.' There was considerable discussion within the party about the need for a new direction for Left-wing politics. As part of these discussions there was an acknowledgement that the old order was not returning. 'The social model of full employment which we had in the 1950s and 1960s is no longer attainable – it has been consigned to history. The challenge now facing trade unions and socialist parties is to embrace a new model of social and economic citizenship which both embraces and incorporates the idea of full employment,' one contributor wrote in a Democratic Left publication late in 1993.[87]

Democratic Left sought to locate a 'third way' between capitalism and socialism. But there was a huge difficulty in moulding the party's ideas with the neo-liberal outlook that had emerged as the economic orthodoxy. As discussed in Chapter 1, policy differences between the Right and the Left narrowed and became less visible for the wider public to see. The failure to offer a tangible alternative goes to the heart of the discussion about the identity crisis in Left politics, where points of difference between Right and Left had became difficult to discern. This lack of radical difference was obvious from comments made in early 1993 by Michael Noonan of Fine Gael. Noonan was complimentary about the agreed Democratic Left/Labour Party policy document arising from their ultimately unsuccessful attempt to form a government with Fine Gael. Interestingly, Noonan's criticisms of the document's economic policies were not based on ideological difference.

> I thought that was a very good policy document and I certainly could agree with the social objectives contained in it. I had very little difficulty with 90 per cent of the social objectives therein and I know that Democratic Left had a major input into this document. What disturbed me, however, was that in spite of the merits of the proposals being made there was no economic policy being put forward by the Labour Party. It is not possible to fulfil social objectives in any democracy without having the economic policies that create the resources to do so. As I see it that is the weakness

in the talks on the formation of a Government – there is no engine to drive the vehicle.[88]

In Michael Laver's expert study analysis Democratic Left was, in terms of economic policy, to the Left of the Labour Party, Fianna Fáil, Fine Gael and the Progressive Democrats in 1992 and 1997. But the margin of difference with the Labour Party was not significant in either 1992 or 1997. Moreover, there was a slight drift to the Right in Democratic Left's economic policy in the 1992–7 period, a movement experienced by most political parties as the economic agenda was framed by the fall-out from the collapse of the Soviet model and the increased prevalence of globalisation. The party had acknowledged the increased political clout of the Right in its 1994 European Parliament election manifesto: 'The New Right is growing. It has an agenda of selfish individualism, racism and na-tionalism. It is attacking all forms of social protection under the guise of labour market flexibility, de-regulation, privatisation and liberal markets.'[89]

But such sentiment aside, Democratic Left essentially bought into the orthodox economic model. The party was able to agree a policy programme with the Labour Party in 1992 and, two years later, to suc-cessfully negotiate a programme for government with Fine Gael and Labour. There were still policy differences, for example in areas like abolishing university fees and setting the corporation rate tax. But, as discussed previously, there were no differences that were so insur-mountable as to prevent agreement being reached with these other par-ties. The economic programme of the Rainbow coalition illustrated how far Democratic Left had moved from a desired radical Left per-spective. For example, the party had campaigned against the 1992 Maastricht Treaty:

> In our view the proposed Treaty is a setback for the concept of a democratic people's Europe and a victory for the most conserva-tive political influences in the EC. On virtually every issue the Treaty is seriously deficient and fails to address the most fundamental political, economic and social problems facing Europe's citizen.[90]

While backing the idea of economic and monetary union, and the creation of a European Central Bank, Democratic Left was strongly critical of the fiscal policy limits ['rigid rules'] in the treaty. Despite this stance, two and a half years later the party signed up to working within these same rules. The 1994 programme for government committed the three coalition parties to 'strict adherence to the Maastricht guidelines regarding Government borrowing and overall debt/GDP ratio'. Not only did Democratic Left sign up to a programme underpinned by the Maastricht criteria but as a member of the Rainbow government in May 1998 the party modified its attitude to the EU by backing the Amsterdam Treaty. 'We would characterise the Amsterdam Treaty as going some way to rectifying the shortcomings of Maastricht and countering the neo-liberal ethos which dominated it.'[91]

Observing this transition in opinion on fundamental policy issues, John Bruton captured the changed environment in the 1990s – post-Berlin and due to increased globalisation – when he remarked that 'the ideological climate of the Left in Europe had changed.'[92] One area where Democratic Left sought to carve out difference was in its support for the state's role in the economy through policy interventions and the ownership of strategic assets. Once again, the party acknowledged the new economic order: 'the role of the state is declining in the global economy ...'[93] To create new jobs the party placed stress on governmental involvement, including backing for an active EU Industrial Policy along the lines of the Common Agricultural Policy. 'The creation of the Single Market and the moves towards economic and monetary union also create a need to develop the economic role of the Union by developing a common industrial policy at European level.'[94] In the 1992 general election manifesto there were proposals for urban renewal schemes with major construction projects, revitalisation of public sector companies and a state-backed community jobs programme to create 50,000 public and voluntary sector positions. The party also backed the idea of a state-controlled 'third banking force' to support Irish enterprise. In a Dáil debate in March 1993 Proinsias De Rossa attacked the Labour Party, which in government with Fianna Fáil had agreed to the sale of some state assets:

> The new Labour Party approach to state companies takes its place alongside its new theory that selling a minority State shareholding in Greencore is not privatisation. Can we deduce from that that the sale of Aer Lingus hotels would not be privatisation either? As far as Democratic Left is concerned, a national aviation policy should be based on one Irish national airline, Aer Lingus. There is no basis for more and any other policy will almost certainly lead

to us having none at all. With deregulation in Europe almost complete, anybody who argues that we need another Irish airline to provide competition either wishes to sabotage Aer Lingus or is out of touch with reality.[95]

But by the time the coalition deal with Fine Gael and the Labour Party was concluded, Democratic Left had modified its own stance on state ownership. The 1994 programme for government stated: 'state assets will be sold where it protects employment and fulfils the strategic interest of the company and its stakeholders ....' A combination of the party's original stance in 1992 and the modification of 1994 were evident in Democratic Left's 1997 general election manifesto, which noted:

> Public ownership of major enterprises has served Ireland well ...
> Democratic Left is opposed to privatisation and in government
> will not agree to state assets being sold except, as the Programme
> for Government said, where it protects employment and is in the
> long-term interest of the company and its stakeholders.

De Rossa's party was not totally opposed to the private sector. The Democratic Left constitution said the party recognised that 'powerful market forces exist, nationally and internationally. At the same time we also recognise that there are no such things as "free markets". All are distorted by various influences, and particularly by multinational companies.' The party had no outright objection to the private sector or to multinational firms locating in Ireland. 'None of us will refuse the employment a multinational company will bring to this country,' Eamon Gilmore told the Dáil in 1993.[96] While the language may still have been more Left-leaning, Democratic Left accepted a mixed economy model. It favoured state ownership but acknowledged the role of the private sector. Stripped bare, the stance was relatively similar to that of the other Leinster House parties. De Rossa's address to the pre-general election Democratic Left annual conference in April 1997 was interesting as much for what he did not say as for what he said. There was no mention of state asset ownership or the type of taxes previously proposed. When Democratic Left was formed there was considerable public criticism of high rates of personal income taxation. Like the other parties Democratic Left policy spoke of the need to reform the tax system. The 1993 party task force report noted that:

Democratic Left's proposals depend firmly on its ability to convince people that the problems of unemployment are not inevitable but political, that taxation is not an evil but a positive, and so on. It is about setting the political agenda and constructing political supports and alliances around *new* priorities.[97]

When the party was founded in 1992 it prepared an economic document which proposed the introduction, for a few years, of a new top income tax rate of 65 per cent to ease the level of national debt. The economic situation had improved sufficiently by 1997 for the 65 per cent rate proposal to be dropped, although the party did not favour reductions in the then top rate of 48 per cent. Like its coalition partners, Democratic Left placed priority on extending bands and allowances, and reducing the lower income tax rate. The party's preference for new forms of taxation featured in numerous policy documents, as did a desire to curb existing reliefs and loopholes. Pat Rabbitte told the Dáil in April 1992:

> Those of us who believe in real tax reform realise that that means broadening the tax base and we cannot come in here and oppose new measures which are designed – however inadequately – to achieve that effect. Many of these reliefs and tax shelters blatantly benefit the rich, the powerful, the better off, and penalise those who work for a wage. They often act as incentives not to promote economic activity or generate wealth but to facilitate easy profits.[98]

Rabbitte was echoing the recently agreed party policy that stated: 'there should be no exemptions or loopholes for anyone. Tax evaders should be seen as social parasites and treated accordingly.' These sentiments were repeated in all party policy statements on taxation from 1992 to 1999. 'Taxes appear to be high because we have low taxes on profits, wealth, inheritance, property and because of loopholes and evasion,' the 1997 general election manifesto stated, adding 'we would eliminate rich people's tax loopholes.'[99] Democratic Left wanted greater taxation of wealth and property. The party made numerous proposals for taxation measures to achieve greater wealth redistribution. For example, the general election manifesto in 1992 referred to the 'introduction of a strengthened Wealth Tax'. The party's Economic Committee published a detailed discussion document on taxation in October 1993, proposing a property tax as well as a wealth tax with a 2 per cent tax on very substantial holdings of wealth.

The idea of a wealth tax did not feature in the 1997 general election manifesto, confirming the expert study finding that there was a moderation in the party's economic policies between 1992 and 1997. The original sentiment remained, with a section in the manifesto entitled 'taxes on wealth and property', but the language and proposals had changed. 'Low tax on inheritance is a disincentive to work and enterprise where children can inherit hundreds of thousands free of any tax. There is also a strong case for effective inheritance taxes to redistribute wealth and to build a society based on merit.' There was repeated endorsement of the idea of a property tax. But the party never succeeded in winning support for the tax, and somewhat cynically joined Fine Gael in making political capital in 1994 at the expense of the Fianna Fáil–Labour coalition over the extension of residential property tax. The tax was a relatively minor form of taxation which, even allowing for its extension in 1994, had a small yield. One study concluded that 'the reaction of the parties to the 1994 budget changes to RPT [residential property tax] indicates responsiveness to middle-class voters to the detriment of the wider community.'[100]

Democratic Left obviously had to be conscious of the economic policies of its coalition partners, particularly Fine Gael. The larger party's taxation stance had prevailed in the government formation discussions in 1994. The Rainbow coalition's programme contained no proposal to increase taxation on wealth, capital or corporate profits. Even during the debate on corporation tax there was a moderation in Democratic Left's attitude, with pragmatism dominating the decision to accept a lower rate. Democratic Left made little headway with its other taxation proposals, particularly a suggestion unique to the party's policy mix – tax on currency speculators. The idea surfaced in the 1993 taxation document and reappeared in the 1997 general election manifesto as 'a small tax on financial transactions of 0.02%'. Again the party made no progress in gaining acceptance for this proposal with either of its coalition partners. Without real success in getting its taxation policies onto the government agenda it was always going to be difficult to convince the wider electorate the party was offering a radically different set of policies. The two larger parties in the 1994–7 coalition set the taxation agenda. Democratic Left had little success with its proposals beyond agreement that taxation was too high for low to middle-income earners, which had, in any event, become the accepted consensus among all the main parties.

Overall, the evolution of party positioning on economic matters indicates that Democratic Left did not seem to have alternative answers to the prevailing economic dogma. The party was good at stressing its opposition to economic developments but it failed to adequately offer alternatives. Traditional social democratic tools driven by a Keynesian approach were made redundant in a new globalised economic environment marked by free capital movements. Des Geraghty acknowledged this new reality in a 1998 party pamphlet:

> Capital has outgrown the nation state, has in many cases liberated itself from the constraints of the production of goods and services and has used technology and globalisation to frustrate labour and indeed citizens generally. It has reasserted its dominance in the global jungle of the 'free markets' after years of social democratic consensus. It now has a mobility and a power which dwarfs all the social forces which seek to impose democratic accountability or restraint.[101]

De Rossa made some interesting observations about globalisation and financial markets at the time of the international currency crisis in 1992 when the British government was forced to devalue sterling:

> The direction and overall control of national economies, not least in Ireland, has escaped the clutches of elected governments and is now in the hands of the financiers who have no interest in the public good, no interest in jobs, no interest in poverty, simply an interest in what can be made out of the latest round of speculation. It is a curious fact that the speculators will make money regardless of whether our currency goes up or down or whether the British economy is in tatters or not. It ought to be the primary objective of our Government to win the co-operation of other national governments in the European Community in re-asserting political control over the financial markets.[102]

There were a number of areas where the party had interesting policy responses that were somewhat ahead of mainstream thinking in Ireland. For example, the party advocated the idea of greater democracy in the workplace, in effect worker participation: 'Workers who are fully involved in decision-making, and properly rewarded for their work, become more efficient and committed to creating a good product or service. This is even more the case for workers who are involved in the ownership and control of their enterprises.'

A proposal for an energy tax was included in the 1993 tax document. Prior to the 1997 general election De Rossa spoke about shifting the tax burden away from income to new eco-taxes. These ideas – which gained greater currency in subsequent years – may have been somewhat before their time but, regardless, Democratic Left did not succeed in establishing a close association between itself and the emerging green agenda. Overall, as the discussion above indicates, in terms of macro-economic or taxation policy it is difficult to discern what was radically different about the party's message to that of the Labour Party in the first instance and also in many respects from the other main parties in Leinster House.

CONCLUSION

Those involved with Democratic Left were reluctant to commit to a new social democratic future in 1992 mainly because of association with the Labour Party. Instead, they sought to forge a new political identity. Over several years the party published policy papers and was active in attempting to define a new political space. The analysis in this chapter has taken three policy areas that were central to Irish public and political life in the 1990s. The situation in Northern Ireland was totally transformed during the seven years in which Democratic Left existed as a political party. In several respects its policy position put Democratic Left in a different political space to the other parties in Leinster House. A case could be made that Democratic Left had a distinctive message in this policy area when the party was founded in 1992. The agenda was unambiguously hostile to nationalism and more accommodating to unionism. The party was possibly unfortunate in that, as a topic, Northern Ireland did not generate greater public interest in electorate terms in the Irish Republic. Moreover, the party's distinctiveness was to reduce as many of the policies which it favoured became part of the mainstream approach to Northern Ireland during the 1990s.

The party faced a similar experience in relation to the main issues on the so-called liberal agenda. Democratic Left was, without doubt, the most liberal party in Leinster House in 1992, as indicated by the Laver-Benoit expert study results discussed previously and also the policies outlined in party documents. But by 1998 when the merger talks with the Labour Party were underway several of the main items on the liberal agenda had been resolved. The main blockers of the liberal agenda in the other parties had been shunted aside as mainstream political opinion reflected an increasingly secular society in, for example, legislating for divorce and making contraception more widely available. The remaining items on the liberal agenda with the exception of abortion failed to generate the same degree of party political controversy.

Democratic Left had some distinctive elements to its economic agenda. It was the only party pushing for a wealth tax and a tax on financial market speculation. But it was unsuccessful in convincing its coalition partners to adopt such ideas in their joint policy programme. Moreover, there was a failure to convince the wider public about the merits of these proposals. As the discussion above indicates, the party moderated its economic policies and by the 1997 general election had a platform which had accommodated itself to the mainstream. The search for a new radical Left, in effect a reformist socialist party, was a challenge which Democratic Left ultimately failed to meet. The conclusion in relation to the three identified policy areas indicates a failure to articulate a policy and ideological position that was genuinely different from social democracy. The party's failure – as with other Left groups in Europe – was never deciding what it wanted to become. Democratic Left very much fits the scenario outlined by March and Muddle, who recorded that, 'as mainstream social democrats have become neo-liberal or social liberal, some West European democratic socialists have become *de facto* social democrats.'[103] It is against this ideological background that the discussion in subsequent chapters will deal with the organisational, leadership, identity and financial challenges faced by small political parties such as Democratic Left.

NOTES

1. Democratic Left, 1993 Task Force Report (draft), section 2.5.
2. Submission to Task Force Committee, 5 April 1993 by Peter McDermott, Gerard O'Quigley, Fearghal Ross and Michael Taft.
3. M. Marsh and R. Sinnott, 'How the Voters Decided', in M. Gallagher and R. Sinnott (eds), *How Ireland Voted, 1989* (Galway: University College Galway, 1990), p.124.
4. R. Sinnott, *Irish Voters Decide: Voting Behaviour in Elections and Referendums Since 1918* (Manchester: Manchester University Press, 1995), p.182.
5. Marsh and Sinnott, 'How the Voters Decided', pp.117–18.
6. P. Mair (ed.), *The West European Party System* (Oxford: Oxford University Press, 1990), p.218.
7. Sinnott, *Irish Voters Decide*, p.73 referring to Mair, *The West European Party System*, pp.214–16.
8. M. Laver, 'Party Policy in Ireland, 1997: Results from an Expert Survey', *Irish Political Studies*, vol. 13 (1998), p.162.

9. Ibid., p.163.
10. Ibid.
11. Ibid.
12. P. Bew and G. Gillespie, *Northern Ireland: A Chronology of the Troubles, 1968–99* (Dublin: Gill & Macmillan, 1999), p.267.
13. Ibid., p.261.
14. Ibid.
15. *The Irish Times*, 17 December 1992.
16. *Hansard*, 6th series, vol. 230, col. 530.
17. Bew and Gillespie, *Northern Ireland: A Chronology of the Troubles*, p.285.
18. D. De Bréadún, *The Far Side of Revenge: Making Peace in Northern Ireland* (London: Collins, 2001), p.31.
19. Interview with Proinsias De Rossa, 7 September 2007.
20. J. Coakley, 'Minor Parties in Irish Political Life, 1992–1989', *Economic and Social Review*, 21, 3 (1990), p.278.
21. Interview with Liz McManus, 18 October 2006.
22. *Dáil Debates*, vol. 421, cols 227–30, 10 June 1992.
23. Democratic Left, *A Programme for Change and Progress*, General Election, November 1992.
24. *Dáil Debates*, vol. 429, col. 65, 1 April 1993.
25. Proinsias De Rossa, Party Leader's Address, Annual Conference, 26 April 1997.
26. *Dáil Debates*, vol. 429, col. 69, 1 April 1993.
27. See *The Irish Times*, 9 September 1994.
28. Proinsias De Rossa, Party Leader's Address, Annual Conference, 26 April 1997.
29. Democratic Left, *A Programme for Change and Progress*, General Election, November 1992.
30. Democratic Left, *Draft Presented by Democratic Left as Basis for Discussion with the Labour Party*, 4 December 1992.
31. De Rossa, President's Address, Democratic Left Annual Conference, 1993.
32. *The Irish Times*, 21 April 1989.
33. BBC Radio Ulster, 'PM Ulster', 26 April 1993.
34. *The Irish Times*, May 1993.
35. De Rossa, President's Address, Democratic Left Annual Conference, 1993.
36. *Dáil Debates*, vol. 437, col. 1288, 17 December 1993.
37. Interview with Proinsias De Rossa, 7 September 2007.
38. *Dáil Debates*, vol. 437, col. 1284, 17 December 1993.
39. *Dáil Debates*, vol. 438, col. 556, 2 February 1994.
40. Interview with John Bruton, 28 March 2008.
41. G. Adams, *Hope and History: Making Peace in Ireland* (Dingle: Brandon, 2003), p.197.
42. Interview with Proinsias De Rossa, 7 September 2007.
43. Interview with Tony Heffernan, 13 September 2006.
44. D. Godson, *Himself Alone: David Trimble and the Ordeal of Unionism* (London: HarperCollins, 2004), p.161.
45. Ibid.
46. Ibid., p.159.
47. Ibid., p.161.
48. See *The Sunday Times*, 22 October 1995.
49. Interview with Proinsias De Rossa, 7 September 2007.
50. Ibid.
51. Interview with Rosheen Callender, 12 September 2006.
52. *Dáil Debates*, vol. 461, cols 1148–56, 13 February 1996.
53. Interview with Proinsias De Rossa, 7 September 2007.
54. Interview with John Bruton, 28 March 2008.
55. *Dáil Debates*, vol. 489, cols 1051–9, 21 April 1998.
56. Democratic Left, 'Policy Position on Northern Ireland', second draft, no date given but most likely early 1994.
57. *Dáil Debates*, vol. 489, cols 1051–9, 21 April 1998.
58. Democratic Left Mission Statement (Draft) July 1998.

59. Interview with Proinsias De Rossa, 7 September 2007.
60. Executive Council meeting minutes, 27 June 1992.
61. Democratic Left, Northern Ireland Report, undated.
62. Correspondence from Proinsias De Rossa to national executive members, 7 July 1993.
63. Interview with Proinsias De Rossa, 7 September 2007.
64. Ibid.
65. B. Girvin, 'An Introduction and Discussion', in B. Girvin and G. Murphy, 'Continuity, Change and Crisis in Ireland: New Perspectives, Research and Interpretation', *Irish Political Studies*, 23, 4 (2008), p.458.
66. B. Chubb, *The Government and Politics of Ireland* (London: Longman, 1992), p.23.
67. See M.P. Hornsby-Smith and C.T. Whelan, 'Religion and Moral Values', in C.T. Whelan (ed.), *Values and Social Change in Ireland* (Dublin: Gill & Macmillan, 1994), p.22.
68. C. T. Whelan, and T. Fahey, 'Marriage and the Family', in C.T. Whelan (ed.), *Values and Social Change in Ireland* (Dublin: Gill & Macmillan, 1994), pp.45–6.
69. Ibid., p.46.
70. J. Burley and F. Regan, 'Divorce in Ireland: The Fear, the Floodgates and the Reality', *International Journal of Law, Policy and the Family*, vol. 16 (2002), p.205.
71. Ibid., pp.207–8.
72. Democratic Left, November 1995.
73. Burley and Regan, 'Divorce in Ireland', p.203.
74. Interview with Liz McManus, 18 October 2006.
75. Interview with Rosheen Callender, 12 September 2006.
76. *Dáil Debates*, vol. 427, col. 109, 26 February 1993.
77. *Dáil Debates*, vol. 419, col. 1403, 13 May 1998.
78. *Dáil Debates*, vol. 422, col. 761, 8 July 1992.
79. Interview with Kathleen Lynch, 10 October 2006.
80. Interview with Eamon Gilmore, 11 September 2006.
81. *Dáil Debates*, vol. 456, col. 204, 17 September 1995.
82. *Dáil Debates*, vol. 456, col. 205, 17 September 1995.
83. C. Keane (ed.), *The Job Crisis: The Thomas Davis Lecture Series* (Dublin and Cork: RTÉ/Mercier Press, 1993), p.10.
84. *Dáil Debates*, vol. 415, col. 331, 29 January 1992.
85. *Dáil Debates*, vol. 415, col. 334, 29 January 1992.
86. Department of Finance, Budget 2000, http://www.budget.gov.ie/2000 (accessed 18 March 2008).
87. P. Teague, 'Full Employment: Attainable and Sustainable?' *Work in Progress, Discussion Journal of Democratic Left* (Dublin: Democratic Left, 1993), p.2.
88. *Dáil Debates*, vol. 425, col. 471, 5 January 1993.
89. Democratic Left, Election manifesto, 1994.
90. Democratic Left, *Europe Deserves Better*, 1992.
91. Democratic Left, *Position Paper on the Amsterdam Treaty*, May 1998.
92. Interview with John Bruton, 28 March 2008.
93. Democratic Left, *301,000 Reasons for Change: Economic Programme*, November 1992.
94. Democratic Left, Election manifesto, 1994.
95. *Dáil Debates*, vol. 427, cols 1957–9, 12 March 1993.
96. *Dáil Debates*, vol. 426, col. 1278, 23 February 1993.
97. Democratic Left, *Towards 2001: Draft Report of the Democratic Left Task Force on Politics, Strategy and Organisation*, April 1993.
98. *Dáil Debates*, vol. 418, col. 2059, 29 April 1992.
99. Democratic Left, *Beyond the Millennium*, 1997.
100. K. Rafter, 'Making It Up as They Went Along: Residential Property Tax and the Process of Policy Change', *Irish Political Studies*, 15, 1 (2000), p.63.
101. D. Geraghty, *New Century Socialism: Fighting for Justice in the Jungle* (Dublin: Democratic Left, 1998), p.10.
102. *Dáil Debates*, vol. 423, col. 545, 9 October 1992.
103. L. Marsh and C. Muddle, 'What's Left of the Radical Left? The European Radical Left After 1989: Decline and Mutation', *Comparative European Politics*, vol. 3 (2005), p.34.

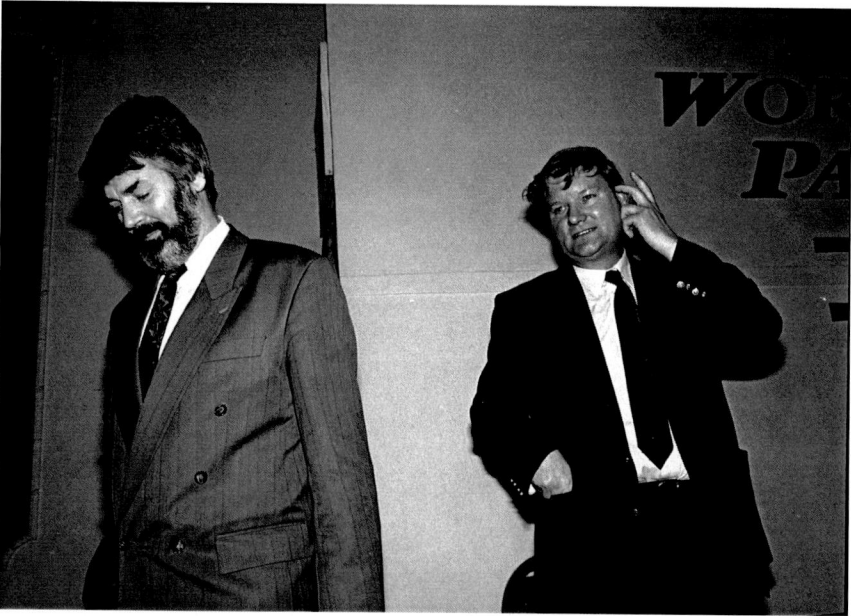

1. Proinsias De Rossa and Des Geraghty at the Workers' Party conference in February 1992 where they failed to get the required two-thirds majority to reconstitute the party.
Source: Photocall Ireland

2. Following the Workers' Party split Eamon Gilmore and Des Geraghty – seen here at the February 1992 reconstitution conference – went on to become influential members of Democratic Left.
Source: Photocall Ireland

NewAgenda

19 - 3 - 1992   Leinster House,
                                                 Dublin 2

Dear Friend,

Your assistance in deciding upon the name of the party would be
very welcome. As you know, we are currently using the working
title of 'New Agenda', which is also one of the suggestions
shortlisted as a possible title.

Our title should signal that we are an open democratic, socialist
party (without <u>necessarily</u> using those words). That we are a new
type of party as outlined in our founding principles, that we are
creative, inclusive and professional in our approach.

Attached is a Questonaire which you are requested to return
IMMEDIATELY, but not later than Mon. Mar. 23rd. The outcome of
this consultation process will be incorporated into the proposal
for a name to be decided at the Launch Conference on Mar. 28th.

QUESTIONAIRE

PART I Should any of the following words or their variations be
used in our title? Draw a line through those you don't want:

DEMOCRACY; SOCIALIST; NEW; AGENDA; PEOPLE; ALLIANCE; PARTY;
PROGRESS; CITIZEN; LEFT.

PART II Which of the following titles (listed alphabetically)
would you prefer? Mark 1,2,3, etc, in order of your choice:

	DEMOCRATIC LEFT
	NEW AGENDA
	NEW DEMOCRACY
	NEW LEFT
	PEOPLE'S PARTY
	PEOPLE'S PROGRESS PARTY
	SOCIALIST PARTY
	SOCIALIST PEOPLE'S PARTY

Have you any alternatives? _____

Signature (optional) _____

3. Operating under the temporary name of 'New Agenda' the De Rossa group sought the help of
members in selecting the permanent name for their new organisation.

4. One of Democratic Left's leading figures Pat Rabbitte at the party's founding conference in March 1992.
Source: Photocall Ireland

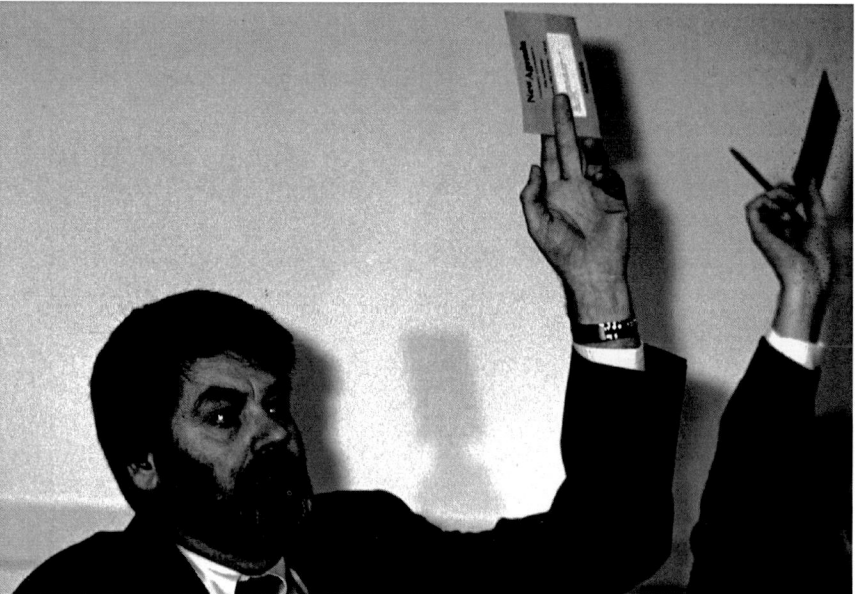

5. Proinsias De Rossa voting at the Democratic Left founding conference in March 1992.
Source: Photocall Ireland

Freddie ... cat row

Bust-up over Freddie Mercury's pussy

EXCLUSIVE

By PIERS MORGAN

FREDDIE Mercury's pet cat is at the centre of a bitter tug of love.

On one side is the tragic Queen singer's ex-neighbour Jo Mundy, the "adopted" ginger tom Oscar, 15, as the star died of AIDS.

On the other side is Freddie's former lover Mary Austin. She inherited his West London mansion, the bulk of his £amillion fortune — and his six cats, including Oscar.

Now Mary, 35, has threatened legal action to recover the moggy, who spent 12 years at Freddie's side.

Queen spokesman Roxy Meade said last night: "She was left Oscar in Freddie's will and wants him back."

But 30-year-old Jo claimed: "She may have more money than me, but I will never give up Oscar."

Jo started caring for Oscar in 1996 when he turned up at her flat overlooking Freddie's Kensington home.

She said: "He was in a terrible state. I thought he was a stray."

Full story — Pages 4 and 5

GATECRASH

Man who beat the ban...smiling Mary shakes hands with Proinsias de Rossa, and gets Albert Reynolds out of a jam

Cool Mary greets

cheeky de Rossa

By PADDY GLANDY

PRESIDENT Mary Robinson spared politicians' blushes by charming a gate-crasher yesterday.

She was being introduced by Taoiseach Albert Reynolds to other party leaders.

But at the end of the line stood Democratic Left boss Proinsias de Rossa.

He was not supposed to be there as Mary arrived on the steps of Leinster House for her historic address to the Oireachtas—a joint sitting of the Dail and Senate.

A special protocol committee had ruled that the Democratic Left was not entitled to a place on the welcoming line, because the party had only six elected TDs.

But de Rossa, who signed Mary's nomina-tion papers when she ran for the presidency, kept good his promise that he would not take a back seat.

For several minutes before the president's arrival, de Rossa stood beside the other dignitaries as photographers prepared to take a picture.

There was no way he could be removed without the moment being captured for the world.

The Taoiseach had no

Continued on Page Two

6. Without an invite Proinsias De Rossa joins other party leaders in welcoming President Mary Robinson to Leinster House as reported by *The Sun* in July 1992.

7. Liz McManus with Proinsias De Rossa, Kathleen Lynch and Eamon Gilmore at a Democratic Left press conference during the November 1992 general election.
Source: Photocall Ireland

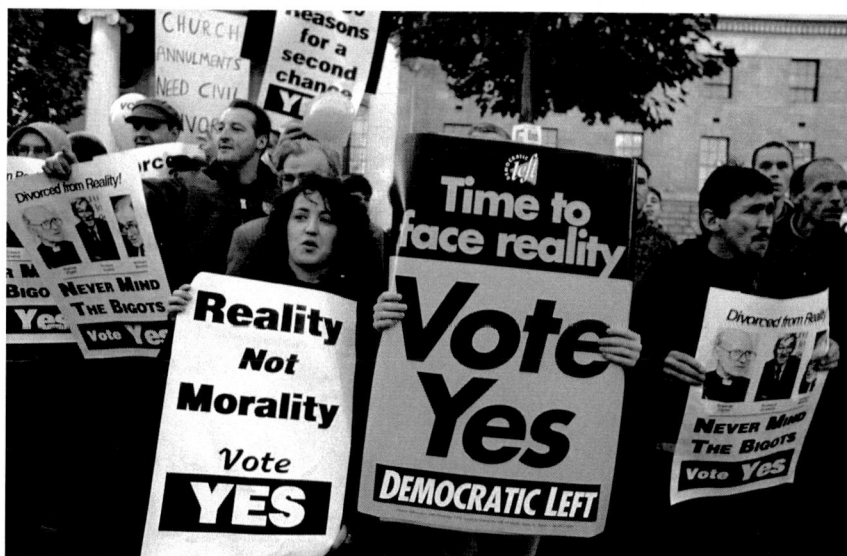

8. Democratic Left championed the so-called 'liberal agenda' and as part of the Rainbow government in 1996 the party campaigned for a 'yes' vote in the referendum to remove the constitutional ban on divorce legislation.

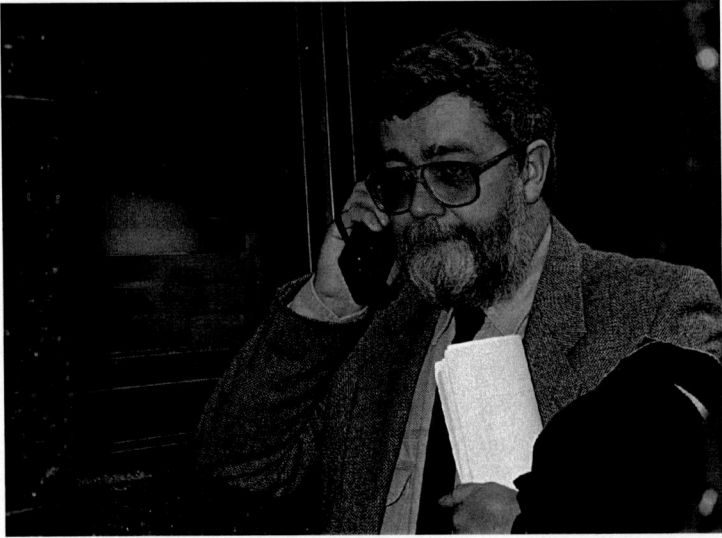

9. Democratic Left advisor Tony Heffernan, who worked for the party in government during the life of the Rainbow coalition.
Source: Photocall Ireland

10. Taoiseach John Bruton and Minister for Social Welfare Proinsias De Rossa welcome US President Bill Clinton to Government Buildings during the life of the 1994-97 Rainbow coalition.

11. The Democratic Left-Labour Party merger discussions as captured by cartoonist Gerard Crowley in the *Sunday Business Post* in July 1998.
Source: Courtesy of Gerard Crowley.

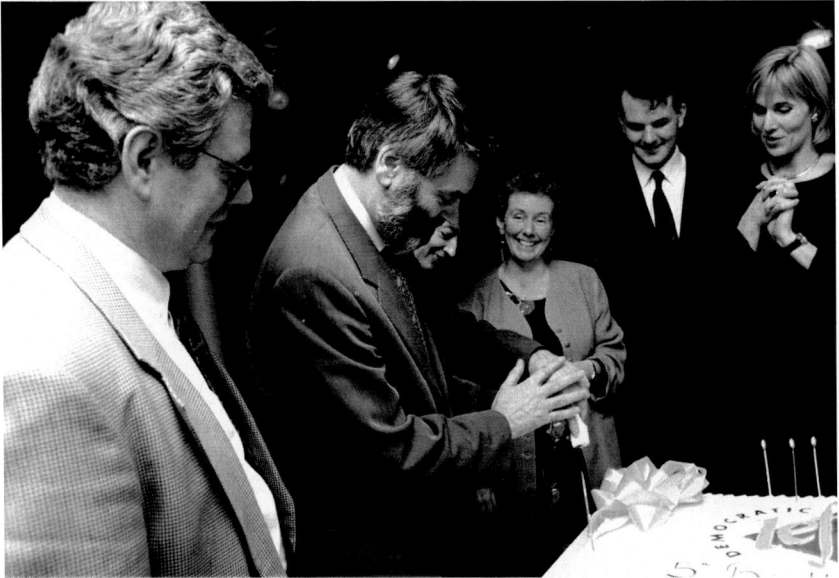

12. Celebrating the party's fifth year in existence in March 1997. (L to R) Eamon Gilmore, Proinsias De Rossa, Catherine Murphy, Helen Lahart, Anthony Creevy and Liz McManus.

13. Having secured the support of their respective parties, Ruairi Quinn and Proinsias De Rossa celebrate the merger. The deal when it became official in January 1999 marked the demise of Democratic Left.
Source: Photocall Ireland

8

Anatomy of a Party I: Organisation, Leadership and Identity

INTRODUCTION

In their anatomy of the ultimately unsuccessful Social Democratic Party (SDP) in the United Kingdom, Ivor Crewe and Anthony King concluded that 'creating a new and durable national party is extraordinarily difficult. Most attempts soon fail ...'[1] The organisation-building efforts of those involved with Democratic Left in Ireland would tend to back this assessment of the SDP experience. Outside of Fianna Fáil, Fine Gael and the Labour Party, the shared experience of most political parties in Ireland is failure. This was very clearly illustrated in John Coakley's examination of minor Irish political parties. Writing prior to the split which gave birth to Democratic Left, Coakley said: 'the remarkable tendency for initial success to be followed by rapid decline is characteristic of all except one of these parties, the Workers' Party, which seems to have established for itself a permanent position as a minor party.'[2] Within three years of this statement the assessment of the Workers' Party was open to revision. Indeed, neither the Workers' Party nor Democratic Left lasted long as prominent parties, and the Workers' Party had little national profile after the events in early 1992.

The ideal organisational requirements – according to Jean Blondel in his 1978 study *Political Parties* – for a successful political party include large size, united membership, dynamic approach and internal democratic structures. Blondel contended that larger parties have more influence and tend to be more effective while united parties avoid unnecessary disruption. He also argued that dynamic parties avoid the public perception that they are 'do nothing' organisations while internal democracy ensures greater responsiveness to party rank and file. Blondel admitted that 'these four requirements are ideal, but they are also somewhat difficult to reconcile ...'[3] They are also open to dispute.

For example, in a coalition-type system it may be that smaller parties get to exert influence over policy formation that is disproportionate to their size. The latter point has some validity in relation to the Democratic Left experience as part of the 1994–7 Rainbow coalition in Ireland.

Considering the four requirements in relation to Democratic Left, it is evident that the party did not meet the Blondel criteria in terms of size. The party had a united membership in the sense that there was little public disagreement between the membership and public representatives. Indeed, throughout 1998 as the discussions intensified about a possible merger with the Labour Party, the lack of public comment indicated remarkably tight internal discipline. This latter outcome may also point towards a strong democratic strand in Democratic Left. However, in one important respect Democratic Left failed the Blondel test: dynamic approach. The party was certainly not a 'do nothing' organisation. If anything the opposite was the case – the drivers of the Democratic Left project debated and discussed constantly what exactly were 'their politics'. But these discussions were unsuccessful in defining a distinctive ideological space, and in failing to convince the voters that they were articulating a different message the party failed to deliver the necessary dynamism to continue as a viable organisation. 'The overall purpose of parties is to implement certain policies, it could be said, without exaggeration that the products of political parties are ideologies and programmes, in much the same way that the products of industrial firms are material goods,' Blondel asserted.[4] Continuing the Blondel comparison, and considering one of the themes in this book about ideological convergence, then the programmes that Democratic Left brought to the political market place failed to secure sufficient public interest.

The party's initial aspirations were never realised. Following their exit from the Workers' Party, those involved in the De Rossa group were confronted with a number of choices. First, they could simply have called a halt to their political involvement and walked away from political activism. Some members, but few of significance, followed this route. The vast majority of the elected representatives and their close confidants wanted to remain politically active. Second, they could have joined the Labour Party – which most ultimately did with the 1999 merger – although at the time of the 1992 split many members thought this route a step too far. As Proinsias De Rossa remarked: 'Some would have been happy enough to do it but the vast majority would not have joined. I certainly didn't want to join the Labour Party at that time.'[5] Third, they had the option of founding a new political movement. In explaining why the third option was chosen, De Rossa told the 1995 party conference that along with his supporters he 'believed that there was a clear role for a new force in Irish politics, a dynamic democratic party of the left'.[6]

The decision to throw their weight behind a new political party also offered De Rossa and his supporters the prospect of a fresh start. But the challenges were enormous. Irish politics – not to mention wider European politics – is littered with the carcasses of failed political endeavours established by well-meaning and well-known figures but ultimately rejected by the voters. Clann na Poblachta remains the best example in recent Irish political history. It was a party that emerged in the late 1940s, entered government in 1948 but within a decade was little more than a banner for a number of politicians who effectively operated as independents. The Progressive Democrats experienced a similar fate in 2009. Those driving Democratic Left acknowledged the disappointing historical experience of other new parties. 'It was seen as a daunting task and people were well aware of the efforts over many decades by different left wing parties to establish themselves and they had all tended to run into the ground, so we were under no illusions,' John Gallagher admitted.[7]

This chapter will examine the elements needed to sustain a new political party, focusing on organisation, leadership and identity. The additional challenges related to funding will be discussed in Chapter 9. The totality of these factors is vital in maintaining a head office, employing full-time staff, attracting members, recruiting candidates and fighting elections. In addition, a new party must have a clear identity to capture the public mood and, most likely in the modern media era, a recognisable leader with a strong personality. Having all these elements in place would be the optimum outcome, but most parties exist with varying strengths and weaknesses in their financial outlook, membership numbers, organisational structure, quality of leadership and clarity of identity. For example, in some circumstances it may be possible to run a successful party with a small membership and little money so long as the party has a charismatic leader and a clearly defined identity. Alternatively, a party with a large membership and strong organisation may compensate for a muted identity with other elements including healthy finances. All four headings – organisation, leadership, identity and money – impacted on the fortunes of Democratic Left.

ORGANISATION: MEMBERSHIP

The 1992 split sundered the ranks of the Workers' Party, although not everyone was prepared to join the new party. 'People followed personal loyalties, personal friends, family relations, that sort of thing,' Tony Heffernan recalled.[8] Along with those who were rooted to the Workers' Party, or committed to following De Rossa, some activists simply walked away from direct political involvement. Heffernan had first hand experience of this. 'My brother-in-law would have been involved in the Workers' Party nearly as long as I had. He just said in 1992, "Look I'm out of here. You're probably right about the Workers' Party but I'm not joining the new party." I knew a couple of people like that.'[9] The reasons why people who were supportive of the De Rossa position walked away from political involvement were varied, as Heffernan explained: 'If you looked at the Workers' Party or Official Sinn Féin in the early nineteen seventies, the average age [of members] was probably early twenties. This [1992] was twenty years on. People had kids, some in secondary school and some going into university. People had devoted a lot of their lives to it, and a lot of people simply said, "you know, it's not for me".'[10]

Democratic Left politicians frequently referred to the difference between their members and those in other political organisations. 'It may well have been that we didn't have mountains of members but the members we had were very committed,' Catherine Murphy argued.[11] But members were thin on the ground, and new members were – according to one assessment – sometimes put off by the commitments demanded of them: 'Some party members of a non-Workers' Party background have remarked on the lengthy nature of party meetings. This may be a cultural throwback from an era when unquestioning devotion to the cause was expected from all members. We should look at how we conduct meetings with a view to greater efficiency in this area.'[12]

Numerous attempts were made to increase the party's membership base. A student conference was held in early 1993 with Eamon Gilmore among the invited speakers. 'The conference was a success in terms of discussion and establishing a core group of active student members within the party,' an internal report noted.[13] The positive tone, however, only masked the poor attendance – 30 students from several third-level institutions including University College Dublin, Trinity College, Dublin and the University of Limerick as well as a south Dublin private secondary school, Gonzaga College, and observers from Northern Ireland. In a sign of how little progress the party made over the following years, an internal note from mid-September 1997 recorded the difficulty in targeting university student members because 'a lot of colleges use a rule that you must have members already present among the student body before being entitled to use facilities or display stands.'[14] The same document noted that setting up a separate 'youth section' in the party in the 1992–7 period had 'not always been successful'.[15]

Various outlets for involvement were available to the party's membership. Being a member of Democratic Left was not just about canvassing. People were encouraged to join policy committees while a summer school was organised to stimulate policy debate. Ways of improving internal communications were also regularly discussed. A working committee was established to examine the feasibility of producing a party magazine. At a meeting of the party executive in May 1992 it was noted that the state training agency FÁS had approved a IR£2,000 (approx. €2,539) feasibility study grant. 'For breakeven the magazine requires a circulation of 5,000 copies monthly. It is planned to have one full-time staff person, with provision for funding from FÁS and the enterprise allowance scheme.'[16] The ambitious plan was never realised, but through the efforts of party activist Paddy Gillen and others, Democratic Left produced on an ongoing basis regular pamphlets and newsletters. The pages of the internal magazine *Times Change* allowed for interesting debate, but an examination of the contributors shows that the same couple of dozen individuals were driving the party.

There was without doubt a heavy reliance on a small pool of active members. As Pat Rabbitte recalled, there was an 'extraordinary workload on a small number of us'.[17] This group – which could be said to number around fifty or so individuals – displayed a huge degree of activity. The party published policy documents on topics as diverse as divorce, reform of the United Nations, community employment, and renewal of the criminal justice system. Campaigns were organised on an array of issues, including the cost of sending children back to school and a government-sponsored tax amnesty. But the same names were associated with all of these activities and events. 'For a variety of reasons, you didn't get the same sort of commitment out of members of Democratic Left that you had out of the Workers' Party,' Tony Heffernan remarked.[18]

In May 1996, a piece in the unsigned 'In Camera' column in the *Sunday Tribune* noted that there was a very poor attendance at a meeting of the party's constituency committee in Dublin North West. 'There were only 11 people at the meeting on 26 February and four of those were members of Proinsias De Rossa's own family,' the article stated.[19] The party was in government at that time but was still struggling to attract member interest, and also to interest new people to become members. There was competition for seats on the National Executive at the 1996 annual conference with thirty-four candidates nominated to contest the twenty vacancies. But a closer examination of the candidate names shows the list included Oireachtas members, local councillors, government advisors and party staff. The party's limited geographical reach was also evident, with the majority of the candidates (twenty-one) representing Dublin constituencies with ten candidates from constituencies outside Dublin and three candidates from Northern Ireland.

In May 1998 De Rossa was critical of membership activity in the referendum on the Belfast Agreement. National Executive minutes record that De Rossa 'said there had been a low level of activity which was unacceptable, particularly given the importance of the Northern Ireland and European situation'.[20] The criticism may be somewhat unfair as a lack of grassroots activism could not just be confined to Democratic Left – while the 56 per cent turnout was good in comparison to other referendums but lower than the turnout levels in general elections. An important categorisation in party membership activity made by Gallagher and Marsh is, however, worth noting.

> We can start by distinguishing two main categories into which members' activity might fall: activity that takes place within the party organisation, and activity that entails engagement with the wider public. The first type of activity covers such behaviour as attending party meetings, giving money to the party, or standing for some position within the party organisation. The second type would mainly involve doing something for the party at elections ... Looked at from the perspective of the party as a whole – if

there is such a thing – it might seem that the most important activity consists of contact with the public.[21]

On this basis, poor attendance at internal Democratic Left meetings should not have been the most serious concern, especially in a small organisation which revolved around a number of key individuals with significant high public profiles. In their 2002 study of Fine Gael, Gallagher and Marsh concluded that 'Party membership figures have been notoriously unreliable in the past, and not just in Ireland.'[22] There is no reason to believe that Democratic Left was an exception in this regard. Membership varied considerably across the country but was largely concentrated in constituencies where the party had elected representatives. The total active membership of the party is difficult to gauge, but one estimate put it at between 300 and 500 in the autumn of 1997.[23] A document prepared ahead of the formal merger with the Labour Party in early 1999 recorded 776 paid-up members on the Democratic Left books. The figure – in Table 8.1 – excluded the Dún Laoghaire constituency, which was one of the most active in the party. But even allowing for Dún Laoghaire having in the region of the 60 to 90 members, the official party membership was in the region of 850.

ORGANISATION: STRUCTURES

In the first half of 1992 Democratic Left leased an office in Middle Abbey Street in central Dublin while the position of general secretary was filled initially by Des Geraghty and subsequently by John Gallagher. The head office operation remained small throughout the party's seven-year history. There was some back-up secretarial support, but volunteer workers were required to attend on a rota basis. 'It was a small operation and constituencies really had to fend for themselves. Head office didn't have the ability to maintain the party effectively, you had Des Geraghty and myself and two part-time secretaries. It [head office] largely fed out information to the constituencies ...' John Gallagher recalled.[24]

Access to equipment and other facilities was determined by money, which was always in short supply. One example of these constraints was found in party minutes which record that in late May 1992 the national executive debated the purchase of equipment including a laser

TABLE 8.1
DEMOCRATIC LEFT MEMBERSHIP, JANUARY 1999

Constituency	Members
Carlow/Kilkenny	9
Clare	1
Cork East	32
Cork North Central	44
Cork South West	2
Cork South Central	14
Donegal (South West and North East)	30
Dublin Central	6
Dublin North Central	13
Dublin North East	20
Dublin North West	65
Dublin North	19
Dublin South Central	86
Dublin South East	12
Dublin South West	67
Dublin South	14
Dublin West	12
Dún Laoghaire	n/a
Galway (East and West)	9
Kerry (South and North)	1
Kildare (South and North)	64
Limerick (East and West)	50
Louth	8
Mayo	1
Meath	20
Sligo	2
Tipperary (South and North)	3
Waterford	45
Wexford	28
Wicklow	93
International	8
Midlands	8
Total	776

Source: From documents in the possession of the author.

printer for head office. The party also agreed to pay half of the cost of a printer for members in Cork city – approval was also given for a bank loan to be obtained, if needed, to cover the other half. With access to the most basic of facilities so limited it was always going to be a difficult challenge to build Democratic Left into a viable political force. For established politicians like Eamon Gilmore and Pat Rabbitte the restricted ability of the central party operation to assist with constituency work and enhancing profile may have been of no significant disadvantage. But in terms of attracting members and growing the party in new areas the constraints on head office placed a considerable limitation on Democratic Left's capacity to seriously challenge the Labour Party's dominance. Des Geraghty admitted that they 'probably underestimated the amount of work' involved in establishing a new party.[25] However, Gilmore, while recognising the difficult head office situation, sought to downplay its significance.

> Centrally we were very poorly positioned. But it didn't make a huge difference. The reason I'm saying this is that we operated our election campaigns when we were in the Workers' Party literally on our own. I never got any assistance from the Workers' Party head office. There was some kind of central arrangement for bulk buying posters for the election but it wasn't any different [after the split]. You were just using a different brand and so on.[26]

The economic situation in the mid-1990s prior to the buoyancy of the so-called Celtic Tiger era should have allowed scope for a party like Democratic Left. Remarkably, one administrative vacancy at head office in early 1993 attracted thirty-eight applications, of which thirty-four were interviewed.[27] This level of interest, however, probably says more about the Irish labour market at that time than it does about interest levels in Democratic Left.

There was considerable internal honesty about the challenges facing the party. Item three on the agenda of a National Executive meeting on 16 January 1993 referred to 'Party Development and Planning'. A variety of views were on offer. Much emphasis was placed on the need to develop policy prescriptions unique to Democratic Left and to 'stimulate the intellectual life of the party'.[28] In a report on Democratic Left's publicity campaign in the 1992 general election there was an admission that 'while we produced a good manifesto and a number of credible policy documents, they did not contain the "new" ideas necessary to capture the attention of the media and the electorate.'[29]

One party member submitted a paper in early 1993, and while much of the document concentrated on organisational structures, an interesting section on 'flagship policies' illustrated the still confused identity of the new party – '… Democratic Left must construct a set of symbols – policies that immediately communicated radical distinctiveness.'[30] The items mentioned included basic income, statutory right to work, national minimum wage, a wealth tax, free GP cover for all and separation of church and state. The first opinion poll of 1993 starkly illustrated the difficulties facing the party. There was no noticeable uplift for Democratic Left. A Market Research Bureau of Ireland (MRBI) poll commissioned by *The Irish Times* in March 1993 showed Democratic Left support levels at 2 per cent. 'Given the high level of dissatisfaction with the Government the poll for DL must be a disappointment. The figures confirm a picture that has remained the same since February of last year,' one private party assessment observed.[31] The conclusion was succinct: 'the politics of why our support has not increased can be debated. The fact that we have remain[ed] stuck over the last year at the 2% level cannot.'[32]

Party officers held two meetings in early 1993 'to consider the new circumstances in which Democratic Left must function' – a reference to the post-general election situation in which Fianna Fáil and Labour were settling into a new coalition arrangement.[33] This internal group led by De Rossa was continuing to seek the 'raison d'être' for the party. A recommendation was made to – and subsequently accepted by – the party's National Executive 'to appoint immediately a small Commission to report on future development of the party's politics, organisation and strategy'. Democratic Left was not yet a year old but already its leadership felt the need to overhaul the party from top to bottom. The deadline for the report was April 1993, while the party membership was to be involved in the discussions 'to consider options open to us and make clear decisions about the party's direction in the period ahead'.[34] The task force examined the party's policies, strategy and organisation. A draft version of the task force report, which restated the core beliefs and values agreed at the founding conference, also noted that in most west European countries a social democratic party was generally:

... flanked by at least one other radical alternative – the effect of which, in practice, has helped maintain a more radical left agenda while simultaneously providing an alternative within the left that helps to sustain the overall vote for that bloc. Today, these social democratic parties are in crisis having abandoned much of their vision [and converged with Christian democratic parties around the political centre].[35]

The challenge for the party was to 'present a convincing case for a left agenda. DL must aim to provide *moral and intellectual leadership*, and win support of a broad section of working class and progressive opinion.'[36] The reality was, however, that despite all the effort to create a new type of politics, the party was struggling to articulate an alternative Left agenda. The issues identified in Chapter 1 about the meaning and direction of Left politics had strong relevance to the challenges faced by Democratic Left. In a telling observation arising from internal discussions about a draft version of the task force report, it was agreed that there was a 'need to create an image of a "re-launch" of the party'.[37] Remarkably, just twelve months following its formation, senior party figures were contemplating a 're-launch'. Like the social democratic parties, described by the task force report as being in 'crisis', it was increasingly clear that Democratic Left and its radical Left agenda was seriously struggling.

The party held its first Annual Delegate Conference at the Royal Marine Hotel in Dún Laoghaire on 15–17 October 1993. The conference focused on what were identified as six flagship areas – jobs, tax, equality, environment, Europe and Northern Ireland. The backdrop to the conference was summarised in a report to the party's general council, prepared a month previously, which concluded that there were mixed views about Democratic Left's progress.[38] A summer school in 1993 had attracted few delegates – 'Attendance may be improved if held in the Spring' – at which there were disappointing reports about membership activity levels: 'Attendance at Executive and at Council is very poor.'[39]

There were repeated criticisms of the internal party structures and that there was a lack of clarity over the role of the executive and the council. 'These roles are never clear, and have become increasingly blurred over time,' one member argued in early 1993. He suggested that the council meet four times a year and concentrate on party policy while monthly executive meetings focus on party management.[40] The party's structure also included numerous committees covering areas such as finance, political organisation and economic affairs. Given the party's size and membership base, there was a valid argument for streamlining the committee structures to take account of the resources available.

Nevertheless, there were some grounds for believing that in the 1993–4 period the party was gradually establishing a political presence based on policy issues and campaigns. The potential for growth was also apparent at election times, as was evident in the various contests in 1994. While De Rossa briefed an Executive Council meeting in June 1994 on the need 'for greater organisational development at local level', the same meeting heard that 'the European, local and by-elections produced an overall good result which had helped to establish the party's public recognition and confirm its base in society.' But that base was, in reality, not very deep. Internally there were ongoing criticisms of the party's organisation, with many – including the authors of the 1997 task force report – focusing on the role of the National Executive. The body was constitutionally the main decision-making authority between annual conferences but it was seen as ineffective, with too many members. The work of party head office was also reviewed in the 1997 task force report, which suggested the appointment of an outside consultant to identify the remit of the head office, an appropriate staffing level, preparation of job descriptions and a review of office technology.[41]

The period in government allowed the party to mask its deficient organisation. But availing of the indirect benefit of government was plainly ignoring the core issue and allowed problems to be sidestepped. Indeed, in early 1995 an article in the internal newsletter *Forum* bluntly described the poor state of the party organisation. The author of the piece observed that members could:

> ... see that the number of party workers is low. Members can see that the party is devoid of a core vote in the working class or any other section of society (not to be confused with personal popularity of individual candidates). Members can see that we have no distinct ideology or identity. In short, the party's structures are weak. It is a house of cards ... [and] ... there is no future at all in being in a Little Labour Party.[42]

One political reporter, who attended the 1995 and 1996 annual conferences, remarked upon similar deficiencies. After the 1996 conference, Denis Coghlan wrote: 'The numbers were small, the age profile worrying. Democratic Left is a party in the doldrums, lacking broad public recognition and new blood. But it may have turned the corner in terms of personal confidence. Last year its annual conference was a shambles – the numbers tiny, the venue dirty and the delegates disillusioned. This year there is a growing confidence that its Ministers have performed well in Government and that the party is making a real impact.'[43] Coghlan attributed this new confidence to the high profile of the party's public representatives. But he still concluded that, such was the weakness in party structures and lack of public recognition for Democratic Left, 'a wave of rejection [at the 1997 general election] could bury the party without trace.'[44] In truth, the public impact of Democratic Left's leading members contributed little to the party brand but rather enhanced the profile of the individuals concerned. By the 1997 general election Democratic Left was less dependent upon its membership base and found itself less a political party and more a group of like-minded independents. None of the party's successful candidates in the June 1997 general election won on the basis of their party allegiance. In that regard, it was obvious that Democratic Left's difficulty went beyond organisation and membership.

IDENTITY

Democratic Left members saw themselves as offering an alternative to the established parties, especially the Labour Party. Yet throughout the party's life its members would time and time again return to the question of what political space did their party occupy. To say the party suffered from an ongoing identity crisis would, in a shorthand way, summarise the difficulty faced by Democratic Left. As early as June 1992 – writing in the aftermath of the referendum on the European Union's Maastricht Treaty – Pat Rabbitte said, 'Clearly Maastricht helped but there remains a Party Identity problem which only time will correct.'[45] For those who remained in the Workers' Party after the 1992 split the apparent lack of ideological definition in Democratic Left was rooted in their view of the motivations for the split. Seán Garland argued:

> We were a socialist party. We were never a communist party. I think in changing to Democratic Left they were saying, 'we are intent on

our own careers.' They had managed to convince people that [we were] you know criminals, Official IRA terrorists, communists and people of that kind. But I didn't see any principle driving the Democratic Left leadership ... and there wasn't a very significant political development for them.[46]

Garland's comments could be taken as a case of sour grapes, but in focusing on Democratic Left's identity dilemma he was not saying anything that was not debated privately in wider Democratic Left circles. The challenge of communicating the new party's message was considerable, especially as those involved had to first deal with the confusion over the emergence of their new political grouping. Even the party leader occasionally slipped up. 'Sometimes I pick up the phone and say, "Hello, Workers' Party". Old habits die hard,' De Rossa admitted in a media interview during the 1992 general election campaign.[47]

Another story recalled by Eamon Gilmore clearly illustrated the enormous challenge in establishing the new party. 'I remember canvassing shortly after Democratic Left was formed and one particular constituent said, "Eamon, I've no problem with you leaving the Workers' Party but joining up with O'Malley [Des O'Malley, leader of Progressive Democrats] is too much for me."'[48] Catherine Murphy in County Kildare shared Gilmore's experience. 'To be honest a lot of people often confused Democratic Left with the Progressive Democrats. The two with the name "democrat" didn't help. And you used to have to say, "No, I'm De Rossa's lot, not Harney's lot." And then they'd say, "Oh, that's alright." So you had to define it [the party] by him [De Rossa] rather than by the name of the party. So that tells you something about your washing powder brand.'[49]

The party's first big challenge was to gain public acknowledgement of its very existence. There was little help from within the political system, where the new party faced constant reminders of its minority status. For example, in July 1992 then president Mary Robinson addressed a joint session of the two houses of the Oireachtas. The Fianna Fáil–Progressive Democrat government issued invitations to all party leaders to participate in the formal welcome reception when the president arrived at Leinster House. De Rossa, however, was excluded. The government said this was because protocol ruled that with only six TDs the leader of Democratic Left was not entitled to attend, as his party did not have formal parliamentary recognition.

The episode generated considerable media coverage. A photograph of De Rossa's handshake with President Robinson was the front-page image on the *Sun* newspaper under the headline, 'Gatecrash'. The newspaper noted: 'De Rossa, who signed Mary's nomination papers when she ran for the presidency, kept good on his promise that he would not take a back seat.'[50] This minor episode is an example of the steep climb faced in gaining acceptance. In truth, throughout its short existence, Democratic Left faced a considerable challenge in putting forward its own distinctive message. This task was the subject of ongoing internal debate, and several internal committees were established in an attempt to overcome confusion and a lack of public clarity about just what Democratic Left stood for.

The same topic was on the agenda when the Dáil Group met for a day-long session in late August 1992. Those present – all six TDs, along with Des Geraghty, Tony Heffernan, John Gallagher and Paddy Gillen – had 'a long discussion on the party to date'.[51] In a document prepared two days prior to this Dáil Group meeting – and circulated to all Executive Council members – Pat Rabbitte observed that the party's economic policy remained undeveloped. 'We have not managed thus far to bring an Alternative Programme and one that distinguishes us from a Labour Party in opposition. The construction of such an Alternative Programme must be (and is being) addressed not merely for electoral purposes but because it goes to the heart of our existence.'[52]

The party's electoral record has been discussed previously, but the difficulties faced as a general election loomed in late 1992 were all too obvious to Democratic Left's leading figures. 'The task of surmounting the recognition barrier – Democratic Left – means that the Campaign must be candidate focused. If budgetary constraints permit, specific steps should be taken now to reduce the name recognition and identification problem. The quickest and most effective way of doing this is through the Public Representatives whose faces and what they stand for are already known to the public.'[53]

These views were mirrored in another internal party assessment prepared around the same time in August 1992. 'While many of the elements of Democratic Left's distinctive political practice and ideology have been enunciated, the party has been unable to define itself in relation to other political forces. As a result morale has not been very high amongst the membership; the media and broader public barely understand why the party exists other than that it emerged from a split.'[54] The unnamed author emphasised a point that was increasingly acknowledged in Democratic Left circles – 'no party can emerge with strength after a split.'

Despite the best efforts of those involved – and the work of a number of internal task forces established to address the issue – no clear understanding emerged as to what exactly was understood by 'Democratic Left'. In his report to the 1993 annual party conference, John Gallagher acknowledged the challenge. 'One of the unsatisfactory aspects for members must be the continuing low poll ratings for Democratic Left. There is no simple explanation for this situation, although it is obvious that the party has still to develop a clear identity in the public mind.'[55] Like others, Gallagher argued that the priority was 'the establishment of the party's profile and identity'.[56]

The identity issue was not one that was easily resolved. It emerged once more in July 1994 in a short internal document – 'Youth Report' – prepared for an executive meeting. 'There is a crisis of identity and purpose in Democratic Left. This has resulted, externally, in continually low voter identification and recognition for the party as a unit, its politics and its policies; internally, with the membership's morale and motivation.'[57] The prescription offered was a variation on a theme repeated time and time again in internal party documents: 'The very immediate task and objective of this party is to clearly establish and define itself as a democratic socialist party on the radical left of the Irish political spectrum. This must be done in an unambiguous and unapologetic way.'[58] Included among the practical solutions put forward to enhance the party's identity was the need for a campaigning section, a party newsletter, promotion of internal debate and a change in the language and symbols of the party.

> The language and symbols should be clear, forceful and emotive. The Party's present sanitised friendly-speak makes us sound more like social workers than socialists. Colours and symbols are important not just in establishing the Party identity but also as an emblem for members and supporters. The new colour should be predominantly red with perhaps green, blue or black. We also need a new logo. We do not propose using clenched fists, chains or hammers and sickles but a triangle is completely meaningless.[59]

The identity problem was widely acknowledged by leading Democratic Left figures. Tony Heffernan said more should have been made of differences with the Labour Party:

> We described ourselves as a democratic socialist party. I suppose we should have tried to explain the difference between that and social democracy, which wasn't all that easy and which wasn't something that the voters were terribly interested in. We should have explained ourselves more in terms of criticising the positions that the Labour Party had taken and criticising the previous record of the Labour Party.[60]

But for others the 'Labour question' was one that did not have an easy answer. 'That bedevilled every left wing party that has emerged because there has always been the Labour Party, and in the mind of the people – "why are you different?" – that certainly was an issue for Democratic Left,' John Gallagher concluded.[61]

The identity issue was again the focus of discussion at the meetings of the post-general election task force that convened in the summer of 1997. 'The precise position and purpose of a socialist party like Democratic Left needs to be re-stated,' the report concluded, adding the recommendation that a new strategic approach involve other like-minded parties to create a Left-led government.[62] In a significant recommendation – and a significant acknowledgement of the troubles facing the party at the time – the task force in 1997 said it 'would favour a change in the Party name but believes that this is not politically practical. However, it recommends that the Party should style itself Democratic Left – the Socialist Party on literature and elsewhere as appropriate.'[63] The party's National Executive did not accept the name change idea, although its members agreed to commission a report 'on projection of our name and policy and the production of a new logo'.[64] But even the recommended new strategic policy focus was not ultimately enough to allow Democratic Left to continue as a viable independent party.

Nevertheless, it is to the credit of those involved that they maintained Democratic Left as a viable political entity for almost seven years. But the lack of a clearly defined identity stifled the party's growth. This situation was even more difficult during the life of the Rainbow government when the points of differentiation with the Labour Party became even more blurred, especially for the electorate.

Paul Sweeney was confronted with this argument at home. 'Eventually, as my wife put it to me – and she isn't particularly interested in politics – "Look, Paul, I find it very hard to differentiate between you [Democratic Left] and Labour ..." It became a big subject in the house and she said, "Really, you can see the party isn't growing and, in fact it is shrinking."'[65] In that regard, a failure to carve out a clear difference of identity in the public mind from the Labour Party meant Democratic Left was never going to achieve its aim of becoming a strong Left alternative in Irish politics.

LEADERSHIP

Proinsias De Rossa became president of the Workers' Party in 1988 having acquired influence and respect over many years as he rose through party ranks stretching back to the late 1950s as a teenage member of the IRA. The bond with his supporters was strengthened during the period in which Democratic Left was formed. There was some media speculation about who would fill the position of leader in the new party. Pat Rabbitte was mentioned as an alternative to De Rossa, although in an interview for this study he dismissed the idea. 'I had no interest in taking over. I had my mind made up at that time that the party [Democratic Left] wasn't viable in the longer term,' he said.[66] The two leading figures in Democratic Left had very different personalities and were very different politicians, as Eric Byrne explained:

> De Rossa was a far more political animal, committed to a political philosophy, and Rabbitte is more a populist type of politician ... He might very well have taken us into the Labour Party more quickly than we went into the Labour Party but I think at that transition De Rossa was needed because he was the only man who could I think effectively handle the old guard. He would have been a better man to ease this split and create a new party and bring as many [people] as possible. I think Rabbitte quite rightly knew that he wouldn't get the leadership at that stage. We would always have envisaged him down the line but, at that stage, it was right that De Rossa was the one.[67]

There may have been some merit in giving greater consideration to a leadership change as part of the process of moving Democratic Left further away from the Workers' Party. De Rossa was firmly rooted in the Workers' Party, although he had led the transformation of the party after he became party president. 'He was probably very pro-Moscow but he hadn't been for a very long time [when he became WP leader],' Paul Sweeney said.[68] A new party with a new leader *might* have generated more excitement and greater public attention. But the downside would possibly have been greater internal dissent. Any move to replace De Rossa at that time would probably have added further division, and may have led more activists to reject the idea of joining a new party. In any event, De Rossa's high internal stature meant the leadership issue was not seriously discussed.

Certainly, there remains strong loyalty towards De Rossa among his former Democratic Left colleagues. 'He was extremely important. There's a slightly Parnell-like quality about him. He was quite distant. He was quite arrogant. But you could trust him completely in his judgement,' Liz McManus said.[69] Des Geraghty was another loyal supporter. 'He was a great asset. He was politically serious, a very committed socialist. He didn't do things to be popular. He wasn't in the mould of kissing babies and slapping backs but he helped put an identification on the party.'[70]

Without doubt, De Rossa gave his party a certain gravitas. He was a serious, policy-minded politician. During his tenure as a government minister he showed how he was different from many of his political peers in displaying a directness in dealing with controversial issues. When he was asked about Fianna Fáil criticism that he supported the adoption of children by homosexual couples, he responded, 'The important thing for the child is a loving parent. Lots of parents who are homosexual have children. It doesn't change the child in any way.'[71] He also displayed a very down-to-earth character. 'From the beginning I made it clear that people would not be holding my coat; that I did not want my bag carried; that I would only use my car for public functions; that I wouldn't use it at weekends,' De Rossa noted.

Despite these attributes, De Rossa could not easily shake off his own past involvements and associations. The break with the Workers' Party did not automatically end questions about criminality and the existence of the Official IRA. In a lengthy interview in *Hot Press* magazine in late 1992 it was put to De Rossa: 'It was only earlier this year ... that you conceded the ongoing existence of the Official IRA. Given that the

RUC and various media outlets, both North and South, had consistently and repeatedly stated this to be the case, how did you manage to remain ignorant of it for so long?' In response, De Rossa stated:

> Well, you see, I still haven't conceded the existence of the Official IRA. If people read what I said at the time, I made the point and I stick to it very clearly, that, as far as I was concerned the Official IRA was disbanded in the early '70s. What became clear to me after I became President of the Workers' Party was that there was very much what I describe as a kitchen cabinet operating within the party ... There were decisions being made outside the normal democratic process of the party ... I was never a member of the so-called Official IRA as such. The Official IRA emerged as a body after the split [with the Provisionals] in 1969. I joined the IRA when I was 16 and I was arrested and interned shortly after my 17th birthday in 1957. I was then kept in The Curragh until shortly before my 19th birthday. A short while after that I resigned from the IRA and joined Sinn Féin, and this was all up to ten years before the Official IRA as a body emerged.

De Rossa explained his decision to leave the IRA by saying:

> It became clear to me that that kind of activity was self-destructive. You know, when you're 16 and you're told that emigration and unemployment were because of the partition of the country, and the only way to fight the partition of the country is to fight the British army, it has a certain appeal. Especially, when at the same time you had people like de Valera calling for an end to partition as well. But as the thing developed it became clear it was nonsense. There was a lot of discussion in The Curragh about freedom and what was it worth to a hungry man and woman and we got discussing socialism and so forth. When The Curragh closed, a whole new direction took place in the republican movement.[72]

But De Rossa's past associations continued to dog Democratic Left. In the autumn of 1992 a letter was sourced in the archives of the Communist Party of the Soviet Union allegedly signed by De Rossa and Seán Garland. It seemed that the Workers' Party had sought money from the communist regime, which had also funded trips to Moscow and

North Korea. The letter, dated September 1986, said that most of the shortfall in the party's finances had been met by 'special activities'.

> Expenditure over a 12 month period is IR£325,000 [approx. €413,000] which covers wages, offices and publications. The bulk of the shortfall has been met by 'special activities' of which it is not possible to detail here because of reasons we are sure you will understand. The 'special activities' are unable always to be effective and so on occasion the party has had to seek loans ... Further the continued growth of the party in the public domain makes 'special activities' more hazardous for the paty [sic] which has more than enough enemies in the establishment ready to pounce on mistakes or difficulties.

The letter-writers continued, 'we would respectfully request a grant of one million pounds (Irish) over the proposed five-year development period.' The letter was signed, 'Yours fraternally, Seán Garland, general secretary; Proinsias De Rossa TD, chairperson, Executive Political Committee'. An internal memo in the Soviet Communist Party files described the Workers' Party as 'the most influential and promising left force in the country'. But there was no offer of financial support, only a 'strengthening of fraternal relations'.

The documentation was held in Moscow and only came to light after the collapse of the Soviet Union. The London *Independent* newspaper contacted De Rossa about the letter in October 1992 to seek confirmation that he had been in Moscow in 1986. While a senior figure in the Workers' Party De Rossa had made several foreign trips, including to the United States in 1984 and to North Korea in 1986, with both legs of that journey via Moscow. He also visited Moscow in 1987 and again in 1989. He told the newspaper that he could not recall any such document as had been discovered in Moscow. *The Irish Times* published a report on the letter on 26 October 1992 but De Rossa denied any knowledge of the letter. Despite the denial, the matter simmered and De Rossa was forced to deal with the controversy during the November 1992 general election. The matter was raised at the party's manifesto launch and, according to one newspaper, 'got a glacial response from Mr De Rossa'.[73] But he had to answer questions from the media:

> Never was it reported that money was sought or received from Moscow. If we were stuck for money we might get money from

the North and we were told that it was money from the clubs. I was in Moscow when the alleged letter looking for money was sent, but I was there to talk to editors of Moscow newspapers telling them that articles that they were running which were sympathetic to the Provos were damaging the left in Ireland and backing the killing of people in Northern Ireland.[74]

In an editorial in the *Sunday Tribune* during the 1992 general election the Moscow letter was used to criticise Democratic Left. 'We stated that we could not recommend a vote for Democratic Left, not because of their policies but because of remaining suspicions concerning the extent of their knowledge of or culpable ignorance of "special activities" conducted by some of their former colleagues attached to the Workers' Party.'[75] For some commentators the Moscow letter took on a different dimension when Democratic Left and the Labour Party commenced discussions about a policy programme for a new government. The Belfast-based *Irish News* concluded that the episode showed that De Rossa was 'clearly not a man equipped to discharge [ministerial] responsibilities'.[76]

Éamon Dunphy, a columnist with the *Sunday Independent*, shared this view. In December 1992 – as talks were underway involving Democratic Left and Labour about possible options for government formation – Dunphy seized upon the Moscow letter as justification to attack the Labour Party for leaving open the possibility of entering government with De Rossa and his colleagues. The article was headlined 'Throwing good money at jobs is dishonest'. Dunphy wrote:

> On one side of the argument are those who would find the idea of Democratic Left in cabinet acceptable. These people are prepared to ignore Democratic Left leader Proinsias De Rossa's reference to the 'special activities', which served to fund the Workers' Party in the recent past. The 'special activities' concerned were criminal. Among the crimes committed were armed robberies and forgery of currency. The people engaged in this business occupied that twilight world where the line blurs between those who are common criminals and others of that ilk who would claim to be engaged in political activity. This world is inhabited by myriad groups, some dealing in drugs, prostitution, protection rackets, crimes of which the weakest members of society are invariably the

victims ... There is evidence ... that De Rossa was aware of what was going on.[77]

Dunphy was a high-profile commentator who attracted controversy. De Rossa believed Dunphy's article was damaging and he instituted libel proceedings in the High Court against the owners of the *Sunday Independent*, Independent News and Media plc. The case dragged on for several years and required a number of retrials and appeals. Just weeks after the 1997 general election, De Rossa told the High Court that he had joined the IRA when he was 16, and left when he was 20. He said his four years as a member of the IRA were 'a bit of an adventure' to him. He said that his membership in the secret and illegal organisation was the 'stuff of storybooks' for an adolescent boy. He said he trained in the use of a Lee Enfield rifle, and in May 1957 was arrested while on a training march in the Wicklow mountains. He served a two-month prison sentence before being transferred to the Curragh internment camp for two more years. He was arrested again in 1960 and spent more time in prison. But when he was freed, he told the court, he moved away from military action and resigned from the IRA.

During the libel trial, De Rossa was asked about Workers' Party links with the communist regime in Moscow, his views on labour camps in the Soviet Union, Garda investigations into counterfeiting, raids on printing premises and money received from the Communist Party in the USSR. He also revealed that in the days after instructing his solicitor to write to Independent Newspapers on 18 December 1992 he had burnt files from his time in the Workers' Party on a bonfire in his back garden. A handwriting expert who had viewed the original letter at the Centre for the Preservation of Contemporary Documents in Moscow also gave evidence. He told the court that the typed letter was on Workers' Party headed paper and bore a watermark. He said he was persuaded that the De Rossa signature was genuine. De Rossa, however, continued to claim that the letter was a forgery.

In July 1997 a jury found the article was defamatory and awarded De Rossa IR£300,000 (approx. €381,000) in damages as well as his legal costs. The award, which was upheld by the Supreme Court, was (up to that time) the highest ever award handed down in a libel case in Ireland and three times the largest libel award previously approved by that court. In a 1998 interview De Rossa laughed as he replied to a question about what he had spent the money on: 'I have given some of it to my family and I bought myself a BMW. That was my revenge. When I put the boot on the brake, I always think of Tony O'Reilly's face.'[78] It was a significant victory for De Rossa but the long-drawn-out controversy had not helped his party as it attempted to create a clear identity away from a Workers' Party past. De Rossa accepted that some damage had been done to Democratic Left as he sought to clear his name in the courts:

> I have no doubt that the *Sunday Independent* had a political agenda ... They assumed that I would never go after them. But certainly it was problematical for DL because DL had actually made a break, definitively, and whatever might be said about me, and we can argue about that, but whatever could be said about me could not be said about Eamon Gilmore or Pat Rabbitte, or indeed most of the members of DL who had no association what-soever with the Official Republican Movement. But having said that I am not convinced it was a significant inhibiting factor for Democratic Left.[79]

Despite the libel case, in terms of the headings identified in this chapter, leadership is the one area which caused Democratic Left the least problems. De Rossa provided the party with a clearly recognised leader. Moreover, in establishing a good working relationship with John Bruton, De Rossa helped to strengthen his party's position in the 1994–7 Rainbow government. In addition, the leadership of the party was not just confined to De Rossa. For a small party, Democratic Left was fortunate in having a collection of high-profile public representatives. The strength of what might be called 'leadership positions' in the party became evident following the January 1999 merger when first Pat Rabbitte and then Eamon Gilmore came to lead the Labour Party.

CONCLUSION

In the opening discussion in this chapter it was stated that among the elements needed to sustain a new political party were money, organisation, leadership and identity. The optimum outcome in these areas for a new political party would be healthy finances, active membership, strong organisation, charismatic leadership and a clearly understood identity. Political parties achieve some of these elements, but more often than not parties do not achieve them all at the same time. In the case of Democratic Left, the party had a small membership (with a very active core group of members) working within a weak organisational structure, had an effective leadership team for public consumption and a leader in De Rossa who played a charismatic role within the party and to a lesser extent externally, and was constrained by an unclear view of its own political identity. The poor state of the party's finances is discussed in the next chapter. One telling assessment of Democratic Left's difficulties was delivered by four party members in April 1993. In a submission to a party task force they titled one section 'Crisis':

> To refound and reconstitute the radical left in Irish politics means facing up to the seriousness of the crisis facing Democratic Left. Leaving aside the precariousness of our financial situation, the Party's organisational and political difficulties are such that the party's continued existence is by no means assured. If the Party does survive there are few indications that Democratic Left is set to become a vibrant, growing movement ...

> Members are fed up. Some of them are falling away; and this includes many who put in long hours at the marathon count in Dublin South Central. It seemed at that juncture that the party was effectively being born under the camera lights at the RDS. But somehow since then, we've gotten lost.

> It is generally accepted that we have an identity problem. Three related criticisms are offered here:

> (a) Democratic Left has done and is doing much which is valuable and worthwhile but there seems to be a missing dimension, a focus which draws together the positive elements.

> (b) Much of the party's output is bland and can be safely confined to the motherhood and apple-pie category. Our political approach is not sufficiently hard-edged and practical.

> (c) Members want a party which is not only qualitatively different from other political parties but is seen to be.

> It is suggested here that the party is perched rather uncomfortably between the Workers' Party of yesterday and the Labour Party of today.[80]

This assessment delivered in April 1993 was never seriously addressed. The issues highlighted once more bring up the question of what type of politics Democratic Left sought to pursue. The identity issue was more fundamental than emblems or logos. At the heart of the Democratic Left project was the ideological revisionism of Left politics. The forces of globalisation and the post-Berlin Wall structural readjustments stripped the Left of an economic language and policy programme. The points of difference were blurred as the core fundamentals of ideologies converged. Like their counterparts elsewhere in Europe, Democratic Left struggled for coherence with its message in this new political environment. Moreover, in failing to clarify where the party was positioned, what emerged in the public's mind was a view that the party was little different from the Labour Party. This identity made the development of the party a constant battle, and one that was eventually lost in the period after the 1997 general election result.

NOTES

1. I. Crewe and A. King, *The Birth, Life and Death of the Social Democratic Party* (Oxford: Oxford University Press, 1995), p.253.
2. J. Coakley, 'Minor Parties in Irish Political Life, 1992–1989', *Economic and Social Review*, 21, 3 (1990), p.293.
3. J. Blondel, *Political Parties: A Genuine Case for Discontent?* (London: Wildwood, 1978), pp.137–42.
4. Ibid., p.141.
5. Interview with Proinsias De Rossa, 7 September 2007.
6. Speech to Democratic Left annual conference, November 1995.
7. Interview with John Gallagher, 15 June 2007.
8. Interview with Tony Heffernan, 13 September 2006.
9. Ibid.
10. Ibid.
11. Interview with Catherine Murphy, 31 August 2006.
12. Proinsias Breathnach, Submission of 1993 Task Force Committee.
13. National Executive meeting minutes, 13 March 1993.
14. Internal Democratic Left memo, 'Towards a DL Youth Committee', September 1997.
15. Ibid.
16. Executive meeting minutes, 23 May 1992.
17. Interview with Pat Rabbitte, 9 January 2007.
18. Interview with Tony Heffernan, 13 September 2006.
19. *Sunday Tribune*, 19 May 1996.
20. Democratic Left, National Executive minutes, 23 May 1998.
21. M. Gallagher and M. Marsh, *Days of Blue Loyalty: The Politics of Membership of the Fine Gael Party* (Dublin: PSAI, 2002), p.80.
22. Ibid., p.56.

23. R. Dunphy, 'A Group of Individuals Trying to Do their Best: The Dilemmas of Democratic Left', *Irish Political Studies*, vol. 13 (1998), p.62.
24. Interview with John Gallagher, 15 June 2007.
25. Interview with Des Geraghty, 9 May 2006.
26. Interview with Eamon Gilmore, 11 September 2006.
27. Executive meeting minutes, 13 March 1993.
28. Officer's Report, undated, most likely January 1993.
29. Tony Heffernan, General Election '92: Report on Publicity, January 1993.
30. Michael Taft, Discussion Paper, no date given but most likely January/February 1993.
31. 'MRBI', internal DL document, March 1993.
32. Ibid.
33. Officer's Report, undated, most likely January 1993.
34. Ibid.
35. Democratic Left, Task Force Report 1993 draft version, Section 2.2.2. The latter section marked [–] was deleted from the task force final report.
36. Democratic Left, Task Force Report 1993 draft version, Section 2.2.3.
37. Correspondence from John Gallagher to task force committee, 30 April 1993.
38. Deputy Party Secretary's Report to General Council, 3 September 1993.
39. Minutes of National Executive, 17 July 1993.
40. Proinsias Breathnach, Submission of 1993 Task Force Committee.
41. Task Force Report, unpublished, September 1997.
42. Eugene Dudley quoted in *Phoenix* magazine, 9 June 1995.
43. Denis Coghlan in *The Irish Times*, 13 May 1996.
44. Ibid.
45. Pat Rabbitte, Memo to council meeting, 'General Election Strategy', 26 June 1992.
46. Interview with Seán Garland, 29 May 2006.
47. *Hot Press*, November 1992.
48. Interview with Eamon Gilmore, 11 September 2006.
49. Interview with Catherine Murphy, 31 August 2006.
50. *The Sun*, 9 July 1992.
51. Meeting of Dáil Group – Report for Council Meeting, 28 August 1992.
52. Pat Rabbitte, Memorandum to National Council Members, Re Electoral Strategy, 26 August 1992.
53. Ibid.
54. 'Democratic Left and Political Strategy', 28 August 1992. Internal DL document, no author given.
55. Secretary's Report, Annual Conference, 1993.
56. Ibid.
57. Youth Report to Executive, July 1994.
58. Ibid.
59. Ibid.
60. Interview with Tony Heffernan, 13 September 2006.
61. Interview with John Gallagher, 15 June 2007.
62. Task Force Report, unpublished, September 1997.
63. Ibid.
64. Democratic Left National Executive minutes, 27 September 1997.
65. Interview with Paul Sweeney, 6 September 2006.
66. Interview with Pat Rabbitte, 10 January 2007.
67. Interview with Eric Byrne, 29 August 2006.
68. Interview with Paul Sweeney, 6 September 2006.
69. Interview with Liz McManus, 18 October 2006.
70. Interview with Des Geraghty, 9 May 2006.
71. *Sunday Tribune*, 19 February 1995.
72. *Hot Press*, November 1992.
73. *Sunday Tribune*, 15 November 1992.

74. *Irish Press*, 19 November 1992.
75. *Sunday Tribune*, 6 December 1992.
76. *Irish News*, 8 December 1992.
77. *Sunday Independent*, 13 December 1992.
78. *Ireland on Sunday*, 6 September 1998.
79. Interview with Proinsias De Rossa, 7 September 2007.
80. Submission to Task Force Committee, 5 April 1993 by Peter McDermott, Gerard O'Quigley, Fearghal Ross and Michael Taft.

9

Anatomy of a Party II: Finances

INTRODUCTION

Political parties in Ireland get money from a number of sources. When Democratic Left was formed in 1992 there was a limited system of state parliamentary funding dependent upon Oireachtas representation but, in general, the main parties relied heavily on private sources and rolling bank debts. Fianna Fáil, Fine Gael and the Progressive Democrats openly sought individual and corporate donations while the Labour Party received funds from the trade union movement. Legislative changes in the mid-1990s led to a significant increase in state funding, with a new arrangement to give parties funds based on their Dáil electoral performance. It was not possible, however, to use these funds for electoral purposes.

Irish politics became increasingly professionalised in the 1990s with the main Leinster House parties adopting more sophisticated campaign strategies. Fianna Fáil, Fine Gael and, to a degree, the Labour Party engaged in more detailed planning, commissioned more research and employed more staff. None of these activities came cheap. David M. Farrell, in a review of the 1992 general election campaign, observed that the available evidence 'demonstrates how expensive campaigning has become'.[1] Farrell also pointed out that, whereas parties in many other European countries had access to state funding, in Ireland political activities at the time of the 1992 general election were largely paid from private and corporate donations. This regime, as mentioned, was modified with the introduction of legislative regulations after 1997, including a new regime for private and corporate donations.

Money was always an issue for a party without access to business support, trade union subscriptions or wealthy benefactors. Democratic Left was opposed to taking business donations and, as such, was dependent on individual donations, membership subscriptions and state grants linked to having TDs in Dáil Éireann. Individual donations were sought in a letter sent on 9 March 1992 to members and supporters about the founding conference. The message was unambiguous: 'A deposit bank account has been opened and donations are eagerly sought.'[2] Democratic Left's life started and ended with few resources available to fund the work of a modern political movement. The disparity between the resources available to the other main parties and Democratic Left became apparent when the new donation disclosure regulations came into place in 1997. Information on donations prior to 1997 is patchy at best. However, Farrell estimated that from the agricultural sector alone between 1987 and 1991 Fianna Fáil received IR£297,000 (approx. €377,000), Fine Gael IR£138,550 (approx. €176,000) and the Progressive Democrats IR£45,000 (approx. €57,000) (1986–91 for the PDs).[3] These corporate donations were said to have represented 10 per cent of Fianna Fáil's income during 1987–91, 7 per cent of Fine Gael's income and 3 per cent of Progressive Democrat total income from 1986 to 1991.

At a state inquiry into planning corruption in May 2008 a former senior Fianna Fáil politician revealed that he was asked to seek donations for the party of between IR£50,000 (approx. €63,500) and IR£100,000 (approx. €127,000) each from a number of business people in 1993. Ray MacSharry said the party was seeking to clear debts of IR£3 million (approx. €3.8 million) ahead of new legislation on political fundraising. 'They all got some contributions because it was coming to the end of corporations providing unlimited resources to political parties,' MacSharry told the tribunal of inquiry.[4] This level of financial support was unimaginable for Democratic Left, which operated on a limited budget at a time when money became increasingly important in determining success or failure in modern politics in Ireland. The discussion in this chapter will show how a lack of funds restricted the party's ability to compete in the political market place.

STRAPPED FOR CASH

Money was an immediate priority for the new party. Indeed, money, or a lack of it, was a major concern throughout Democratic Left's existence. In 1992 De Rossa and his colleagues had to find the funds to pay for a new head office and staff as well as other activities associated with party political activism, including electioneering and policy formation. The financial position was not good. 'We were a fairly cash strapped party,' was John Gallagher's assessment of the 1992 to 1999 period.[5] Gallagher worked in head office, and along with Des Geraghty he was privy to the consequences of the party's difficult financial situation. Geraghty recalled: 'I was one of the people involved in trying to find the money. We were to the pin of our collar. It was unbelievable, and it was, I remember, a horror story. I mean we were trying to operate out of a shoe box.'[6]

The new party survived on a tight budget, especially when set against the level of funding mentioned previously which was available to its main competitors. A IR£5,000 (approx. €6,350) bank overdraft was sought for the Maastricht referendum campaign in June 1992.[7] There was a general view that the money was well spent. 'It was felt the campaign had been successful and of considerable benefit to building the party's profile and members' morale.'[8] However, an internal review of the Maastricht Treaty campaign, prepared for Democratic Left's Central Council, exposed the lack of funds at all organisational levels. The party memo noted that, after the referendum, the 'constituencies have financial difficulties ...'[9]

Funds were raised from a variety of sources. The party's membership subscription was low. It could never be counted upon to generate anything near the type of funds needed to run a well-organised and professional political movement. 'It was a case of making do,' John Gallagher admitted, 'the TDs helped out the party financially. They used to contribute but the party had no income. There were membership subscriptions and a draw but they turned over a pretty low level of money.'[10] The party's annual national collection – a feature of fundraising for most political organisations in Ireland – was expected to generate some money. An internal party document stated in 1992: 'The importance of raising money in the national collection was emphasised, a leaflet is being prepared centrally.'[11] The response was, however, a disappointment. Several months later, Pat Rabbitte admitted: 'It is not evident that the National Collection mobilised the general membership despite the goodwill towards the Party evident on the doorsteps.'[12] Over subsequent years many constituencies actually stopped taking up a national collection. An internal report in 1997 recommended that the party 'return to more vigorous fund-raising, including the holding of an annual collection'.[13]

Democratic Left was limited in its ability to raise funds by a party ban on taking corporate donations. Des Geraghty recalled that corporate donations were 'studiously avoided ... we literally turned down financial donations.'[14] Early in the life of the new party, Geraghty was approached by a representative of a leading financial institution about making a political donation. 'He said that they tended to give money to political parties. I rang Proinsias De Rossa, and said, "we could do with a few bob" and [that] I had this person on the phone to me. But Proinsias said, "Ah no, that would be tainted, we won't accept."'[15]

Interestingly, several years later, in 1997 an internal task force suggested that 'the party should agree in principle to seek appropriate corporate funding especially for specific projects; such as the Autumn School'.[16] The proposal, which was discussed by the National Executive on 27 September 1997, was accepted 'subject to drawing up ethical guidelines'.[17] The change in policy on corporate donations was taken for financial reasons. The decision to change a deeply held stance is a clear sign of the party's increasingly desperate financial situation. Table 9.1 shows the party's financial position at the end of 1996 and at the end of 1997. Table 9.2 shows the party's outstanding debts on 30 October 1998. The figures in the two tables confirm that as the discussion in Democratic Left in 1998 increasingly centred on the party's future, a lack of money – while not the principal factor – was one of the factors which eventually pushed De Rossa and his colleagues into merger talks with the Labour Party.

WORKERS' PARTY DEBT

Right from when the party was formed in 1992 Democratic Left was at a financial disadvantage. But the new party's financial plight was not helped by the debts several leading members were repaying from their previous existence in the Workers' Party. Senior figures in the new party were saddled with heavy bank debts transferred from the Workers' Party on which they had given personal guarantees. The Workers' Party was reported to have had bank debts totalling some IR£400,000 (approx. €508,000) at the start of 1992.[18] These media estimates were accepted by David M. Farrell, who observed that 'Prior to the split the WP debt was estimated at lying between IR£300–500,000 [approx. €381–635,000]. It is not clear just how much of that had been inherited by the DL.'[19]

Crucially for those individuals intent on establishing a new political party, around IR£65,000 (approx. €83,000) of the total debt was personally guaranteed by several leading figures in the new entity, including Proinsias De Rossa, Pat Rabbitte, Tony Heffernan, Séamus Lynch and Des Geraghty. Others who were liable for this debt with Allied Irish Bank (AIB) were Tomás MacGiolla and Seán Garland. In the aftermath of the split the financial institutions, which held the personal guarantees, were naturally interested in recovering their money, as De Rossa explained:

> The banks are looking to see if we will meet our guarantees. Different individuals have guaranteed different amounts. There were a number of different loans, one of which I personally guaranteed. The debts were incurred in order to get people elected as members of the Workers' Party. Therefore, we believe they should be covered by the Workers' Party.[20]

Seán Garland, however, had other ideas. In his role as national treasurer of the Workers' Party, Garland wrote to those former members who had given personal guarantees on bank loans for party activities. Indeed, Garland wasted little time in seeking to deal with the outstanding debt. His correspondence was dated 3 March 1992 – just over a week after the split was confirmed.

> The Party [the WP] has now been deprived of substantial income from the Dáil and European Parliament because of the defection of six TDS. As you are aware part of this income was used to repay some of the substantial debt the party incurred in recent years contesting elections and securing seats in the Dáil and European Parliament. We have now made an assessment of the various loans and leases outstanding for which you signed personal guarantees – this is AIB Dame Street who are owed a total of [IR]£65,000 [approx. €83,000]. We would now like to know how you intend to discharge the sums owing for which you gave personal guarantees.[21]

A representative of the Workers' Party was quoted as saying that the issue of personal guarantees was a matter between the financial institutions and the persons concerned.[22] Democratic Left had no responsibility for the debts but the matter was important for the new party. With a policy of refusing corporate donations, Democratic Left was from its foundation going to be heavily dependent upon the financial goodwill of its membership and elected representatives. By June 1992 the AIB debt – with interest applied – approached IR£70,000 (approx. €89,000). This situation was obviously going to limit the generosity of several party figures in funding the new organisation.

The AIB loan was not the only debt causing concern. For example, in May 1992 the executive meeting minutes recorded, 'Christy Gorman loan: a loan taken out by him on behalf of the Workers' Party has caused some difficulties. The WP have paid the most recent instalment. It is to be monitored.'[23] Yet despite the financial amounts involved, De Rossa was bullish when questioned about the debts. 'The Democratic Left will not pay a penny. That's for sure. As regards the individuals concerned, I cannot rule anything out. The banks have been quite reasonable about this to date.'[24] The reality was somewhat different. The outstanding loans were to restrict the ability of some members to contribute financially to Democratic Left. Des Geraghty was one of those paying off debts.

> I had three loans that I owed as a result of money that had been borrowed for the Workers' Party because I was chairman of the Dublin region at one stage and we had a region account [and] we had to put money up for various elections. So we were all privately in hock, you know, in terms of personal finances, a disaster ...[25]

Alongside the debts incurred while they were members of the Workers' Party, a number of individuals including Tony Heffernan and John Gallagher continued to receive correspondence from solicitors representing the Workers' Party 'seeking possession of certain files and equipment'.[26] This matter was discussed at a party meeting in August 1992.

> Arising from this there was a wider discussion on the position of TDs and others who had signed personal guarantees for Workers' Party debt. One of the solicitors' letters referred to an 'anxiety on the part of the Workers' Party to finally sort out all matters relating to property'. In view of this it was suggested that Des Geraghty and an accountant who had been advising some of our people regarding the debts should contact the solicitor to try to establish if this was a serious proposal.[27]

The financial and legal parting from the Workers' Party was not straightforward for those who embarked on the formation of Democratic Left. The amounts involved were small by comparison with the monies available to other parties with representation in Dáil Éireann, but the burden of repaying bank loans limited the funds available for the new party.

MAKING ENDS MEET

The limitations imposed by a lack of resources were not altogether new. Many involved in the Workers' Party had operated under financial restrictions as Tony Heffernan explained: 'It is one of the myths about the Workers' Party but there wasn't a huge amount of money and the reason we had debts to bring with us was that people had signed up to borrow money for the Workers' Party.'[28] Eamon Gilmore shared this view. 'We'd always run election campaigns on a very modest budget so it didn't make a huge difference,' he said.[29]

There were, however, others who had a different experience, including John Gallagher. While Gallagher supported Gilmore and Heffernan's general assessment, he did so only in relation to the 1992 general election. 'I don't know if having a lot of money in 1992 would have produced a different outcome. That's my view. It would have made everyone's lives a lot easier. We would not have had to worry about bills.'[30] In Gallagher's opinion the importance of money should be judged by its impact on the party's capacity to develop.

> It became increasingly a problem as time moved on. You can live on a nervous energy for a time but the absence of cash to do anything [was a problem] in doing all the things that political parties increasingly need to do. We were increasingly aware that we had no money.[31]

The lack of financial resources may not have impacted on established party figures but, according to Gallagher, the absence of money was a real issue for new members.

> The people who joined Democratic Left perhaps would have noticed the lack of resources more than the people who came out of the Workers' Party and, as a result, might have become more easily disillusioned. We lost some of those members. Somebody comes into a party and the first thing they find is that they're being

approached for a standing order or a donation and being told there's no money for this, that and the other. That becomes their highlight rather than the great political debate, which is why they may have joined.[32]

A lack of money was frequently compensated for through the use of imaginative campaign posters and slogans. The Workers' Party had an excellent record of relying heavily on activists for as much benefit-in-kind work as possible, including literature design and artwork. The party also received praise for maximising the impact of its allocated broadcast time on RTÉ television at election times. For example in 1989, Peter Mair noted that 'it was generally accepted that the most impressive PPB [party political broadcast] in the campaign was that of the Workers' Party which, involving minimal expenditure, developed the theme of the popular quiz programme, Mastermind.'[33] Democratic Left continued in this vein. When urging a 'No' vote in the 1992 Maastricht Treaty referendum – which was dominated by controversy over abortion and the right to travel to have a pregnancy termination outside the jurisdiction – the party's poster featured a photograph of a stern-looking judge complete with wig and accompanying slogan, 'With Maastricht, women will have to deal with a new kind of travel agent'.

The campaign, with 15,000 posters, cost IR£25,000 (approx. €32,000) and received favourable media mention. 'We're inundated with phone calls from people wanting copies of the posters for themselves, particularly the one of the Judge. It's humorous but there's a serious reality behind it and it's proving especially popular,' Tony Heffernan told the *Sunday Press* newspaper.[34] There were other examples of 'thinking outside the box' to promote the party on a limited budget. Some party members decided to exploit the 'Trip to Tipp' music festival in the summer of 1992. The amusing episode was captured in a report written for party head office:

> Because it was an event attended mostly by young people it was decided to have 'Condom' tee shirts incorporating the Democratic Left logo designed ... We ordered 1,000 tee shirts, at no stage did we envisage selling all the tee shirts, as things worked out it was a long haul but we felt we did reasonably well, selling 300 shirts, it must be remembered this was our first time. What we had not considered was the huge competition we faced from other groups

i.e. the hundreds of Traders who were there flogging their cheap, imitation tee shirts. Also, we had started out trying to sell them for IR£7 [approx. €8.88] but this was a non starter and we reduced them to IR£6 [approx. €7.62].[35]

The party's membership and support base was too thin for merchandising to become a reliable form of party finance. But the report continued by noting that a member of the Sawdoctors band made a purchase and that there was good feedback from the various bands who were left free t-shirts in their dressing rooms. This type of endeavour had novelty value. But it was not suitable as a mainstream fundraising exercise. At a special meeting of the National Executive – called to discuss preparations for the November 1992 general election – the minutes recorded: 'the party does not have any substantial financial resources.'[36] The meeting also agreed to produce a leaflet explaining the party's stance on the abortion referendums to be decided on the same day as the general election poll but it was decided that a 'separate poster would not be produced'. It can only be assumed that the decision was based on the costs involved.

Money was again mentioned at the first National Executive meeting in January 1993 when Joe Sherlock's decision to contest the Seanad Éireann election was discussed. In a report prepared by John Gallagher it was noted that 'the campaign has been run at little cost to the party.'[37] Correspondence to members in April 1993 referred to fundraising functions for local elections in Northern Ireland and an imminent Dáil by-election contest in the Dublin South Central constituency. Among the events planned was 'a sponsored hill walk', which may also have been a reflection on the political task still facing party members.[38] Three hundred people participated in a development draw in 1993. But the returns were insufficient to transform the party's finances. An internal party report in September 1993 noted that projected expenditure for the year was IR£46,000 (approx. €58,000), which was to cover expenses such as wages, rent, heating, leaflets and conferences. Income was derived from several sources, including a party draw, standing orders, public representatives' contributions and membership fees. It was estimated that total income in 1993 was going to be IR£40–42,000 (approx. €51–53,000) – leaving a shortfall of IR£4–6,000 (approx. €5–7,600). The redeployment of a staff member to the Oireachtas payroll helped ease the income shortfall but the party did not expect to balance its books in 1993. 'The valley period of December to January may result in a cash flow problem for Head Office,' the party report observed.[39]

As previously mentioned, finances, or rather a lack of finance, impinged on the party's growth. When planning for the 1994 European Parliament elections, Eamon Gilmore recommended that 'emphasis be put on Dublin and that, barring exceptional circumstances that the other Euro-constituencies not be contested, on the grounds of cost and on the need to concentrate the party's planning and resources'.[40] Finances were again the motivating factor in deciding to limit the party's conference in 1994 to a one-day affair, but the decision was eventually reversed when it emerged that 'no financial savings will accrue from dropping Fri [day].'[41]

The period in government between 1994 and 1997 helped Democratic Left in that its ministers had access to the benefits of office, which compensated for a lack of party money, while several paid and unpaid party staff and advisors were taken onto the public payroll. The party returned to the opposition benches after the 1997 general election, and while there was now for the first time annual state funding based on the election outcome, Democratic Left's own financial situation did not prosper. Indeed, after the 1997 general election Democratic Left representatives were once more faced with their party's precarious financial position.

Table 9.1 clearly illustrates this worsening financial situation. At the end of 1996, when the party was in government, income exceeded expenditure by IR£82,827 (approx. €105,169). Twelve months later, the situation had been transformed, with expenditure exceeding income by IR£104,950 (approx. €133,259). Income increased between 1996 and 1997 – largely by constituency payments arising from the general election. But the party's expenditure rose significantly from IR£95,129 (approx. €120,789) in 1996 to IR£319,867 (approx. €406,147) in 1997. Spending on the 1997 general election and the presidential contest in the same year added almost IR£150,000 (approx. €190,000) to expenditure levels. But there were other new costs associated with the party returning to the opposition benches mid-year in 1997. A number of party-type expenses were largely covered by governmental activity in 1996. For example, the cost of the leaders and whips' offices appear in the 1997 figures (the party exited government in June 1997) but in the preceding year these costs were obviously related to the governmental offices of the respective ministers. Being in government helped subsidise the activities of the party in office. In that

TABLE 9.1
DEMOCRATIC LEFT INCOME AND EXPENDITURE, 1996 AND 1997

	As at 30 Dec 1996 IR£	As at 30 Dec 1997 IR£
Income		
Parliamentary Allowance	97,881	93,258
Oireachtas Funding	20,500	27,235
Donations	24,600	17,985
Party Fundraising	3,840	5,239
Party Draw	12,000	10,000
Standing Orders	14,290	14,425
Rent (premises sublet)	3,538	2,383
General Election Constituency Payments	-	43,100
Party Conference	-	1,110
Other income	1,307	182
Total Income	177,956	214,917
Expenditure		
Staff	49,593	64,617
Rent and Rates	8,380	6,949
Light and Phone	3,297	4,999
Office Equipment/Supplies	857	16,002
Repairs	1,578	-
Party Conference	4,205	13,951
Bank Fees and Interest	916	3,311
Travel	2,634	5,093
Press Conferences/Receptions	8,523	7,029
Election Campaigns	9,720	-
General Election	-	122,195
Presidential Election	-	27,687
Leaders' and Whips' Offices	-	9,560
Party Development	-	9,742
Research	-	1,200
Publicity/Promotions	3,222	13,712
Insurance	-	9,922
Miscellaneous	2,204	3,897
Total Expenditure	95,129	319,867
Excess of Expenditure over Income	82,827	(104,950)

Source: From documents in the possession of the author.

way, opposition brought more than just a political cost – the loss of power had a real financial impact on Democratic Left.

The 1997 financial situation was unsustainable for a small organisation such as Democratic Left. Steps were taken to address the situation. Staff numbers at the party's head office were cut as a cost-saving measure. In September 1997, the National Executive was told that 'the party's debt has nevertheless been reduced from in excess of IR£100,000 [approx. €127,000] immediately following the general election to a little over IR£80,000 [approx. €102,000] at present …'[42] Almost half of the IR£80,000 (approx. €102,000) debt in September 1997 was accounted for by a bank loan which was being repaid over a two-year period to the summer of 1999. However, by December 1997 the party was seeking to extend its bank facilities due to a IR£30,000 (approx. €38,000) outlay arising from its involvement in Adi Roche's ultimately unsuccessful presidential election campaign.

The party had sought to limit its financial exposure in the Roche campaign to IR£10,000 (approx. €12,700).[43] An internal note prepared in late October 1997 contained a number of justifications for a change to the 2:1:1 cost ratio agreed between the Labour Party, the Green Party and Democratic Left. The note even went so far as to argue that by applying the general election results (Labour 10.4 per cent; Greens 2.7 per cent; Democratic Left 2.5 per cent) the ratio would be changed to 4:1:1. This new ratio would have reduced Democratic Left's financial outlay to between IR£13,000 (approx. €16,500) and IR£16,000 (approx. €20,315), although it seems that the two other parties, which backed Roche, were not supportive. In correspondence with Ruairi Quinn in February 1998, Proinsias De Rossa proposed discharging Democratic Left's 25 per cent debt by means of a 'standing order of IR£1,000 [approx. €1,270] per month'.[44] When the two parties formally merged later in 1998 the IR£20,000 (approx. €25,000) outstanding was subsumed into the new party organisation.

In the 1997–8 period as discussions about future strategy and direction were underway, Democratic Left party meetings were hearing bleak financial reports – and not just about the central organisation. At a meeting on 5 December 1997 it was reported that the Wexford constituency had debts which totalled approximately IR£6,000 (approx. €7,600). Some IR£5,000 (approx. €6,350) of the total amount was a bank loan, half of which had been used to contribute towards head office election bills. 'They are seeking central assistance,' an internal memo observed, although no record is available to indicate if assistance was forthcoming, but given head office's limited funds the probability of help was limited.[45]

By the end of 1997, outstanding debts relating to that year's general election forced the party to increase its bank loan to IR£50,000 (approx. €63,000), while it was clear that 'pressure on cash flow will arise in the new year, related to costs on the Limerick by-election and Presidential election.'[as they fell due][46] The party was also facing a scheduled rent review of its leased head office premises in Dublin city centre. The news was not good. 'The landlords have now confirmed a proposal of IR£15,000 [approx. €19,000] p.a., up from a current IR£6,000 [approx. €7,600],' a party memo recorded.[47] The proposed rental rate was too high, and a decision was taken to seek alternative accommodation. The financial situation was so bad that consideration was given to operating without a formal head office premises. But the National Executive ultimately decided 'that operating from a Box Office number would not be appropriate'.[48]

Several fundraising initiatives were organised, including a draw limited to 300 members at a cost of IR£100 (approx. €127), or IR£10 (approx. €12.70) a month for ten months, with a guaranteed monthly prize of IR£1,000 (approx. €1,270). 'It was agreed that all constituencies should seek additional subscribers and that the Draw should go ahead by the end of June.'[49] The reality was, however, that no small gain from a members' draw was ever going to generate the type of money required to sustain and build the party organisation.

The finances were simply not in good order. An examination of the party's books undertaken by the Labour Party in October 1998 as part of the merger negotiations showed outstanding debts of IR£72,000 (approx. €91,000). It is difficult to see what action Democratic Left could have taken to reverse its financial plight, with significant debts relative to its size and a day-to-day operation where expenditure exceeded income. The breakdown of the party debt is shown in Table 9.2, which also indicates the continued generosity of the party's public representatives.

As well as making regular contributions to Democratic Left, TDs like Proinsias De Rossa and Pat Rabbitte also lent the party money to pay its bills.

TABLE 9.2
DEMOCRATIC LEFT DEBTS, 30 OCTOBER 1998

Creditor	IR£
AIB Loan	32,000
Labour Party (Presidential Election)	20,000
Rent	6,000
Proinsias De Rossa	6,000
Pat Rabbitte	2,000
Miscellaneous	6,000
Total	72,000

Source: From documents in the possession of the author.

STATE FUNDING

Reforms aimed at introducing greater transparency into the financing of politics and regulating the funding of political life were introduced in the late 1990s. Funding under the Electoral Act, 1997 was issued for the first time in 1998 in addition to the existing party leaders' allowance scheme from which payments were made to qualifying political parties with Oireachtas representation. The state-funded schemes guaranteed a minimum budgetary level for Democratic Left, although none of the money could be spent on electioneering.

A political party receiving at least 2 per cent of the first-preference votes at the 1997 general election received Electoral Act payments. The amount of funding payable was determined by the share of the total first-preference vote secured by the qualifying parties. The funds had to be spent in the following defined areas: general party administration; research, education and training; policy formulation; co-ordination of the activities of branches and members of the party. It was also possible to use the funds to promote the participation by women and young people in political activity.

As shown in Table 9.3, Democratic Left received almost IR£29,000 (approx. €37,000) from the Electoral Act scheme under the first annual round of payments in 1998. Democratic Left received a further IR£1,942.41 (€2,466.35) up to 24 January 1999 when the party was formally removed from the Register of Political Parties.

There had been considerable controversy in 1992 about the party

TABLE 9.3
ELECTORAL ACT PAYMENTS, 1998

Political Party	Total Payment (IR£)
Fianna Fáil	449,437.36
Fine Gael	317,257.42
Labour Party	118,799.00
Progressive Democrats	53,475.01
Green Party	31,528.62
Sinn Féin	29,158.81
Democratic Left	28,643.64

Source: Standards in Public Office Commission, 1998.

leaders' allowance scheme, the allocation from which is based on Oireachtas representation. The Workers' Party received IR£99,243 (€126,012) from this scheme in 1991. But following the split which led to the formation of Democratic Left, the new party was denied funding as it did not have the minimum number of TDs necessary for qualification. However, the rules were subsequently changed during the life of the Rainbow coalition. The party received IR£191,140 (€242,697) from the leaders' allowance scheme in 1997, IR£116,481 (€147,900) in 1998 and IR£7,247 (€9,202) up to its merger with the Labour Party in January 1999. The new merged party had hoped to receive the combined allowances previously available to the Labour Party and Democratic Left. But following contacts with the relevant authorities the rules were interpreted as meaning the Democratic Left allowance was exclusive to that party and could not be carried forward.

Both state funding sources were useful in providing Democratic Left with a minimum annual budget. The monies involved were, however, inadequate to cover the costs of running a modern political party, especially as the political environment in Ireland became increasingly professional in the 1990s. The main parties were spending greater amounts on backroom activities in areas such as opinion polling, policy research and media. In addition, the rules governing both schemes precluded money being used for electoral purposes. As Table 9.1 showed in relation to Democratic Left's expenditure in 1996 and in 1997, the biggest cost for most political parties is contesting elections. The reality was that a small party such as Democratic Left had to raise funds elsewhere – in the type of areas discussed previously – in order to meet its operating costs and fund its election campaigns. The ability, or inability, of Democratic Left to attract private donations is discussed below for 1997 and 1998. Regulations governing electoral spending limits and the disclosure of donations received by political parties and election candidates were introduced in 1997. The spending limits did not apply to the 1997 general election. These were introduced for the first time in a number of Dáil by-elections held in 1998, including Dublin North and Limerick East. These were the final electoral contests in which Democratic Left nominated candidates.

Research undertaken in more recent elections in Ireland – that is, following the 1999 Democratic Left–Labour Party merger – clearly indicates the importance of money in electoral success in Ireland. Having examined the spending patterns at the June 1999 local elections, Benoit and Marsh observed: 'Our essential substantive conclusion is that spending matters. It matters in particular for the candidates. The god of elections is a mercenary one who rewards those most who make the largest monetary sacrifices. The candidates who spend a larger share in their constituencies win a larger share of the constituency vote.'[50]

The spending totals for the various parties and independent candidates in the Limerick East and Dublin North by-elections are shown in

TABLE 9.4
BY-ELECTION EXPENDITURE, 1998 (IR£)

	Dublin North	Limerick East
Democratic Left	9,233	16,050
Fianna Fáil	16,408	19,757
Fine Gael	14,348	21,947
Labour Party	17,497	18,990
PDs	5,565	17,694
Sinn Féin	4,336	4,186
Green Party	1,454	914
Socialist Party	6,498	N/A
Christian Sol.	3,475	N/A
Natural Law	60	N/A
National Party	N/A	1,727
Independents	9,994	3,560

Source: Standards in Public Office Commission, 1999.

Table 9.4. The new expenditure limits meant candidates in the five-seat Limerick East constituency could spend a maximum of IR£20,000 (€25,000), while the spending ceiling was set at IR£17,000 (€21,500) in the four-seat Dublin North constituency.

As Table 9.4 indicates, the Democratic Left candidate in the Dublin North by-election spent IR£9,233 (€11,700). It was an expensive outing, as Joe Holohan only received 225 first-preference votes. This translated into a sizable IR£41 (€52) per vote. By way of comparison, Seán Ryan of the Labour Party, who won the by-election, spent IR£17,497 (€22,217), equating to IR£1.51 (€1.92) for each first-preference vote. In Limerick East, the Democratic Left candidate John Ryan spent IR£4.15 (€5.27) for each of his 3,868 first-preference votes. The successful candidate, Jan O'Sullivan of the Labour Party, spent IR£1.79 (€2.27) for each of her first-preference votes. In the two contests, Democratic Left spent less than the candidates representing Fianna Fáil, Fine Gael and the Labour Party. The party also spent less than the Progressive Democrats in Limerick East. The money available to Democratic Left by-election candidates was generally raised locally. The party's policy until 1998 had been to decline corporate donations, so supporters and members were the main source of non-state funding.

The new donation disclosure regulations also came into place in 1997. Political parties had to declare all annual donations exceeding

TABLE 9.5
DONATIONS DISCLOSED BY POLITICAL PARTIES, 1997 AND 1998

Political Party	1997		1998	
	Total donations (IR£)	Number of donations	Total donations (IR£)	Number of donations
Fianna Fáil	237,125 +US$10,000	30	432,501	36
Sinn Féin	7,229 + US$122,933	5	24,750 + US$256,208	3
Fine Gael	27,500	2	63,528	5
Labour	26,600	3	51,741	3
PDs	10,000	1	5,000	1
Dem. Left	5,000	1	5,000	1

Source: Standards in Public Office Commission, 1997 and 1998.

approx. (€5,079), while elected representatives had to declare any
donation in excess of IR£500 (€635). The disparity between Democrati
Left and the other Leinster House parties was clearly evident from the
1997 donation declarations, as Table 9.5 illustrates. The disparity was
even starker as the single Democratic Leftdonation actually came from
Proinsias De Rossa. The 1998 donation of IR£5,000 (€6,350) was
received from Irish Life, which made a number of payments to the main
political parties for their referendum campaigns to promote support
for the Belfast Agreement.

Pat Rabbitte was the only Democratic Left TD to make a donation
disclosure in 1998 above the IR£500 (€635) limit. He was in receipt
of a single donation of IR£1,000 (€1,270). By way of comparison, in
the same year eleven Labour Party TDs disclosed donations above the
IR£500 (€635) threshold, which totalled almost IR£45,000 (€57,000).
The total value of all donations exceeding the IR£500 (€635) threshold in 1998 for all Dáil members was IR£253,378 (€321,724).

CONCLUSION

The merger of Democratic Left and the Labour Party was motivated by
numerous factors. While finances were not one of the main issues identified by the leading party figures, a lack of money certainly impinged upon
the ability to Democratic Left to organise and develop as a political party.
An internal Democratic Left memo from late in 1997 was very honest in
explaining the party's financial plight: 'tell the truth – the cupboard is
bare.'[51] It is a real possibility that if Democratic Left had had access to
greater resources the party may have continued to exist as an independent political entity after 1999. Research has shown that money counts in
modern political life and it did so increasingly in the 1990s in Ireland.
State funding, while helpful in parliamentary and organisational terms,
did not level the political playing field. Indeed, it may well be that finances
– and access to state funding – now act as a new barrier to entry in
contemporary Irish politics, as argued in 2010 by Desmond O'Malley, the
founding leader of the Progressive Democrats:

> ... public funding is based on votes and seats won at the last general
> election. So if you did not fight the last general election, you get
> nothing. If you get nothing, you can't fight the next election,
> unless you have some source of mysterious, unaccountable

foreign finance or other even dodgier sources of funds. The system has been devised to favour the status quo. It discriminates in favour of what I consider a somewhat stifling incumbency. It is an indefensible manipulation of public funds to support a status quo that has not inspired any great confidence that it can remedy the ills that now beset our economy and our public administration. Truth is that it is probably easier today to start a new political party in Iraq than it is in Ireland.[52]

Starting and developing a new political party is an enormous undertaking, and without sufficient financial resources the challenge of getting a message to the electorate is incredibly daunting. Monies from the state schemes came too late in the life of Democratic Left for a proper assessment of their impact on the party, but the new system would still have been inadequate to prevent disbandment, particularly as the monies were not available to pay for the main expenditures – electoral costs. From its formation Democratic Left had none of the financial advantages which assisted its opponents in the electoral arena. The party opponents included the similarly politically small and niche Progressive Democrats. The financial position of the two parties differed in one important respect – the Progressive Democrats was a party of business. The figures for agricultural sector donations between 1986 and 1991 clearly show the PDs' ability to attract corporate donations. The disclosed donations in 1998 published under the new rules show the PDs receiving IR£10,000 (€12,270) in 1997 and IR£5,000 (€6,350) in 1998. The party would also have received corporate donations below the IR£4,000 (€5,079) disclosure threshold, and it is probable that the donations from the non-agricultural sectors were of an even greater order.

Pat Rabbitte was aware of the impact money made on the ability of the two parties to compete in the political market place: 'The difference between DL and the PDs, which commanded a similar amount of electoral support, would be that the PDs would have commanded infinitely more financial resources, and maybe one is as a result of the other ... It costs to run the party organisation and to fight elections, and there was a viability question, in my opinion.'[53] Without access to adequate financial resources Democratic Left struggled, and as its finances indicate, the party was struggling badly by the time the merger with the Labour Party was concluded in late 1998. De Rossa provided what can be described as an accurate summary of the impact of money on the party's progression: 'There is no doubt that it was an impediment but wasn't necessarily the fatal impediment.'[54]

The demise of the Progressive Democrats in 2009 adds strength to De Rossa's statement. Despite over a decade as a participant in coalition governments, the Progressive Democrats grappled with poor organisational structures, personality clashes among its leading figures and an increasingly uncertain political identity. After the loss of several leading members in the 2007 general election, the party found it difficult to overcome these organisational problems or to reshape its pro-business and tax-cutting agenda which had been poached to varying degrees by both Fianna Fáil and Fine Gael. Senior figures in the Progressive Democrats identified insufficient membership and a lack of leadership as the main weaknesses which led to the decision to wind up the party: 'Where is the strong leadership going to come from? Unfortunately that wasn't apparent in the hall and therefore that's why the motion was carried.'[55] Democratic Left and the Progressive Democrats differed in many important respects – the latter party still apparently had an ability to attract private and corporate donations. But money was not enough to maintain the Progressive Democrats as an independent party. While money is hugely important, it may be surmised that on its own money is not sufficient to maintain a small political party – issues such as leadership, organisation and identity also have a significant role to play in determining a party's longevity. As the case of the Progressive Democrats illustrates, a message – identity – and having an organisation to get that message to the voters is an even more fundamental challenge than raising money. The problem for Democratic Left was that the party faced a potent combination of these issues – weak organisation, uncertain identity and little money.

NOTES

1. D.M. Farrell, 'Campaign Strategies', in M. Gallagher and M. Laver, *How Ireland Voted, 1992* (Dublin: PSAI, 1993), p.21.
2. Letter from Steering Committee to membership, 9 March 1992.
3. Farrell, 'Campaign Strategies', p.32.
4. Reported in *The Irish Times*, 8 May 2008.
5. Interview with John Gallagher, 15 June 2007.
6. Interview with Des Geraghty, 9 May 2006.
7. Executive Council meeting minutes, 23 May 1992.
8. Executive Council meeting minutes, 27 June 1992.
9. Report to Central Council by Eamon Gilmore, 27 June 1992.
10. Interview with John Gallagher, 15 June 2007.
11. Executive Council meeting minutes, 27 June 1992.
12. Pat Rabbitte, Memo to council meeting, 'General Election Strategy', 26 June 1992.
13. Task Force Report, unpublished, September 1997.
14. Interview with Des Geraghty, 9 May 2006.
15. Ibid.
16. Task Force Report, unpublished, September 1997.
17. Minutes of Extended National Executive, 27 September 1997.
18. *Sunday Business Post*, 23 August 1992.
19. Farrell, 'Campaign Strategies', p.33.
20. *Sunday Business Post*, 23 August 1992.
21. Letter from Seán Garland to various DL figures, 3 March 1992.
22. *Sunday Business Post*, 23 August 1992.
23. Executive Council meeting minutes, 23 May 1992.
24. *Sunday Business Post*, 23 August 1992.
25. Interview with Des Geraghty, 9 May 2006.
26. Meeting of Dáil Group – Report for Council Meeting, 28 August 1992.
27. Ibid.
28. Interview with Tony Heffernan, 13 September 2006.
29. Interview with Eamon Gilmore, 11 September 2006.
30. Interview with John Gallagher, 15 June 2007.
31. Ibid.
32. Ibid.
33. P. Mair (ed.), *The West European Party System* (Oxford: Oxford University Press, 1990), p.57.
34. *Sunday Press*, 7 June 1992.
35. Report on Féile 1992, no date given.
36. Minutes of Special Executive meeting, 8 November 1992.
37. Seanad Éireann Report [to National Executive], John Gallagher, 16 January 1993.
38. Head Office correspondence, 15 April 1993.
39. Deputy Party Secretary's Report, 3 September 1993.
40. Minutes of General Council, 3 August 1993.
41. Report on preparation for ADC, John Gallagher, undated.
42. General Secretary Report, 27 September 1997.
43. Democratic Left National Executive minutes, 27 September 1997.
44. Letter from Proinsias De Rossa to Ruairi Quinn, 18 February 1998.
45. General Purposes Committee, Points for Discussion, 5 December 1997.
46. Democratic Left National Executive minutes, 29 November 1997.
47. General Purposes Committee, Points for Discussion, 5 December 1997.
48. Democratic Left National Executive minutes, 29 November 1997.
49. Democratic Left National Executive minutes, 23 May 1998.
50. K. Benoit and M. Marsh, 'Campaign Spending in the Local Government Elections of 1999', *Irish Political Studies*, 18, 2 (2003), pp.19–20.

51. Notes for General Purposes Committee, 22 November 1997.
52. Desmond O'Malley, *The Irish Times*, 2 April 2010.
53. Interview with Pat Rabbitte, 9 January 2007.
54. Interview with Proinsias De Rossa, 7 September 2007.
55. *The Irish Times*, 10 November 2008.

PART 3
Death

10

Merger I: A Return to Opposition

INTRODUCTION

In the aftermath of the 1997 general election serious questions were being asked within Democratic Left about the party's future, not to mind its future direction. Some members believed they had a role to play as a critical niche political party offering an alternative on the Left to the more moderate Labour Party. This argument was ultimately rejected by several senior party figures who were no longer able to distinguish real differences between themselves and their counterparts in the Labour Party. These two schools of thought were, however, united in appreciating the task involved in rejuvenating the party after the disappointing election results in 1997 which had seen Democratic Left exit government and return to the opposition benches in Leinster House.

The analysis in this chapter focuses on the post-1997 general election debate in Democratic Left and considers the viewpoints of several leading party members on their future direction as well as the different attitudes – which still prevailed at that time – to the Labour Party. The evidence shows that the discussions after the 1997 general election – and debate provoked by an internal party task force report – led ultimately to the conclusion that Democratic Left did not have an independent future. Initial steps in the direction of the Labour Party were undertaken, although the ultimate merger idea took some time to emerge as the majority view within the leadership tier in Democratic Left.

The 1997 general election results had a significant impact on Democratic Left, with the loss of two Dáil seats and no obvious areas of electoral growth. 'There was a deflation after the election. It was a serious blow,' John Gallagher summarised.[1] Tony Heffernan was one of those who was conscious of the uncertain political future facing Democratic Left:

> I think that [the results] raised questions about the viability of the
> party. As well when we came out of government we found it more
> difficult to maintain the party structures. People just drifted off,
> people were dropping out – 'well, the election is over and I did my
> bit so then I'll go off and play golf or whatever' – which was the
> natural human reaction.[2]

The question why Democratic Left failed to survive as a separate political entity produces different responses from those involved with the
party. Certainly by the end of 1997 there was a realisation among many
leading party figures that the process of rebuilding was going to be very
difficult. Des Geraghty was not alone in addressing the scale of the
work and effort being shouldered by a small group of individuals, and
the resulting pressure this generated. 'I think we were faced by just too
many elections, too quickly, and then there was the strain in a very
small party, intellectually, physically and mentally ...'[3] Eamon Gilmore
also referred to the energy required to maintain the party when, for
many senior members and the vast majority of the electorate, the party
was no different from the Labour Party.

> We can be very proud of the party but in 1997 we were out of
> government and you were saying to yourself, 'right what am I
> going to put my energy into here?' I mean we certainly saw no
> future in effectively two Labour parties with little or no difference
> ... We worked together on the 1997 presidential election but the
> tick-tacking was going on between us.[4]

Others were more hopeful that the party would be able to develop in
the aftermath of the 1997 general election outcome. Liz McManus –
who had resigned her membership of the Labour Party in the 1960s
over the party's positive attitude to coalition with Fine Gael – was
initially opposed to a merger. 'I was very happy to keep pottering on.
We'd been through worse times, and we certainly had, I mean I was in
the Workers' Party since 1971 ...'[5] Rosheen Callender was also initially
hopeful that a separate party could be preserved:

> I remember being quite hopeful at the time. We generated a lot of
> discussion and re-enthused people with ideas, but even at the end of
> that process we were already talking to the Labour Party about the
> merger. So it all happened very quickly really and quite suddenly. It's

not that it hadn't been discussed before but, suddenly, the discussion just took off and I think those of us who'd been struggling to keep this very small party going – and the high level of work – I suppose just began to get tired, and sort of felt this couldn't be sustained.[6]

The hostility between the two parties reduced significantly during the 1994–7 Rainbow coalition. Many involved mention increased trust and the development of friendships between individuals who previously would have had no opportunity to associate with each other. 'I do know that we worked well together after that initial kind of stand-offishness … we worked pretty well with the Labour people …' Rosheen Callender admitted.[7] The period in government also only served to highlight the perception issue, that is, how the voters saw the two parties. 'The public wouldn't have been able to understand the difference [between Labour and Democratic Left],' Des Geraghty said.[8] Eric Byrne, who lost his Dáil seat in the 1997 general election, was fully aware of the party's precarious existence and the nascent movement in the direction of the Labour Party:

I think everybody was accepting, at different stages, that what you had representing Democratic Left was just individually committed and powerful public representatives who managed to win seats in the Dáil. And they could win for any political party. I think what happened was inevitable. Once it went into government it could never replace the Labour Party and if you couldn't replace the Labour Party … I don't think anyone would have seen it any other way than to merge.[9]

Eamon Gilmore had reached a similar conclusion.

There was a sense that when it [the 1997 general election] was over the game was up. I remember meeting soon after the election an individual on the street, and you know [our conversation] it was a case of 'look Labour had a very poor election and we didn't have a good election.' It was very much a sense of the two Labour parties were better off working together.[10]

The assessments of both Byrne and Gilmore point once more to the thesis that the journey embarked upon in 1992 was one involving movement into the moderate social democratic space occupied by the

Labour Party. Membership of the Labour Party was not an option for most people associated with De Rossa in 1992. But after the experience of the Rainbow coalition and the poor general election results in 1997 the viability of Democratic Left as a separate entity was questionable. The party had not carved out a distinctive political niche and was increasingly confronted by a failure to explain real difference with the Labour Party. This identity conundrum was set alongside the ongoing organisational and mounting financial challenges. The party's future was leading in one direction, according to John Gallagher: 'The Labour Party had moved on. In 1992 there would have been a more confrontational view of the Labour Party. But by 1997 a lot of old battles were over and [many] constituency battles had also sorted themselves out ...'[11]

A SECOND TASK FORCE AND TWO BY-ELECTIONS

The idea of merging with the Labour Party was reached slowly. In the aftermath of the 1997 general election the national executive at its July meeting took the decision to establish a task force 'to take stock of the current position of Democratic Left'.[12] The group was chaired by trade unionist and senior party member Pat Brady and met on ten separate occasions during the summer of 1997.[13] Submissions were received from several party members. The completed report was divided into three sections: Policies and Political Strategy; Organisation; and Implementation. The document recommended a new strategic approach, while noting that:

> The purpose and strategic aim of Democratic Left should become the construction of a new progressive majority in Irish politics. This should be achieved through a series of alliances with progressive parties, groupings and individuals in national and local politics. Obvious partners in such a strategy are the Labour Party, the Greens and progressive independents. The alliance will be a third force in Irish politics and challenge the stranglehold of the other two main parties on the political agenda ... The long-term goal of this approach is the creation of a national alliance capable of creating a progressive majority in a coalition government of the future. Democratic Left can be the ideological and strategic engine of this new majority by campaigning on its own policies and seeking their inclusion in the programme of the alliances.[14]

A number of 'flagship policy headings' – identified by the task force – included a basic income, a statutory right to work, free health care and universal pre-school education. The report was circulated to members of the National Executive ahead of a meeting on 27 September 1997 at the ATGWU trade union hall at Middle Abbey Street in central Dublin. The meeting was briefed on the document, which was followed by 'an initial general discussion on the overall content of the report, during which points were made concerning the need to define what the party's role is, the development of political alliances and the political objectives of Democratic Left'.[15] A decision was taken to first debate section 3 of the report, which dealt with organisational matters. Following a general discussion, each recommendation was addressed separately. Among the decisions agreed was that an audit of local organisations be undertaken, a renewed focus be placed on recruitment and an external review be commissioned on the operation of party head office. The discussion took up so much time that consideration of section 1 of the task force report on policies and political strategy was deferred and eventually took place in late November 1997.

In the intervening period briefings were organised with various constituency groups. The audit to determine the level of constituency activity was undertaken, with head office preparing a detailed questionnaire which had to be returned by 10 December 1997. Although no information on the returns received is available, it can only be assumed that whatever evidence was gathered only served to confirm what many in the party were acknowledging in private – Democratic Left was in deep organisational and financial trouble, with the continuing subject of its identity still unresolved.

The debate about the future of the party continued at the national executive meeting on 29 November 1997. Proinsias De Rossa led the discussion and observed that it was 'important that discussion is brought to a conclusion as speedily as possible to allow people concentrate on necessary campaigns and policy implementation'.[16] The minutes of the same meeting noted that Eamon Gilmore 'proposed that the party identify what is the political agenda of the Left in Ireland, how to deliver on it, and what is the appropriate vehicle or vehicles for ensuring that the Left's agenda is brought forward'.[17] Gilmore's contribution was moving the debate into a wider context which ultimately was to involve use of the word 'merger'.

The discussion about forging a wider alliance on the Left to restart the Democratic Left project found little interest with some activists, among them John Gallagher. 'That was genuine but I thought it was bullshit. Those on the Left continually had these discussions but the people hadn't voted for it. I had been faced too often with the practicalities. I had formed the view that Labour was where the party [DL] should go ...'[18] Nevertheless, key Democratic Left figures continued to insist that a merger was not the only outcome of this process. According to Tony Heffernan:

> It wasn't as if everyone woke up one morning and said, 'we could merge with the Labour Party.' It started off from a position of saying, 'can we work out some sort of closer relationship with Labour that will benefit us?' Then as the discussions and negotiations went on, I suppose, people had come around to the view that the merger was probably the best option. I think there would have been a degree of realisation that if we had to face into another election in the short term then there was a danger we would have been wiped out.[19]

There was a poor attendance at some of these crucial meetings, which may be taken as another indication that the party was struggling. 'I regret to say that the seriousness of this process has not been reflected in the attendance pattern of a number of executive members,' Pat Brady wrote in January 1998, adding 'the attendance at the last meeting was deplorable and some Executive members seem to pay little or no heed to the starting time of the meeting. Given what is at stake this really is not good enough.'[20]

The debate about the future direction of Democratic Left was not just confined to meetings of the party's national executive, no matter what attendance level the body achieved each month. Party members and likeminded supporters were invited to a series of regular Sunday morning meetings early in 1998 which were aimed at facilitating discussion and debate in key policy areas. Held under the title 'New Century Socialists!' these gatherings in Bewley's Café on Grafton Street in Dublin city centre were known as the 'Candid Coffee Circle'. Those attending heard contributions on the elimination of poverty, wealth redistribution, the role of the United Nations and gender equality. While the gatherings may have been intellectually stimulating, the initiative only stressed Democratic Left's organisational problems. 'The recent coffee mornings, on top of a declining audience from week to week as the novelty of dialogue wore thin, showed only one thing – that we are not a coherent group of people with a joint view of the world and political action.'[21] In late March 1998, Philip O'Connor – an activist in Dublin North Central who was heavily involved in the party's international committee – wrote to De Rossa, Rabbitte, Gilmore, McManus and Gallagher.

> The time has come to take a decisive step and operate for the last time as a block in Irish politics. Because DL is internally dysfunctional and incapable of coherent activity (finally proven by the non-event of the 'Task Force' report), you are the only people who can do it. It is now your historic duty to ensure that the left tradition you represent does not again fizzle out (as so often before), and also your political duty – both to yourselves personally and to us your colleagues – to ensure that the essential transition is carried out with strength, dignity and political effect. What is required is for you to meet with Ruairi Quinn now and offer a block merger of DL and Labour.[22]

A radically different course of action was proposed by academic Richard Dunphy, who attributed a 'demoralisation of the members and a loss of self-confidence' to a 'failure to forge a clear political identity' coupled with 'a failure of leadership within the party'.[23] Dunphy argued strongly against any move to dissolve the party ahead of members joining the Labour Party. He was optimistic that by sharpening the party's ideological profile, membership numbers and activity levels would increase.

> We are small and we are currently weak. But we have a radical edge to our politics and the capacity to mount a sharp and necessary critique of society. No other party comes remotely close to filling that role. If we take a hard-nosed and cool-headed look at our situation; if we take the decisions necessary to restore morale and revitalise the party within realistic limits; then I believe we can still turn the party around, recruit some new members and re-inspire some existing members, and remain a small but vital and influential force in the years ahead.[24]

These written contributions are important in that they provide two records of the widely differing viewpoints held by Democratic Left members in early 1998 as a debate was underway about the party's future. While this debate was ongoing across the membership, the task force report provided cover for the wider discussions about the party's next move. The report was discussed in some detail at several National Executive meetings in the early part of 1998. 'This is a vital crossroads for our organisation,' Pat Brady stated in correspondence ahead of a meeting to conclude discussion on 4 April 1998.[25] A minute from that meeting, which was attended by most of the leading figures in the party, gives a real sense of the crucial juncture that had been reached.

> Pat Brady introduced discussion, in the context of an assessment of initiatives undertaken since last September, including the Task Force report, the promotion campaign and the results of the by-elections. He stated that the overall outcome of the above had not been successful and that a better approach must be identified. A discussion followed during which the following principal points were made, including that there had been successes, including the interest in the intellectual life of the party as evidence in the coffee mornings, that the party must be prepared for the long haul, the need for a party like DL to deal with the issues, structural problems such as the size of the NEC [National Executive Committee], the need to relaunch and reorganise, disappointment with continual debate about problems. Diverging views were expressed that the party's high expectations have not been fulfilled, we must address the option of a new arrangement with Labour, tackling the issues of tax, poverty, employment requires power and how best can we achieve this is the issue. A further view was expressed that the issue of our future should be dealt with a [sic] speedily as possible.[26]

The debate – which started the previous summer in the aftermath of the 1997 general election – was about to move into a new phase. It was also about to take on a new seriousness. A motion proposed by De Rossa and seconded by Rabbitte was agreed at the National Executive meeting on 4 April 1998. It approved the start of internal consultations to ascertain 'the options open to DL and how the party will address these options' with a May deadline, while another motion from Gilmore was also adopted which called for the commencement of 'a process of discussion on the future of the party and the future of the Left in Ireland'.[27] Neither motion made direct reference to the Labour Party, but a process had commenced which would lead within eight months to the end of Democratic Left as a separate independent political party.

Nevertheless, in the early months of 1998 the day-to-day work of a separate and independent party was still being done despite the task force-inspired talk about different future directions. Preparations for forthcoming local elections were underway, while proposals for a fundraising draw were being developed. The party had also debated the most appropriate strategy to adopt in relation to two by-elections caused by the resignation of Fianna Fáil's Ray Burke in Dublin North and the death of Limerick East TD Jim Kemmy of the Labour Party. The matter was discussed at a General Purposes Committee meeting on 11 February 1998 and the question of money was to the fore. The minutes recorded: 'Limerick East: Update presented on campaign. Need to ensure proper accounting of spending emphasised. Dublin North: Encourage Joe Holohan to contest, in contest of Dublin North offer to provide funding.'[28]

Polling in the two by-elections – the first contests since the 1997 general election – was held on 11 April 1998. The results were hugely disappointing for Democratic Left, as has been discussed previously. Coming as they did at a time when an internal soul-searching of sorts was already underway, the poor performance at the polls further raised the issue of the party's future. Tony Heffernan summarised: 'We had great hope for John Ryan in Limerick East. He did OK but never came near winning a seat. But the other candidate Joe Holohan in Dublin North got 200 votes, which was sort of a wipeout, although we invested a fair bit of money and effort in it. I think that caused a lot of people to question whether or not it was viable for us to continue.'[29]

The by-election results were discussed at a National Executive meeting in early April 1998. The meeting decided to consult the party membership on the way forward. 'Nothing can be discounted, nor can any assumption be made before the party review is completed,' Rabbitte said publicly, although, as is discussed in the next chapter, the Democratic Left TD was at that time privately indicating to Ruairi Quinn that a merger was an achievable outcome.[30]

UNCERTAIN FUTURE

At the beginning of May 1998 De Rossa addressed a meeting of the
party's Dublin membership. He did not explicitly mention the merger
issue but stated the need to 'spell out how we are going to carry through
a major reconstruction of the Democratic Left organisation, transforming it into the agency for radical change which we set out to do in
March 1992'.[31] As a reminder of the ambitions of those who had been
motivated to attend the party's founding conference, he quoted from
this own speech on that day.

> Since then [1992] we have played an important and progressive role
> in the political life of this country; in opposition and, to everyone's
> surprise, in Government. We have had election successes and losses.
> In five years we have also had policy successes beyond everyone's
> expectations. But we have not had the political, organisational or
> electoral growth that we set for ourselves.[32]

De Rossa argued strongly that the party's lack of electoral growth could
not be explained by either an end of ideological division or an absence
of exclusion and injustice, or even a failure of a socialist critique of
society. But crucially in his written address, the Democratic Left leader
did not provide his own explanation; rather he opted for a non-specific
rallying call to party members to 'rediscover and renovate the univer-
salist socialist values' as he added:

> I know that the combined resources of this party; its membership,
> elected representatives, intellectual capacity, history and comrade-
> ship if properly mobilised are capable of rising to the challenge
> … It will not be easy; decisions on key questions should not,
> indeed cannot be reached overnight. It will take time.[33]

Numerous media reports noted that a majority in Democratic Left,
including the party leader, favoured the retention of their own separate
identity. Indeed, only days before the decision was taken to seek talks
with the Labour Party, Kathleen Lynch was predicting that 'Democratic
Left intends to double its Dáil representation to eight seats next time
round …'[34] There was a strong desire in sections of Democratic Left to
see any discussions go beyond talk of a merger to encompass other
groups on the Left of Irish politics so as to agree a progressive political
programme capable of delivering greater electoral success. In an

unpublished paper prepared for a meeting of party activists in Dún Laoghaire on 21 May 1998, Eamon Gilmore argued that, 'This project is bigger than DL, bigger than the Labour Party – and bigger than a merger between both.'[35] Gilmore's paper – which was also sent to De Rossa, Rabbitte McManus and Heffernan – was written just days prior to the Democratic Left national executive meeting at which the idea of opening talks with the Labour Party was due to be debated. Gilmore wrote:

> To move this project forward, the Executive of the Party should decide on Saturday:
>
> - To commit ourselves to help build a larger Left movement in Ireland.
> - To commence exploratory discussions with the Labour Party to explore how a larger Left might be developed.
> - To involve people from outside both parties in the process – trade union, community, social activists.
> - To report back on any progress made or response received and to ensure that the process and any outcome is subject to approval by the Executive, and by the membership.
> - To continue our work in developing policy, preparing for the Local Elections and general political activity.[36]

The issue of the party's future direction was discussed at an extended national executive meeting held at the Royal Dublin Hotel on O'Connell Street in Dublin on Saturday 23 May 1998. A number of different motions were submitted for consideration, including one from John Ryan in Limerick East calling on the party to enter into six weeks of 'exploratory discussions with the Labour Party with the aim of establishing a new formulation of the left in Ireland'.[37] Another motion in the name of the task force chairman Pat Brady sought 'a new formation on the Irish left, built on a foundation of Democratic Left and the Labour Party ...'[38] There was even more ambition in an unsigned, handwritten note entitled 'Draft motion for Sat. meeting' which stated that 'the time is ripe for a major new initiative on the Irish left, North and South, in order to ensure a pre-eminent position for "new century socialism" in Ireland. To this end our Party Leader should, as a matter of urgency, approach Ruairi Quinn and John Hume and others ...'[39]

What all these motions shared in common was a desire for an initiative to help revitalise Democratic Left. They were, however, withdrawn in favour of a motion tabled in the name of the party's four TDs. This motion endorsed the idea of exploring with the Labour Party 'the possibility of developing a new political formation which would be significantly larger than the sum of our two parts …'[40] It was discussed in the context of a letter from Ruairi Quinn to Proinsias De Rossa – and read to the meeting – 'supporting the concept of a new formation on the Left'.[41] The motion from the four TDs made reference to several developments which facilitated the move, including progress in cementing European Union integration, the peace process in Northern Ireland and the decline in support for Left parties at the 1997 general election. By moving towards a 'new political formation' with Labour, the members of Democratic Left were signalling their desire to take advantage of these developments and also to create a political environment in which a Left-led government might finally emerge.

The motion eventually approved by the national executive with one vote against and no abstentions had actually gone through a number of different drafts which contained a significant number of variations in terminology and in language. For example, the first typed draft stated that any new initiative would ensure the growth of 'new century socialism' which changed in the second draft to 'democratic socialism/the Left in Ireland'. By the third draft this concept was edited to 'democratic socialism', and so it remained in the final draft of the motion. Similarly, in the first draft it was stated that the national executive 'resolves that Democratic Left should invite the Labour Party to enter into discussions with a view to agreeing a common programme and strategy for the growth and development of the Left with the objective of creating a new political entity that would be significantly larger than the sum of our two parts and that the objective should be to have this process completed (by the end of 1998) in time for preparations for the 1999 local government elections …'

The timeframe was deleted from the second draft while, rather than Democratic Left inviting Labour to participate in the initiative, the wording was also changed so that 'Democratic Left should explore with the Labour Party.' More significantly, however, the objective in the first draft to create 'a new political entity' was revised to 'a new political formation'. These drafting changes can be seen as introducing a degree of protection for Democratic Left in the event of unsuccessful talks with the Labour Party. Moreover, the party was not at that time indicating in writing what was its preference for the eventual outcome of the initiative. The initial inclusion of a deadline and an emphasis on 'a new political entity' may in some quarters have been seen as a signal that Democratic Left members were desperate to find a new political home. Ultimately, the absence of a deadline and the reference to 'a new political formation' left open the belief that something less than a merger, or even takeover, was being sought. Yet despite these text changes in the drafting process, the meeting on 23 May 1998 formally accepted that there was, in effect, an elephant in the room. The future of Democratic Left was being discussed not just in terms of party revitalisation as outlined in the September 1997 task force report but also in terms of closer relations with the Labour Party. A merger, while not mentioned in public, was a realistic outcome of this process and crucially had been mentioned by Ruairi Quinn in private correspondence with De Rossa on 12 May 1998, which is discussed in detail in the following chapter.

A small group including De Rossa, Geraghty, Callander and Paddy Gillen met the day after the national executive meeting – 24 May 1998 – to discuss how progress could be made. A note of this private meeting, headed 'New Formation', refers to the 'medium to long term objective' as a Left-led government.[42] The discussion, however, was very much about the practical steps to progress the decision taken the previous day. There was agreement on the need for regular meetings between the leaders and spokespersons of the two parties (Labour and Democratic Left) as well as for Democratic Left to talk to other groups, including the trade unions. The meeting decided: 'Various people to talk to friendly Labour people to encourage support for New Formation.'[43]

A copy of De Rossa's 23 May 1998 media statement was subsequently sent to all party members. In an accompanying letter De Rossa observed that, 'this is a very exciting time for politics in Ireland. We on the Left have an unprecedented opportunity to create a new politics ... and of promoting the socialist values on which we were founded as values that underpin society in general.'[44] Events were now moving at a speedy pace. Leading party figures attended constituency meetings on the future of Democratic Left, while all the time the discussion was increasingly focusing on the basis for contact with the Labour Party.

CONCLUSION

In June 1998 Des Geraghty prepared an action plan of sorts for the discussions about the party's future direction. He observed that, 'The project we are now engaged in is about "Growing the Left". It is not a Democratic Left/Labour merger, although that could turn out to be one of the options – but not necessarily the only one for Democratic Left.'[45] The programme of activities envisaged by Geraghty included internal action – 'increase political dialogue [and] increase political visibility on key political issues' – and a strengthened external profile. While there was considerable speculation that the engagement with the Labour Party would end with a merger, Geraghty was keen that all options were kept open: 'most importantly is the necessity to make it known that we are still in business and still – indeed more than ever – have a serious political agenda to address now and in the future, and that we want more people involved in the process.'[46] Geraghty was not alone in believing that the exercise with the Labour Party also opened up room for debate about key issues in Irish society and what political response could be offered by Democratic Left. But the party's future was never too far away. 'On an organisational level, we need hard information from all our constituencies about what the current position actually is vis-à-vis Labour, independents or other left groups, provos etc.'[47]

Once the Labour Party option – however, constituted – was out in the open a variety of views were heard at party meetings. The constituency council in North Kildare where Catherine Murphy was a local councillor based in Leixlip agreed on 12 June 1998 that 'Democratic Left should continue as an independent political party with its own constitutions and party programme.'[48] A motion from Murphy's constituency for consideration of the party's national executive bluntly stated:

> ... that achieving Democratic Left's objectives and remedying the fundamental defects in Irish society ... requires energetic and radical action; that the history and composition of the Irish Labour Party demonstrates clearly that it is not capable of such radical political action; that given the current organisational strengths of the Irish Labour Party and Democratic Left, that any form of merger (whether formal or informal) between the two parties will

not be conducive to the achievement of Democratic Left's long-term goals, given the inherent social conservatism and commitment to short-term electoral advantage of the great majority of the Labour Party organisation.[49]

But this view was quickly overtaken by events. The internal questioning underway since the 1997 general election – and debate provoked by the party task force – had facilitated only one serious scenario. By the autumn of 1998 the talks between the two parties had moved into the realm of a merger agreement between Democratic Left and the Labour Party. The specific role played by Pat Rabbitte and Ruairi Quinn in progressing the merger deal is dealt with in Chapter 11 while the negotiations leading to the eventual deal are the subject of Chapter 12.

NOTES

1. Interview with John Gallagher, 15 June 2006.
2. Interview with Tony Heffernan, 13 September 2006
3. Interview with Des Geraghty, 9 May 2006.
4. Interview with Eamon Gilmore, 11 September 2006.
5. Interview with Liz McManus, 18 October 2006.
6. Interview with Rosheen Callender, 12 September 2006.
7. Ibid.
8. Interview with Des Geraghty, 9 May 2006.
9. Interview with Eric Byrne, 29 August 2006.
10. Interview with Eamon Gilmore, 11 September 2006.
11. Interview with John Gallagher, 15 June 2007.
12. Task Force Report, unpublished, September 1997.
13. The other members of the Task Force were Proinsias Breathnach, John Gallagher, Alex Klemm, Bernard Lynch, Fiachra Ó Ceilleachair, Emer O'Sullivan, Michael Taft and Noel Ward.
14. Task Force Report, unpublished, September 1997.
15. Democratic Left National Executive minutes, 27 September 1997.
16. Democratic Left National Executive minutes, 29 November 1997.
17. Ibid.
18. Interview with John Gallagher, 15 June 2007.
19. Interview with Tony Heffernan, 13 September 2006.
20. Pat Brady, letter to all National Executive members, 13 January 1998.
21. Philip O'Connor, letter to De Rossa, Rabbitte, Gilmore, McManus and Gallagher, 29 March 1998.
22. Ibid. Pat Rabbitte showed a draft of this document to Ruairi Quinn at a private meeting of the two men on 20 March 1998.
23. Richard Dunphy, letter to Democratic Left, undated.
24. Ibid.
25. Pat Brady, correspondence to Democratic Left National Executive members, 27 March 1998.
26. Democratic Left National Executive minutes, 4 April 1998.
27. Ibid.
28. Democratic Left General Purposes Committee minutes 11 February 1998.
29. Interview with Tony Heffernan, 13 September 2006.
30. *The Irish Times*, 22 April 1998.

31. Proinsias De Rossa, address to Dublin membership, 5 May 1998.
32. Ibid.
33. Ibid.
34. *Examiner*, 21 May 1998.
35. Eamon Gilmore, unpublished policy paper, 21 May 1998.
36. Ibid.
37. John Ryan, letter to John Gallagher, Democratic Left head office, 19 May 1998.
38. Pat Brady, draft motion submitted to Democratic Left head office, 20 May 1998.
39. No author identified, draft motion submitted to Democratic Left head office, undated.
40. Democratic Left National Executive motion, 23 May 1998.
41. Democratic Left, minutes of National Executive, 23 May 1998.
42. Unpublished note of ad hoc meeting, 24 May 1998.
43. Ibid.
44. Proinsias De Rossa, letter to party membership, 25 May 1998.
45. Des Geraghty, unpublished memo, 1 June 1998.
46. Ibid.
47. Ibid.
48. Correspondence from Catherine Murphy to Proinsias De Rossa, 16 June 1998.
49. Ibid.

11

Merger II: Pat Rabbitte and Ruairi Quinn

INTRODUCTION

The merger between Democratic Left and the Labour Party was very much a 'top-down' exercise. There were strong pockets of membership support in both organisations for moves in the direction of a merger – more prevalent in Democratic Left – but it was by no means an initiative driven by the grassroots members in either party. Indeed, given the localised hostility between members in various constituencies it is doubtful if grassroots momentum would have led to fruitful discussions between the two organisations, not to mind a successful conclusion. This 'top-down' exercise was driven by two key individuals, Pat Rabbitte and Ruairi Quinn. Both politicians played crucial roles in progressing movement towards the start of merger discussions in their respective parties. A strong sense of loyalty within Democratic Left had prevented individual TDs deflecting to the Labour Party. But the loyalty of ambitious TDs like Rabbitte was severely tested in the aftermath of the 1997 general election, with no clear sense about Democratic Left's future direction. Moreover, the idea of individual party TDs joining the Labour Party did not appeal to Quinn. The Labour Party leader wanted the 'big bang' which, he believed, a merger would create.

The involvement of Rabbitte and Quinn is the main focus of the discussion in this chapter. Their preference for a merger deal and the contacts between the two men is examined, as is Rabbitte's role in ensuring that Proinsias De Rossa, despite his personal sceptical views, backed the proposal. Without the active involvement of Rabbitte and Quinn – in late 1997 and throughout 1998 – it is unlikely that the merger idea would have advanced as quickly as it did, nor would the negotiations have moved to a point where by the autumn of 1998 an agreement was within reach.

PAT RABBITTE AND THE MERGER IDEA

The post-1997 general election period not only raised serious doubts about the future of Democratic Left but also gave rise to questions about the future intentions of the party's four TDs. The possibility that some of them individually would seek to join the Labour Party was always an option, with Pat Rabbitte and Eamon Gilmore considered the most likely to deflect. Indeed, in the weeks prior to the calling of the 1997 general election Ray Kavanagh and Jim Kemmy had discussed approaching Rabbitte about the Democratic Left minister of state switching parties. The move was not pursued. At that time, it would have done huge damage to the joint electoral approach favoured by the three parties in the outgoing Rainbow coalition.

When asked did he give consideration to leaving Democratic Left to join the Labour Party after the 1997 general election, Gilmore replied, 'No, I didn't. I wouldn't have done that.'[1] The response illustrates the strong personal and political loyalty shared by those who had formed Democratic Left in early 1992.

> The people I was in Democratic Left with were people I had worked with going back to the time of the Workers' Party. There was a loyalty between us. And wherever we were going, we were going together, particularly people in my own constituency. The other thing was I had great regard and great loyalty to De Rossa. We had gone through all of that together and I certainly was not going to do something on my own. I wasn't going to say, 'right, I resign from DL and I'm joining the Labour Party.' We were going to do it as a party. We went through a lot together and we were going to do it together.[2]

Pat Rabbitte had held a similar view since 1992 despite his personal belief at that stage that those departing the Workers' Party should have joined the Labour Party.

> There was a question of loyalty involved, if we were to move we were going to move together. It was certainly argued but nobody was going to break ranks. I had a clear preference and I had pretty much made up my mind but, I mean, I wasn't going [alone].[3]

Despite the loyalty stance from Rabbitte and Gilmore, neither man was convinced about the ability of Democratic Left to break out from its underachieving record. Indeed, since late 1992 Gilmore had been unconvinced about the long-term viability of having two similar parties on the Left of the Irish political spectrum. But Gilmore was only prepared to move in conjunction with his parliamentary colleagues. The view of many senior figures in Democratic Left was that Rabbitte and Gilmore rather than De Rossa ultimately pushed the merger idea. Eric Byrne subscribed to this assessment:

> De Rossa would have been far more cautious, and that's not to say that he wouldn't have recognised that it had to happen, it would have been a bigger disappointment for him ... Rabbitte wouldn't have held and never did hold the ideological line as strongly as De Rossa did. So when the talk of a merger [emerged] it was clear to everybody that the Rabbittes and Gilmores of this world would have been most prone to the acceptance of a merger than De Rossa. But De Rossa, knowing this was the swing and this was the direction, didn't try to stop it.[4]

Catherine Murphy shared Eric Byrne's view:

> The person I talked most to about it was De Rossa. And he certainly wasn't the original architect of it. I have no doubt that the Rabbitte/Gilmore axis is where it came from. They had obviously got close to others in the Labour Party during the period of government.[5]

Rabbitte was the principal driver of the process. He set out some of his thoughts in a paper prepared for Democratic Left's national executive in April 1998. 'Whatever about its individual public representatives, the Party has failed to strike a responsive chord with the electorate or put down roots in Irish society,' Rabbitte wrote in an analysis that offered a bleak outlook for Democratic Left.

> Inequality is still deeply rooted in our society ... In Ireland the least educated and early school leavers tend to be geographically clustered in areas mainly unplugged from the real economy. As a consequence and especially given the level of abstention in the voting process this 20% is not influential in determining the character of Government. This analysis would appear to have led the Labour Party to direct its main electoral appeal towards the 'coping classes'. And whereas Democratic Left has not similarly abandoned the unemployment black spots, the electoral dividend has been diminishing. The main factors contributing to this diminution includes the level of sustained

indigenous organisation required to service the clientelist expectations in these areas and the emergence of Sinn Féin as self-pro-
claimed defenders of these communities on issues such as drug
pushing. Accordingly the protest element of the vote in these areas
has significantly transferred to Sinn Féin and in some areas to candidates campaigning under the banner of the Socialist Party. Poverty
in Ireland is concentrated in, but is not exclusive to, these areas.
However, these areas alone cannot sustain a Party whose main platform is economic justice. Such a Party has to be able in order to sustain itself win votes outside of the marginalised areas. This challenge
distinguishes parties determined to win power to shape political
and economic policy from protest parties or single-issue candidates.[6]

Democratic Left was engaged in an internal review of its future political strategy in late 1997 – discussed in Chapter 10 – when Rabbitte
sought to shift his party in the direction of its longstanding rival. 'We
were offering to run a parallel Labour Party. I really couldn't see the
point in that,' he explained.[7] Rabbitte raised the idea of a merger. But
he did so not within his own party but by privately contacting Ruairi
Quinn, the newly elected leader of the Labour Party. This move may
have been sparked by the tragic death of Michael Enright in a car acci-
dent in early October 1997. Enright had been a member of Wexford
Corporation since 1985 and was one of those who left the Workers'
Party to join Democratic Left. A teacher by profession, he was also active in trade union politics. He had served for a short period as a member of Seanad Éireann, having been nominated by John Bruton in June
1997 to fill a vacancy which arose following the election of an incumbent nominee to Dáil Éireann. He was an active member of the Democratic Left national executive and his sudden death shocked his party
colleagues. The tragic event seems to have been a seminal
moment for Rabbitte, as several weeks later when he approached
Ruairi Quinn about a merger proposal he mentioned the discussion at
his late colleague's funeral. Some of Rabbitte's colleagues in Democratic Left were aware that he was increasingly convinced by the
merits of a merger. Liz McManus recalled talking with Rabbitte at
Michael Enright's funeral:

> I know in Pat's mind the idea was growing … I remember Michael
> Enright died and I went to his funeral. It was a great turnout, and

I turned to Pat and I said, 'you know this is the party and you're saying there's no party left.' And he said, 'we can't survive on this.' And he was right. We couldn't have gone on.[8]

Over the following months Rabbitte took the lead in pursuing contacts with the Labour Party. His actions were independent of his party leader but they added impetus to the process and eventually convinced De Rossa to accept the merger idea.

RUAIRI QUINN BECOMES LABOUR PARTY LEADER

The election of Ruairi Quinn as Dick Spring's successor as Labour Party leader in November 1997 made the prospect of a merger somewhat easier to discuss. Quinn was perceived as having a less hostile attitude to Democratic Left than displayed by Spring. Liz McManus, who was not in favour of a merger, stressed the importance of Quinn's election as Labour Party leader.

> The fact that Ruairi Quinn was there for the merger made a difference. He wasn't as forceful as Dick Spring [who] was very abrasive, and he would cut you down for absolutely no reason except that he wanted to, you know, it just made him feel good. When Ruairi Quinn came in, he was so facilitating and so easy going that that actually made things a bit easier.[9]

Despite the perception about Spring's attitude to Democratic Left, he played a role in opening up discussions with the smaller party. When he departed as Labour Party leader Spring had said he favoured closer co-operation with Democratic Left as the two parties 'now share virtually all of the same values'.[10] Quinn was seized by the possibility of such a proposition. He had seen the positive outcomes from previous merger deals with smaller Left organisations. Over the previous decade, the Democratic Socialist Party in Limerick led by Jim Kemmy and Declan Bree's independent socialist organisation in Sligo had merged with the Labour Party. Both of these groupings were more locally based than Democratic Left and were very much single constituency units based around a prominent individual. What was being contemplated with Democratic Left was a more fundamental realignment to potentially produce significant electoral and political gains.

Despite Quinn's interest, at that stage in late 1997 De Rossa was not entertaining a merger between the two parties. He confirmed his position in correspondence with his Labour Party counterpart. The Democratic Left leader wrote to Quinn on 18 November 1997 offering congratulations on the party leadership outcome. De Rossa told Quinn he would 'appreciate an early opportunity to meet you formally to discuss matters of mutual concern to both our parties on which we could co-operate. I think that it would be best to meet initially without a specific agenda.'[11] The meeting between the two leaders took place on 27 November 1997. They agreed to work towards closer political and parliamentary co-operation. But the two parties were preserving their respective separate identities: 'Labour and Democratic Left had distinctive roles to play as independent parties.'[12] Quinn was left with the impression that De Rossa 'felt quite threatened' by the interaction between the two parties.[13]

Arising from the leaders' meeting, an ad hoc group to find common ground on policy between the two parties was established. 'Close co-operation was considered by both of us as highly desirable. We agreed, if possible, a policy foundation should be established, shared by our two parties, dedicated to developing a clearly left critique of Irish society,' Quinn recalled.[14] A joint Democratic Left/Labour Party study group was eventually established in April 1998. Quinn wanted the group to 'discuss how the broad Left recaptures the intellectual high ground we lost to the Right in the 1980s'.[15] The group reported back to the two party leaders in mid-July 1998 with a paper representing 'a useful basis for developing a broad left programme for the new millennium'.[16] The theme is similar to that discussed in Chapter 1 of this study – finding a role for Left politics in a post-1989 political landscape.

> There is no end of ideology. There is no end of Left and Right. There is no triumph of markets. There is no triumph of pragmatism. There are as many serious problems in the world today as twenty years ago. Communism has collapsed, but capitalism is not triumphant. Much progress has been achieved, but new problems have arisen. Great tracts of the Left's agenda on the welfare state, health, housing, education, training and social issues have been achieved. They have been accepted by the Right and the resultant consensus may have made it appear as if there is an end of ideology. But there is still a deep division on how to develop society and the economy.[17]

The document was prepared against the backdrop of a possible closer relationship between the two parties. Moreover, the study group outcome once more provides evidence of the uncertainty in Left politics over its own distinct agenda. Democratic Left was not alone in this endeavour as the Labour Party was also seeking to clarify its ideological position in light of the changing political landscape across Europe in the 1990s. The ultimate objective from the contacts was the establishment of a think tank or policy foundation – an undertaking which would feature in the subsequent merger discussion. The study group played a useful role in facilitating new communications lines between the two parties at a crucial time in their nascent relationship.

At the start of 1998 there had been a delay in establishing the study group and, interestingly, it was finally set up after a letter dated 10 February 1998 from Rabbitte to Quinn, De Rossa and Brendan Howlin, the deputy leader of the Labour Party. Rabbitte wrote that he had information that some private money might be available to fund a Left-leaning research institute. He was seeking views on the idea. Whatever about the merits of a research institute, Rabbitte's intervention in February 1998 can be seen as a sign of increasing impatience with the political status quo in Democratic Left. The fact that he suggested that the body would examine topics 'from a broadly social democratic perspective' was in itself a clear indication that he wanted all kinds of barriers between the parties removed. Eight days after Rabbitte's circular correspondence, on 18 February 1998 De Rossa wrote to Quinn with the names of the Democratic Left members of the proposed study group, although Quinn only nominated his party's representatives on 1 April 1998.

Rabbitte's interest in progressing links between the two parties on a research institute followed an independent move he made in late 1997 in seeking to advance the process. Closer political co-operation between Democratic Left and the Labour Party had been discussed by the two party leaders in November 1997 immediately after Quinn's election as Labour Party leader. But the Quinn–De Rossa contacts took on an additional dimension some days later when Rabbitte contacted Quinn seeking a confidential meeting. The two men met in the parliamentary party meeting room of the Labour Party in Leinster House. In his memoir, *Straight Left*, Quinn recalled that the Democratic Left TD said that he:

> ... was there entirely in his own personal capacity. He just wanted me to hear something that I might not have heard. Welcoming the

meeting between De Rossa and myself, he then went on to say that something more fundamental than a declaration of closer co-operation might be available between the two parties.[18]

According to Quinn, Rabbitte referred to the recent discussions that had taken place among Democratic Left colleagues who attended the funeral of Michael Enright, when 'the talk turned from Michael's life to the future of many of those present.'[19] Quinn then recounted the key moment in their conversation:

> As I continued to listen, Pat looked at me straight, 'If you were open to it,' he said directly, 'we could be talking about a merger of our two parties and not just co-operation. The Labour name, the Labour brand,' he went on, 'has a historical validity and a tra-dition that could never be replaced. We tried in Democratic Left and it did not work. A merger is now possible with you as leader. While Spring was there, it simply was inconceivable.'[20]

The idea of a merger greatly interested Quinn, although he was aware that a by-election contest in Limerick East early in 1998 was problem-atic. The vacancy had been caused by the death of Labour TD Jim Kemmy. Democratic Left had hopes of winning the by-election. 'Any suggestions of our conversation becoming public before that's con-cluded would be disastrous,' Quinn told Rabbitte.[21] The discussions at the December 1997 meeting were not progressed until 20 March 1998 – eight days after the Limerick East by-election won by Labour's Jan O'Sullivan with John Ryan of Democratic Left polling poorly. Once again, Rabbitte contacted Quinn seeking a private meeting. They met in O'Reilly's bar in Sandymount near Quinn's home in south Dublin. Quinn recalled the conversation:

> Pat soon got to the point. 'This thing that I spoke to you about has moved much more quickly than I thought. Limerick simply con-firmed it to us. If a strong, dedicated hard-working guy like John Ryan cannot do it, then where are we going?'[22]

Rabbitte asked Quinn to read from a document which the Labour leader subsequently learnt had been written by Democratic Left activist Philip O'Connor. Quinn recalled their conversation:

> 'Read that section there,' he [Rabbitte] indicated. The piece was

a commentary on the evolution of the European Project and the positive future of the Party of European Socialists, with, in passing, some kind references to me. 'What's this?' I said half jokingly. 'Flattery?' 'No, no, but an indication of the way thoughtful people in our party are reacting.'[23]

This document was sent to several key Democratic Left members on 29 March 1998 – eight days after Rabbitte and Quinn met – as part of the internal debate about the party's future. The author was strongly in favour of approaching Quinn about a merger. The 'flattery' in the material Quinn read on 20 March 1998 can be seen from the theme of the paper in which the author observed: 'Quinn is not the Irish Blair but an Irish Jospin. He is completing the construction of a new Labour Party and now is the time to join and help shape it!'[24] Quinn was right to be flattered as he asked Rabbitte to continue.

> He looked at me intensely as he laid his cards on the table. There were many people on his side who wanted to do business but they needed reassurance. If the project advanced, would I be generous? Would they have a role? Would we respond openly? I had no difficulty in immediately replying, 'For my part, most certainly yes.'[25]

These two meetings were the precursor to wider talks between the two parties, and according to Quinn,

> the decisive, but informal, contact with Pat [Rabbitte] was soon followed by a formal exchange between De Rossa and myself ... It seemed to me that, initially, Proinsias was quite reluctant and distant about the whole idea ... [although] ... because of promptings from within his own party [he advanced the process].[26]

Prompted by Rabbitte's contact – and now being privy to the internal dynamic within Democratic Left – Quinn was in a strong position when he contacted Proinsias De Rossa. Quinn had already settled in his own mind where he wanted the discussions to conclude. Even before news of talks between the Labour Party and Democratic Left went public in late May 1998 – and despite his less than specific public comments – Quinn favoured a merger between the two parties. Following his private meetings with Rabbitte, Quinn sought to advance the process by directly contacting De Rossa. Previously unpublished correspondence, dated 12

May 1998, shows that Quinn very clearly placed the idea of a merger
on the table.

> I am aware of the discussions which have commenced within your
> own Party concerning the future of Left politics in Ireland in the
> next millennium and within that the role of Democratic Left.
> Despite media speculation and numerous requests for comments
> from myself and others, we have decided to remain silent. We have
> taken this course of action out of respect for the internal process
> of your own Party. We are not indifferent to its outcome. On the
> contrary, we would welcome moves to consolidate and strengthen
> the Left in Ireland by bringing closer together the Labour Party
> and Democratic Left ... I want you to know, at this stage of the
> process of discussion within your own Party, that I would welcome
> a transformation on the Irish Left which would undoubtedly
> result from a merging of Democratic Left with the Labour Party
> ... I am sure that all of the operational and organisational difficul-
> ties associated with such a coming together could be overcome
> with sensible and sensitive transition arrangements.[27]

So even before the membership of the respective parties got to digest
news of discussions about a possible new working relationship, the
Labour Party leader had, in private at least, formally pressed for a
merger. De Rossa was less forthcoming in his reply, and here a clear
difference of approach with Rabbitte emerged. While Rabbitte was
actively promoting the merger idea, De Rossa, in his actions and words
at least, appeared to have been open to different future directions for
Democratic Left. In correspondence dated 15 May 1998 De Rossa
acknowledged Quinn's letter but he made no reference to the merger
proposal. 'I appreciate the approach you and your party are adopting
to the current media interest in our internal debate. I expect some conclusion will be drawn before too long and I would obviously sit down
and talk with you then whatever these conclusions might be.'[28] Despite his
obvious preference to preserve his party's independence, De Rossa was
confronted with the reality that Democratic Left's future as a separate
entity was under threat. There is little doubt that the intervention of
Rabbitte had a crucial impact on subsequent developments. News that
Rabbitte had made contact with Quinn reached some of his Democratic
Left colleagues. 'I heard Rabbitte had made overtures ... in fairness once

he did it I knew we were finished ... so the best thing was, instead of fading away, was probably to join with Labour,' Paul Sweeney recalled.[29]

There was a bold sentiment in De Rossa's letter to Quinn on 15 May 1998 – to maintain Democratic Left's independence – but the two leaders were talking within ten days of the correspondence being sent. The internal pressure within Democratic Left to resolve the party's future ultimately forced a decision. Some members favoured an attempt to rejuvenate the party. But eventually – and influenced by senior personnel like Gilmore and Rabbitte – there was acceptance that Democratic Left as a project was no longer viable. Crucially, De Rossa came to accept the importance of Rabbitte's opinion on the party's future.

> It was Pat Rabbitte who first mooted the idea that there should be a merger. And it was clear from the way it had been put that he had already put out soundings. My initial response was no. I didn't think it was the right thing to do. I went home and thought about it. And it seemed that, taking everything into account and given our experience in government, the development of Left politics and so on, it didn't make sense to have two parties vying for the same electorate. It wasn't doing anything for progressive politics. And it seemed that if we didn't [merge] then we were going to lose people like Pat Rabbitte. So it seemed far better to lead an orderly merger provided we could negotiate elements of the DL position into the Labour Party position.[30]

Once De Rossa had accepted the Rabbitte position, formal discussions were started with the Labour Party about establishing a new relationship on the Irish parliamentary Left. The national executive of Democratic Left passed a motion on 23 May 1998 that referred to the possibility of creating 'a new political formation'. It was the first signal that the contacts of the previous months were entering a crucial phase. The formal announcement of merger talks was made two days later on Monday 25 May 1998 following a meeting between Quinn and De Rossa.

In separate media statements, both leaders said that the timing of their exploratory talks was in the context of the signing of the Belfast Agreement between most of the main parties in Northern Ireland. The developments north of the border had 'the potential to have a profound impact on the politics in the Republic,' De Rossa predicted.[31] He said there would not be a 'simple merger', adding, 'It is the first step towards creating a bigger Left in Ireland. How that may emerge we cannot tell now.'[32]

> We feel strongly, however, that there is now an opportunity to join forces with our sister party to pursue a new Left agenda for the coming decades. This will not be achieved by one party swallowing the other but through a partnership and the pooling of the physical and intellectual resources of both which would acknowledge the broad similarity of our objectives and respect the diversity of our traditions.[33]

In a media statement, Quinn described the talks as 'positive and constructive'. He said the two parties had:

> ... divergent traditions and histories. However, we also share common goals and ideals. The Labour Party will enter into discussions with Democratic Left in a spirit of goodwill and openness and we will work constructively to develop a Left strong enough to take on the two traditional parties.

The talks had three possible positive endings – a formal merger, a common electoral platform or the creation of a new political party. While a merger appeared the most likely outcome from the contacts – and media commentary certainly accepted such an eventuality – a spokesman for the Labour Party was urging caution. 'We will respond to Democratic Left in due course after reflecting on the proposal throughout all parts of the party. Nothing has been decided with Democratic Left at this point.'[34] Quinn, however – as his correspondence of 12 May 1998 with De Rossa showed – was already set on achieving a merger from the talks. A memo prepared for Quinn by his party's legal advisor plotted the options from a Labour Party perspective. These options were simple absorption, complicated absorption, and merger requiring constitutional change in the Labour Party.[35] Simple absorption would occur where 'DL TDs and most of their members sign up to join the Labour Party, without pre-conditions.' Complicated absorption would 'involve there being pre-conditions to the DL TDs and members joining the [Labour] Party'. The advice in the legal memo noted that 'neither of ... [these] ... options would be sufficient'. The advice favoured a merger in which 'a joint agreement would be reached at leader and [Executive] Council level ... [which] would include a policy statement and a draft new party constitution'. One party to the talks would be formally wound up as part of the deal – winding up the two entities to create a new third party was impractical, and would ensure continuous legal ownership of property and lower taxation bills.

When news of the talks between Democratic Left and the Labour Party emerged in late May 1998 there was favourable editorial mention but the challenges involved were identified. 'More problematic for both Democratic Left and Labour will be to redefine the meaning of the word "left" Labour is clearly moving to a form of what has come to be called Blairism, but Blairism is very poorly defined. But it will be fascinating to see how the two parties set about redefinition. And nothing but good can come of it,' the *Irish Independent* observed.[36] There was a note of caution from journalist Damien Kiberd, writing in the *Sunday Business Post*:

> It has yet to be explained by Quinn what percentage there is in signing itself with a party which is severely diminished in scale (and was never large to begin with) and which is inextricably linked in many voters' minds with the dog-eared socialism that prevailed in eastern Europe for decades.[37]

In a newspaper opinion article, academic Michael Laver noted that mergers between two organisations almost never take place on equal terms and one is generally more needy than the other. 'In this case, DL almost certainly has most to fear from the future. How long can a party with no national vote share to speak of continue to survive on the sheer willpower of four high-profile and very able TDs with well-tended local support bases?'[38]

Laver concluded that the Democratic Left politicians would have a more secure future but, more significantly, a larger party on the Left 'could hammer home a more coherent electoral message. The ideological polarisation between right and left would become more clear-cut, while economies of scale could allow a more effective use of scarce campaign resources.' There was, however, a very stark message for those involved in the nascent merger discussions. 'When the prospective partners take instruction on the political reality of mixed marriages they will find almost no European example of two parties which have merged and gone on to increase their combined electoral strength. Nearly always, the new party's vote share is less than the sum of its component parts.'[39]

THE LABOUR PARTY RESPONSE

The possibility of a merger with Democratic Left was first formally mentioned at the Labour parliamentary party on 27 May 1998. The long history of bitter rivalry between the Labour Party and the Workers' Party/Democratic Left was well known and has been discussed previously, and will emerge once more in the analysis in Chapter 12. Nevertheless, the experience of working together in the Rainbow coalition had improved relations, in particular between senior political and backroom figures in both parties. Ruairi Quinn and Brendan Howlin drove the exercise from within the Labour Party. 'My European overview of left wing history and politics – and a sense of what was going on elsewhere – was probably greater by a factor of 10 than most of the other people in the parliamentary party at that time, and that was probably influencing me,' Quinn admitted.[40]

Some senior figures in the Labour Party questioned the discussions with Democratic Left. Difficulties existed, although these were largely related to personality clashes and constituency rivalries. The party's general secretary Ray Kavanagh was among those sceptical of the benefits of a merger. He subsequently observed that there has been 'no attempt to analyse the effects of the merger from an intellectual or political viewpoint,' while adding that Ruairi Quinn 'was reacting to someone else's initiative lured by the bait of four seats'.[41] One of the main arguments against the merger – political self-preservation – was evident in another observation made by Kavanagh. He admitted: 'The practical problems of a merger were centred on candidate strategy.'[42]

A confidential internal party paper prepared by Kavanagh in April 1998 examined the scenarios arising from a merger. In the section dealing with 'Democratic Left TDs as Labour Candidates' he identified numerous constituency problems. A hostile view of Democratic Left runs through the analysis. For example, the solution in the three-seat Dublin North West where De Rossa and Roisin Shortall were sitting TDs was for the Democratic Left leader to 'retire or find an alternative career'.[43] It was suggested that Rabbitte move constituencies to Dublin Mid West – 'we have no candidate there and he would be a superb gain' – while trouble was predicted in Dún Laoghaire ('a lot of work would have to be done laying the ground here'), in Wicklow (a 'major rift and a possible split') and in Cork North Central ('already quite a headache').[44] Kavanagh's document noted that two staff at the Democratic Left head office would have to be 'subsumed'. Moreover, the party's press officer Tony Heffernan 'would be a terrific gain though there would be personnel problems on our side ... He is closely associated with Prionsias [sic] De Rossa and shares his IRA background so he might be hesitant to move himself.'[45]

Constituency matters were also raised at the Labour parliamentary party meeting on 27 May 1998. Kavanagh recalled: 'Those deputies most affected by it, namely the Dublin ones, were the most wary.'[46] Several Labour TDs were unconvinced of the benefits accruing from a merger. Brian O'Shea (Waterford) predicted that a merger would only provide a short-term electoral boost. Roisin Shortall (Dublin North West) argued that the Democratic Left vote would not transfer automatically to a merged party but would more likely switch to Sinn Féin or the Socialist Party.

Difficulties in the Labour Party were said to exist in Dublin North West, Dublin South West, Dublin South Central, Wicklow, Cork East and Cork North Central. In several of these constituencies the two parties were seen to be fighting for a single seat. The task for those driving the merger idea was to convince their members that in constituencies with four and five seats a united party could hope to win two seats.

Among the critics of the merger proposal, Pat Upton led the internal opposition within the Labour Party. He had a long and difficult relationship in Dublin South Central with Eric Byrne of Democratic Left. There was significant hostility between supporters of the two men. These constituency differences were always going to be more problematic than anything else in concluding a merger deal, although the Democratic Left historical narrative was also raised as a concern. 'Pat Upton said, "Why don't you let them join one-by-one?" I said I didn't want a defeated troop of individual deserters. I wanted whatever they had left as a force. That was my sentiment,' Quinn recalled.[47]

Upton was unconvinced, and it was no great surprise that the Dublin South Central TD was one of those who broke ranks publicly. He identified two problems with the proposed merger. 'There is enough evidence from European elections to confirm that when small parties amalgamate, they amount to something less than the sum of the two parts. Furthermore, I would not be comfortable with the culture of Democratic Left, because of certain associations they have had in the past.'[48] There was little support for Upton's position from his party leader.

'When pressed [he] could give little constructive argument why. He just didn't like the people and didn't like the idea,' Quinn observed.[49]

Despite Quinn's stance, similar doubts to Upton's were also raised by some figures in Democratic Left. Catherine Murphy, a longstanding local councillor in County Kildare, expressed concerns about the different ethos in the two existing parties. 'If I wanted to join Labour I'd have done it 15 years ago. That party carries a lot of tradition with it. I would find them highly opportunistic. I look for substance over style, whereas with Labour you get style over substance.' Murphy added that she would not join a new merged arrangement. 'If the merger happens, I will part company with my colleagues in Democratic Left. I feel Labour is part of the establishment. I see myself as a politician of the anti-establishment tradition.'[50] The Labour Party organisation in Murphy's Kildare North constituency concluded that the merger move 'would be positive and should be welcomed'.[51] The fact that they believed that Murphy and her supporters would not join the Labour Party – wrongly as it turned out – probably influenced their assessment.

In mid-June 1998 Quinn wrote to party members seeking their views on the talks with Democratic Left. His Dublin South East constituency welcomed the merger, noting that it would bring a strengthened parliamentary party. The membership in Limerick East backed the move 'as it was felt there was little or no ideological reasons for not doing so'.[52] But there was also considerable unease at the proposition, mirroring what several party TDs had said at the earlier parliamentary party meetings. The Labour Party organisation in Dublin North West (where Roisin Shortall was the party's TD) provided a nine-point list of objections to a proposed merger which was viewed as offering a 'life-line to vulnerable DL TDs'. Echoing Pat Upton's warning, the Dublin North West constituency council noted that 'many members and voters have very genuine concerns about the origins, history and behaviour of DL and the potential for embarrassment to Labour.'[53]

The Labour Party members in East Wicklow were unanimously opposed to the proposed merger. The party had no Dáil representation in Wicklow, having lost its seat at the 1997 general election, where Liz McManus effectively replaced former minister Liam Kavanagh as the main Left politician. A summary of remarks made at a constituency meeting was sent to Labour Party head office. '"Impossible to see our enemies being welcomed" – Liam Kavanagh; "Throwing them a life-line at a time when they are in decline" – George Newsome; "DL will do Trojan Horse, we'll end up working for them" – John O'Brien.'[54]

The matter of illegal activities and criminality was raised in several other items of correspondence, some of which contained very serious and detailed accusations against named members of Democratic Left. Even where there was support for a proposed merger, a number of issues were signalled as either non-negotiable or requiring further clarification arising from the ongoing discussions. These matters included that the name of any new group would be 'The Labour Party'; clarity on responsibility for Democratic Left debts; assurances about future candidate selection; and assurances about the structures of new constituency organisations. Overall, the assessment of the party organisation in the Cavan/Monaghan constituency provided a good summary of the Labour Party membership views: 'proceed with caution, but proceed.'[55]

Quinn acknowledged the different views in his party ranks, although he revealed that in the negotiations there was 'agreement in ideological terms' – in effect confirming that opposition was motivated by personal and constituency considerations. This conclusion is supported by the nature of the opposition from constituencies such as Dublin North West, Dublin South Central and Wicklow. But the Labour Party leader was not for turning. 'I have to take the broader and historical view, minimising the difficulties that may be there,' Quinn said.[56]

Several newspaper stories were published reporting opposition to the idea of the merger within the Labour Party. For example, in early August the *Irish Independent* stated that 'several sources within Labour said some constituencies were ready to fight "tooth and nail" against the merger.'[57] Writing in the letters page of *The Irish Times*, Labour's organiser in Cork North Central, Alan Kelly, observed that 'the anticipated joining of Democratic Left with our party is to be welcomed. However, politics is about values and those of my party are certainly not up for negotiation.'[58] Kelly's remarks were framed in the context of the merger implications for the Cork North Central constituency, where he accepted that Democratic Left's 'Kathleen Lynch would be the most obvious candidate for a merged party in the future ...' but significantly the welcome came with a warning – 'Whether Cllr Lynch can represent these values for the Labour Party in Cork North Central in the future remains to be seen.'[59]

In late September 1998, ahead of the new Dáil session, *The Irish*

Times reported that there was 'strong opposition' among members of the Labour parliamentary party members to the merger. An unidentified source was quoted as saying, 'There is great unhappiness about this in the party. Frankly, it is not on. It has the potential to blow the party asunder and must be stopped before it is too late. About six or seven members of the parliamentary party oppose it outright.'[60]

There was, however, reluctance among sitting TDs to openly criticise the merger talks. Few TDs went on the record with their views, while the negotiating teams from the respective sides worked on the nascent deal. Two former Labour Party government ministers became the most senior party figures to publicly question the merger in early September 1998. 'I am opposed to the merger taking place before the encouragement of greater co-operation. I am afraid of the practical problems we will face,' Liam Kavanagh noted with reference to the Wicklow constituency where he had lost out in 1997 while Democratic Left's Liz McManus held on.[61] This concern – again based on the implications for constituency matters – was echoed by Niamh Breathnach, another former minister who lost her seat at the 1997 general election in Dún Laoghaire where Gilmore represented Democratic Left. The former Labour Party TD, however, went further with her reservations:

> We have to protect our proud brand image which is based on openness and consultation. I do not believe that four TDs coming in from a democratic centralist background are going to lead to a consolidation and development of the left in Ireland. I am doubtful to say the least.[62]

Others associated with the party, however, went public to offer a very different perspective. Longtime party advisor Fergus Finlay openly backed the idea of a merger based on the benefit that would arise by ending the situation where two Left-wing parties were in competition without meaningful influence and power:

> For as long as they like, the two parties can occupy their own comfortable niches, and maybe from time to time they can have separate negotiations with others about government formation. But if they're serious about growth, they're going to have to swallow hard, and start growing as one ... There is a fantastic opportunity now to mix the resolve and professionalism of DL with the traditions, history and structure of the Labour party.[63]

Despite pockets of resistance – and unease in certain constituencies – Finlay's view reflected the assessment of the leadership in the Labour Party as the merger talks moved towards a deal.

CONCLUSION

The merger between Democratic Left and the Labour Party was very much a 'top-down' exercise rather than an initiative driven by the grassroots in either organisation. The personal commitment to the merger option by Pat Rabbitte and Ruairí Quinn drove the process. Rabbitte's involvement convinced others in Democratic Left that a deal with the Labour Party offered their best future route. He was also vital in ensuring that Proinsias De Rossa backed the proposal. In a similar view, Quinn pressed the merger idea within the Labour Party in the face of internal resistance.

Without the involvement of Rabbitte and Quinn it is unlikely that the merger idea would have advanced as quickly as it did, or that it would have ended as it did. As the negotiations moved into the autumn of 1998 there was an increasing sense that a deal was within reach. On the Democratic Left side Catherine Murphy spoke with her party colleagues about the direction in which events were moving. 'I had several discussions with De Rossa and then Rabbitte just said to me, "Look, sometimes you're better off making the decision to either go or don't go ..."'[64] There was more resistance to a deal within Labour Party ranks. But the fact that opposition was associated with individuals from constituencies where competition with Democratic Left was greatest only served to lessen the influence of critics of a deal. With the backing of the leadership tier in both parties, and the strong support from key individuals like Quinn and Rabbitte, it was always going to be difficult to derail the process once any sort of momentum was achieved.

NOTES

1. Interview with Eamon Gilmore, 11 September 2006.
2. Ibid.
3. Interview with Pat Rabbitte, 9 January 2007.
4. Interview with Eric Byrne, 29 August 2006.
5. Interview with Catherine Murphy, 31 August 2006.
6. Pat Rabbitte, 'Economic Social and Political Developments at Entry to the New Millennium', unpublished, April 1998.
7. Interview with Pat Rabbitte, 9 January 2007.
8. Interview with Liz McManus, 18 October 2006.
9. Ibid.
10. *Irish Independent*, 6 November 1997.

11. Letter from De Rossa to Quinn, 18 November 1997 in Ruairi Quinn files.
12. Press release, issued 27 November 1997.
13. Interview with Ruairi Quinn, 5 February 2008.
14. R. Quinn, *Straight Left: A Journey in Politics* (Dublin: Gill & Macmillan, 2006), p.378.
15. Ruairi Quinn, letter to Proinsias De Rossa, 1 April 1998.
16. Deirdre O'Connell, letter to Ruairi Quinn, 13 July 1998.
17. Democratic Left/Labour Party Study Group, *Left Politics in the New Century*, July 1998.
18. Quinn, *Straight Left*, p.378. In an interview for this study in January 2007, Pat Rabbitte said Quinn's account was 'more or less accurate'.
19. Quinn, *Straight Left*, p.379.
20. Ibid.
21. Ibid.
22. Ibid., p.380.
23. Ibid.
24. Philip O'Connor, letter to De Rossa, Rabbitte, Gilmore, McManus and Gallagher, 29 March 1998.
25. Quinn, *Straight Left*, p.380.
26. Ibid., p.381.
27. Ruairi Quinn, letter to De Rossa, 12 May 1998, in Ruairi Quinn files.
28. Proinsias De Rossa, letter to Quinn, 15 May 1998.
29. Interview with Paul Sweeney, 6 September 2006.
30. Interview with Proinsias De Rossa, 7 September 2007.
31. Democratic Left Press Office statement, 25 May 1998.
32. Ibid.
33. See *The Irish Times*, 26 May 1998.
34. See *The Irish Times*, 27 May 1998.
35. Memo entitled 'Labour and DL: The Options', dated 'early summer 1998', in Ruairi Quinn files.
36. *Irish Independent*, 26 May 1998.
37. *Sunday Business Post*, 31 May 1998.
38. *The Irish Times*, 26 May 1998.
39. Ibid.
40. Interview with Ruairi Quinn, 5 February 2008.
41. R. Kavanagh, *Spring, Summer and Fall: The Rise and Fall of the Labour Party, 1986–1999* (Dublin: Blackwater Press, 2001), p.216.
42. Ibid., p.214.
43. Report entitled *Scenarios Resulting from a Merger between the Labour Party and the Democratic Left Party*, Ray Kavanagh, April 1998.
44. Ibid.
45. Ibid.
46. Kavanagh, *Spring, Summer and Fall*, p.214.
47. Interview with Ruairi Quinn, 5 February 2008.
48. *Sunday Business Post*, 27 September 1998.
49. Quinn, *Straight Left*, p.382.
50. *Sunday Business Post*, 27 September 1998.
51. Letter from Labour Party, Kildare North to Ray Kavanagh, 8 August 1998.
52. Letter from Labour Party, Limerick East to Ruairi Quinn, 30 June 1998.
53. Letter from Labour Party, Dublin North West to Ray Kavanagh, 15 September 1998.
54. Letter from Labour Party, Wicklow Area Council to Ray Kavanagh, 8 June 1998.
55. Letter from Labour Party, Cavan/Monaghan to Ruairi Quinn, 19 June 1998.
56. *The Irish Times*, 23 September 1998.
57. *Irish Independent*, 12 August 1998.
58. *The Irish Times*, 11 August 1998.
59. Ibid.
60. *The Irish Times*, 21 September 1998.
61. *Sunday Business Post*, 13 September 1998.
62. Ibid.
63. *The Sunday Times*, 9 August 1998.
64. Interview with Catherine Murphy, 31 August 2006.

12

Merger III: The End of a Party

INTRODUCTION

In early July 1998 Democratic Left and the Labour Party signalled their intention to establish a Left-wing policy think-tank, which would operate irrespective of the merger talks. The idea was developed from a specially established Democratic Left/Labour Party study group. The think-tank idea eventually emerged in October 1998 as a policy and research foundation with the challenge 'to generate ideas and initiatives for consideration by the Left generally in its policy formation process'.[1] Ciarán Benson, a well-known figure in the arts world, agreed to serve as the independent chairman of the body, while the other board members were closely associated with the two sponsoring parties, including trade unionist Pat Brady and academic Paula Clancy from Democratic Left.

Work on agreeing the establishment of the research body had taken place in the summer of 1998. But the contacts between the two parties were about more than a research body. Meetings were held between Proinsias De Rossa and Ruairi Quinn as well as between the committee set up to explore the potential for a new political initiative. 'The party leader has written to over 100 individuals informing them of developments and inviting them to become involved in the process,' a Democratic Left newsletter recorded in July 1998.[2] It is worth recalling that there had been continuing mention of a possible merger right since the weeks leading to the eventual formation of Democratic Left back in early 1992. In the days after the split in the Workers' Party the prospect of joining the Labour Party was examined, although not in a genuinely serious way. The scenario was somewhat different in 1998 and not just because the two parties had enjoyed a period together in government. As Kathleen Lynch explained, 'The only reason why we had any leverage joining, I suppose, was because we joined as a very cohesive group, and it was a negotiated merger. If we had joined earlier, after the split [in

1992] with the Workers' Party, I think the group that went with Proinsias would have split further.'[3]

The talks between the two parties entered an important stage in the autumn of 1998. 'There was a lot of chess being played and a lot of poker, waiting for people to move and not move ...' Quinn admitted.[4] De Rossa, by his own admission, was a still reluctant convert to the idea of merging Democratic Left with the Labour Party. Even after accepting that his party could not continue as an independent entity, De Rossa was among those in Democratic Left who favoured the creation of a broader alliance on the Left, one that went beyond both Democratic Left and the Labour Party. In the latter regard, informal contacts were made in late May 1998 with the Green Party to seek their involvement in the discussions about creating a new formation. The public response from Green Party TD John Gormley was negative. Gormley told *The Irish Times* that 'tentative and informal approaches' had been made to his party to hold discussions but that these approaches were 'rejected outright'.[5]

'We have no interest in talking to Labour or Democratic Left on co-operation. Their stance on the Amsterdam Treaty was further evidence, if such were required, that our parties have very little in common. Democratic Left obviously sees Labour as an electoral lifeline,' Gormley stated. Interestingly, a Labour Party spokesperson told the newspaper that they had no knowledge of any contact with the Green Party about a new political formation. Democratic Left declined to comment, but privately there was considerable annoyance with Gormley's public statement. A disappointed Proinsias De Rossa prepared a response to send to Gormley and his party colleague in Dáil Éireann, Trevor Sargent.

> To put it mildly I was taken aback by the vehemence and alacrity with which you went to the press to reject our informal approach to your party to discuss the Democratic Left idea of a New Formation on the left ... our idea is much broader than the electoral aspirations of individuals. Our objective is a left led government. I feel that a green component would be important in such a project ... I suggest therefore that the basis of your peremptory rejection of the Democratic Left approach is based on a false premise.[6]

Despite the negative response from the Green Party, by July 1998 Democratic Left had prepared a draft 'mission statement' which presented a revised set of objectives for a new broadly based party.

Our purpose is to bring into being a creative egalitarian society which provides for the needs and aspirations of all the people. Our mission is to create a radical, participatory, political movement in Ireland and in Europe which will seek to redirect the dynamism and innovation in the economy in order to bring about social and economic justice, the protection of the environment, and the wise use of the scarce resources of the planet. The first step is to create a credible political formation, which will include the Labour Party, Democratic Left with others including trade unions, community activists and individuals on an agreed platform, which will seek to achieve those objectives. The achievement of a left-led government is essential for the transformation of Irish society and is our major political objective.[7]

The discussion in the previous chapter showed the commitment of Pat Rabbitte, Eamon Gilmore and others in Democratic Left to achieve a political future with the Labour Party. Proinsias De Rossa was a reluctant convert to the latter viewpoint. Even as the discussions with the Labour Party were underway, De Rossa was considering a future beyond a merger deal. Indeed, the ultimately unsuccessful attempt to bring the Green Party into the discussions is an indication that the De Rossa group within Democratic Left knew a major initiative was required to re-start the process embarked upon in 1992. But they were not wildly enthusiastic about merging only with the Labour Party and continued to favour a pan-Left realignment. The Rabbitte/Gilmore group was somewhat more realistic, accepting that Democratic Left had run its course, and believed that the time had arrived to merge with the Labour Party. With the Green Party rejection of involvement in a new alliance, the two-party merger option was increasingly the most likely outcome as the negotiating teams from the two sides met to discuss their agenda.

By early autumn the talks with the Labour Party had firmly advanced into the arena of a merger. The general council of the Labour Party met on 24 September 1998 and backed further discussions. 'There are difficulties but they are not insurmountable,' Ruairi Quinn said after the meeting where formal reference was made to a 'merger' as opposed to the previous description of the talks as leading to an 'alliance'.[8] Indeed, an internal memo prepared for Quinn by a senior member of his staff on 30 September 1998 recorded: 'we have successfully moved to the final stage of negotiations with Democratic Left ... It is now time to think of how the project will be launched publicly.'[9] There was a slightly less emphatic assessment in Democratic Left, where there was still a view that the negotiations could lead to different outcomes besides the merger option. De Rossa and Gilmore reported on the discussions to Democratic Left's national executive on 26 September 1998. The relevant minute of the meeting is worth restating as it is the first written indication in Democratic Left files that the 'new formation' would be something very different and along the lines of the merger suggested by Quinn.

> Eamon Gilmore reported verbally on discussions with Labour. There is recognition that the two parties separately cannot effectively build the Left in Ireland and of the need to create a new formation comprising DL, Labour and individuals who share our views. The proposal is to put together the first two components with the aim of attracting the third subsequently. The central understanding of the talks is that the two parties committing together will involve a sharing of control, there will be no 'take-overs', and that its form will be such as to be meaningful for the members of both organisations. A wide range of issues are being dealt with including policy, rule and structural changes, integration of Executives, election and candidate strategy, name of the new organisation, etc. Proinsias De Rossa reported on two meetings with the Labour Party leader. He pointed out that what was emerging was two options – a fusion of the two parties or continuing separately; formation of loose alliances would not work.[10]

The contributions from Gilmore and De Rossa were followed by a discussion of the options available to the party. A motion in the names of the party's four TDs was passed without a vote, which authorised De Rossa to:

> … advance the discussions with the Labour Party with a view to bringing about a union of the two parties as a basis for the new political formation we envisage; [and] That this union will be backed on (a) an agreed mission statement which will have as its objective the formation of a Left-led government, (b) a shared leadership and (c) an agreed programme and agreed priorities for political action and practice.[11]

The leadership had reached a formulation of words which encompassed both the Rabbitte and De Rossa positions. At the time this debate took place – despite their fine sentiments about future development – the reality was that the leadership was negotiating from a weakened position. The party was in financial trouble with expenditure levels running considerably ahead of available income while outstanding debts were considerable and unsustainable. The party was also organisationally weak and, despite the fine sentiments in the 1997 task force report, there was little internal confidence about the future. Moreover, there was the continuing question of 'identity' which had never clearly been resolved. The prospect of a merger with the Labour Party offered financial stability, organisational security and the resolution of the identity issue in terms of joining a social democratic-leaning, Left party. 'They had nowhere else to go,' Ruairi Quinn concluded.[12] The assessment of the Labour Party leader – supported by several leading Democratic Left figures – was emerging as the majority view.

When the idea of merging with Democratic Left was first mooted with the Labour Party membership the responses sent by various units of the organisation offered what, for many, were bottom-line issues. Most important, as indicated in Chapter 11, was that the name of any new entity would be 'The Labour Party'. An internal Labour Party memo indicated that Ruairi Quinn and his colleagues were teasing out just what exactly was the Democratic Left bottom line. It was noted that the name of the Labour Party was 'non-negotiable' by Quinn – and accepted by De Rossa. But other questions posed in private among senior Labour Party figures were framed in the memo as: 'Do they wish to have their leader as Deputy Leader of the Labour Party or indeed as joint Leader of the Labour Party? Do DL members of the Dáil believe that they must be appointed to specific senior opposition portfolios and if so which ones? Are they seeking guarantees of ministries in the event of the Party entering government?'[13]

There was some media commentary about a Democratic Left demand for 'a shared leadership' and what was understood by the phrase, which had been left undefined. There was also public speculation about what positions would be offered to leading Democratic Left figures in a new arrangement. 'The high price being sought by DL, particularly in relation to a shared leadership, could prove a big stumbling block to agreement because there is already some opposition in the Labour Party to the deal,' one newspaper report noted.[14] Interestingly, in

his memoir, Ruairi Quinn recalled that by the end of October the negotiating teams had narrowed 'the issues to what level of posts the Democratic Left would get as part of an enlarged parliamentary party'.[15] It
would appear that Quinn was willing to be generous but Pat Rabbitte's
request to be finance spokesman in a new merged party was strongly
resisted by the Labour Party leader. Quinn was, after all, dealing from
a position of strength. His initial discussions with Rabbitte had left him
in no doubt that senior figures in Democratic Left had concluded that
they had no political future outside the Labour Party. Moreover, after
several months of contacts the Labour Party leader had a deepened
sense of confidence that few stumbling blocks would prevent Democratic Left reaching agreement.

> There was a strong view that we should press home our victory ...
> At one stage I remember Brendan Howlin saying, 'Jesus, Eamon
> Gilmore has notionally left the DL and has already joined the
> Labour Party.' Brendan said, 'Gilmore is not going to be able to get
> back from here if the merger doesn't go through.' He had kind of
> emotionally crossed the line.[16]

Nevertheless, there were difficult moments when it seemed that the
negotiations could collapse, as Quinn also recalled: 'I got this letter from
De Rossa saying, "Fuck off. Its all over." Something to that extent. And I
rang Pat Rabbitte and I said "I have just got this letter. We're very far gone
down the road. I'm not going to respond. And if I don't respond, he's got
nothing to react to."'[17] Quinn's strategy obviously worked, as by mid-
October 1998 the two parties were close to a deal. A draft agreement was
prepared which stated: 'The Labour Party and Democratic Left agree to
unify and to constitute a single political party, which will form the core of
the new political formation.'[18] According to the draft document the
'union' would come into effect not later than 1 February 1999, although
interestingly the section dealing with the party's name read, at that stage,
as 'The name of the unified party shall be _____ '[19]
    The draft document indicated that considerable progress had been
made, and agreement apparently reached, on the mission statement and
organisation of the new entity as well as the necessary transition phase to
take account of candidate selection arrangements in contentious constituencies. A detailed analysis of the negotiations was provided to the
Democratic Left national executive on 31 October 1998 at which it was

confirmed that the agreement would lead to 'the formation of a single party'.[20] Eamon Gilmore informed those present that a transitional period would be in place for a number of years before the full integration of the two parties occurred, while Democratic Left staff would be retained and guarantees would be provided regarding candidates at the next local elections and general elections. The meeting passed a vote endorsing:

> ... the work undertaken to date by the DL negotiating team ... subject to further clarification or negotiation on the issues of the name of the new party, resources/debts – particularly at constituency level, the development of policy and committee work and participation and mechanisms for election to a new Executive.[21]

After several months of seeking an alternative, Proinsias De Rossa had finally come to accept the merger idea. 'If you cannot discern a significant difference between what you're saying and the other main Left party, then it makes sense to work together rather than against each other. So that was the way I came to it,' De Rossa admitted.[22] Once the Democratic Left leader had reached this point, the game was in effect up for his party. The endgame was played out in the latter months of 1998. The final phase of the negotiations dealt with two particular issues – De Rossa's status in the new merged party and candidate selection in various constituencies arising from the merger.

ISSUES OF ORGANISATION AND LEADERSHIP

While the talks were underway during 1998 between the negotiating teams from the Labour Party and Democratic Left, both parties had proceeded with their separate preparations for the European and local elections which were scheduled for June 1999. A Democratic Left National Executive meeting in late September ratified 25 local election candidates while the Labour Party selected European Parliament candidates. Questions remained unanswered as to how these decisions would be accommodated in the event of a merger deal being concluded prior to June 1999. It was generally accepted that for a merger to be successful – and fulfil its objective of growing the Left's vote – the new entity would have to be seeking to win more than a single Dáil seat in many constituencies. The negotiating teams reached agreement about candidate selection in all constituencies, with two-candidate strategies proposed for several four- and five-seat constituencies with strong Labour Party and Democratic Left candidates, including Wicklow, Dublin South Central and Kildare.

The resistance of Labour's Pat Upton has already been noted. But within the Democratic Left organisation in Dublin South Central there was also unease. In a letter sent to Eamon Gilmore on 13 October 1998, the constituency secretary warned that at a party meeting a week earlier 'a number of concerns were raised about the implications of the current talks with the Labour Party.'[23] None of the matters raised, however, related to ideological issues. They were concerned about the protection of the role of Democratic Left activists within a new party structure, guarantees about officer board positions and the treatment of existing constituency bank loans which totalled just over IR£3,000 (approx. €3,800) to be repaid by 2001. The main concern, however, was candidate selection. 'Eric Byrne to be guaranteed a nomination for the upcoming local elections in Crumlin and for Dublin South Central in the next general election. This is a core demand and I do not think that the branch membership would accept a compromise on this,' the Dublin South Central memo recorded.[24]

The situation was even more complicated in Dublin North West, the constituency shared by two sitting TDs, Proinsias De Rossa and Roisin Shortall, which had been reduced to a three-seater following the 1997 general election. Hostility to a merger was strong within Labour ranks in the constituency. The local Labour Party organisation requested an early selection convention in what was seen as an attempt by supporters of Shortall to gain a tactical advantage over De Rossa. Shortall insisted, however, that her stance was not entirely motivated by personal political considerations.

> The experience in other European countries is that the combined representation of merged parties is often less than was achieved as separate entities. In the 1992 general election there were constituencies where Labour and Democratic Left each won seats through each having our own distinctive appeals.[25]

The situation in Dublin North West was one of the final remaining items when negotiations on the draft deal were concluded in the middle of November 1998. Quinn did not accept Shortall's arguments about the validity of the merger but he was not prepared 'to sacrifice' the established Labour Party TD. 'Roisin had a genuine problem and I could recognise the legitimacy of her [constituency] concerns,' Quinn admitted.[26] The impasse was eventually resolved following contacts between De Rossa and Quinn. In private correspondence sent on 19 November 1998, De Rossa acknowledged that 'the process of negotiation for the unification of Democratic Left and the Labour Party has proceeded very satisfactorily.'[27] He then moved to address the remaining issue ahead of agreeing the draft deal, namely his own electoral future. Two options were offered:

> I am also conscious of concerns which you have expressed to me about the electoral implications of the union for the next general election in Dublin North West and I have given considerable thought and consideration to how I might assist in resolving this difficulty ... I have been considering, for some time, the possibility of standing on behalf of Democratic Left in the elections to the European Parliament. As you know, the proposed agreement provides, inter alia, for Democratic Left to nominate a candidate in the Dublin Constituency. However, this would only be an option if there is a clear strategy to win two seats for the united party and if the Labour incumbent accepts, and publicly endorses such a strategy. In such circumstances, I would be willing to offer for selection as the Democratic Left nominee for the European elections under the terms of the proposed agreement. Obviously, if elected, I would not intend to stand in Dublin North West in the next general election. An alternative strategy would be to seek to maximise the number of seats by defending the existing two seats in Dublin North West, but that in the event of either incumbent not holding a seat, that they would be offered a Seanad nomination.[28]

The strategy outlined by De Rossa was sufficient to conclude the draft deal between the two parties, as it was made public the following day, 20 November 1998. Before the deal was published, however, there was further private correspondence between Quinn and De Rossa. Quinn acknowledged the solution offered by his Democratic Left counterpart in terms of the European parliament elections without making any reference to the alternative option of offering a Seanad nomination to either De Rossa or Shortall in Dublin North West. He also asserted his desire to see two Labour candidates secure seats in the Dublin constituency at the following year's European elections.

If, however, you do not win a Euro seat, it is my personal wish, and
I believe that of the party at large, that you would continue to have
a leading role in national politics. To achieve this end, the party will
ensure that you will receive a nomination to contest, on an agreed
basis, a seat in the next Oireachtas other than Dublin North West.[29]

Interestingly, in his earlier letter De Rossa had not made any reference to
his future in Dáil Éireann should he not secure election to the European
Parliament. Nevertheless, when replying to Quinn's correspondence,
the Democratic Left leader stated: 'Your response is generous and fully
endorsed by me.' In a media statement, also issued on 20 November
1998, De Rossa revealed that he would not stand in Dublin North West
in the next general election irrespective of the outcome of the June
1999 European Parliament elections.[30]

Alongside the difficulty of accommodating Shortall and De Rossa in
Dublin North West, there was the question of the merged party's leadership. Quinn was aware of the need to resolve this issue. 'But what does
an ex-party leader do in a new party having allowed his party to merge
with a larger one?' Quinn asked, while acknowledging that this matter
was 'about status and perception'.[31] There was media speculation that
two deputy leaders would be appointed in the new arrangement to
accommodate De Rossa and Brendan Howlin, the existing deputy
leader of the Labour Party. Howlin eventually suggested the creation of
a new position of party president to be filled by the Democratic Left
leader, although De Rossa initially rejected the idea. But the talks had
gone too far to allow this problem to bring about an end to the negotiations. 'A collapse at this stage was simply inconceivable. In some
ways, Eamon Gilmore and Pat Rabbitte had already, psychologically,
joined the Labour Party. But I resisted the suggestion from some in my
own quarter to encourage a collapse in the negotiations and to accept
individual applications for membership,' Quinn said.[32]

Speculation about a new position of party president drew an angry
response from Brian Fitzgerald, a former Labour TD in Meath who
called for a suspension of the negotiations. 'To even consider such a
proposal would be seen as a "slap in the face" to many loyal Labour
Party members ... who fought for many years against the efforts of Mr
De Rossa and his colleagues to bring us down,' Fitzgerald said, although
there was no evidence of great public support within his party's ranks
for this stance.[33] Fitzgerald subsequently resigned from the Labour

Party over the merger deal, as did another former Dáil deputy, John Ryan in Tipperary North. But the leadership issue was not enough to collapse the talks. The text of the published merger agreement confirmed De Rossa as party president for a two-year period during what was intended to be a transitional timeframe for consolidating the merger and 'to facilitate the smooth integration of the two parties and to advance the development of the larger formation ...'[34]

THE MERGER DEAL

The aspirations in the 'Agreement on the Union of the Labour Party and Democratic Left' were broad, and in many respect non-contentious. The mission of the new Labour Party was 'to build in Ireland, a fair, safe and prosperous society'. The document noted: 'Democracy, Economic and Social Justice, Equality, Sustainability, Pluralism, Community Solidarity. These are our enduring values and we want to apply them to our challenging, new times.' In many respects the document sought broad accommodation. For example, acceptance of the current economic model rested alongside free market capitalism: 'the Global Market Economy, despite its dynamism and innovation, is widening the gap between Rich and Poor.' There was little by way of the language or sentiment of the radical Left.

According to the document, the new merged party was to be managed by a 'shared leadership team' involving Quinn, De Rossa, Howlin, Stagg and another representative nominated by Democratic Left. The transitional leadership group was to exist until 2001 with powers to adjudicate on any organisational matter that arose from the merger. The published agreement allowed Democratic Left to nominate candidates in eight constituencies to contest alongside candidates from the Labour Party. These constituencies were Cork East, Cork North Central, Dublin South Central, Dublin South West, Dún Laoghaire, Kildare North, Limerick East and Wicklow. Interestingly, confidential legal advice received by the Labour Party about the merger from barrister Frank Clarke argued that in strict legal terms the arrangement was not a merger at all.

> The new political entity will, therefore, remain the same party as it was in legal form sense, and will not require any new registration

under the provisions of the 1992 Electoral Act. That does not
mean that, as a matter of political substance, it is appropriate to
describe the arrangements as anything other than a merger.[35]

Having given an initial welcome to the negotiations, the response of several media editorials to the merger deal was far from positive. 'This was
no merger – it was a simple takeover of a declining party, past its sell-by
date, by its bigger left-wing brother,' one editorial writer concluded.[36]
Another asserted, 'What has happened … is a quite unprecedented rescue
operation.'[37] Eamon Gilmore took exception to such commentary.

> I think it's wrong to describe it as the death of the party. What hap-
> pened was that Democratic Left and the Labour Party merged. There
> was an interim constitution. The mission statement of Democratic
> Left was part of the constitution of the Labour Party. So it wasn't
> that we decided that we were going to say, 'Look let's close down
> Democratic Left and join the Labour Party', that's not what we
> decided.[38]

In his public response to the announcement, De Rossa was far more
upbeat than the media assessments as he recorded his pride at the record
of Democratic Left in national and local politics since 1992: 'The new
arrangement we are proposing will enable us to continue and intensify
our contribution to Irish politics and to the development of the Left.'[39]

The draft agreement required the backing of the respective party
executives followed by two delegate conferences which were scheduled
for early December.[40] The ruling bodies of Democratic Left and the
Labour Party overwhelmingly endorsed the proposals at separate meetings
on 26 November 1998. Labour TD Roisin Shortall and Dublin MEP
Bernie Malone abstained on the vote, with fifty members in favour and
no votes against. There were four dissenting voices at the Democratic
Left meeting, with twenty-two members in favour and a single absten-
tion. These respective party votes paved the way for separate delegate
conferences in central Dublin – Labour members met in the National
Conference Hall while the Shelbourne Hotel was the venue for the
Democratic Left gathering. Both conferences took place on 12 December 1998. Ruairi Quinn told Labour members that the two parties
shared 'the same view of where this country should go. We have the
same analysis and the priorities.'[41] The Labour Party leader saw the
merger as the conclusion of a transition begun in the late 1980s.

The union of Labour and Democratic Left marks the end of another political division. It recognises the end of the historical rivalry across Europe among the different parties of the Left following the collapse of the Berlin Wall. Today you have the opportunity to unite the two dominant traditions of the Irish Left: Labour and radical republicanism.[42]

Liz McManus, who had delivered the opening address at Democratic Left's founding conference in 1992, was first to the platform at the party's concluding event. Her contribution, like those from other senior party figures, sought to place the merger in a positive light. 'Far from entailing a move to the centre by those on the Left, it has meant, over the years, the centre has shifted in our favour,' she claimed. A neutral observer could have asked, if the party had made such progress why was it bringing down the shutters on its existence.

De Rossa formally proposed the merger at his party's conference. 'You can be proud of the agreement we have before us today. You can measure it against the values of Jim Larkin ... even against the values of Marx and you will not be disappointed,' he said, adding, 'This is not about merging with the Labour party; it's about mobilising various elements to create a situation where values of the Left will be pursued by a Left-led government.'[43] Tony Heffernan had – like De Rossa – been a member of the various parties which preceded Democratic Left from the 'pre-split Sinn Féin in 1968'. His thirty-year involvement included twenty-two years as a full-time officer, 'trying to build a separate party, an alternative on the Left to the Labour Party'. He identified the period in government as showing the shared political ambitions within the two parties.

Only two speakers from the thirty or so who spoke from the podium opposed the proposal. 'The Labour Party has no commitment to socialism or left-wing policies and that is not going to be changed by the introduction of a few Democratic Left TDs,' Brian Kenny from Dublin South Central said.[44] Despite these sentiments, outright dissent was limited, but several delegates acknowledged that they had only reluctantly come to accept the merger idea. 'In Democratic Left, the reality is we have lost more members than we have gained,' Hugh McConville said. He also lamented the party's failure to 'develop the potential of the membership and the people who voted for us'. Another delegate said the party 'started to atrophy not so long after birth'. He added that the reason 'why we are here today' was because the leadership had come to the conclusion that Democratic Left had no future. Writing in *The Irish Times*, reporter Mark Brennock captured the mood at the conference.

> The delegates were in the Shelbourne Hotel not to conduct a traditional conference but to wind up their party … Much of the debate was low key and quiet, with many delegates treating it as a social occasion, hanging around in an area at the back of the hall talking to old friends. There was some expectation but considerable sadness.[45]

When a vote was called at the end of a two-hour debate, 171 delegates (89 per cent) backed the merger deal while 21 (11 per cent) voted against. The numbers voting only represented 20 per cent of the party's membership as confirmed by Democratic Left head office to the Labour Party on 31 January 1999. The decision brought Democratic Left to an end as an active political party, with differing reactions from leading party figures. 'I suppose the argument we used in favour of the merger was that we could radicalise the Labour Party. [They] were desperately in need of talent and, I suppose, Democratic Left was in need of a home,' Kathleen Lynch stated.[46] Eamon Gilmore expressed a similar view. 'It wasn't difficult because we both shared – and there might have been differences in language or emphasis – a common outlook.'[47] For Tony Heffernan the decision to support the merger of Democratic Left and the Labour Party had been far easier than the decision to leave the Workers' Party:

> We put a lot more – 15 to 20 years – work into building the Workers' Party. I always thought that the Democratic Left was to some extent an artificial creation that was created only because certain things weren't possible within the Workers' Party.[48]

Having concluded their respective conferences, the two groupings met later on 12 December 1998 for a joint social function. De Rossa and Quinn were photographed smiling and chatting at the bar in the Riverside Centre in Dublin. Author Gerry Stembridge presided over the evening, which included a poetry reading by Michael D. Higgins and a performance by comedian Dara Ó Briain who had some fun over the speculation about how spokespersons' positions would be allocated in the new arrangement. Frank McNally recorded the atmosphere for *The Irish Times*:

> Ó Briain looked for a volunteer from the audience – 'preferably a media-shy person' – and picked Pat Rabbitte. If [Derek] McDowell

– Labour's finance spokesman – had not already joined the queue at the bar, this might have driven him there. But publicity can be a mixed blessing and when Rabbitte – DL's finance spokesman – was invited to play the part of an eight-year-old on the Late Late toy show, he made a fatal mistake. Asked, Gay Byrne-style, how many marks out of 10 he would give a certain toy, Rabbitte said 'three' and then explained in his best eight-year-old's voice: 'I can't count any higher.' Whereupon Ó Briain, sharper than the crease in Rabbitte's trousers, shot back: 'No finance portfolio for you, so.' The joke was greeted by loud laughter (and that was only Derek McDowell).[49]

With the agreement of the two parties finally in place, it was decided to formally merge Democratic Left and the Labour Party early in the New Year. There was obviously work still to be concluded but there was apparently a lack of urgency among the senior party figures as the Christmas break approached. The 'Shared Leadership Team' had not met by 22 December 1998, a fact which led Tony Heffernan to prepare a memo warning that the 'full potential will not be realised unless some person or persons takes responsibility for "driving" the operation ...'[50]

The aspiration of the new party was to form a Left-led government. But the merger was very much a 'rescue Democratic Left' exercise. This reality was unintentionally confirmed in an internal document prepared for the merger group by party officials who had been asked to agree a new corporate identity for the new organisation. 'Given the fact that the name of the party and its key personalities are not new, then in the initial stages of its existence, the design will be heavily relied upon to represent the newness of the Party. In addition, it will be some time before new policies will be developed for public presentation.'[51]

The document confirmed that, despite all the sentiment from the main politicians in the two parties, what they had agreed was a process to allow the Labour Party take over Democratic Left while giving De Rossa and his colleagues a degree of protection for their positions and standing. The ruse was clearly exposed in the discussions about a new identity. The post-merger party was relying on a new identity to convey the message that a new party had actually been formed. The lack of depth to the undertaking was further confirmed by a consultant's report on the new 'corporate identity'.[52] It argued for retaining the Labour Party's rose as the new party's symbol as part of continuity with the Labour Party's history and traditions. The rose as a symbol – the consultants wrote – was recognisable as the symbol of the party, had historical as well as emotional linkages, its red colour reminded the party's audiences of its traditions and values and had 'none of the now negative connotations of more radical imagery'. Moreover, the new identity and message was to be 'positioned to avoid any association with the branding of "New Labour" in Britain'. The discussions about the corporate identity were highly revealing about the merger process. In essence, for the Labour Party it was business as usual having made room for the arrival of senior figures from Democratic Left.

The merged party was formally launched on 24 January 1999 in the Pillar Room of the Rotunda Hospital in Dublin. Ruairi Quinn said the event marked 'a beginning not an end'. But for Democratic Left it was the end. The formal confirmation came with a letter from the Office of the Registrar of Political Parties in Leinster House. In his capacity as general secretary of Democratic Left, John Gallagher had written to the registrar, Kieran Coughlan, on 22 January 1999. Coughlan replied five days later.

Dear Mr Gallagher,

I wish to acknowledge receipt of your letter dated 22 January regarding your Party ceasing to function as a separate Party. I confirm that I have amended the current register accordingly.

Yours sincerely,

Kieran Coughlan
Registrar of Political Parties

CONCLUSION

Despite the initial reservations of some of his colleagues, Eamon Gilmore saw the merger as a final stage in a near seven-year political journey for those who opted to leave the Workers' Party in 1992.

I must say that the discussions between Labour and Democratic Left in the post-1992 general election, that's what really brought about the merger. We agreed a common programme with the Labour Party and it wasn't that difficult to agree. We had, you know, the same issues, the same objectives and so on. So what we did then in 1992 was have one Labour Party in government and one [Democratic Left] in opposition, in effect.[53]

It took another seven years – and a term in government – for the pressures on Democratic Left to force an internal party decision on its future. A lack of money, a weak organisation and in particular a crisis over political identity all combined to force the issue. Despite some internal resistance, the decision of Rabbitte and Gilmore, among others, to talk about a possible merger agreement with the Labour Party influenced De Rossa and helped to crystallise his thinking about the future of the parliamentary Left in Ireland. Once De Rossa came to accept Rabbitte's analysis the dye was cast for Democratic Left, and the inevitable steps were taken towards an eventual deal with the Labour Party.

In subsequent years, several leading Democratic Left figures have held senior positions in the Labour Party – De Rossa was its first president while Rabbitte replaced Quinn as party leader in 2002 and was himself succeeded five years later by Gilmore. Liz McManus also served as deputy leader from 2002 to 2007. But there was no electoral bounce from the merger, as was evident in the results of the 2002 and the 2007 general elections. Interestingly, opinion poll data commissioned at the time of the merger deal had been less than reassuring about its outcome. When asked for their opinion, only 29 per cent of respondents to an MRBI survey considered the merger a good idea. Some 21 per cent thought the merger a poor idea while a significant 50 per cent offered no opinion. Some 47 per cent of Labour Party supporters thought the merger a good idea, 24 per cent a poor idea and 30 per cent had no opinion. The corresponding figures for Fianna Fáil were 27 per cent good idea, 25 per cent poor idea, 48 per cent no opinion; and for Fine Gael 33 per cent, 21 per cent and 46 per cent. The MRBI poll respondents were offered a list of reasons for the merger deal. Some 50 per cent said the reason was motivated to create a more effective and strengthened party while 23 per cent said the merger was because the two parties had the same or similar policies. This convergence of belief was one of the principal drivers of the merger process, but unfortunately for those involved, the coming together of the Labour Party and the Democratic Left by itself did not lead to a more effective or strengthened party.

NOTES

1. Press Release 'Labour and Democratic Left name interim board of policy and research foundation', 5 October 1998.
2. Democratic Left, Members' Newsletter, July 1998.

3. Interview with Kathleen Lynch, 10 October 2006.
4. Interview with Ruairi Quinn, 6 February 2008.
5. See *The Irish Times*, 27 May 1998.
6. Proinsias De Rossa, draft letter to John Gormley, 8 June 1998.
7. Democratic Left Mission Statement, July 1998 (draft).
8. *The Irish Times*, 25 September 1998.
9. Ronan O'Brien, memo to Ruairi Quinn, 30 September 1998.
10. Democratic Left, National Executive minutes, 26 September 1998.
11. Democratic Left, statement, 26 September 1998.
12. Interview with Ruairi Quinn, 6 February 2008.
13. Memo re. negotiations between Labour Party and Democratic Left, undated.
14. *Sunday Tribune*, 29 September 1998.
15. R. Quinn, *Straight Left: A Journey in Politics* (Dublin: Gill & Macmillan, 2006), p.383.
16. Interview with Ruairi Quinn, 6 February 2008.
17. Ibid.
18. Draft Agreement (DL/LAB), 16 October 1998 (unpublished).
19. Draft Agreement (DL/LAB), 16 October 1998 (unpublished).
20. Democratic Left, National Executive minutes, 31 October 1998.
21. Ibid.
22. Interview with Proinsias De Rossa, 7 September 2007.
23. Correspondence from David Hobson to Eamon Gilmore, 13 October 1998.
24. Ibid.
25. *The Irish Times*, 26 September 1998.
26. Interview with Ruairi Quinn, 6 February 2008.
27. Correspondence from Proinsias De Rossa to Ruairi Quinn, 19 November 1998.
28. Ibid.
29. Correspondence from Ruairi Quinn to Proinsias De Rossa to Ruairi Quinn, 20 November 1998.
30. Democratic Left, media statement, 20 November 1998.
31. Quinn, *Straight Left*, p.384.
32. Ibid.
33. Brian Fitzgerald, media statement, 10 November 1998.
34. 'Agreement on the union of the Labour Party and Democratic Left', p.7
35. Frank Clarke, correspondence to Labour Party, 3 December 1998.
36. *The Sunday Times*, 22 November 1998.
37. *Sunday Business Post*, 29 November 1998.
38. Interview with Eamon Gilmore, 11 September 2006.
39. Democratic Left, media statement, 20 November 1998.
40. In late October 1998, Democratic Left postponed its planned national conference – due on 14 November – to allow moves towards the merger proceed, with an end-of-year deadline.
41. Media statement issued on 12 December 1998.
42. Ibid.
43. *Ireland on Sunday*, 31 May 1998.
44. *Examiner*, 14 December 1998.
45. *The Irish Times*, 14 December 1998.
46. Interview with Kathleen Lynch, 10 October 2006.
47. Interview with Eamon Gilmore, 11 September 2006.
48. Interview with Tony Heffernan, 13 September 2006.
49. *The Irish Times*, 14 December 1998.
50. Memo written by Tony Heffernan, 22 December 1998.
51. Document titled 'Labour/DL New Identity Design Brief', undated but from early December 1998.
52. Public Communications Centre, 'Final Brief for the Design and Implementation of a Corporate Identity', December 1998.
53. Interview with Eamon Gilmore, 11 September.

Conclusion

During the 1992 calendar year, Proinsias De Rossa and his supporters established a new political party, contested a general election and engaged in discussions about possible governmental involvement. Yet, despite all this activity, 1992 still closed with party activists uncertain about the political future of their new undertaking. In the post-election period, and in the aftermath of unsuccessful government talks, senior member Des Geraghty did not mince his words: 'We are sore, battered and weary; we are not soaring in the popularity charts, we had a poor election result and we are hardly financially solvent.'[1] It was a brutally honest summary of a year in the life of the new party – its first year – and an experience shared by most of the small political parties that have challenged the electoral and governmental stranglehold of Fianna Fáil, Fine Gael and the Labour Party.

Geraghty's written assessment submitted to a Democratic Left national executive meeting in early 1993 referred to party members as 'suffering from uncertainty, insecurity and self-recrimination (when we are not exchanging recriminations)'. He did see some positives from the initial twelve months – optimistically noting, 'we are still alive' – and arguing that the Democratic Left name had been established while the party had 'a small but first-class team of public representatives, and more importantly a small but dedicated membership which has demonstrated its capacity to overcome adversity'. These attributes were, however, little good without confidence that the party had a future. Geraghty side-stepped the very question he posed – 'the politics we represent must have a future' – but his paper did confront the dilemma faced by the Democratic Left leadership: did their politics and aspiration towards a progressive, Left agenda actually need an independent party?

As the discussion in this study has shown, Democratic Left was established at a time when the wider European Left in all its various hues was engaged in debate about forging a new radical identity in response to the challenges arising from the collapse of communism and the rise of financial globalisation where the mobility of capital found favour with the free market dogma of the New Right. But there was – and remains – on the Left, a failure to find a consistent and coherent voice. Democratic Left – like many other Left groups in Europe – never decided what it wanted to become; never offering a coherent explanation of how it would use a given set of policy instruments to deliver its stated goals. Globalisation left nation states less powerful, national budgets less influential. A new message to replace Keynesianism never emerged, as was shown most recently during the post-2008 global financial crisis. The so-called 'credit crunch' crisis fundamentally challenged the philosophy championed by Ronald Reagan and Margaret Thatcher, but there has been little to suggest that a new model is emerging from a Left perspective.

The short but eventful life of Democratic Left was shaped by this debate in European Left politics. The blurring of ideological identity had an impact on the achievement of the goals set down at the party's founding conference. As the rules of the game changed in the 1990s, Democratic Left found itself unable to articulate a distinct message for Irish voters. The party was further hindered because in early 1992 those involved were reluctant to commit to a new social democratic future mainly due to past associations with the Labour Party. This political space, however, became their ultimate destination when the two parties formally merged at the start of 1999. The exit from the Workers' Party was also prompted by a specific local issue – criminality – and there is little doubt that those embarrassing revelations created a climate in which, having failed to reconstitute the party, the formation of a new political grouping was inevitable. But even if the reconstitution had been accepted, it is likely that a stronger Workers' Party would also have been confronted by the same issues which challenged Democratic Left. In such a scenario it might have been possible to move beyond the criminality allegations, but a reformed Workers' Party would also have had to explain what were the substantive policy differences with the Labour Party.

Democratic Left sought to establish a political foothold in an

Ireland undergoing considerable change. The various socio-economic and political changes underway in Irish society in the 1990s had a significant impact on the ability of the backers of the new party to carve out a distinctive political agenda, and in particular one that was distinct from the Labour Party. In the history of twentieth-century Ireland this final decade was defined by tremendous transformation but it was also a time of resolution, as if there was a rush to settle matters on so many different fronts before the new millennium dawned. Ultimately, the new party was stripped of its distinctiveness arising from the resolutions of social and moral controversies, and the emergence of the peace process in Northern Ireland. The failure to articulate a new policy agenda in areas such as the economy and the environment only contributed to a perception – and indeed, perhaps a reality – that Democratic Left had come to accept the framework of the larger political parties. The period in government from 1994 to 1997 only assisted this convergence process. As the discussion throughout this study has shown, Democratic Left viewed itself by reference to the Labour Party so it should not be a surprise that Des Geraghty in his 1993 review paper followed in a similar vein: 'My own view is that the answer to whether we need an independent party ... depends, in part, on how the Labour Party – still an untried force, in its new size and shape – performs in government.'

In the absence of a radicalised Labour Party, Geraghty concluded that the time was not right to contemplate a merger between the two parties. 'I believe we should continue for the time being in a fraternal relationship with Labour, as a supportive but critical and separate party.' Geraghty was, however, conscious of potential developments: 'If the Labour Party actually does take on the mantle of a modern socialist party with a vision of the future open to change and development, there would be a strong case for a merger.' Geraghty was writing in early 1993 but a merger with the Labour Party was still several years away. The unsuccessful 1992 government discussions were ultimately to prove hugely important in improving relations between the two parties. Those talks facilitated successful government negotiations two years later, and assisted the development of important personal relations between the leading politicians in both parties. By the mid-1990s the blurring of ideological differences between Democratic Left and the Labour Party was increasingly accepted in private by many senior figures in each party. The expert surveys in 1992 and 1997 support the thesis that there were few substantive policy differences between the two parties. Eventually, the weaknesses in Democratic Left's organisational position, a lack of resources and an inability to outline identity difference moved the party in the direction of a merger. This journey that has been undertaken by several other small political parties, all of which initially established a national and governmental relevance in Irish politics. But none was able to create a sustainable niche in the Irish political system. The Democratic Left experience shows that a coherent identity is vital to sustaining a political party, especially a party in the shadow of a similarly minded opponent. Moreover, a well-structured organisation supported by an active membership assists in prolonging a party's life. But what the story of Democratic Left also shows is that to function today as an active political party in Ireland, access to money is important. In the absence of sufficient resources, internal pressures mount and limitations are placed on a party's ability to compete with its rivals. Small parties fail when the burden of these pressures becomes too great over time for the limited number of individuals involved, regardless of their dedication or commitment. It is possible that greater certainty over identity would have allowed the party to continue as an independent political entity Undoubtedly, certainty over identity would have assisited in expanding the party's membership base – thereby injecting renewed energy into the organisation, reducing the workload on established members, creating a pool of new candidates and, possibly, enhancing fundraising opportunties. The more recent demise of the Progressive Democrats – a far better resourced organisation than Democratic Left – similarly illustrates the importance of identity in party political self-preservation.

The search for a new radical agenda was a challenge which Democratic Left ultimately failed to meet. The party was bedevilled by unresolved issues relating to its political identity – shaped primarily by its membership of a political family impacted by tremendous uncertainty. Challenging the dominance of Fianna Fáil, Fine Gael and the Labour Party in Irish electoral and governmental history is extremely difficult. These three main parties in the Irish Republic have proven to be remarkably durable in political and electoral terms. They each benefit from having established roots in the political system with national, or near-national, organisations and loyal membership bases, as well as long experienced abilities to 'shape-shift' on policy to match the threat of new entrants.

Over the last eighty years several new parties have attempted to mount a sustained challenge to the established political order – to date, all have failed, including Democratic Left.

NOTE

1. Des Geraghty, undated and untitled note to the National Executive, most likely early 1993.

Appendix I
Main Characters

Proinsias De Rossa was president of the Workers' Party until early in 1992. He was leader of Democratic Left from March 1992 to January 1999. He was minister for social community and family affairs in the 1994–7 Rainbow government. De Rossa had a long history with the republican movement – he joined the IRA in 1956 when he was 16 years of age and spent time in prison during the 1956–62 border campaign. He was adopted onto the Árd Comhairle of Sinn Féin in July 1962, continued to have an active involvement in republican politics and in later years emerged as a senior public figure for Sinn Féin The Workers' Party. He was first elected to Dáil Éireann in February 1982 and held his seat in Dublin North West until he left national politics in 2002 to concentrate on his membership of the European Parliament. A serious, policy-minded and liberal politician, De Rossa received huge loyalty from his party colleagues, although few, if any of them, would admit to being personally close to him. Following the merger deal in 1999, De Rossa became president of the Labour Party, a position he held until 2002.

Pat Rabbitte unsuccessfully contested the November 1982 and 1987 general elections before winning a Dáil seat in the 1989 general election as a Workers' Party candidate in Dublin South West. Born in Mayo in 1949 he was active in student union politics at University College Galway and served as president of the Union of Students in Ireland (USI) from 1972 to 1974. He had been a member of the Labour Party until 1976 but he came to political prominence through his involvement with the Workers' Party. Following the end of his student union activities Rabbitte became a trade union official with the Irish Transport and General Workers' Union (now SIPTU). This college and career history – which was very similar to that of Eamon Gilmore – led Rabbitte and others to be labelled 'the Student Princes' during the debates over the future direction of the Workers' Party. He was a founding member of Democratic Left in 1992 and was a minister of state in the 1994–7 Rainbow government. He was often described as a 'super junior minister' because this position allowed him to attend cabinet meeting in a non-voting capacity. His ministerial title was minister of state to the government and at the department of enterprise and employment with special responsibility for commerce, science and technology and consumer affairs. A witty and incisive parliamentary debater, Rabbitte established a reputation as a commanding media performer. His intellectual abilities have been evident during his contributions on several Oireachtas committees, including the inquiry into DIRT tax evasion. He was leader of the Labour Party from October 2002 to September 2007.

Eamon Gilmore was a founding member of Democratic Left and a minister of state in the 1994–7 Rainbow government. He was elected as a Workers' Party TD in 1989 for the Dún Laoghaire constituency having failed to secure election in November 1982 or in 1987. Born in Galway in 1955, Gilmore was very active in student union politics in the mid-1970s and was president of the Union of Students in Ireland from 1976 to 1978. He was subsequently employed by the Irish Transport and General Workers' Union and worked as a trade union official until his election to Dáil Éireann. Gilmore was on the modernising wing of the Workers' Party and was a prominent member of the De Rossa group which formed Democratic Left. As a minister of state in the 1994–7 period he was based at the department of the marine where he had responsibility for port development, pollution and nuclear hazards. He became leader of the Labour Party in October 2007.

Tony Heffernan was a founding member of Democratic Left and was a full-time party advisor until the merger with the Labour Party in January 1999. He had a long association with the Official republican movement. Documents in Seán Swan's history of Official Irish republicanism record his arrest along with other leading republicans in 1972.[1] He served as general secretary of Sinn Féin The Workers' Party in the 1970s and opposed the dropping of Sinn Féin from the party name in 1982.

Throughout the 1980s he headed up the party's offices in Leinster House and oversaw its media operation. He was assistant government press secretary during the life of the Rainbow coalition. Heffernan is a fount of knowledge about contemporary Irish politics and is recognised by his colleagues as having an encyclopedic grasp of dates and events. Following the merger in 1999 he worked with the Labour Party staff in Leinster House.

Eric Byrne was elected as a Workers' Party TD in 1989 for the Dublin South Central constituency having unsuccessfully contested the five previous elections. He was a founding member of Democratic Left in 1992 but narrowly lost his Dáil seat in a dramatic and prolonged count in the general election held later that same year. Born in April 1947, Byrne was a prominent member of the new party and in a successful by-election victory in 1994 he was returned to Dáil Éireann. Along with Kathleen Lynch – who was also a new TD – he was a backbench TD during the life of the Rainbow coalition. Also like Lynch, he lost his Dáil seat in the 1997 general election. He supported the merger in 1999 but failed to secure a return to national politics, remaining an active member of Dublin City Council as a Labour Party representative.

Kathleen Lynch was elected a member of Cork City Council in 1985 and unsuccessfully contested two Dáil Éireann elections as a Workers' Party candidate prior to the 1992 split. Some of her family members were involved in the Official republican movement. Born in Cork in June 1953, she was an active member of the new party's internal committees, and won a by-election in late 1994 in Cork North Central only weeks before the formation of the Rainbow coalition. Despite being a new TD, she was a prominent backbencher on the government side as Democratic Left attempted to keep a distinct public profile during its period in office. Lynch lost her seat at the subsequent general election. She supported the merger in 1999 and three years later regained her Dáil seat as a Labour Party candidate.

Liz McManus, who was born in Canada in 1947, came to prominence through the women's rights campaigns in the 1970s. She was also a well-known writer, newspaper columnist and media commentator. She was a successful local election candidate for the Workers' Party in

County Wicklow before becoming a founding member of Democratic Left. She won a Dáil seat in the 1992 general election and was a minister of state in the 1994–7 Rainbow government. In the latter role she had responsibility for housing and urban renewal. She was deputy leader of the Labour Party from 2002 to 2007.

Catherine Murphy was elected as a Workers' Party councillor in 1991. She joined Democratic Left when the party was founded in 1992. She was an active party member and unsuccessfully contested the 1992 and 1997 general elections. She joined the Labour Party after the 1999 merger but subsequently resigned from the party. She was elected as an Independent candidate in a by-election in Kildare North in March 2005 but lost her seat in the 2007 general election.

Des Geraghty was a member of the Workers' Party prior to the split in 1992. He represented Democratic Left in the European Parliament after 1992 but did not contest the 1994 European elections. A senior party figure, he also worked as general secretary in the Democratic Left head office. Geraghty was president of the SIPTU trade union from 1999 to 2004.

Rosheen Callender was a senior Democratic Left member. She worked as a policy advisor to Proinsias De Rossa in the 1994–7 Rainbow government. She has held several senior positions with the Irish Congress of Trade Unions.

John Gallagher worked as Democratic Left's assistant general secretary and general secretary. He was a member of the team which negotiated the merger deal with the Labour Party.

Paul Sweeney was a trade union economic advisor. He backed the reconstitution of the Workers' Party in 1992 and was an active member of Democratic Left.

Tomás MacGiolla stood down as president of the Workers' Party in 1988. He was the only one of the party's seven TDs who did not support the decision to form Democratic Left in 1992.

Seán Garland was a senior figure in the Workers' Party who opposed the proposal to reconstitute the organisation in 1992. He remained with the Workers' Party after the split.

Ruairi Quinn was minister for finance in the 1994–7 Rainbow government. He was elected leader of the Labour Party in November 1997.

John Bruton became leader of Fine Gael in 1990. He served as taoiseach in the 1994–7 coalition government involving Fine Gael, the Labour Party and Democratic Left.

Eoghan Harris was a leading figure in the Workers' Party from the early 1970s until the late 1980s. He was one of the pivotal figures in the party's Research Section and was also a well-known television producer with RTÉ.

NOTE

1.   S. Swan, *Official Irish Republicanism, 1962–82* (Belfast: Lulu, 2008), p.347.

Appendix II
Draft Constitution of Democratic Left, March 1992

1. General

1.1 The name of the party is XYZ.

1.2 XYZ is a democratic, secular, socialist party.

1.3 XYZ is organised in both states on the island of Ireland. Branches may be organised in other states as appropriate.

1.4 Membership is open to all those who subscribe to the principles set out in this constitution.

2. Objectives

2.1 The objectives of XYZ are:

(a) The development of a democratic, secular, socialist society in Ireland.

(b) To contribute to the development of democratic socialism in Europe and throughout the world.

(c) An egalitarian, tolerant, pluralist society within which everyone is afforded the means and the opportunity to participate as an equal citizen.

(d) To produce the conditions to facilitate self-expression and participation in cultural life.

(e) The elimination of all manifestations of patriarchy and the creation of conditions of genuine equality between men and women.

(f) The elimination of all forms of exploitation based on disability, gender, age, class, creed, sexual orientation or ethnic or racial origin.

(g) The incorporation of ecological principles into economic and political decision-making.

(h) Economic equality through democratic control of resources and the elimination of poverty in all its forms.

(i) A positive neutrality, opposition to war and to military blocs and the development of global collective security.

(j) To actively work for third-world development.

3. Means

3.1 XYZ pursues its objectives through democratic political activity.

3.2 Our strategy involved co-operation with a wide range of democratic organisations and participation in alliances on a principled basis.

4. Principles of Organisation

4.1 XYZ is a member-centred party governed by democracy from the bottom up.

4.2 The Annual Delegate Conference is the policy decision-making body of the party.

4.3 Open and free debate is encouraged and as much use as possible made of consensus decision making. Where necessary, decisions are made by majority vote. Collective decision implies collective responsibility for implementing these decisions.

4.4 The leadership of the party is elected democratically and is accountable to the membership.

4.5 Party rules are an appendix to this constitution. They may be changed by a simple majority of valid vote at the Annual Delegate Conference.

4.6 Changes to this interim constitution will require a simple majority of the valid vote at the ADC.

Bibliography

PRIMARY SOURCES

Selected Democratic Left Publications and Documents

Democratic Left, *Europe Deserves Better*, Maastricht Treaty referendum manifesto, 1992

Democratic Left, *301,000 Reasons for Change Economic Programme*, November 1992

Democratic Left, *A Programme for Change and Progress*, general election, November 1992

Democratic Left, *Draft Presented by Democratic Left as Basis for Discussion with the Labour Party*, 4 December 1992

Democratic Left, *Europe Deserves Better*, 1992

Democratic Left, *Task Force Report* (draft), 1993

Democratic Left, *Towards 2001: Draft Report of the Democratic Left Task Force on Politics, Strategy and Organisation*, April 1993

Democratic Left, *Election Manifesto*, 1994

Democratic Left, *Policy Position on Northern Ireland*, second draft, no date given but most likely early 1994

Democratic Left, *Setting a New Agenda: A Framework for Agreement on Northern Ireland*, September 1994

Democratic Left, *Local Government Democracy and Development: A Discussion Document*, 1994

Democratic Left, *A Government of Renewal: Discussion Notes on DL Priorities*, memorandum, 30 January 1995

Democratic Left, *Human Rights are Women's Rights*, November 1995

Democratic Left, *Towards Policing in A Peaceful Society*, March 1995

Democratic Left, *Stick With a Winning Team*, draft party document, April 1997

Democratic Left, *Beyond the Millennium*, 1997
Democratic Left, *Make the Future Work: Achievements in Government, 1994–97*, May 1997
Democratic Left, 'Task Force Report' (unpublished), September 1997
Democratic Left, 'Labour/DL: New Identity Design Brief' (unpublished), undated but from early December 1998
Democratic Left, *Position Paper on the Amsterdam Treaty*, May 1998
Democratic Left/Labour Party Study Group, *Left Politics in the New Century*, July 1998

Newspapers and Periodicals

An Phoblacht
Belfast Telegraph
Dungarvan Observer
Ireland on Sunday
Irish Independent
Irish News
Irish Press
Magill
Phoenix
Sunday Business Post
Sunday Independent
Sunday Tribune
Sunday World
The Cork Examiner
The Examiner
The Irish Times
The Sun
The Sunday Times

Broadcast Media

BBC Radio Ulster, 'PM Ulster', 26 April 1993
BBC1 Northern Ireland, 'Spotlight', 27 June 1991
RTÉ Radio News, 17 October 1991

Official Documents and Manuscripts

Dáil Debates

House of Commons Debates
Irish Labour History Museum and Archives

Private Collections
Tony Heffernan
Ruairi Quinn

Interviews
Des Geraghty
Rosheen Callender
Paul Sweeney
Tomás MacGiolla
Seán Garland
Proinsias De Rossa
Pat Rabbitte
Eric Byrne
Liz McManus
Catherine Murphy
Kathleen Lynch
Eamon Gilmore
Tony Heffernan
Eoghan Harris
Ruairi Quinn
John Bruton

SECONDARY SOURCES

Adams, G. *Hope and History: Making Peace in Ireland* (Dingle: Brandon, 2003)
Andrews, D. *Kingstown Republican* (Dublin: New Island, 2007)
Arter, D. 'Scandinavia: What's Left is the Social Democratic Consensus', *Parliamentary Affairs*, 36, 1 (2003), pp.75–99
Arthur, P. *Special Relationships: Britain, Ireland and the Northern Ireland Problem* (Belfast: Blackstaff Press, 2002)
Barrington, H. 'New Parties in Britain: Why Some Live and Most Die', *International Political Science Review*, 6, 4 (1985), pp.441–61
Bell, D. and Shaw, E. (eds), 'Introduction', in special issue on 'What's Left? The Left in Europe Today', *Parliamentary Affairs*, 56, 1 (2003), pp.1–5

Bell, D.S. 'France: The Left in 2002 – The End of the Mitterrand Strategy', *Parliamentary Affairs*, 56, 1 (2003), pp.24–37

Benoit, K. and Laver, M. 'Estimating Irish Party Positions Using Computer Wordscoring: The 2002 Elections', *Irish Political Studies* 18, 1 (2003), pp.97–107

Benoit, K. and Laver, M. 'Mapping the Irish Policy Space: Voter and Party Spaces in Preferential Elections', *Economic and Social Review*, 36, 2 (2005), pp.83–108

Benoit, K. and Marsh, M. 'For A Few Euros More: Campaign Spending Effects in the Irish Local Elections of 1999', *Party Politics*, 9, 5 (2003), pp.561–82

Benoit, K. and Marsh, M. 'Campaign Spending in the Local Government Elections of 1999', *Irish Political Studies*, 18, 2 (2003), pp.1–22

Bew, P. and Gillespie, G. *Northern Ireland: A Chronology of the Troubles, 1968–99* (Dublin: Gill & Macmillan, 1999)

Bew, P., Hazelkorn, E. and Patterson, H. *The Dynamics of Irish Politics* (London: Lawrence & Wishart, 1989)

Bishop, P. and Mallie, E. *Provisional IRA* (London: Heinemann, 1987)

Blair, T. *The Third Way: New Politics for the New Century* (London: Fabian Society, 1998)

Blondel, J. *Political Parties: A Genuine Case for Discontent?* (London: Wildwood, 1978)

Bolleyer, N. 'Small Parties: From Party Pledges to Government Policy', *West European Politics*, 30, 1 (2007), pp.121–47.

Bouvet, L. and Michel, F. 'Pluralism and the Future of the French Left', in G. Kelly (ed.), *The New European Left* (London: Fabian Society, 1999)

Broughton, D. and Donovan, M. (eds), *Changing Party Systems in Western Europe* (London: Pinter, 1999)

Browne, V. (ed.), *The Magill Book of Irish Politics* (Dublin: Magill, 1981)

Browne, V. (ed.), *The Magill Book of Irish Politics* (Dublin: Magill, 1982)

Buelens, J. and Hino, A. 'The Electoral Fate of New Parties in Government', in K. Deschouwer (ed.), *New Parties in Government: In Power for the First Time* (London: Routledge, 2008)

Bull, M.J. 'Whatever Happened to Italian Communism? Explaining the Dissolution of the Largest Communist Party in the West', *West European Politics*, 14, 4 (1991), pp.96–120

Bull, M.J. 'The West European Communist Movement in the Late Twentieth Century', *West European Politics*, 18, 1 (1995), pp.78–97

Bull, M.J. 'Italy: The Crisis of the Left', *Parliamentary Affairs*, 36, 1 (2003), pp.58–75

Burley, J. and Regan, F. 'Divorce in Ireland: The Fear, the Floodgates and the Reality', *International Journal of Law, Policy and the Family*, vol. 16 (2002), pp.202–22

Butler, A. *Transformative Politics: The Future of Socialism in Western Europe* (London: St Martin's Press, 1997)

Callaghan, J. 'Social Democracy in Transition', *Parliamentary Affairs*, 56, 1 (2003), pp.125–40

Chubb, B. *Cabinet Government in Ireland* (Dublin: Institute of Public Administration, 1974)

Chubb, B. *The Government and Politics of Ireland* (London: Longman, 1992)

Coakley, J. 'The Significance of Names: The Evolution of Irish Party Labels (1)', *Études Irlandaises*, vol. 5 (1980), pp.171–81

Coakley, J. 'Minor Parties in Irish Political Life, 1922–1989', *Economic and Social Review*, 21, 3 (1990), pp.269–97

Coakley, J. and Gallagher, M. (eds), *Politics in the Republic of Ireland* (Dublin: Blackwater Press, 1992)

Coakley, J. 'The Rise and Fall of Minor Parties in Ireland', *Irish Political Studies*, 25, 4 (2010), pp.503–40

Cohen, N. *What's Left?: How the Left Lost its Way* (London: Harper Collins, 2007)

Collins, N. (ed.), *Political Issues in Ireland Today* (Manchester: Manchester University Press, 1999)

Collins, N. and Cradden, T. *Irish Politics Today* (Manchester: Manchester University Press, 1997)

Comisso, E. 'Crisis in Socialism or Crisis of Socialism?', *World Politics*, XLII, 4 (1990), pp.563–607

Coogan, T.P. *The IRA* (London: Harper Collins, 2004)

Coogan, T.P. *Ireland in the Twentieth Century* (London: Palgrave, 2004)

Copus, C., Clark, A., Reynaert, H. and Steyvers, K. 'Minor Party and Independent Politics Beyond the Mainstream: Fluctuating Fortunes but a Permanent Presence', *Parliamentary Affairs*, 62, 1 (2008), pp.4–17

Crewe, I. and King, A. *The Birth, Life and Death of the Social Democratic Party* (Oxford: Oxford University Press, 1995)

Crosland, A. *The Future of Socialism* (London: Robinson Publishing, 2006)

De Bréadún, D. *The Far Side of Revenge: Making Peace in Northern Ireland* (London: Collins, 2001)

Delaney, E. *Accidental Diplomat: My Years in the Irish Foreign Service, 1987–1995* (Dublin: New Island, 2001)

Department of Finance *Budget 2000*, http://www.budget.gov.ie/2000 (accessed 18 March 2008)

Desmond, B. *Finally and in Conclusion: A Political Memoir* (Dublin: New Island, 2000)

Duignan, S. *One Spin on the Merry-Go-Round* (Dublin: Blackwater Press, 1996), pp.91–118

Dunphy, R. 'The Workers' Party and Europe: Trajectory of an Idea', *Irish Political Studies*, vol. 7 (1992)

Dunphy, R. 'From Eurocommunism to Eurosocialism: The Search for a Post-Communist European Left', *University of Dundee Occasional Papers*, Series 1:7 (1993)

Dunphy, R. 'A Group of Individuals Trying to Do their Best': The Dilemmas of Democratic Left', *Irish Political Studies*, vol. 13 (1998), pp.51–75

Eley, G. *Forging Democracy: The History of the Left in Europe, 1850–2000* (Oxford: Oxford University Press, 2002)

English, R. *Armed Struggle: The History of the IRA* (Oxford: Oxford University Press, 2003)

Farrell, B. *Chairman or Chief? The Role of Taoiseach in Irish Government* (Dublin: Gill & Macmillan, 1971)

Farrell, B. 'The Formation of the Partnership Government', in M. Gallagher and M. Laver, *How Ireland Voted, 1992* (Dublin: Political Studies Association of Ireland (PSAI), 1993), pp.146–61

Farrell, D. 'Ireland: A Party System Transformed?', in D. Broughton and M. Donovan (eds), *Changing Party Systems in Western Europe* (London: Pinter, 1999), pp.30–47

Farrell, D.M. 'Campaign Strategies', in Gallagher and Laver, *How Ireland Voted, 1992*, pp.21–38

Ferriter, D. *The Transformation of Ireland, 1900–2000* (London: Profile, 2004)

Finlay, F. *Snakes and Ladders* (Dublin: New Island, 1999)

Fisher, S. L. 'The "Decline of Parties" Thesis and the Role of Minor Parties', in P. H. Merkl (ed.), *Western European Party Systems* (New York: Free Press, 1980)

FitzGerald, G. *All in a Life: An Autobiography* (Dublin: Gill & Macmillan, 1991)

Flackes, W.D. and Elliott, S. *Northern Ireland: A Political Directory, 1968–88* (Belfast: Blackstaff, 1989)

Foster, R. *Luck and the Irish: A Brief History of Change, 1970–2000* (London: Penguin, 2007)

Fukayama, F. 'The End of History?', *National Interest*, vol. 16 (Summer 1989), pp.3–18.

Fukayama, F. *The End of History and the Last Man* (New York: Free Press, 1992)

Gallagher, M. *The Irish Labour Party in Transition, 1957–1982* (Manchester: Manchester University Press, 1982)

Gallagher, M. *Political Parties in the Republic of Ireland* (Manchester: Manchester University Press, 1985)

Gallagher, M. 'The Election Results and the New Dáil', in M. Gallagher and R. Sinnott, *How Ireland Voted, 1989* (Galway: PSAI Press, 1990)

Gallagher, M. 'The Election of the 27th Dáil', in Gallagher and Laver, *How Ireland Voted, 1992*, pp.57–78

Gallagher, M. 'The Results Analysed', in M. Marsh and P. Mitchell, *How Ireland Voted, 1997* (Dublin: PSAI, 1999)

Gallagher, M. and Laver, M. *How Ireland Voted, 1992* (Dublin: PSAI, 1993)

Gallagher, M. and Marsh, M. *Days of Blue Loyalty: The Politics of Membership of the Fine Gael Party* (Dublin: PSAI, 2002)

Gallagher, M. and Sinnott, R. (eds), *How Ireland Voted, 1989* (Galway: University College Galway, 1990)

Garry, J. 'The Demise of the Fianna Fáil/Labour Partnership Government and the Rise of the Rainbow Coalition', *Irish Political Studies*, vol. 10 (1995), pp.192–9

Garry, J. and Mansergh, L. 'Irish Party Manifestos', in Marsh and Mitchell (eds), *How Ireland Voted, 1997*, pp.82–10

Garvin, T. *The Evolution of Irish Nationalist Politics* (Dublin: Gill & Macmillan, 1981)

Geraghty, D. *New Century Socialism: Fighting for Justice in the Jungle* (Dublin: Democratic Left, 1998)

Geraghty, D. 'A Peace Policy for Europe: Constructing a New Model of Security', *Work in Progress: Discussion Journal of Democratic Left* (Dublin: Democratic Left, 1993)

Girvin, B. 'The Road to the Election', in Gallagher and Laver, *How Ireland Voted, 1992*, pp.1–20

Girvin, B. 'The Campaign', in Gallagher and Sinnott, *How Ireland Voted, 1989*

Girvin, B. and Murphy, G. 'Continuity, Change and Crisis in Ireland: New Perspectives, Research and Interpretation', *Irish Political Studies*, 23, 4 (2008)

Godson, D. *Himself Alone: David Trimble and the Ordeal of Unionism* (London: Harper Collins, 2004)

Godson, R. and Haseler, S. *Eurocommunism: Implications for East and West* (London: Macmillan, 1978)

Gottfried, P. *The Strange Death of Marxism: The European Left in the New Millennium* (Columbia: University of Missouri, 2005)

Government Information Service, *A Government of Renewal: Agreed Programme for Government between Fine Gael, the Labour Party and Democratic Left*, December 1994

Government Information Service, *Public Opinion and the Budget*, 28 February 1995

Hanley, B. and Millar, S. *The Lost Revolution: The Story of the Official IRA and the Workers' Party* (Dublin: Penguin, 2009)

Hayek, F.A. *The Fatal Conceit: The Errors of Socialism – The Collected Works of F.A. Hayek*, edited by W.W. Bartley III (Chicago: University of Chicago Press, 1991)

Holmes, M. 'The Establishment of Democratic Left', *Irish Political Studies*, vol. 9 (1994), pp.148–56

Holmes, M. 'Organisational Preparation and Political Marketing', in M. Marsh and P. Mitchell (eds), *How Ireland Voted, 1997* (Oxford: Westview Press, 1999)

Hopkins, S. and Dunphy, R. 'The Organizational and Political Evolution of the Workers' Party of Ireland', *Journal of Communist Studies and Transition Politics*, 8, 2 (September 1992), pp.91–118

Horgan, J. *Labour: The Price of Power* (Dublin: Gill & Macmillan, 1986)

Horgan, J. *Broadcasting and Public Life: RTÉ News and Current Affairs, 1926–1997* (Dublin: Four Courts Press, 2004)

Hornsby-Smith, M.P. and Whelan, C.T. 'Religion and Moral Values', in C.T. Whelan (ed.), *Values and Social Change in Ireland* (Dublin: Gill & Macmillan, 1994)

Hudson, K. *European Communism Since 1989: Towards a New European Left?* (London: Palgrave, 2000)

Ishiyama, J.T. 'Communist Successor Parties', *Politics and Society*, 34, 1 (March 2006)

Ishiyama, J.T. and Bozoki, A. *The Communist Successor Parties of Central and Eastern Europe* (London: M.E. Sharp, 2000)

Kavanagh, R. *Spring, Summer and Fall: The Rise and Fall of the Labour Party, 1986–1999* (Dublin: Blackwater Press, 2001)

Keane, C. (ed.), *The Job Crisis: The Thomas Davis Lecture Series* (Dublin and Cork: RTÉ/Mercier Press, 1993)

Kindersley, R. 'In Lieu of a Conclusion: Eurocommunism and "the Crisis of Capitalism"', in R. Kindersley (ed.), *In Search of Eurocommunism* (London: Macmillan, 1981)

Larkin, P. 'Sticking to their Guns', in *A Very British Jihad: Collusion, Conspiracy and Cover-Up in Northern Ireland* (Belfast: Beyond the Pale, 2004)

Laver, M. 'The Relationship between Coalition Policy and Party Policy', *European Journal of Political Economy*, vol. 1 (1985), pp.243–69

Laver, M., Mair, P. and Sinnott, R. (eds), *How Ireland Voted: The Irish General Election, 1987* (Dublin: Poolbeg, 1987)

Laver, M. and Shepsle, K.A. 'Election Results and Coalition Possibilities in Ireland', *Irish Political Studies*, vol. 7 (1992)

Laver, M. 'Party Policy in Ireland, 1997: Results from an Expert Survey', *Irish Political Studies*, vol. 13 (1998), pp.159–71

Lawson, K. and Merkl, P. *When Parties Fail: Emerging Alternative Organisations* (Princeton, NJ: Princeton University Press, 1988)

Lee, J.J. *Ireland, 1912–1985* (Cambridge: Cambridge University Press, 1989)

MacGiolla, T. *Struggle for Peace, Democracy and Freedom* (Dublin: Repsol, 1976)

McGraw, S. 'Managing Change: Party Competition in the New Ireland', *Irish Political Studies*, 23, 4 (December 2008)

MacStíofáin, S. *Memoirs of a Revolutionary* (Edinburgh: Gordon Cremonesi, 1975)

Mair, P. *The Changing Irish Party System: Organisation, Ideology and Electoral Competition* (London: Pinter, 1987)

Mair, P. (ed.), *The West European Party System* (Oxford: Oxford University Press, 1990)

Mair, P. 'The Electoral Universe of Small Parties', in F. Müller-Rommel and G. Pridham (eds), *Small Parties in Western Europe: Comparative and National Perspectives* (London: Sage, 1991)

Mair, P. 'The Irish Party System in the 1990s', in Gallagher and Sinnott (eds), *How Ireland Voted, 1989*

Mair, P. 'Fianna Fáil, Labour and the Irish Party System', in Gallagher and Laver, *How Ireland Voted, 1992*

Mair, P. 'The Party System', in J. Coakley and M. Gallagher (eds), *Politics in the Republic of Ireland* (Dublin: Folens, 1992)

Mair, P. *Party System Change: Approaches and Interpretations* (Oxford: Oxford University Press, 1997)

Manning, M. *Irish Political Parties: An Introduction* (Dublin: Gill & Macmillan, 1972)

Marsh, L. and Muddle, C. 'What's Left of the Radical Left? The European Radical Left After 1989: Decline and Mutation', *Comparative European Politics*, vol. 3 (2005), pp.23–49

Marsh, M. and Sinnott, R. 'How the Voters Decided', in Gallagher and Sinnott (eds), *How Ireland Voted, 1989*

Marsh, M. and Sinnott, R. 'The Voters: Stability and Change', in Gallagher and Laver (eds), *How Ireland Voted, 1992*

Marsh, M. and Mitchell, P. (eds), *How Ireland Voted, 1997* (Dublin: PSAI/Westview, 1999)

Marsh, M. and Sinnott, R. 'The Behaviour of the Irish Voter', in Marsh and Mitchell, *How Ireland Voted, 1997*

McCartan, P. 'On the Campaign Trail', in Gallagher and Sinnott (eds), *How Ireland Voted, 1989*

McKittrick, D., Kelters, S., Feeney, B., Thornton, C. and McVea, D. *Lost Lives: The Stories of the Men, Women and Children who Died as a Result of the Northern Ireland Troubles* (Edinburgh: Mainstream, 1999)

McManus, L. 'On the Campaign Trail', in Gallagher and Laver, *How Ireland Voted, 1992*

Milotte, M. *Communism in Modern Ireland: The Pursuit of the Workers' Republic Since 1916* (Dublin: Gill & Macmillan, 1984)

Moller, T. 'The Swedish Election 1998: A Protest Vote and the Birth of a New Political Landscape?', *Scandinavian Political Studies*, 22, 3 (1999), pp.261–76

Murray, G. *John Hume and the SDLP* (Dublin: Irish Academic Press, 1998)

O'Donnell, C. *Fianna Fáil, Irish Republicanism and the Northern Ireland Troubles, 1968–2005* (Dublin: Irish Academic Press, 2007)

O'Malley, D. 'It is easier to set up a new party in Iraq than it is in Ireland', *The Irish Times*, 2 April 2010

O'Malley, E. 'Punch Bags for Heavyweights? Minor Parties in Irish Governments', *Irish Political Studies*, 25, 4 (2010), pp.541–64

Ó Murchú, E. 'The Workers' Party: Its Evolution and its Future', *Irish Socialist Review* (September 1982)

Padgett, S. 'Germany: Modernising the Left by Stealth', *Parliamentary Affairs*, 36, 1 (2003), pp.38–57

Paterson, W.E and Thomas, A.H. (eds), *The Future of Social Democracy: Problems and Prospects of Social Democratic Parties in Western Europe* (Alderley: Clarendon Press, 1986)

Paterson, W.E. 'Reprogramming Democratic Socialism (Rethinking Social Democracy in Europe)', *West European Politics* (January 1993)

Patterson, H. *The Politics of Illusion: A Political History of the IRA* (London: Penguin, 1997)

Pedersen, M. N. 'Towards a New Typology of Party Lifespans and Minor Parties', *Scandinavian Political Studies*, 5, 1 (1982), pp.1–16

Puirséil, N. *The Irish Labour Party, 1922–73* (Dublin: University College Dublin Press, 2007)

Quinn, R. *Straight Left: A Journey in Politics* (Dublin: Gill & Macmillan, 2006)

Rafter, K. *The Clann: The Story of Clann na Poblachta* (Cork: Mercier Press, 1997)

Rafter, K. 'Making It Up as They Went Along: Residential Property Tax and the Process of Policy Change', *Irish Political Studies*, 15, 1 (2000), pp.63–82

Rafter, K. *Martin Mansergh: Biography* (Dublin: New Island, 2002).

Rafter, K. *Sinn Féin, 1905–2005: In the Shadow of Gunmen* (Dublin: Gill & Macmillan, 2005)

Rafter, K. *Fine Gael: Party at the Crossroads* (Dublin: New Island, 2009)

Robertson, D. *Penguin Dictionary of Politics* (London: Penguin, 1993)

Rooney, E. 'From Republican Movement to Workers' Party: An Ideological Analysis', in C. Curtin, M. Kelly and L. O'Dowd (eds), *Culture and Ideology in Ireland* (Galway: Officina Typographica, 1984), pp.79–98

Sassoon, D. *One Hundred Years of Socialism: The West European Left in the Twentieth Century* (New York: New Press, 1996)

Sassoon, D (ed.), *Looking Left: West European Social Democracy after the Cold War* (New York: Tauris, 1997)

Sassoon, D. 'Introduction: Convergence, Continuity and Change on the European Left', in G. Kelly (ed.), *The New European Left* (London: Fabian Society, 1999)

Shaw, E. 'Britain: Left Abandoned? New Labour in Power', *Parliamentary Affairs*, 36, 1 (2003), pp.6–23

Sinn Féin The Workers' Party, *The Great Irish Oil and Gas Robbery: A Case Study of Monopoly Capital* (Dublin: Repsol, 1977)

Sinn Féin The Workers' Party, *The Irish Industrial Revolution* (Dublin: SFWP, 1977)

Sinnott, R. *Irish Voters Decide: Voting Behaviour in Elections and Referendums Since 1918* (Manchester: Manchester University Press, 1995)

Smith, G. 'In Search of Small Parties: Problems of Definition, Classification and Significance', in F. Müller-Rommel and G. Pridham (eds), *Small Parties in Western Europe: Comparative and National Perspectives* (London: Sage, 1991)

Sunberg, J. 'The Enduring Scandinavian Party System', *Scandinavian Political Studies*, 22, 3 (1999), pp.221–41

Swan, S. *Official Irish Republicanism, 1962–82* (Belfast: Lulu, 2008)

Teague, P. 'Full Employment: Attainable and Sustainable?' *Work in Progress, Discussion Journal of Democratic Left* (Dublin: Democratic Left, 1993)

Ware, A. *Political Parties and Party Systems* (Oxford: Oxford University Press, 2001)

Whelan, C.T. 'Values and Social Change', in C.T. Whelan (ed.), *Values and Social Change in Ireland* (Dublin: Gill & Macmillan, 1994)

Whelan, C.T. and Fahey, T. 'Marriage and the Family', in Whelan (ed.), *Values and Social Change in Ireland*

White, J.H. *Church and State in Modern Ireland* (Dublin: Gill & Macmillan, 1980)

Index